THE EXPERTS

THE EXPERTS

CLYDE EDWIN PETTIT

"Madness in great ones must not unwatch'd go."
—*Hamlet*, III, 1

LYLE STUART, INC. / SECAUCUS, N.J.

Copyright © 1975 Clyde Edwin Pettit
Library of Congress Card No. 73-90777
ISBN No. 0–8184–0153–2

Queries regarding rights and permissions should be addressed
to Lyle Stuart, Inc., 120 Enterprise Avenue, Secaucus, New
Jersey 07094

Published by Lyle Stuart, Inc.
Manufactured in the United States of America

For my Parents,

And for those who fought,

And for those who fell on all sides,

In Indochina,

Because of The Experts

Contents

Foreword

This is a book about power and the men who wield it. It is about the press and those who control it. It is about young men sent to foreign fields to shed blood, each cell stamped with the genetic uniqueness that once made them individuals. It is about old men who sent them there, secure in their own immunity and that of their sons.

It is also about ourselves: our own credulity and the inexplicable tendency in all of us to believe what we are told and to follow those whose ambitions are to lead. It is about our forgetfulness of the history of our species—the record that there is no morality among nations and the only law is the law of the jungle.

After the outbreak of the First World War, the former German chancellor, Prince von Bülow, asked his successor, "How did it all happen?" The famous reply was, "Ah, if only one knew."

As historians begin to ask how Vietnam happened, the quotations which follow form a chronicle of its genesis and what followed. Cut as film is edited, and removing remarks from context out of editorial necessity, the original meaning is preserved throughout. The sources are the press accounts of the time, official documents such as *Public Papers of the Presidents,* the broadcast media, press releases by the U. S. and other governments, and books. Of the tens of millions of words researched from hundreds of thousands of pages of printed text, recorded tape and microfilm, some minor errors are inevitable. In all cases they are mine and not the publisher's.

The reader may come to his own conclusions and may decide that the brightest and the best of men simply make mistakes, or that life is a pointless existential joke, or an outrage, or the reader may decide that the contrary is the case, or that there is no lesson to be derived at all.

As the story of the Indochina wars is far from ended, it will, of course, remain for historians of the far distant future to assess the long-range effects, economic and otherwise, on the United States, on Asia, and on the rest of the world.

But some conclusions would seem warranted already. The Vietnam War is a textbook example of history's lessons: that there is a tendency in all political systems for public servants to metamorphose into public masters, surfeited with unchecked power and privilege and increasingly overpaid to misgovern; that war is necessary to any élite corps, which has no reason to exist without it; that even free peoples are inevitably led to death and maiming because they do not have the intelligence to realize that all wars are against their interests; that there may be some dark and perverse tropism in our very natures that makes us turn toward the senseless destruction of war; that wars, once started, may become inundating forces of nature, inexorable and beyond the control of any of the participants.

At any rate, here they are: the high officials with their *hubris,* the captains of industry with their contracts, the battalion commanders with their body counts, the men who made the munitions and the top brass who bought them, the haruspices of the press with their predictions, the mandarins of the foundations and the think-tanks, the men who made the mistakes and the men who made the money, the politicians and the pundits, the establishmentarians, the rich and powerful, the respected— all hellbent on a suicide course, with a tiger by the tail which they would not let go.

Here is the chronological account of a crusade doomed to certain failure before it began and those who were too blind to recognize it.

Here are those who were destined never to turn the tide and never to see the light at the end of the tunnel.

Here are The Experts.

CLYDE EDWIN PETTIT

PRELUDE

EDITOR'S NOTE: *The Experts* is chronologically arranged, but some entries throughout the book were written long after the period or era which they concern; in such cases the time of publication is omitted to avoid the possible confusion of having the narrative seem to "zig-zag" back and forth in time.

The Vietnamese encounter with Christ is considerably prior to the colonial intervention of the French. The first missionaries to embark for Vietnam were the Spanish and Portuguese in the 16th century . . . the first evangelization . . . was renewed by the Jesuits in the 17th century.

— Piero Gheddo, *The Cross and the Bo Tree*

In 1658, a Vicar Apostolic was appointed by the Pope in Rome, and he also made the Catholic Church in Vietnam an extension of the Church of France.

— A. C. Crawford,
Customs and Culture of Vietnam

The conquest of Vietnam . . . was but part of the larger struggle then going on between the French and Portuguese clergy for dominance in China and the Far East. . . . [There were] intense struggles by Portuguese and Italian missionaries, already on the scene, to keep French missionaries out of the country. . . . The Dutch, who controlled the Straits of Malacca, successfully resisted efforts by the French East India Company to establish a trading post in southern Vietnam in 1664–5. Other French commercial ventures in Vietnam in 1682 and 1684 were similarly thwarted by the Dutch. Finally in 1749–50, a treaty was concluded with Annam granting trade concessions to the French East India Company.

— Senator Ernest Gruening, Democrat of Alaska,
Vietnam Folly

The kings of Tonkin and Cochin China . . . saw that the missionaries . . . were destroying the bases of local society . . . they hastened to expel them. . . . The Indochinese Church continued to survive with the help of missionaries who secretly entered the country. . . . Vietnam was unified under one Emperor, Gia-Long, who granted freedom to the missionaries and to the Christians since he had conquered the country with the aid of the French . . . Gia-Long himself called France "the

1

protectress of the Christians." . . . In exchange for their help, the French held the port of Tourane (today Danang) and had freedom of trade throughout the country.

— Peiro Gheddo, *The Cross and the Bo Tree*

I, Ming-Mang, the king, declare this. Men from the West have been for many years spreading the Christian religion and thus deceiving the people. . . . They have lost respect for Buddha and have no reverence for their ancestors. That is a great blasphemy. . . . The religion of Jesus deserves our contempt. . . .

— Emperor Ming-Mang, edict, 1833

Our country has always been known as a land of deities; shall we now permit a horde of dogs to stain it? . . . From the moment they arrived with their ill luck, happiness and peace seem to have departed from everywhere.

— Vietnamese appeal for resistance against French, 1864

The conquest of the country by France, "the Elder Daughter of the Catholic Church," understandably increased the influence of Catholicism throughout Vietnam.

— Ellen J. Hammer,
Vietnam: Yesterday and Today

The Vietnamese are ripe for servitude.

— Paul Doumer, French Minister of Finance, 1867

Colonization is for France a question of life and death.

— Pierre Leroy-Beaulieu, French economist, 1882

The colonial policy is the daughter of the industrial policy. European powers of consumption are saturated. New masses of consumers must be made to arise in other parts of the world, or else bankruptcy faces modern society and the time will approach for a cataclysmic social liquidation of which we cannot calculate the consequences.

— Jules Ferry, French premier and colonialist, 1890

That which it behooves us to introduce into our colonies is neither philosophical theories nor social institutions of a contingent value, but simply our manufactured products.

> — Auguste Billiard, French economist,
> *Politique et Organisation Coloniales,*
> Paris, 1899

[America's] Pacific era . . . destined to be the greatest of all, is just at its dawn.

> — President Theodore Roosevelt,
> San Francisco, 1903

The colonist brings the techniques and capital, the soil furnishes the raw materials, the native alone supplies the labor.

> — Joseph Chailley-Bert, French economist,
> June 20, 1904

Those who believe that Indochina could become a rival of metropolitan France fail to see that Indochinese products have a natural outlet, a sure and profitable market, in China, that immense territory with its 400 million population, and that these products would go at very little cost to China, from which they are only separated by a few hundred kilometers instead of the considerable distance that separates them from the French market, where they would have to compete with the natural products weighed down by costly freight charges. Hence French industry has nothing to fear from the proposals being discussed in Tongking, and which, it is to be hoped, the future will see in full bloom. [But the native economy must be improved] to enable the natives to afford the products that France wishes to sell.

> — Albéric Neton, French economist, 1904

The Vietnamese are slaves by nature. They have been ruled by us and now they are ruled by the French. They can't have a very brilliant future.

> — Sun Yat-sen, leader of Chinese revolution,
> founder of modern China, to Japanese
> statesman Ki Tsuyoshi Inukai, Tokyo, 1911

We take the liberty of . . . setting forth the claims of the Annamite people on the occasion of the Allied victory. We count on your great kindness to honor our appeal by your support. . . . Since the victory of the Allies, all subject peoples are frantic with hope at the prospect of an era of right and justice which should begin for them . . . in the struggle of civilization against barbarism.

> — Ho Chi Minh (then named Nguyen Ai Quac),
> letter to Secretary of State Robert Lansing in
> Paris; letter, in French, now in National
> Archives; it never received reply; the date:
> June 18, 1919

When the Versailles Peace Conference started work, Ho . . . drew up an eight-point program for their country's emancipation and forwarded it to the conference secretariat in January 1919. Today, this plan, inspired by President Wilson's 14 Points, sounds extremely moderate. It asked for permanent representation in the French parliament; freedom of the press; freedom to hold meetings and form associations; amnesty and release of political prisoners; government by law instead of . . . decree; equality of legal rights between French and Annamese. When Ho tried to argue their case with Wilson himself at Versailles he was unceremoniously shown the door.

— Jean Lacouture, *Ho Chi Minh*

You all have known that French imperialism entered Indochina half a century ago. In its selfish interests, it conquered our country with bayonets. Since then we have not only been oppressed and exploited shamelessly, but also tortured and poisoned pitilessly. Plainly speaking, we have been poisoned with opium, alcohol, etc. I cannot, in some minutes, reveal all the atrocities . . . inflicted on Indochina. Prisons outnumber schools and are always overcrowded with detainees. Natives . . . are arrested and sometimes murdered without trial. . . . Vietnamese are discriminated against. . . . We have neither freedom of press nor freedom of speech. Even freedom of assembly and freedom of association do not exist. We have no right to live in other countries or to go abroad as tourists. We are forced to live in utter ignorance and obscurity because we have no right to study. In Indochina the colonialists find all ways and means to force us to smoke opium and drink alcohol to poison and beset us. Thousands of Vietnamese have been led to a slow death or massacred to protect other people's interests. . . . Such is the treatment inflicted upon more than 20 million Vietnamese, that is more than half the population of France. And they are said to be under French protection!

— Ho Chi Minh,
Tours, France, December 26, 1920

Out of four prisoners, we had to kill three; out of ten, we had to kill nine and keep only one for interrogation. These were our orders.

— Soldier LeGallic, testimony before Hanoi
court concerning uprisings against French,
who killed 10,000 Indochinese in reprisal, 1931

The roots of the story go back to the French and the ruins of the nation they destroyed. . . . It was not the classic avarice, extortion and expropriation of colonial life that offended so much. Nor the fact that the

French budgeted their opium monopoly at a larger sum than the budget for hospitals, schools and libraries combined. It was the sight of people—the casual quality of cruelty, the simple slapping by white men, smack across the face, of grown Vietnamese rickshamen and servants as if they were naughty children. The sullen quality of native faces repudiated the beauty of the city; the splendid French boulevards ran like causeways above a basin of hate.

> — Theodore H. White,
> "Saigon," *Life*, September 1, 1967

It is indeed pleasant for an American when motoring . . . to stop at a little hamlet . . . and to find . . . rows of familiar brands of California fruits and fish which . . . may be eaten with American crackers. . . . About one out of five automobiles are American. . . . The clerks . . . are pounding away on American typewriters. . . . It is no longer a novelty . . . to see American tractors.

> — "Saigon—The Pearl of the Orient,"
> *Export Trade & Finance*, November 1932

As a force capable of acting against the public order, Communism has disappeared.

> — Pierre Pasquier, governor general of
> Indochina, speech, December 17, 1932

The French carry France to their colonies. . . . The Frenchman has deep down in him a persuasion that all men are equal and that mankind is a brotherhood . . . a feeling that the native . . . is of the same clay as himself. . . . He is friendly with him without condescension and benevolent without superiority. . . . Every young Annamite is . . . convinced that outside France there is neither art, literature, nor science. . . . The Annamites admire the French. . . . At Hanoi I found nothing much to interest me.

> — W. Somerset Maugham, *The Gentleman in the
> Parlour*, 1933

It can be taken as established that the population lives at the borderline of famine and misery.

> — Pierre Gourou, French authority on Tonkin, in
> *Les paysans du Delta Tonkinois*, Paris, 1936

In 1929 . . . we were bound for Haiphong in Indo-China. . . . We hired a car and drove to Hanoi. Here we were not allowed out of the hotel as there was a revolution in progress. . . . We hired a car and driver and set off the next day down the length of Indo-China to Saigon.

The journey took the best part of a week. . . . We were deeply impressed by the admirable French colonization which enabled us to procure excellent coffee and rolls in the remotest villages.

— Noel Coward, *Present Indicative*, 1937

1940–1954

French colonial policy . . . was largely shaped by the concept of Indochina as a profitable economic enterprise to be exploited for the benefit of the mother country. The economy was dominated by a combination of private French investors and the Bank of Indochina, which developed into the real political and financial nerve center of all Indochina . . . the instrument for channeling metropolitan capital into the colony and directing its investment at highly profitable rates. French interests permeated all sectors of the economy but exercised almost exclusive control over mineral extraction, the rubber industry, and manufacturing . . . land was concentrated in large estates. . . . The French colonial system also acted to destroy the village as a social and economic unit. . . . The traditional mode of life was further modified by the process of urbanization; this gave rise to a rootless indigenous proletariat and . . . wealthy landowners.

— George Kahin, *Government and Politics of Southeast Asia*

Japan would not dare make a military attack [on Indochina] at this time.

— Secretary of State Cordell Hull, July 1, 1940, a few weeks before Japanese attacked Indochina, midnight, September 22, 1940

[There was] an open revolt under the Viet Minh banner in December 1940. The French at that time were already under the pressure of Japanese penetration and were being attacked by the Siamese in the west. They were unable or unwilling to oppose effectively either the Japanese or the Siamese, but they turned with ruthless cruelty on the revolting Annamites. During the repressions, some 6,000 were killed or wounded and thousands more arrested. French courts-martial for months afterward were grinding out condemnations to long years of penal servitude or to death.

— Harold Isaacs, *No Peace for Asia*

9

The vision of America as the dynamic leader of world trade has within it the possibilities of such enormous human progress as to stagger the imagination. Let us not be staggered by it. Let us rise to its tremendous possibilities. Our thinking of world trade today is on ridiculously small terms. For example, we think of Asia as being worth only a few hundred million a year to us. Actually, in the decades to come Asia will be worth to us exactly zero—or else it will be worth to us four, five, ten billions of dollars a year. . . . America . . . will send out through the world its technical and artistic skills. Engineers, scientists . . . developers of airlines, builders of roads. . . . Throughout the world . . . this leadership is needed and will be eagerly welcomed. . . . We must undertake now to be the Good Samaritan of the entire world. It is the manifest duty of this country to undertake to feed all of the people of the world . . . all of them, that is, whom we can from time to time reach consistently with a tough attitude toward all hostile governments. For every dollar we spend on armaments, we should spend at least a dime in a gigantic effort to feed the world. . . . Throughout the 17th century and the 18th century and the 19th century, this continent teemed with manifold projects and magnificent promises. Above them all and weaving them all together into the most exciting flag of all the world and of all history was the triumphal purpose of freedom. . . . All of us are called . . . to create the first great American Century.

— Henry R. Luce, "The American Century," *Life*, February 17, 1941

If Japan was the winner, the Japanese would take over French Indochina. And if the allies win, we would take it.

— Admiral William D. Leahy to French, quoting himself from memoirs *I Was There*, July 1941

1840: 420,000 baptized; 1890: 708,000 baptized; 1933: 1,365,000 baptized; 1941: 1,638,000 baptized.

— Piero Gheddo, *The Cross and the Bo Tree*

Eyes must look far ahead, and thoughts be deeply pondered.
Be bold and unremitting in attack.
Give the wrong command, and two chariots are rendered useless.
Come the right moment, a pawn can bring you victory.

— Ho Chi Minh, *Prison Diary*, 1943

We should do nothing with regard to resistance groups or in any other way in relation to Indochina.

— President Franklin D. Roosevelt, memo to Secretary of State Cordell Hull, October 13, 1944

Ho's first wartime contact with American officials came in late 1944. During that year the Viet Minh, a guerrilla army as well as a group of political parties, began small scale guerrilla attacks against the Japanese. In his capacity as leader of the only significant guerrilla force in Indochina and a "provisional government," Ho went to Office of Strategic Services (O.S.S.) headquarters in Kunming, China . . . "seeking arms and ammunition in return for intelligence, sabotage against the Japanese and continued aid in rescuing shotdown Allied pilots." . . . Ho eventually did receive the American aid he sought from the Special Operations (S.O.) branch of O.S.S. China. In the spring of 1945, the first O.S.S. officers parachuted into Ho's jungle headquarters 75 miles north of Hanoi.

— Senate Foreign Relations Committee Staff
Study, "The U.S. and Vietnam; 1944–1947"

I still do not want to get mixed up with any Indochina decision. It is a matter for postwar. By the same token, I do not want to get mixed up in any military effort toward the liberation of Indochina from the Japanese. You can tell Halifax that I made this very clear to Mr. Churchill. From both a military and civil point of view, action at this time is premature.

— President Franklin D. Roosevelt to Secretary
of State Cordell Hull, January 1, 1945, quoted
in *Diplomatic Papers, 1945*

Bring in troops, more troops, as many as you can.

— General Douglas MacArthur to General
Leclerc, French commander, Indochina, 1945

If there is anything that makes my blood boil, it is to see our allies in Indochina and Java deploying Japanese troops to reconquer the little people we promised to liberate. It is the most ignoble kind of betrayal.

— General Douglas MacArthur, 1945

FEBRUARY 16, 1946

DEAR MR. PRESIDENT:

Our VIETNAM people, as early as 1941, stood by the Allies' side and fought against the Japanese and their associates, the French colonialists.

From 1941 to 1945 we fought bitterly, sustained by the patriotism, of our fellow-countrymen and by the promises made by the Allies at YALTA, SAN FRANCISCO and POTSDAM.

When the Japanese were defeated in August 1945, the whole Vietnam territory was united under a Provisional Republican Government, which immediately set out to work. In five months, peace and order were restored, a democratic republic was established on legal bases, and adequate help was given to the Allies in the carrying out of their disarmament mission.

But the French colonialists, who betrayed in wartime both the Allies and the Vietnamese, have come back, and are waging on us a murderous and pitiless war in order to reestablish their domination. Their invasion has extended to South Vietnam and is menacing us in North Vietnam. It would take volumes to give even an abbreviated report of the crises and assassinations they are committing everyday in this fighting area.

This aggression is contrary to all principles of international law and the pledges made by the Allies during the World War. It is a challenge to the noble attitude shown before, during and after the war by the United States Government and People. It violently contrasts with the firm stand you have taken in your twelve point declaration, and with the idealistic loftiness and generosity expressed by your delegates to the United Nations Assembly, MM. BYRNES, STETTINIUS, AND J. F. DULLES.

The French aggression on a peace-loving people is a direct menace to world security. It implies the complicity, or at least the connivance, of the Great Democracies. The United Nations ought to keep their words. They ought to interfere to stop this unjust war, and to show that they mean to carry out in peacetime the principles for which they fought in wartime.

Our Vietnamese people, after so many years of spoliation and devastation, is just beginning its building-up work. It needs security and freedom, first to achieve internal prosperity and welfare, and later to bring its small contribution to world-reconstruction.

These security and freedom can only be guaranteed by our independence from any colonial power, and our free cooperation with all other powers. It is with this firm conviction that we request of the United States as guardians and champions of World Justice to take a decisive step in support of our independence.

What we ask has been graciously granted to the Philippines. Like the Philippines our goal is full independence and full cooperation with the UNITED STATES. We will do our best to make this independence and cooperation profitable to the whole world.

I am, Dear Mr. PRESIDENT,

Respectfully Yours,

(Signed) Ho Chi Minh

— President Ho Chi Minh, letter to President
Harry S Truman, February 16, 1945 (never
answered, never declassified until 1972)

The President said that the Indochinese were people of small stature, like the Javanese and the Burmese, and were not warlike.

> — President Franklin D. Roosevelt to Marshal
> Josef Stalin, Livinia Palace, Yalta, USSR,
> 1945, recorded by Charles E. Bohlen, FDR's
> interpreter; from Minutes of the Far East
> Discussions

The first thing I asked Chiang was, "Do you want Indo-China?" . . . He said, "It's no help to us. We don't want it. They are not Chinese. They would not assimilate into the Chinese people." . . . With the Indochinese, there is a feeling they ought to be independent, but are not ready for it.

> — President Franklin D. Roosevelt to
> Generalissimo Chiang Kai-shek, on board
> U.S.S. *Quincy*, returning from Yalta
> Conference, February 23, 1945, quoted by
> Judge Samuel I. Rosenman, *The Public Papers
> and Addresses of FDR*

From the point of view of national interest, I willingly envisaged that hostilities would commence in Indochina . . . in view of our position in the Far East, I thought it essential that the conflict should not end without us having become . . . belligerents. . . . French blood shed on Indochinese soil would give us an important voice [in later settlements]. . . . I desired that our troops should fight, no matter how desperate their situation.

> — General Charles de Gaulle, concerning
> surrounding French troops by Japanese,
> March 9 and 10, 1945, when 4,200 of 13,000
> overwhelmed French troops were massacred;
> from *Memoires de Guerre*

FDR had offered China *all* of Indochina (including the "Hinduized" states of Cambodia and Laos!) as an outright grant. It is to Chiang Kai-shek's honor (or an indication of his political realism) that he turned down the gift. Mindful of China's previous experience with the Vietnamese—of which the President and his advisers seemed unaware—Chiang explained his refusal by pointing out that the Indochinese were "not Chinese. They would not assimilate into the Chinese people."

> — Bernard B. Fall, citing Henry A. Wallace and
> Samuel I. Rosenman as authority for FDR's
> offer of Indochina to Chiang

The government of the Republic has always considered that Indochina was called upon to occupy a special place in the organization of the

French community. . . . The Government considers it its duty now to define the status Indochina shall have. . . . The Indochinese federation will comprise, together with France and the other sections of the community, a "French Union" whose foreign interests will be represented by France. . . . The inhabitants of the Indochinese Federation will be . . . citizens of the French Union.

> — French government, declaration, translated
> from *Notes Documentaires et Etudes*, No. 115,
> Serie Coloniale XV, Ministière de
> l'Information, Paris, March 23, 1945

The Japanese have taken over Indo-China. . . . It would look very bad if we excluded the French from participation in our councils as regards Indo-China.

> — Prime Minister Winston Churchill, message to
> President Franklin D. Roosevelt day before he
> died, April 11, 1945

The record is entirely innocent of any official statement of this government questioning, even by implication, French sovereignty over Indo-China.

> — Secretary of State Edward R. Stettinius to
> French foreign minister, San Francisco,
> May 8, 1945

In my last conference with President Roosevelt . . . I told him that the French, British and Dutch were cooperating to prevent the establishment of a United Nations trusteeship for Indo-China.

> — Ambassador Patrick J. Hurley, letter to
> President Harry S Truman, May 28, 1945

The United States recognizes French sovereignty over Indochina.

> — Department of State,
> policy statement, June 1945

At Potsdam in July 1945 a precise line of demarcation was defined: south of latitude 16° N., South-East Asia Command was responsible, and north of that line the Chinese. Thus a precedent for the partitioning of Indo-China was established.

> — *Documents Relating to British Involvement in
> the Indo-China Conflict, 1945–1965*

Apprehension . . . is inevitable on the part of the French who have the second largest empire in the world but lack the means to defend it. Hence the concern about the fate of Indo-China, and the suspicions provoked by every American allusion to bases. . . . French touchiness on the subject of Indo-China is kept acute by American comments like that cited today by the newspaper *Combat*. . . . *Combat* says *The Washington Times Herald* asserted that "the United States did not conquer Japan to give back to European countries their lost colonies." . . . *Combat* . . . wonders whether idealism will become "the best ambassador of business men," an allusion to what the French call American economic imperialism.

> — Harold Callender, dispatch by wireless to *New York Times*, Paris, August 15, 1945

The French Government is taking steps in Washington and London to have its position in Indo-China fully recognized. . . . Gen. Charles de Gaulle and his colleagues realize that . . . the fate of Indo-China is going to be settled within the near future. . . . Soon after the Berlin Conference, the Paris authorities learned from outside sources that, in the initial talks that they had before Premier Stalin's arrival, President Truman and Prime Minister Churchill agreed on the advisability of re-establishing all French rights and prerogatives in the Indo-Chinese Union. This brought great relief, since French colonial circles have long feared that the colony might be turned to . . . international trusteeship.

The decision reached by Messrs. Truman and Churchill was interpreted to mean that all such schemes had been abandoned so far as Indo-China was concerned. . . . Nevertheless, during the past few days, the French have found fresh reasons to worry. . . . Tonking might become a field of operations for the Chinese army if Japanese troops holding that area should not readily comply with General MacArthur's orders. The Chinese, if they had a chance to rule Tonking . . . would, of course, endeavor to profit from France's helplessness of today and try to recapture a region that slipped out of their overlordship some 60 years ago. . . .

> — Pertinax, North American Newspaper Alliance, dispatch from Washington, *New York Times*, August 17, 1945

Dear Lt.:

I feel weaker since you left. Maybe I'd have to follow your advice—moving to some other place where food is easy to get, to improve my health.

I am sending you a bottle of wine, hope you like it.

Be so kind as to give me foreign news you got.

Please be good enuf to send to your H.Q. the following wires.

1. Daivet [a pro-Japanese nationalist group] plans to exercise large terror against French and to push it upon shoulder of VML [Viet Minh

League]. VML ordered 2 millions members and all it population to be watchful and stop Daivet criminal plan when & if possible. VML declares before the world its aim is national independence. It fights with political & if necessary military means. But never resorts to criminal & dishonest acts.

2. National Liberation Committee of VML begs U.S. authorities to inform United Nations the following. We were fighting Japs on the side of the United Nations. Not Japs surrendered. We beg United Nations to realize their solemn promise that all nationalities will be give democracy and independence. If United Nations forget their solemn promise & don't grant Indochina full independence, we will keep fighting until we get it.

         (Signed) LIBERATION COMMITTEE OF VML

Thank you for all the troubles I give you. . . . Best greetings!

Yours sincerely,

Hoo [*sic*]

— Ho Chi Minh, letter to American OSS liaison
officer "John," quoted by Robert Shaplen;
letter sent late August 1945

[Ho] would talk about American ideals and how he was sure America would be on his side . . . he thought that the United States would help in throwing out the French and in establishing an independent country. . . . He was convinced that America was for free, popular government all over the world; that it opposed colonialism in all its forms . . . and he seemed sincere in his desire to have our help.

— R. Harris Smith, *O.S.S.: The Secret History of
America's First Central Intelligence Agency*

I have always been impressed with your country's treatment of the Philippines. You kicked the Spanish out and let the Filipinos develop their own country. You were not looking for real estate, and I admire you for that. I have a government that is organized and ready to go. Your statesmen make eloquent speeches about helping those with self-determination. We are self-determined. Why not help us? Am I any different from Nehru, Quezon—even your George Washington? I, too, want to set my people free.

— Ho Chi Minh, quoted by René J.
Defourneaux,
Look, August 9, 1966

During the long years of the Japanese occupation, the Vietminh carried on increasingly strong underground activity under the slogan: "Neither the French nor the Japanese as masters! For the independence of Vietnam!" The French and Japanese joined in an equally persistent but unsuccessful attempt to stamp out the movement. . . . The Japanese collapse was the Vietminh opportunity. The puppet regimes in Saigon and Hanoi all but collapsed at the same time.

The Vietminh moved in to take over. A Vietminh congress was held at Caobang . . . the week the Japanese surrendered. A provisional government was formed. On August 19 . . . this government took power in Hanoi.

Bao Dai, for 20 years the puppet king of Annam under the French and briefly under the Japanese, wearily and gladly laid down his scepter. . . . The new banner of the republic, a yellow star on a red field, fluttered throughout the city. . . . In the South, at Saigon, the Vietminh on August 25 called for a popular demonstration. . . . More than 100,000 turned out . . . under banners proclaiming the new power of the Vietnam Republic. . . . The Vietminh was solidly in power in the north and south.

— Harold Isaacs, *No Peace for Asia*

British official sources said today that French Indo-China will be administered immediately after its liberation from the Japanese, by Chinese forces and representatives of Admiral Lord Louis Mountbatten's Southeast Asia Command, and not by French authorities. This decision . . . is likely to provoke considerable criticism in Paris.

— From Herald Tribune Bureau (London), *New York Herald Tribune*, August 23, 1945

We have declared ourself ready for any sacrifice. . . . We have decided to abdicate. . . . Upon leaving our throne . . . we request the new Government take care of the dynastic temples and royal tombs. . . . As for us, during 20 years' reign, we have known much bitterness. Henceforth, we shall be happy to be a free citizen in an independent country [France]. We shall allow no one to abuse our name or the name of the royal family.

— Emperor Bao Dai, abdication statement, Hué, August 25, 1945

"All men are created equal. They are endowed by their Creator with certain inalienable rights, among these are Life, Liberty, and the pursuit of Happiness."

This immortal statement was made in the Declaration of Independence of the United States of America in 1776. . . .

The Declaration of the French Revolution made in 1791 on the Rights of Man and the Citizen also states: "All men are born free and with equal rights. . . ."

Those are undeniable truths.

Nevertheless . . . the French . . . abusing the standard of Liberty, Equality and Fraternity, have violated our fatherland and oppressed our fellow-citizens. They have acted contrary to the ideals of humanity and justice.

In the field of politics, they have deprived our people of every democratic activity.

They have enforced inhuman laws; they have set up three distinct political regimes in the North, the Center and the South of Vietnam in order to wreck our national unity. . . .

They have built more prisons than schools. They have mercilessly slain our patriots; they have drowned our uprisings in rivers of blood. They have fettered public opinion. . . .

To weaken our race they have forced us to use opium and alcohol.

In the field of economics, they have fleeced us to the backbone, impoverished our people, and devastated our land.

They have robbed us of our rice fields, our mines, our forests, and our raw materials. They have monopolized the issuing of banknotes and the export trade.

They have invented numerous unjustifiable taxes and reduced our people, especially our peasantry to a state of extreme poverty. . . . In the autumn of 1940, when the Japanese Fascists violated Indochina's territory to establish new bases in their fight against the Allies, the imperialists went down on their bended knees and handed the country over to them.

Thus, from that date, our people were subjected to the double yoke of the French and the Japanese. Their sufferings and miseries increased. The result was that from the end of last year to the beginning of this year . . . more than two million of our fellow-citizens died from starvation. . . .

On several occasions before March 9, the Vietminh League urged the French to ally themselves with it against the Japanese. Instead of agreeing to this proposal, the French colonialists so intensified their terrorist activities against the Vietminh members that before fleeing they massacred a great number of our political prisoners. . . .

Notwithstanding all this, our fellow-citizens have always manifested toward the French a tolerant and humane attitude. Even after the Japanese putsch of March 1945, the Vietminh League helped many Frenchmen to cross the frontier, rescued some of them from Japanese jails, and protected French lives and property.

From the autumn of 1940, our country had in fact ceased to be a French colony and had become a Japanese possession.

After the Japanese had surrendered to the Allies, our whole people rose to regain our national sovereignty and to found the Democratic Republic of Vietnam.

The truth is that we have wrested our independence from the Japanese and not from the French.

The French have fled, the Japanese have capitulated, Emperor Bao Dai has abdicated. Our people have broken the chains which for nearly a century have fettered them and have won independence for the Fatherland. Our people at the same time have overthrown the monarchic regime that has reigned supreme for dozens of centuries. In its place has been established the present Democratic Republic.

For these reasons, we, members of the Provisional Government, representing the whole Vietnamese people, declare that from now on we break off all relations of a colonial character with France; we repeal all the international obligation that France has so far subscribed to on behalf of Vietnam and we abolish all the special rights the French have unlawfully acquired in our Fatherland.

The whole Vietnamese people, animated by a common purpose, are determined to fight to the bitter end against any attempt by the French colonialists to reconquer their country.

We are convinced that the Allied nations which at Teheran and San Francisco have acknowledged the principles of self-determination and equality of nations, will not refuse to acknowledge the independence of Vietnam.

A people who have courageously opposed French domination for more than eighty years, a people who have fought side by side with the Allies against the Fascists during these last years, such a people must be free and independent.

For these reasons, we, members of the Provisional Government of the Democratic Republic of Vietnam, solemnly declare to the world that Vietnam has the right to be a free and independent country—and in fact it is so already. The entire Vietnamese people are determined to mobilize all their physical and mental strength, to sacrifice their lives and property in order to safeguard their independence and liberty.

> — Declaration of Independence, Democratic
> Republic of Vietnam, September 2, 1945

The question of the government of Indochina is exclusively French. Civil and military control by the French is only a question of weeks.

> — General Douglas D. Gracey, Commander of
> British occupation troops in Indochina, before
> leaving India for Saigon, September 8, 1945

The British army proclaimed martial law throughout south Indo-China today in a move to head off a threatened uprising by anti-French

nationalists. Maj. Gen. Douglas D. Gracey, commander of British forces
in Indo-China . . . backed up his stern order by posting heavily-armed
Gurkha patrols throughout Saigon and the territory controlled by the
British to replace the native and Japanese police. The proclamation was
apparently intended to squelch native Annamite nationalists in prepara-
tion for the crucial moment when French authorities resume control of
their former colony and protectorates in Indo-China. Observers believed
the greatest danger of an explosion would come when the French
re-enter Indo-China and the Annamese see their last hope of independence vanishing.

> — *Washington Times-Herald,*
> UP dispatch from Saigon,
> September 20, 1945

Nowhere did the coming of Americans, in this case a mere handful of
them, mean so much to a people as it did to the population of northern
Indo-China. To Annamites, our coming was the symbol of liberation not
from Japanese occupation but from decades of French colonial rule. For
the Annamite government considered the United States the principal
champion of the rights of small peoples, guaranteed so promisingly by
the United Nations conferences. . . . Our prowess in the war, our vast
production abilities, our progressiveness in technical and social fields—
all were known by the Annamites, to a surprising degree. In their
blueprint for self-government they envisaged American trade bringing
them peacetime products.

American technicians to help them industrialize Vietnam, American
consultants in the political, medical and social sciences. Essentially, they
feel that the French did not develop the resources of the country for the
benefit of the people themselves, and in their own planning have
emphasized their intention to throw Vietnam open to American commercial penetration. As a matter of practical preference they would like to
see the economy of Vietnam geared to our own if that were possible or
desirable to us. Above all they want the good will of the American
people and our government. From the top of the Annamite leadership to
the bottom of the social scale in Tonkin, every person made a visible
effort to please American officers and men. They offered courtesies and
simple gestures of friendship at every opportunity.

The C.B.I. patch on the shoulder of an American was his ticket to a
warm welcome and good treatment. . . . Annamites asked for all sorts of
advice—how to run a newspaper, how to repair and operate machinery,
how to run a street-cleaning department most efficiently—even though
they were managing quite well indeed in operating utilities and other
physical functions of government. They inquired about our schools, our
courts, our elections, about the workings of both houses of the Congress.

They seemed to feel that every American contained within himself all the virtues and accomplishments of the nation they wanted most to emulate. . . .

The public grew to hate and to fear individual Japanese; the Annamites were happy to get rid of them, yet they maintained a respect for Japan as a seemingly undefeated loser of the war. This feeling was increased by the knowledge that British and French forces in the Saigon area were virtually allies of the Japanese in the fighting against native forces. . . . It is strongly recommended that a United States information service be established in Indo-China as soon as possible.

While the Annamites are not at present anti-Caucasian, the danger of such an attitude developing in the months to come is not remote. Nor is it fantastic to admit the possibility of an Asia-wide, sweeping revolt against all Westerners in a color war of the future. . . . Incidents such as the recent shipment of French troops to Saigon in American vessels must have impaired considerably the great prestige in the eyes of the Annamites we enjoyed at the cessation of hostilities with Japan.

> — Arthur Hale, U.S. Information Agency, report
> on visit to Hanoi, Fall 1945, Gallagher Papers,
> Department of the Army, classified until 1972

British army forces intervened in the dispute between Nationalist Annamites and French authorities today after two days and nights of street fighting. The British commander of Allied forces in southern Indo-China ordered Gurkha troops under his command to disarm insurgent Annamites. The French charged that the Annamites had been armed by the Japanese.

> — UP dispatch from Saigon,
> September 25, 1945

I believe the situation in Indo-China is now in hand and developments in Cambodia and Laos are relatively satisfactory.

> — French Minister of Colonies Paul Giacobbi to
> cabinet, Paris, September 25, 1945

A violent uprising of Annamite (Indo-Chinese independence) forces occurred today and the British fired mortars and heavy machine guns in efforts to halt the disturbance. . . . NBC Correspondent Guthrie Janssen, according to the United Press, reported from Saigon that the Japanese were firing on the French as well as the Annamites and said the French regard the trouble as "all Jap-inspired." . . . The British said recently that their only role in Indo-China was to keep order until sufficiently large French military forces arrived to assume control.

Correspondents were informed that Japanese troops in southern French Indo-China are still armed and guarding Allied property.

> — *Washington Post*, AP dispatch from Saigon,
> September 26, 1945

General Gracey, British Commander of Allied Forces in Southern Indo-China, reported today that the riotous native uprisings in Saigon had subsided somewhat. He issued stern orders to Field Marshal Terauchi, Commander of the Japanese Southern Armies, the keep the peace. General Gracey said he had "ordered the Japs to disarm the Annamese but they failed to do so." . . . Lieut. Gen. Takazo Numata, chief of staff and spokesman for Terauchi, conceded that Japanese soldiers had supplied arms to the Annamese after Japan's surrender. . . . Japanese soldiers had furnished the Annamese with mortars, light machine-guns, rifles and grenades, had taught the natives how to use them, and in some cases had posed as natives and participated in the fighting. A French division and a British division are due in Saigon early in October, when the Japanese will be disarmed and started for home.

> — *Washington Times-Herald*, AP delayed
> dispatch from Singapore, September 29, 1945

Admiral Lord Louis Mountbatten, chief of the Allied Southeast Asia Command, has hastened the shipment of British troops . . . to Indo-China, where Annamites have been rioting for weeks, it was disclosed today. . . . Admiral Mountbatten called to his headquarters Maj. Gen. D. D. Gracey, British commander in Indo-China, and Col. J. H. Cedille, head of a French mission that parachuted into the colony in August, for conferences on the riots in Indo-China.

> — *Washington Times-Herald*,
> UP dispatch from Singapore,
> September 29, 1945

I didn't come back to Indochina to give Indochina back to the Indochinese.

> — General Jean Leclerc, Saigon,
> September 30, 1945

Headquarters of the Southeast Asia Command announced today that an agreement had been reached for the cessation of hostilities in Indo-China by Annamite forces. . . . Saigon itself was reported quiet for the past 24 hours.

> — *Washington Times-Herald*,
> INS dispatch from Kandy (Ceylon),
> October 2, 1945

Fighting has broken out again in Indo-China. . . . The Annamese originated around Yunnan in southern China and were pushed south and east by the Chinese who helped make them what they are today: small-featured, delicate, energetic and sometimes effeminate. . . . Annamese don't carry umbrellas. A fellow caught in a downpour steps off the path and plucks a banana leaf. This gives him all the protection he wants. . . . Annamese like to eat bananas and bamboo shoots.

> — *Washington Times-Herald*,
> Scripps-Howard story,
> October 15, 1945

Viet-Minh, as its first move after seizure of the government, sought a united front against French imperialism. . . . Frenchmen . . . think that by . . . labelling Viet-Minh "Communist," they have summed up the situation to the disadvantage of the Vietnam government. There is considerable communist influence in Viet-Minh. . . . The national salute is very nearly the raised right arm salute of communists. Posters, banners, have been adapted from Western leftist art. . . . But at the same time there is ample evidence of an equally strong influence from the United States. The American experience in the Philippines has been brought to the people, down to the smallest village, by radio and newspaper. Policy statements and declarations by the government are obvious imitations of American techniques of democratic government. In short, the Viet-Minh leadership seems to have used communist methods of appeal . . . to arouse the masses behind a program for an independent democracy. To the casual observer Viet-Minh seems to have been successful . . . its campaigns of education and propaganda has reached the Annamite masses, to whom the program offers an outlet for French feelings that were long repressed and the positive goal of self-government. Certainly . . . it could not correctly be said that the people were not aroused by this campaign of the Viet-Minh and the government did not have their roots in the people.

Obviously, the basic feeling of the average Annamite toward the French is an old resentment. . . . The feeling was universal, excepting only the elite who enjoyed personal favor in the French government or in lucrative business connections. . . . The native people were contemptuous of the westerners who had boasted of their protection and improvement of a backward country only to turn that country over to the Japanese without a fight. During the three and a half years of Japanese occupation, hatred of the French mounted. When on March 9, 1945, the former rulers let themselves be ousted from government and virtually be confined to house prison, without even token opposition, contempt and hatred reached the boiling point. "You sold out the country twice," the Viet-Minh government has repeatedly accused in press and radio, "And now you want back the position you wouldn't defend, the unfair oppression of the Vietnamese who alone fought the enemy with whom you collaborated." The feeling of the Annamites against the French in Indo-China is a strong, active one. It was typified by the ricksha coolie whom observers saw refuse to carry a French civilian. He glared spitefully at the well-dressed Frenchman, spat on the walk, and with his head high pulled his vehicle away. Also typical was the cold refusal of an Annamite shopkeeper to sell her goods to a Frenchman and woman. A moment later she produced her entire stock of goods to show with great cordiality to two GI's.

> — Arthur Hale, U.S. Information Agency, report
> on visit to Hanoi, Fall 1945, Gallagher Papers,
> Department of the Army, classified until 1972

British forces beat off an Annamese threat to capture the Saigon airport, Saigon's only link with the outside world, as sharp fighting continued today between rebellious Indo-Chinese and British and French reoccupation troops. . . . Gurkhas of the British Indian Army repulsed an Annamese attempt to cross the Saigon River. . . . The Annamese have appealed to the United Nations on the grounds that they had been sold out by the Vichy Administration before the outbreak of the Pacific war. They asserted that Vichy had signed an economic agreement with the Japanese, aimed at "undermining the national front and repressing liberation." When the Allies landed in Normandy, the Japanese ceased to trust French colonial rule and disarmed and arrested French forces in Indo-China almost without opposition, the Annamese maintain. The Viet Minh party took the position that this act had ended 80 years of French rule, as far as the Annamese were concerned.

> — *New York Times*, AP dispatch from Saigon,
> October 15, 1945

Late in 1945 Ho had proclaimed the independence of the State of Vietnam "within the French Union." . . . The arrival of the first French troops December 19th and the way they arrived further darkened the scene. Under the Yalta agreement, British troops from the Indian Army constituted the Allied Occupation Force in the south of Vietnam, below the 16th parallel. In Tonkin the Chinese had been given the occupation assignment. The Chinese, under Marshal Lu Han, who was also called the "other Chinese Gimo," had devoted themselves to looting the country systematically of everything of value they could find.

> — Frank M. White, former major, OSS, part of
> American intelligence group working with Ho
> Chi Minh

[Could I send] to the United States of America a delegation of about 50 Vietnam youths with a view to establishing friendly cultural relations with the American youth on the one hand, and carrying on further studies in Engineering, Agriculture as well as other lines of specialization on the other. They have been all these years keenly interested in things American and earnestly desirous to get in touch with the American people whose fine stand for the noble ideals of international Justice and Humanity, and whose modern technical achievements have so strongly appealed to them.

> — President Ho Chi Minh, letter to Secretary of
> State James Byrnes, Hanoi, November 1, 1945

Since the autumn of 1940 our country has ceased to be a colony and has become a Japanese outpost . . . we have wrested our independence from the Japanese and not from the French. The French have fled, the Japanese have capitulated, Emperor Bao Dai has abdicated, our people have broken their fetters which for over a century have tied us down; our people have . . . overthrown the monarchic constitution . . . and instead have established the present Republican government.

> — President Ho Chi Minh, 1945

TOP SECRET

Ho Chi Minh handed me 2 letters addressed to President of USA . . . request USA as one of United Nations to support idea of Annamese independence according to Philippines example, to examine the case of the Annamese, and to take steps necessary to maintenance of world peace which is being endangered by French efforts to reconquer Indochina. . . . The petition ends with the statement that Annamese ask for full independence in fact and that in interim while awaiting UNO decision the Annamese will continue to fight the reestablishment of French imperialism.

> — American diplomat in Hanoi, identified as
> Landon, cablegram to State Department,
> February 27, 1946

TOP SECRET

In an interview with source, General Le Clerc ... expressed confidence that there would be no major Annamite resistance to French return.

> — Strategic Services Unit, War Department,
> Intelligence Dissemination No. A-66441 (SSU
> assumed some OSS functions after latter was
> disbanded in September 1945); the date:
> March 21, 1946; classified until 1972

TOP SECRET

Ho Chi Minh is firmly convinced that what his country needs most in its struggle for independence is the sympathy and understanding of the American people.

> — Strategic Services Unit, War Department, Intelligence Dissemination No. A-66610, March 27, 1946, classified until 1972

Ho Chi Minh spoke at various times of the aid which he hoped to get from the United States . . . he explained that the riches of his country were largely undeveloped, he felt that Indochina offered a fertile field for American capital and enterprise. He had resisted and would continue to resist the French desire for a continuation of their policy of economic monopoly. He was willing to give the French priority in such matters as advisers, concessions, and purchases of machinery and equipment, but if the French were not in a position to meet his country's needs he would insist on the right to approach other friendly countries. He hinted that the policy might apply to military and naval matters as well and mentioned the naval base at Cam Ranh Bay.

> — George M. Abbott, first secretary, American Embassy, Paris, memorandum to Ambassador Jefferson Caffery on conversation with Ho Chi Minh, September 12, 1946, classified until 1972

The old colonialism was out of date. . . . It was not the view of [French High Commissioner for Indochina] Admiral d'Argenlieu or most of the men around him. . . . The majority of the Frenchmen in Indochina, colonists and administrators alike, refused to recognize that their position in the country had changed. . . . The Vietminh took military and political steps to consolidate itself in power. . . . Relations with France worsened rapidly in the fall of 1946. . . . There was no mutual trust between the French and the Vietnamese, and the uneasy armistice inaugurated by the March 6 Agreement could not go on indefinitely. It was breached violently at Haiphong. . . . On orders from the French high command, which decided to teach the Vietnam Republic a lesson. The French bombarded the city on November 23, killing thousands of Vietnamese.

> — Ellen J. Hammer, *The State of Asia*

Attempts at conciliation . . . are out of season. The moment has come of giving a severe lesson to those who have treacherously attacked you. Make use of all the means at your disposal to master Haiphong and to bring the leaders of the Vietnamese to a better understanding of the situation.

> — General Valluy to Colonel Dèbes, French commander, Haiphong, November 21, 1946

I have learned with indignation of the recent attacks at Haiphong and Langson. . . . I bow down before our great, dead soldiers. I salute the wounded . . . the Government of the Republic and the whole country . . . realize the extraordinary difficulties you have met and the exceptional merits of our Expeditionary Corps, which will surmount them. . . . We shall never retreat or give up.

> — Admiral G. Thierry d'Argenlieu, French High Commissioner, Indochina, about Viet Minh attacks against French seeking to reimpose colonial rule, November 24, 1946

He spoke of his friendship and admiration for the United States and the Americans he had known and worked with in the jungle, etc., and how they had treated the Annamese as equals. He spoke of his desire to build up Vietnam in collaboration with the French so that his people might be better off, and so to that end they wanted independence to seek friends among other countries as well as France and to secure the capital needed to develop their country, which France was now too poor to give them. He said he knew that the United States did not like Communism, but that that was not his aim. If he could secure independence that was enough for his life time. "Perhaps 50 years from now the United States will be communist; and then the Vietnam can be also" or "then they will not object if the Vietnam is also." He spoke in English, but I am not sure of his exact words. The intent, at any rate, was a smiling, and friendly "Don't worry"—which coincides with the ablest French views (not the popular view) that the group in charge of Vietnam are at this stage nationalists first.

> — Abbot Moffat, chief of State Department's Division of Southeast Asian Affairs, conversation with Ho Chi Minh, Hanoi, December 14, 1946; Ho's last conversation with American diplomat and summary from Moffat private papers were classified until 1972

France does not intend in the present stage of evolution of the Indo-Chinese people to give them . . . independence, which would be an action prejudicial to the interests of both parties. . . . [Vietnamese nationalists] have increased the numbers and arms of their army; their political chiefs have conducted propaganda. . . . The French Government will not tolerate such grave and such flagrant breaches.

> — Admiral G. Thierry d'Argenlieu, special Christmas message, quoted by Reuters, Saigon, December 25, 1946

The situation is growing no worse. French forces in Indochina are carrying out an energetic action with caution.

> — Minister of National Defense Andre
> LeTroquer of France, Paris,
> December 26, 1946

The situation is well in hand.

> — Minister of Overseas Territories
> Marius Moutet of France,
> Saigon, December 26, 1946

The main Red forces [of Mao Tse-tung] will be annihilated within one year.

> — Generalissimo Chiang Kai-shek,
> New Year's Eve address to nation,
> Nanking, December 31, 1946

Ho Chih-minh [sic] . . . with his little goat beard, looks something like a Mongoloid Trotsky. . . . Onetime photographer, cabin boy, Ho has a War Minister named Vo Nguyen-giap, who hates the French, because, he says, his wife perished in a French jail. . . . At week's end, there was talk of weakening rebel resistance and furtive peace feelers.

> — *Time*, January 6, 1947

It is untrue to speak of war in Indochina. The truth is that operations with a view of re-establishing order are being undertaken.

> — Admiral G. Thierry d'Argenlieu,
> January 10, 1947

Frankly we have no solution to the [Indochina] problem to suggest.

> — Secretary of State George C. Marshall,
> cablegram drafted by P. T. Culbertson, French
> desk, Division of Western European Affairs,
> State Department to American Embassy,
> Paris, February 3, 1947; declassified, 1972

Only in April 1947 did the French government reply to a Vietnamese proposal for an armistice with a concrete offer of terms, brought secretly to Ho by Paul Mus, a noted scholar. This led to a brief but fleeting optimism among the Vietnamese, until they discovered that it was a demand for capitulation. . . . Despite early French victories, it was soon evident that the French could not hope to win by military means alone in Vietnam; they found themselves at a military stalemate. . . . In a memorandum to the Paris government soon after full-scale fighting broke out on December 19, d'Argenlieu proposed returning Bao Dai to the throne. . . . The ex-emperor, in 1947, was living in Hong Kong, where he laid the foundations of the reputation that caused critics to label him the "night-club emperor." He had little personal following in Cochin China or Tonkin. Even in Annam, the seat of the imperial dynasty, his support was not widespread. But Bao Dai seemed the one person around whom a number of minor disaffected political groups might be rallied in opposition to Ho. . . . The French envisaged Bao Dai as a key figure, the majority of the country, however, still supported Ho. Despite the strong and entrenched Communist minority in the Republican government, by far the greater part of non-Communist Vietnamese nationalists regarded Ho as their only possible leader of the struggle against the French.

> — Ellen J. Hammer, *The State of Asia*

Turn Catholic and have rice to eat.

> — Vietnamese proverb during French colonial
> rule

Negotiations with Bao Dai dragged on in 1949. . . . The French . . . urged Bao Dai, who was then in France, to go home and rally his people around him. . . . Bao Dai departed for home, ending his three years of self-imposed exile on April 28, 1949. . . . He acted as though he had never abdicated, announcing his intention to retain provisionally the title of emperor. . . . In the meantime he proclaimed himself chief of state. . . . Some 150,000 soldiers were fighting on the French side in Vietnam. . . . They included not only Frenchmen, but also a number of Indochinese; there were Germans who had exchanged the swastika for the tricolor of the French Foreign Legion, and Moroccans and Senegalese from Overseas France. . . . The French were spending more than half of their military budget in Indochina, but still the guerrilla war went on, and by the end of 1949 the greater part of the country was in the hands of the Ho forces.

> — Ellen J. Hammer, *The State of Asia*

There is no longer a military problem in Indochina.

> — French Minister of Defense Paul Coste-Floret,
> May 13, 1947

France will remain in Indochina, and Indochina will remain in the French Union.

> — Emile Bollaert, French High Commissioner,
> Indochina, quoted in *Le Monde*, May 17, 1947

Present actions are only a police action.

> — Paul Coste-Floret, October 15, 1947

[There should be] no difficulty in raising at once adequate Annamite forces to defeat Ho Chi Minh.

— William Bullitt, former ambassador to France,
    Life, December 29, 1947

There were various reasons why the Democratic Republic of Vietnam could not find any champions. . . . The United States did have a tremendous stake in France, which it regarded as a key to the defense and recovery of Western Europe. The State Department, as a result, despite American traditional opposition to colonialism, was sympathetic when Frenchmen argued that if they lost Vietnam, they would lose North Africa and most of their empire as well.

— Ellen J. Hammer, *The State of Asia*

The French claim that their situation in the northern state of Tonkin is greatly improved as a result of their offensive last fall. . . . Neutral observers see three factors indicating that Bao Dai may be able to win over a majority of the resistance. They are: (1) The prestige of the Emperor among his former subjects. (2) A growing weariness of fighting, noted among the peasantry and among the guerrillas themselves. (3) A growing sense of urgency among the French. . . . Ho Chi Minh and his Viet Minh party . . . remain a major and unknown quantity.

— AP dispatch, Saigon, March 13, 1948

No matter what else we have of offensive or defensive weapons, without superior air power America is a bound and throttled giant; impotent and easy prey to any yellow dwarf with a pocket knife.

— Congressman Lyndon B. Johnson, Democrat
    of Texas, speech in House of Representatives,
    March 15, 1948

TOP SECRET

Since V-J day . . . the Vietnamese have stubbornly resisted the reestablishment of French authority. . . . We have not urged the French to negotiate with Ho Chi Minh, even though he probably is now supported by a considerable majority of the Vietnamese people, because of his record as a Communist. . . . Ho Chi Minh is the strongest and perhaps the ablest figure in Indochina and any suggested solution which excludes him is an expedient of uncertain outcome. We are naturally hesitant to press the French too strongly or to become deeply involved so long as we are not in a position to suggest a solution or until we are prepared to accept the onus of intervention.

— Department of State, policy statement,
    September 27, 1948, from *U.S.–Vietnam
    Relations, 1945–1967*, declassified for House
    Armed Services Committee by Department of
    Defense

This House must now assume the responsiblity of preventing the onrushing tide of Communism from engulfing all Asia.

> — Congressman John F. Kennedy, Democrat of
> Massachusetts, speech in House of
> Representatives, January 25, 1949

His Holiness the Pope is praying for Emperor Bao Dai of Vietnam.

> — Vatican announcement, November 1949

Indochina is a prize worth a large gamble. Ever since World War II, Indochina has yielded an annual interest of $300 million. In the North are exportable tin, tungsten, zinc, manganese, coal, lumber, and rice, and in the South are rice, rubber, tea, pepper, cattle, and hides. . . . From the military standpoint Indochina is equally important, forming an 800-mile long bridge between Communist China and Malaya and with a common frontier with both Burma and Thailand. Its two main harbors, Hai Phong and Saigon, are excellent bases.

> — *New York Times*, February 12, 1950

Ho [is] the mortal enemy of native independence in Indochina.

> — Secretary of State Dean Acheson, quoted in
> *Department of State Bulletin*,
> February 13, 1950

Viet Namese Premier Nguyen Phan Long promised today to defeat what the French say are Communist-led Nationalists in six months if his government got United States military and economic aid.

> — *New York Times*, February 15, 1950

I do not think conditions in Indo-China are hopeless at all. They could become very good.

> — Robert Allan Griffin, head, U.S. aid mission,
> Singapore, March 16, 1950

The United States Government . . . considers the situation to be such as to warrant its according economic aid and military equipment to the Associated States of Indochina and to France in order to assist them in restoring stability.

> — Secretary of State Dean Acheson,
> Paris, May 8, 1950

The Government of the United States has decided to initiate a program of economic aid to the States of Cambodia, Laos, and Vietnam . . . to restore stability . . . the U.S. Government is establishing, with headquarters in Saigon and associated with the U.S. Legation, a special economic mission . . . working with . . . the French High Commissioner. . . . The approval of these agreements will be subject to legal conventions existing between the Associated States and France. . . .

> — American chargé d'affaires, Saigon, note to chiefs of state, Vietnam, Laos, and Cambodia, May 24, 1950

It is [Emperor] Bao Dai's mission—and the U.S.–French hope, to rally his countrymen to the anti-Communist camp of the West. In this undertaking he needs time. "Nothing can be done overnight," he says.

> — *Time*, Bao Dai cover story, May 29, 1950

The attempted assassination of a Cabinet member yesterday moved . . . Bao Dai's Vietnam state today to embark on total war against Ho Chi Minh's . . . guerrillas. . . . The new crackdown includes imprisonment without trial for knowing underground terrorists. . . . The authoritarian policy is an acknowledgement of Vietnam failure to woo some nationalistic factions with arguments that under Ho Chi Minh they were fighting for Moscow communism instead of nationalism.

Almost all over Indo-China, regular forces are in control in daylight. Terrorists take over at night. . . . Persons charged with subversive political activity will be sent to concentration camps by executive order. . . . The first measure put into effect by Bao Dai has clamped censorship on the French-language press. The nationalistic Vietnamese press has criticised the Bao Dai Government and some sections are clearly on the side of Ho Chi Minh.

> — *New York Times*, AP dispatch from Saigon, June 7, 1950

I have . . . directed acceleration in the furnishing of military assistance to the forces of France and the Associated States in Indochina and the dispatch of a military mission. . . .

> — President Harry S Truman, statement on violation of 38th Parallel in Korea, June 26, 1950

There have been no requests, suggestions, nor plans for sending American military units to Indo-China.

> — Major General Graves B. Erskine, commander, 1st Marine Division, ranking Defense Department representative, U.S. military mission, Indochina, July 20, 1950

I think that 150,000 elite French troops should have settled the issue in about four months.

> — General Douglas MacArthur, commander, U.S. forces, Far East, Wake Island, October 15, 1950

The United States and Great Britain . . . were anxious to stem the spread of Communism. The French recognized this and, hoping for help in their war against Ho, emphasized that they were not fighting a colonial war in Vietnam, but an anti-Communist war. They were the defenders of Western civilization in the Far East, they insisted, and as such were entitled to American aid, not only in Europe (where Marshall Plan dollars released francs for expenditures in the Vietnamese war), but also in Indochina.

— Ellen J. Hammer, *The State of Asia*

Diem came to the United States . . . early in 1951. He lived mostly at the Maryknoll Seminary, a Catholic men's school located in New York state. . . . Diem made powerful friends in Catholic circles. These friends included Francis Cardinal Spellman, Senator John F. Kennedy (D., Mass.), Senator Mike Mansfield (D., Mont.), Joseph P. Kennedy, the father of the Senator and a powerful behind-the-scenes political figure in the United States, and a host of others. Earlier, he had greatly impressed Mr. Justice William O. Douglas of the Supreme Court who, after a trip to Vietnam, had written in praise of Diem's abilities.

— Senator Ernest Gruening, Democrat of Alaska, *Vietnam Folly*

We will have victory in 15 months.

— General Jean de Lattre de Tassigny, mid-December 1950

Ho is a dangerously able soldier and administrator trained in France . . . it was he who set up the original Viet Nam Republic, immediately after the conclusion of the war. With Ho are most of the Indo-Chinese who (a) hate the French, (b) hate economic despotism, (c) hate the past. . . . Americans, by and large, do not understand Asia. . . . We must be practical . . . in Indo-China, where we would deliver that country to communism if we withdrew our support of the French.

— John Gunther, in *Look*, January 2, 1951

The Communist drive for Hanoi has been smashed completely and the situation now rests in our hands.

— General Jean de Lattre de Tassigny, French commander in chief, Indochina, January 5, 1951

Reds in North Vietnam are up against this situation: *Food shortage* is acute.

— *U.S. News & World Report*, January 6, 1951

General Jean de Lattre de Tassigny, the new French Commander in Chief in Indo-China, is both energetic and optimistic. . . . A fatalistic and defeatist philosophy that had permeated too much French thought and a lack of original political and military thought or vigorous political and military action have contributed to the development of the present serious situation. General de Lattre has . . . both energy and courage; perhaps new minds in Indo-China may supply the tough, swift and novel methods that the crisis demands.

— Hanson W. Baldwin, *New York Times*,
January 10, 1951

Chanting "there is no God but Allah," fierce Moroccan mountaineers swept into Vietminh Communist rebels in the battle raging 32 miles from Hanoi. . . . Overhead, French King Cobra fighters strafed Vietminh troops in foxholes.

— *Washington Times-Herald*,
Reuters dispatch from Hanoi,
January 17, 1951

Last week . . . came brighter news. In Indo-China, where France has committed half of all her armed strength . . . a new broom suddenly began to sweep. An aggressive, five-star French general named Jean de Lattre de Tassigny, a complete stranger to Indo-China, had just been made the country's commander in chief after a succession of incompetents. . . . De Lattre arrived . . . counterattacked and generally began acting like a man who likes to fight. These tactics . . . imparted some of De Lattre's brimming confidence to the Indo-Chinese. . . . The De Lattre strategy is to hit them where they are.

— *Life*, January 22, 1951

This month 30 Sherman tanks, Hellcats and newly arrived B-26s were supporting the French counteroffensive. . . . The French had for the moment more than balanced the situation in their favor. For the time, De Lattre's gamble had paid off.

— Dean Brelis, *Life*, January 22, 1951

Premier René Plevin told President Truman today that French forces had every expectation of staying on in Indo-China and fighting off the Communists.

— *New York Times*, January 29, 1951

Bao Dai, Chief of State of Vietnam, outlined his ideas for social, political and economic progress in a lunar New Year radio address to the nation here tonight. . . . Bao Dai's speech ushered out the "Year of the Tiger" and heralded the "Year of the Cat" for the Vietnamese and he predicted steady future progress in the pacification and the general well-being.

> — Tillman Durdin, dispatch from Saigon,
> *New York Times*, February 5, 1951

Arms aid from the U.S. is playing an important role in helping the French in Indo-China resist the Communist-led Vietminh forces, Brigadier General Francis G. Brink declared at the Pentagon today. General Brink is chief of the U.S. Military Assistance Mission in Indo-China. . . . General Brink told reporters today that French authorities in Indo-China were optimistic about the prospects of turning back the Vietminh insurgents and in this connection that Vietminh troops were poor defensive fighters. . . . General Brink observed that, "This is the first time I've seen people really fighting Communism in Asia."

> — *New York Times*, dispatch from Washington,
> February 6, 1951

The French have lately displayed increased ability to deal with the attacks of the Vietminh insurgents.

> — Tillman Durdin, dispatch from Saigon,
> *New York Times*, February 9, 1951

A military solution to the stalemate in the fighting is probable in the reasonably near future. . . . Progress already accomplished by the Associated States of Vietnam, Laos and Cambodia in every field is remarkable and will not fail in the long run.

> — Ambassador Donald R. Heath, Paris,
> March 20, 1951

The French command here is capable of handling the American military aid. . . . Plans for the future here seem to be well-formed.

> — General Mark W. Clark,
> U.S. commander in chief, Far East,
> Saigon, March 20, 1951

General of the Army Douglas MacArthur's criticisms of the French Army in Indo-China . . . have caused pain, surprise and resentment in French quarters here. Gen. MacArthur's . . . estimate that the French should have been able to clean up the insurgents in 4 months are rejected as displaying a lack of understanding of the actual conditions.

> — *New York Times*, dispatch from Hanoi,
> May 1, 1951

The Communist assault in Indochina has been checked by the free people of Indochina with the help of the French.

> — President Harry S Truman, May 7, 1951

French Union forces have beaten back three attacks by Indochina's Viet Minh insurgents stabbing at the underbelly on the French-held Tonkin delta in a seven-day battle for possession of the rice harvest . . . [in] the Viet-Namese Catholic provincial capital of Phatdiem, 75 miles southeast of Hanoi. . . . The French said the garrisons, manned by Catholic partisans, had fought with desperate gallantry.

> — *Washington Times-Herald*, Reuters dispatch
> from Hanoi, June 3, 1951

Gov. Thomas E. Dewey arrived today and told reporters the defense of Indo-China from Communist aggression was the keystone of Southeast Asia defenses. The touring New York governor said that if Indo-China, where the French and Vietnamese were engaged in a long war with Vietminh guerrillas . . . should fall to communism, Southeast Asia would be lost spiritually, if not militarily.

> — *New York Times*, AP dispatch from Canberra,
> Australia, August 6, 1951

With the assured support of as great a power as the United States, the people of Indo-China should get more of the confidence they badly need.

> — General Jean de Lattre de Tassigny,
> September 13, 1951

I am absolutely sure that it is a question of months, perhaps one or two years, but we shall dominate the problem surely. . . . We are putting [in] . . . something between two and three billion of dollars every year. . . . We have 38,000 killed in Indochina and more than a hundred thousand lost in all. . . . It's a question of months. . . . The citizens of those countries are very desirous to make the national armies and I do all that I can to help them—and they know it. But you see to make national armies . . . it is necessary to have soldiers. Our French and French Union soldiers . . . they are splendid soldiers. . . . The American Mission in Indochina helps me with the equipment. . . . The Chief of that Mission, General Brink . . . is for me a great friend, a great supporter, a great help.

> — General Jean de Lattre de Tassigny,
> *Meet the Press*, NBC, September 16, 1951

Plans to smash half a million Communist rebels in a big 1952 Indochina offensive are awaiting the outcome of the current visit to the U.S. of Gen. Jean de Lattre, the 62-year-old commander of Indochina's 380,000 strong French Union army. Gen. De Lattre has halted the rebels' advances in eight months, spending more than a billion French francs a day. Now, he wants to . . . turn Indochina into another successful Greece inside a year. To inject into his army the firepower "boost" which he believes it needs for this task, Gen. De Lattre is expected to ask the U.S. joint chiefs of staff for more military aid.

> — Reuters dispatch from Saigon,
>   September 17, 1951

There will be victory within 18 months to two years. Once Tongking is lost, there really is no barrier before Suez. . . . The loss of Asia would mean the end of Islam. . . . The fall of Islam would mean upheavals in North Africa. . . .

> — General Jean de Lattre de Tassigny
>   to National Press Club, Washington,
>   September 20, 1951

The French are defending Indochina now with 140,000 troops, and they're doing an awful lot of dying.

> — Governor Thomas E. Dewey, Republican of
>   New York, *Meet the Press*, NBC,
>   October 14, 1951

There is no question that the Communist menace in French Indo-China has been stopped.

> — General J. Lawton Collins, chief of staff,
>   U.S. Army, Taipei, Taiwan, October 27, 1951

It is generally agreed in the United States that we should support and assist the armies of France and the Associated States in meeting the armed threat in Indochina. . . . We are trying to build, the enemy is trying to tear down.

> — Assistant Secretary of State for Far Eastern
>   Affairs Dean Rusk, November 1951

In Indochina we have allied ourselves to the desperate effort of the French regime to hang on to the remnants of empire. There is no broad general support for the native [Bao Dai] Government among the people of the area.

> — Senator John F. Kennedy,
>   Democrat of Massachusetts, November 1951

I have just come back from a visit to Indochina recently and I would

say that certainly conditions within Indochina have greatly improved
since General de Lattre went there.

> — General J. Lawton Collins,
> *Meet the Press*, NBC,
> December 23, 1951

French Finance Minister René Mayer asked . . . that the U.S. grant
France $400,000,000 as aid in the Indo-Chinese war in the coming year.

> — *New York Times*, December 28, 1951

An American delegate to the United Nations said today that France
wants to withdraw from Indo-China, but is remaining "at the insistence
of the United States." Rep. Mike Mansfield (D.) of Montana made this
statement after conferring in France with both French and American
leaders. . . . The congressman added: "They are remaining at our
insistence . . . French leaders are in agreement that [withdrawal] would
be hailed everywhere with acclaim." Mansfield, a member of the House
foreign affairs committee, continued: "The French have committed in
Indo-China . . . their very best men, the cream of their army. Their
casualties exceed ours in Korea. . . . They are pouring into the conflict
there in money the equivalent of what they are receiving from the United
States in Marshall plan funds." The Montana Democrat stated that the
French feel their financial interests in Indo-China are not sufficiently
important now to warrant the sacrifice they are making in men and
money. He added that the United States has asked the French
government to remain in Indo-China and in return has agreed to furnish
the French colonial army and its native allies with armaments. Mansfield
termed Indo-China "a key to power in Southeast Asia. If the Communists take over Indo-China, then they will have a clear path to the rubber
and oil of Southeast Asia, including the East Asia."

> — INS,
> December 31, 1951

We're actually at war in Asia today and not at war in Europe. . . . We
are helping in the development of Vietnamese forces in Indochina.

> — W. Averell Harriman, presidential adviser,
> *Meet the Press*, NBC, January 27, 1952

Indo-China, torn by war for five years, is sapping the strength of
France. Here France has spent about 2.5 billion dollars. That's about the
equivalent of U.S. aid to France since World War II. A force of 350,000
men fights Communist-led rebels in Indo-China. Lives lost by anti-Com-

munists so far total more than 30,000, including nearly 1,500 French officers, the flower of the French Army.

> — *U.S. News & World Report*, January 18, 1952

Many in the Thah Hoa area believe that Ho Chi Minh, Vietminh leader, is dead.

> — *New York Times*, February 10, 1952

It is vital that further American aid be given anti-Communist Vietnamese in Indo-China.

> — C. Douglas Dillon, ambassador designate to
> France, before Senate Foreign Relations
> Committee, February 18, 1952

Laos is making steady progress in cleaning up insurrectionary forces within her borders.

> — Tillman Durdin, dispatch from Vientiane,
> Laos, *New York Times*, February 18, 1952

The French are holding Indo-China, without which we would lose Japan and the Pacific.

> — Governor Thomas E. Dewey, Albany,
> February 19, 1952

France does not refuse to talk with the Vietminh, but we will not take the first step.

> — Jean Letourneau, Minister of Overseas France,
> February 25, 1952

The strategical, geographical position of the area, as well as the vitally important raw materials, such as tin and rubber, which it supplies, makes it important for us to maintain an effective support of the French Government.

> — Secretary of Defense Robert S. Lovett,
> March 13, 1952

Ngo Dinh Diem is revered by the Vietnamese because he is honest and independent and stood firm against the French influence.

> — Supreme Court Justice William O. Douglas,
> *North From Malaya*, 1952

We shall need much help from the United States and France in creating our army.

> — General Nguyen Van Hinh,
> Saigon, April 27, 1952

The military situation appears to be developing favorably. . . . The tide is now turning in our favor. . . . We can anticipate continued favorable developments. . . . Aggression has been checked.

> — Secretary of State Dean Acheson, June 1952

Results of the Tonkin hostilities since last December have been decidedly positive. We are much stronger than at the beginning of last winter. . . . Not only do I not fear the Vietminh offensive, but I look forward to it because it will suffer the same fate as all of its predecessors without being as troublesome for us. . . . A new setback for the Vietminh runs the risk of being decisive. . . . We have dealt the enemy their heaviest defeat since the start of the Indo-China war. . . . It is now evident that they suffered more during the last campaign season than appeared to be the case.

> — General Raoul Salan, commander in chief,
> French Union forces, Indochina, Saigon,
> June 6, 1952

The reinforcement of the French Expeditionary Force, particularly its aviation, thanks to American aid, no longer leaves any hope for the Viet-Minh. . . .

> — Philippe Devilliers, French journalist,
> Paris, 1952

M. Jean Letourneau, Minister of the Associated States for the French Government, has been spending the last few days in Washington. . . . I would like to share with you the feeling of encouragement and confidence which M. Letourneau inspires. . . . The military situation appears to be developing favorably. . . . The effort has made great progress. . . . The national armies . . . look forward with confidence and determination to assuming an increasing share of the burden of carrying on the struggle. Their effectiveness fully justifies the program of expansion to which the governments concerned are committed and underlines, I believe, the soundness of our own decision to render increasing assistance. . . . Favorable developments have not been confined to the fighting fronts and to the national armies. There are increasing evidences of the growing vitality of the Associated States in handling their political, financial and economic affairs. M. Letourneau's account . . . was heartening. . . . We are doing our best. . . . The Communist . . . aggression has been checked and recent indications warrant the view that the tide is now turning in our favor. Once again the policy of meeting aggression with force is paying off and I can, I believe, be confident . . . we can anticipate continued favorable developments.

> — Secretary of State Dean Acheson,
> news conference, June 18, 1952

The Washington conference on Indo-China ended today on an optimistic note. . . . The discussions preface a new and more hopeful phase in the seven-year war that has torn the rich and strategically important Indo-China area. The reasons for optimism are two . . . U.S. aid . . . also because of improved policies. . . . The native forces fighting with the French are being strengthened greatly. . . . More and more the burden of fighting . . . is being transferred to the Vietnamese.

For the first time . . . the French . . . can count the campaign season just ended as a definite victory . . . a victory in the sense of tactical successes . . . a victory in the campaign of attrition. . . . Ho Chi Minh's Communist forces suffered very severely. . . . French leadership, American aid and strengthened native forces far more than offset French losses. . . . The most hopeful aspect of the Indo-Chinese situation is the increasing utilization of native troops. . . . The process of organizing Asiatic armies to halt Asiastic Communism has been well-begun in Indo-China.

> — Hanson W. Baldwin, military editor,
> *New York Times*, June 19, 1952

There was unanimous satisfaction over the vigorous and successful course of military operations.

> — *Department of State Bulletin*, June 30, 1952

France may be obliged to abandon Indo-China. . . . It should not be allowed to suggest, however, that the situation in Indo-China is one of approaching catastrophe. . . . The actual military position is getting better, not worse. . . . It has been possible . . . to prevent any large-scale Communist occupation of rice-harvest areas. The position, therefore, is considerably better than it was a year ago. . . . The improved position has two elements of strength. First, there has been an important increase in the training and equipping of a Vietnamese army . . . attracting more recruits than ever . . . training of Vietnamese officers and non-coms is going forward at an accelerated rate.

There is no reason why the manpower balance should not swing steadily toward Vietnam. . . . The second element is the increased pace of United States military assistance. There has been an actual step-up in the rate of deliveries. . . . The equipment of the Vietnamese forces has been affected for the better. There is need for a further build-up and for even more rapid deliveries, but there is assurance that it will be forthcoming. The line in Indo-China is being held. . . . The French . . . are not right if they suggest that they can, or will, abandon this commitment. . . . The French, and we, will unquestionably continue.

> — Editorial, *New York Times*, August 2, 1952

The situation in Indo-China is better than last December and possibly
the best since hostilities started.
> — Admiral Arthur W. Radford,
> commander in chief, U.S. Pacific Fleet,
> New Delhi, November 7, 1952

In the small and troubled Communist land of North Viet Nam . . .
salaries and taxes are still computed in bags of rice. . . . In Hanoi, rice is
still rationed, and beggars, though forbidden by law, swarm the streets.
The dong has sunk so low—7,000 to the dollar—that it may well be the
worst currency in the world.
> — *Time*, December 1, 1952

We only pray they will attack us.
> — General Jean Giles, commander,
> Nasan fortress, December 24, 1952

The reoccupation of Dien Bien Phu must constitute in the forthcoming
period the first step for the regaining of control of the T'ai country and
for the elimination of the Viet-Minh from the area west of the Black
River.
> — General Raoul Salan,
> Directive No. 40, December 30, 1952

We have a mission there now, and the French are paying more
attention than was originally the case, I might say, to our general views
. . . in the matter of handling the Vietnamese troops.
> — General J. Lawton Collins, U.S.
> Representative to NATO, *Meet the Press*,
> NBC, January 3, 1953

The future of our military actions is now secured.
> — General Raoul Salan,
> quoted by *Time*, January 5, 1953

Beneath the wan lights of flare shells, the war in Indo-China moved
into the seventh year. Said a red-haired Foreign Legionnaire: "We now
have the oldest war in the world." . . . In a dugout mess 25 feet
underground, Nassan Commander Two-Star General Jean Giles passed
out cigars and liquors to his staff. Said bearlike General Giles: "We've
done a nice job here." . . . Straws in the wind: the native Viet Nam
soldiers are coming into their own. French officers, once hostile to their
small, thin allies, now speak enthusiastically of the Viet Nam soldiers,
report them gaining in strength and spirit. . . . If, in the seventh year of

fighting, the French could command the confidence and support of native peoples, there was hope for Indo-China.

> — *Time*, January 12, 1953

All over war-racked Viet Nam from secure Saigon to tiny towns barely out of sound of Red gunfire . . . local elections gave Emperor Bao Dai's anti-Communist government a thumping vote of confidence. . . . "Even in my dreams I didn't expect such popular success," said Viet Nam's Premier Nguyen Van Tam.

> — *Time*, February 9, 1953

Military shipments should be stepped up considerably to that area . . . Indo-China is at this time the most important area on the continent of Asia. Its loss would start a chain-reaction.

> — Senator Mike Mansfield,
> Democrat of Montana,
> Senate Foreign Relations Committee,
> February 21, 1953

The more arms are given to Bao Dai, and the more the United States attempts to get "Asians to fight Asians," the more arms and recruits will come to the People's Army.

> — President Ho Chi Minh, February 1953

This is a difficult job. . . . I am thinking of helicopter units. . . . I am also impressed by the French military plans, by the apparent Vietnamese determination to fight. . . . I could not make any better plans than those already in existence here. . . . You know it is a policy of my Government to help those who help themselves—and the Vietnamese Government is doing just that.

> — General Mark W. Clark, U.S. commander in
> chief, Far East, after 4-day visit to Indochina,
> Hanoi, February 24, 1953

C. Douglas Dillon, new Ambassador to France, indicated today that the U.S. would supply more military aid toward helping the French. . . . Mr. Dillon said after a call on President Eisenhower that the Administration's "general feeling was that Indo-China aid should be increased."

> — *New York Times*,
> UP dispatch from Washington,
> February 27, 1953

With our new Vietnamese battalions, we think we shall be able to clear the Red River Delta by 1955. . . . After that, we shall move northward into the Communist rear territory. . . . We see a turning tide in Indo-China.

> — General Raoul Salan, Saigon, March 6, 1953

The progress already accomplished by the Associated States of Vietnam, Laos and Cambodia in every field is remarkable and will not fail in the long run to create a sure and solid barrier against the onslaught of totalitarian Communism.

> — Ambassador Donald R. Heath, Paris,
> March 20, 1953

We are trying to develop the national Vietnam army in order that we may one day bring back to Europe the greater part of the French Expeditionary Force.

> — Premier René Mayer of France, Paris,
> March 20, 1953

We will . . . reach victory in Indochina.

> — Premier René Mayer of France,
> quoted by *New York Times*, March 26, 1953

I am confident we can hold this area.

> — Colonel André Gillard, commander,
> French Union troops, Laos, March 29, 1953

The French here are making really efficient use of arms we deliver to them, and surely don't need to be stuffed with advice on how to use them.

> — General Mark W. Clark, after 3-hour briefing
> by General Raoul Salan and Vietnamese Chief
> of Staff Nguyen Van Hinh and 25-minute chat
> with Emperor Bao Dai, quoted by *Time*,
> March 30, 1953

I should like to underline once more my unshakable conviction that the Associated States [of Indochina] will be successful in protecting their freedom and a military solution is possible within the reasonably near future.

> — Ambassador Donald R. Heath,
> quoted by *Time*, March 30, 1953

A somewhat larger expenditure might be necessary.

> — Secretary of State John Foster Dulles,
> April 13, 1953

The situation is serious. The Viet Minh have introduced new complications in Laos. But the Viet Minh will be defeated. They must be.

> — Admiral Arthur W. Radford, after conference
> with General Raoul Salan, Hanoi,
> April 25, 1953

If today the French had the same military system . . . set up in Britain—two years military service and the power to send conscripts beyond Europe—they would, I believe, have much less difficulty in maintaining their position in Indo-China.

> — Winston Churchill, quoted in *New York Times*,
> May 12, 1953

What will enable us to defend Laos is the impossibility of the Vietminh's maintaining more than 20,000 to 25,000 men there.

> — General Raoul Salan, memorandum to
> General Henri Eugène Navarre, new
> commander in chief, French Union forces,
> Indochina, May 1953

[The Vietminh] is done for.

> — General Henri Eugène Navarre to
> General Raoul Salan, May 21, 1953

My decisions are made within a certain framework established in France before I took command. The framework is secret and personal. . . . Observe, our casualties are only half what they were in the same period last year. I am sending these charts to Paris.

> — General Raoul Salan,
> quoted by *Time*, May 25, 1953

General Henri Eugène Navarre . . . was a cavalryman . . . a small, shy man . . . he hardly showed himself to the troops, and he evaded newsmen. . . . Then, last week General Navarre completed his review of the Indo-China battlefront and made one of the most aggressive declarations yet to come from a French officer in that theater [since] the late Marshal de Lattre had said: "We shall not let go of one inch of terrain." Navarre's plans were well-received by French Union soldiers, who have become discouraged by continuous caution. Said a delighted staff officer: "One must not forget that his weapon is cavalry. And in cavalry, one attacks!"

> — *Time*, June 29, 1953

We shall take the offensive. We shall give back to our troops the mobility and aggressiveness that they have sometimes lacked. Our units have become too heavy. Certainly our troops have preserved their supremacy in pitched battle—when they are offered it by the Viet Minh. But this is not enough. Henceforth our troops will seek the enemy in the very heart of their jungle and paddies. They will impose battle on the enemy. . . . Our infantry must have confidence in itself, in its weapons and its officers. There may be a real problem of confidence among our troops. If this problem presents itself, it will be resolved. We shall renew the war.

> — General Henri Eugène Navarre,
> quoted by *Time*, June 29, 1953

I shall not make the same mistakes as my predecessors.

> — General Henri Eugène Navarre,
> last Sunday in July 1953

Our forces have delivered a crushing blow to the Vietminh.

> — General René Cogny, commander, French
> Union forces, northern Indochina, Hanoi,
> July 20, 1953

Now the cabinet is in deep discussion of a series of proposals by General Henri Navarre, commander in chief in Indochina, that the war be increasingly turned over to the Vietnamese themselves, permitting France to reduce the burden on its manpower and economy.

> — *Life*, August 3, 1953

Now let us assume that we lose Indochina. If Indochina goes, several things happen right away. The Malayan peninsula . . . would be scarcely defensible—and tin and tungsten we so greatly value from that area would cease coming. . . . All of that weakening position around there is very ominous for the United States, because finally if we lost all that, how would the free world hold the rich empire of Indonesia? So you see, somewhere along the line, this must be blocked. That is what the French are doing. . . .

So, when the United States votes $400 million to help that war, we are not voting for a giveaway program. We are voting for the cheapest way that we can to prevent the occurrence of something that would be of the most terrible significance for the United States of America—our security, our power and ability to get certain things we need from the riches of . . . Southeast Asia.

> — President Dwight D. Eisenhower,
> remarks at Governors' Conference, Seattle,
> Wash., August 4, 1953

860,000 refugees—more than 500,000 of them Catholics—began to pour into what was now rapidly becoming "South Viet-Nam."
— Bernard B. Fall, *Viet-Nam Witness*

His [Diem's] brother, Monsignor Thuc, was more successful, however, with the Catholic hierarchy. Francis Cardinal Spellman became interested in the far-away country with its small but fiercely militant Catholic community and became a strong advocate of American support for Diem over the following years. . . . Dr. Walter H. Judd, then a representative from Minnesota, Senator Mike Mansfield, and Senator John F. Kennedy, soon became his devoted advocates. But the time was not yet ripe. Diem left the United States in May, 1953, to return to Belgium, where he took up quarters in the Benedictine monastery of Saint-Andre-les-Bruges, which is also a key center of missionary activity in the Far East. His close association with Father Raymond de Jaegher, a Belgian priest who has in recent years often acted as one of his advisers, may date from that period.
— Bernard B. Fall, *The Two Viet-Nams*

I am confident that the French-trained Vietnam Army when fully organized will prevail over the rebels.
— General John W. (Iron Mike) O'Daniel, chief, U.S. military mission, Saigon, Fall 1953

A year ago none of us could see victory. There wasn't a prayer. Now we see it clearly—like light at the end of a tunnel.
— General Henri Eugène Navarre, quoted by *Time*, September 28, 1953

Ten thousand young German soldiers are fighting for France in Indo-China. They represent some 70 per cent of the French Foreign Legion which has the best fighting record of all the regiments in the country. Others who wear the distinctive white pill-box cap of the Legion are Spaniards, Italians, Poles and a few French, Americans and Britons. . . . The Legion has played a major part in almost every battle of the 7-year-old Indochina war and in the process has suffered more losses than any other fighting unit in the country.
— *Washington Times-Herald*, Reuters dispatch from Saigon, October 3, 1953

To speak of negotiations is the surest means of raising the morale of the adversary and of demoralizing our own troops.
— Deputy Raymond Dronne, French Parliament, *Journal Officiel*, October 23, 1953

Victory is possible, certain, and almost immediate if, right away . . .
Vietnamese officials will resolutely launch into the necessary political
and social reforms and correct their mistakes.

> — Deputy René Kuehn, French Parliament,
> *Journal Officiel*, October 27, 1953

The Vietminh can be turned back if U.S. military aid is continued.
This aid is justified and essential.

> — Senator Mike Mansfield,
> Democrat of Montana, October 27, 1953

Vice President Richard M. Nixon urged the Vietnamese today to make
greater efforts in the war.

> — *New York Times*, dispatch from Saigon,
> November 1, 1953

We shall never abandon the Indo-Chinese peninsula to a foreign
power.

> — Maurice Dejean, French commissioner
> general, Hanoi, November 4, 1953

We want to see to it that no supplies are lacking for the Indo-China
war. . . . I will make suggestions to President Eisenhower.

> — Vice President Richard M. Nixon,
> statement to press, Hanoi, November 4, 1953

It is impossible to lay down arms until victory is completely won. I am
impressed by the high morale of the French Union troops. . . . The U.S.
would vigorously disapprove any negotiations for peace in Indochina.

> — Vice President Richard M. Nixon, at dinner
> given in his honor by French Commissioner
> General Maurice Dejean, Hanoi, November 4,
> 1953; dispatch headed NIXON WARNS
> AGAINST TRUCE IN INDOCHINA,
> *Washington Times-Herald*, November 5, 1953

We want to make perfectly clear to the enemy that he has not a single
chance of obtaining by force the departure of our troops. . . . I think
that it will be possible for us to maintain the initiative of widespread
operations and to improve our situation rapidly, until the national
(Vietnamese) armies have developed enough for their weight to be felt in
battle. . . . The war will not end by extermination, but by the
discouragement of one of the two belligerents, and causes for discourage-

ment are, in the long run, smaller on our side than on theirs. My government is prepared to seize every opportunity for making peace.

— Premier Joseph Laniel of France,
address to French Assembly,
quoted by *Time*, November 9, 1953

We've taken the place [Dienbienphu] and we shall stay there. We will have enough mobility to turn the tide in our favor in the dry season from September 1954 to May 1955. I foresee final victory in the spring of 1956.

— General René Cogny, commander,
French Union forces, northern Indochina,
November 20, 1953

Catholics form the backbone of resistance to Viet Minh rebels. Native Catholic bishops now are openly militant in their opposition to the Viet Minh. . . . Monasteries have been converted into basic training camps, troop quarters, supply centers and ammunition dumps. Priests join army officers in waging psychological warfare among the villagers. In areas where the Viet Minh rebels are strong, cathedral compounds are barricaded and become the redoubts. . . . Col. Pham Van Dong, a promising 34-year-old officer . . . heads a new experiment in the Indo-Chinese war. Completely native forces . . . to clean out pockets of Viet Minh resistance and to "pacify" areas . . . under French-Vietnamese control.

Col. Dong works with local Catholics. . . . He seeks especially close relations with the Catholics. . . . They have facilities in which he can base his light battalions. . . . In Buichu, capital of a province of the same name . . . the weapons carriers and jeeps from America, the United States–equipped guards and the French-type Catholic cathedral looming in the background symbolize the two forces which are rallying the Viet Namese to battle. . . . Col. Dong took me to see a basic training camp.

A few more steps past the honor guard and we were in the compound of what had formerly been a monastery. In a corner at the left was a parish church, another handsome structure, with one tower. Along the outer perimeter of the church square were low lines of buildings. They had once been the quarters of young men studying for the priesthood. Now they were barracks for Viet Namese basic trainees. In the center of the square a Viet Namese sergeant was drilling a platoon of trainees. . . . In the barracks . . . at the side of each soldier's sleeping area was a Catholic religious symbol, a figure of Christ on the cross, the Virgin Mary or some other saint. In the center of the room was a little shrine centering around the Virgin. People who have spent Christmas with

Catholic Viet Namese troops say that each soldier makes his own tiny manger and worships at it in his foxhole or dugout throughout the Christmas season.

> — Earle H. Voss, *Washington Evening Star*,
> November 22, 1953

In Indochina we believe the tide is now turning.

> — Assistant Secretary of State for Far Eastern
> Affairs Walter S. Robertson,
> New York City, December 2, 1953

The deception of the enemy has been of great help to us in successfully carrying out evacuation by air.

> — General René Cogny, on French retreat and
> evacuation of northwest provincial capital Lai
> Chau, dispatch from Reuters, Hanoi,
> December 11, 1953

We are ready for a showdown with the Vietminh.

> — French High Command, Hanoi,
> December 14, 1953

We would all like to think the war there might be successfully concluded in the next calendar year.

> — Secretary of State John Foster Dulles,
> Paris, December 14, 1953

Our mission in Paris is directly observing the use of these funds in relationship to the Indochina war. . . . We know the money we are supervising under the President's program is going toward the winning of the Indochina war.

> — Harold E. Stassen, director,
> Foreign Operations Administration,
> *Meet the Press*, NBC, December 27, 1953

In Cambodia, French Union forces have the situation well in hand.

> — Maurice Dejean,
> French commissioner general,
> Hanoi, December 28, 1953

The situation is not at all bad.

> — French Foreign Ministry official spokesman,
> Paris, quoted by AP, December 29, 1953

I do not believe that anything that has happened upsets appreciably
the timetable of General Navarre's Plan [for French success]. There is no
reason I am aware of for anybody to get panicky about what has
happened.

> — Secretary of State John Foster Dulles,
> December 29, 1953

No canvas shoes on his feet and his toes wriggled voluptuously in the
warm mud of the shelter. Glatigny's reaction was that of a regular officer.
He could not believe that this *nha que* squatting on his haunches and
smoking foul tobacco was, like him, a battalion commander with the
same rank and the same responsibilities as his own. This was one of the
officers of the 308th Division, the best unit in the People's Army. It was
this peasant from the paddy fields who had beaten him. Glatigny, the
descendant of one of the great military dynasties of the West, for whom
war was a profession and the only purpose in life.

> — Jean Lartéguy, *The Centurions*

The war must stop being a French war supported by Vietnam and
become a Vietnamese war supported by France.

> — Vice Premier Paul Reynaud of France, 1953

I fully expect victory . . . after six more months of hard fighting.
Having lost all hopes of winning a decisive battle in the Red River Delta,
the Viet Minh disperses its forces. . . . We have the advantage. . . . A
campaign begun under such conditions can but turn in our favor.

> — Major General Henri-Eugène Navarre,
> Hanoi, January 2, 1954

The French Command is sure of inflicting a serious defeat on the Viet
Minh at Dien Bien Phu. We expect a long hard fight. We shall win.

> — General René Cogny, Hanoi,
> quoted by AP, January 2, 1954

The battle . . . offers us genuine chances of success. So far, General
Giap's army has never dared face a mission as formidable as that of
attacking Dien Bien Phu.

> — Maurice Dejean, French commissioner
> general, cablegram to Paris,
> January 3, 1954

This is a war without issue.

> — Former Premier Edouard Daladier of France,
> speech to French Assembly, quoted by
> *Washington Times-Herald*, January 4, 1954

Some developments beyond our shores have been equally encouraging. Communist aggression, halted in Korea, continues to meet in
Indo-China the vigorous resistance of France and the Associated States,
assisted by timely aid from our country.

> — President Dwight D. Eisenhower,
> State of the Union Address, January 7, 1954

French General Henri Navarre was talking . . . of victory in 1954.

> — *Life*, January 11, 1954

I am hoping for a fight at Dien Bien Phu. Admittedly, the Vietminh
artillery may bother us for awhile, but we shall silence it. As he can't go
to Laos in force for fear that our forces will close in behind him, Giap is
obliged to attack. I shall do everything to make him bite the dust and
cure him of his desire to try his hand at grand strategy.

> — General René Cogny,
> quoted by UP, Hanoi, January 15, 1954

General Henri Navarre's French Union forces are expected to
abandon their fixed positions and carry the fight to . . . Vietminh rebels.
. . . On-the-spot observers reported Sunday that Navarre is determined
to recapture the initiative from the rebels.

> — Reuters dispatch from Hanoi,
> January 19, 1954

For several years all French military actions have been of a defensive
nature. This phase is ended. . . . The French command has succeeded in
grouping sufficient forces to take the initiative in an offensive.

> — French High Command, communiqué,
> January 21, 1954

The French High Command announced Monday that 93,337 . . .
Vietminh troops have been killed. . . . The French added that 113,987
rebels were captured. . . . The French also said they had seized more
than 57,000 rifles, machine guns and other automatic weapons.

> — AP dispatch from Hanoi, January 24, 1954

We cannot afford to permit the situation in Indochina to drift any
longer. A few months ago I said on my return from that area that the
issue there could be met successfully by a three-pronged effort of the
Indochinese, the French, and the United States. . . . I fully approve
the sending of additional B-26 bombers. I am glad that 25 C-47s were
sent last December. I see nothing wrong in sending 200 technicians to

assist the 125 technicians who have been there, working under the Military Assistance Advisory Group. . . . I think that is good, sound policy.

> — Senator Mike Mansfield, Democrat of
> Montana, debate in Senate,
> February 8, 1954

I do not believe the United States Government would, in any event, send ground forces to that area.

> — Senator William F. Knowland, Republican of
> California, debate in Senate, February 8, 1954

Step by step, we are moving into this war in Indochina, and I am afraid that we will move to a point from which there will be no return. . . . We are going to war inch by inch.

> — Senator John C. Stennis, Democrat of Missis-
> sippi, speech in Senate, February 9, 1954

The press and everyone I have spoken to are indignant that the French government has spent several billion dollars in fighting this war but has failed to build housing for the growing population of Paris. The majority in parliament has long demanded "peace by negotiation" with Ho Chi Minh, leader of the Vietminh opposing French forces. Criticism of Premier Laniel and . . . with the President [Eisenhower] offering huge sums to France to carry on the war, sharp criticism has been leveled against the United States. "Why must we spend billions and lose thousands of lives in a war 10,000 miles away that we can never win while thousands of our people in France are exposed to death by freezing and privations?" newspaper editorials ask. "How dare the United States order us to keep fighting in Indochina after they have ended their own war in Korea? Are we mercenaries to shed the blood of our sons merely to obey the policy of Washington regarding communism?" the papers say. . . . Leftists have called the struggle in Indochina "the dirty war" on the ground that it is carried on for the sole benefit of the Banque d'Indochine, the Michelin rubber plantations, and a dozen other powerful interests which exploit the natural resources of the colony and have a stranglehold on imports, exports and finance.

The Associated States of Laos, Cambodia and Viet Nam, as the colony is now called, have never paid their way. But they have proved a fabulous asset for the "great bank," for rich and powerful colonists, and the horde of men who operate the opium, illicit gold, and similar rackets. . . . For years the war cost France a million dollars a day. Now waste, inefficiency, and graft have swelled the cost to $1.5 billion a year, of which the U.S. forks over nearly $800 million. Another $800 million has

been promised for the fiscal years 1954–1955. A great part of this huge
sum goes to raising a native Indochinese army. These battalions are
expected to reinforce the French units and achieve victory. But French
newspaper correspondents on the scene insist that the native battalions
are practically worthless. The war correspondents state that the Vietnam
soldiers will not fire on their Vietnam brothers and either quit or desert
with their arms. France has 200,000 natives under arms and expects to
have 325,000 by the end of the year. She also has 200,000 "French
troops" who are mostly Algerians, Moroccans, Senegalese, and Foreign
Legionnaires.

> — Henry Wales, CTPS dispatch from Paris,
> February 9, 1954

General O'Daniel's most recent report is more encouraging than is
given to you through French sources. I still believe that . . . most needed
for success [is] French will.

> — President Dwight D. Eisenhower, cablegram to
> Secretary of State John Foster Dulles in
> Berlin, February 10, 1954, quoted by
> Eisenhower in *Mandate for Change*

What we are doing is supporting the Vietnamese and the French in
their conduct of the war. . . . Now, recently, some of our equipment
shipped to Indochina has involved airplanes, and they just didn't have
the people to take care of them. So we increased that particular body by
some airplane mechanics, who are to be returned from there no later
than June 15th. . . . They are not only maintenance troops, but I see no
opportunity of them even getting touched by combat.

> — President Dwight D. Eisenhower,
> news conference, February 10, 1954

It has been critical for so long [in Indochina] that it is difficult to point
out a period when it is more than normally critical.

> — President Dwight D. Eisenhower,
> February 14, 1954

Our job is to get the Viet to come down. Once he comes down, we'll
catch him.

> — Colonel Christian de Castries, commander at
> Dienbienphu, quoted in *Le Monde*, Paris,
> February 14, 1954

The Vietnamese National Army will soon assume much greater
responsibility in the Indo-Chinese war.

> — General Nguyen Van Hinh, chief of staff,
> Vietnamese National Army,
> Saigon, February 16, 1954

The war is going fully as well as we expected at this stage. I see no reason to think Indochina will be another Korea. I believe success in Indochina will not only be possible but probable.

> — Secretary of Defense Charles E. Wilson,
> February 17, 1954

Vietminh prospects for victory in Indochina are non-existent. . . . The French have developed a broad strategic concept which within a few months should insure a favorable turn in the course of the war.

> — Admiral Arthur W. Radford, chairman, Joint
> Chiefs of Staff, to House Foreign Affairs Sub-
> committee, closed session, February 18, 1954

The Vietminh offensive is slack, or at about its peak. The Vietminh has reached the highest point of its pretensions and . . . furnished proof that it has exceeded its logistic possibilities. Giap's offensive is blocked.

> — General Henri Eugène Navarre,
> news conference, Saigon, February 19, 1954

Victory in Indochina, in short, is within . . . grasp . . . in the opinion of most American experts.

> — *U.S. News & World Report*,
> February 19, 1954

United States officials said Saturday they have "strong evidence" that . . . Ho Chi Minh is dead and that the Reds are using a "voice from the grave" as a symbolic rallying point for the war against France in Indochina. Officials wondered whether the western Big Three allies will be negotiating with a ghost [at] Geneva. . . . Far Eastern experts said that . . . Ho Chi Minh . . . has not been seen alive by any responsible person on this side of the "bamboo curtain" since 1946. Washington . . . officials said that careful checks of the last voice broadcast raised a question as to whether the Ho Chi Minh voice was not being mimicked by a "stand-in." . . .

The mysterious "Uncle Ho" was described as being a man of incredible longevity if he is still alive. United States records show that he was described by a British government doctor in the Hong Kong crown colony in 1930 as being a "hopeless tubercular." Ho was jailed there and released after 18 months imprisonment "dying of tuberculosis." Officials said that the physician attending Ho said he had an advanced case of TB and had begun smoking opium heavily. . . . The physician said that Ho's addiction to opium was such that he "didn't know whether Ho would die first of opium poisoning or of TB."

> — INS,
> February 21, 1954

The military situation is favorable. Contrary to some reports, the recent advances by the Viet Minh are largely "real estate" advances. Tactically, the French position is solid and the officers in the field are confident of their ability to deal with the situation.

> — Under Secretary of State Walter Bedell Smith, speech to Chicago World Trade Conference, February 23, 1954

Ho Chi Minh is about to capitulate; we are going to beat him.

> — Foreign Minister Georges Bidault of France to Deputy Alain Savary, beginning of March 1954

Shall we [sic] accept a stalemate in Indochina and lose all of Asia by making another truce? . . . Or shall we go on to victory in Indochina . . . ? Our side can win the war in Indochina. There are native troops in abundance to fight for freedom. . . . There is, indeed, no substitute for victory.

> — David Lawrence, editorial, U.S. News & World Report, March 5, 1954

I returned from the Far East with the strong conviction that the forces of freedom are growing stronger and that the Communist position is weakening. This is true in both an economic and a military sense.

> — Harold E. Stassen, AID administrator, March 5, 1954

I will say this: There is going to be no involvement of America in war unless it is the result of the Constitutional process that is placed upon Congress to declare it. Now, let us have that clear; and that is the answer.

> — President Dwight D. Eisenhower, March 10, 1954

The Navarre Plan is being successfully accomplished. . . . Later this year the victories should begin.

> — Malcolm MacDonald, British High Commissioner, Southeast Asia, Saigon, March 11, 1954

French Union forces in Indochina will be successful over a period of time. . . . I am optimistic about the outcome. Vietnamese forces fighting alongside the French will be more than doubled by 1955.

> — Admiral Arthur W. Radford, March 12, 1954

The United States is carrying 78 percent of the cost of the Indo-Chinese war.

> — Deputy Christian Pineau,
> French National Assembly,
> Paris, March 16, 1954

Last week we were talking about Indochina, and I believe the question was concerning the possibility of one of our men, or one or two, getting killed, and what that would mean. I tried to reply very emphatically and I still don't back away from the generalization I made in this general sense. Strange and weird things are happening in this war. . . . I haven't really asked my G-2 boys to give me their interpretation of the movement [of the Vietminh against the French]. . . . I have no exact interpretation of these things, as none of us has.

> — President Dwight D. Eisenhower,
> March 17, 1954

If the Communists continue to suffer the losses they have been taking, I don't see how they can stay in the battle.

> — General Paul Ely,
> chief of staff, French armed forces,
> Washington, March 20, 1954

The French are going to win. It is a fight that is going to be finished with our help.

> — Admiral Arthur W. Radford, March 22, 1954

[The French at Dienbienphu] are writing, in my opinion, a notable chapter in military history. . . . I do not expect that there is going to be a Communist victory in Indo-China. . . . We have seen no reason to abandon the so-called Navarre plan. . . . There is no reason to question its inherent soundness. . . . [It will produce] decisive military results . . . at least a year from now. . . . The upper hand will probably be gained by the end of the next fighting season.

> — Secretary of State John Foster Dulles,
> news conference, Overseas Press Club,
> New York City, March 23, 1954

You shall therefore win. You shall delay the attack, you shall win the offensive battle and you shall break out of Dien Bien Phu. You will then go over to the exploitation phase for, at the very least, you will be able to reduce the strength of their organization. . . .

> — General René Cogny, commander, French
> Union forces, northern Indochina, to General
> Christian de Castries, March 24, 1954

[On April 4, 1954] at a Sunday night meeting in the upstairs study at the White House Eisenhower had agreed with Dulles and Radford on a plan to send American forces to Indochina under strict conditions.

— Sherman Adams, *First Hand Report*

[Indochina] is rich in many raw materials such as tin, oil, rubber and iron ore. . . . The area has great strategic value. . . . It has major naval and air bases.

— Secretary of State John Foster Dulles, March 29, 1954

I expect all the troops to die at the positions assigned to them rather than retreat an inch.

— Brigadier General Christian de Castries (promoted from colonel previous week), Dienbienphu, Indochina, March 30, 1954

One of the world's richest areas is open to the winner in Indochina. That's behind the growing U.S. concern . . . tin, rubber, rice, key strategic raw materials are what the war is really about. The U.S. sees it as a place to hold—at any cost.

— "Why U.S. Risks War for Indochina: It's the Key to Control of all Asia," *U.S. News & World Report*, April 4, 1954

The important thing is that the coalition must be strong and it must be willing to join in the fight if necessary. I do not envisage the need for any appreciable ground forces on your or our part. . . . With warm regards, Ike.

— President Dwight D. Eisenhower to Prime Minister Winston Churchill, April 5, 1954

TOP SECRET

The Special Committee . . . believes that defeat of the Viet Minh in Indo-China is essential . . . to demonstrate that ultimate victory will be won by the free world. . . . The Western position in Indo-China must be maintained and improved by a military victory. . . . The Special Committee wishes to reaffirm the following recommendations which are made in NSC 5405. . . . (1) It be U.S. policy to accept nothing short of a military victory in Indo-China. (2) It be the U.S. position to obtain French support of this position; and that failing this, the U.S. actively oppose any negotiated settlement in Indo-China at Geneva. (3) It be the

U.S. position in event of failure of (2) above to initiate immediate steps with the governments of the Associated States aimed toward the continuation of the war in Indo-China, to include active U.S. participation and without French support should that be necessary. . . . The Special Committee also considers that all possible political and economic pressure on France must be exerted as the obvious initial course of action to reinforce the French will to continue operatings [sic] in Indo-China. The Special Committee recognizes that this course of action will jeopardize the existing French Cabinet, may be unpopular among the French public, and may be considered as endangering present U.S. policy with respect to EDC. . . . The U.S. should, in all prudence, take the following courses of action in addition to those set forth. . . . Ensure that there be initiated no cease-fire in Indo-China prior to victory whether that be by successful military action or clear concession of defeat by the Communists.

— Memorandum, Special Committee on the
Threat of Communism, April 5, 1954

What is it we are going to fight for and to defend? I am a Senator and I don't know. The Democratic Senators on the Armed Services and Foreign Relations Committees don't know.

— Senator Wayne Morse, Republican of Oregon,
April 5, 1954

On February 5th, 1951, the late Brigadier General Francis G. Brink, then head of USMAAG in Indochina, told us of the favorable turn of events in that area. . . . Every year we are given three sets of assurances: 1st, that the independence of the Associated States is not complete; 2nd, that the independence of the Associated States will soon be completed under steps "now" being undertaken; and, 3rd, that military victory for the French Union Forces in Indochina is assured, or is just around the corner, or lies a year off. . . . The time has come for the American people to be told the blunt truth about Indochina.

— Senator John F. Kennedy, Democrat of
Massachusetts, speech in Senate, April 6, 1954

A new foreign aid program of $3,497,000,000, one-third of which would be spent to support anti-Communist forces in Indo-China, was submitted to Congress today. . . . [Mr. Stassen] . . . disclosed today . . . that the biggest single item in the program was $1,133,000,000 for Indo-China. Of this amount, $500,000,000 would be for direct support of the anti-Communist fighting forces, allocated through France;

$300,000,000 for equipment supplied to the fighting forces; $21,185,000 for economic assistance, and the rest for technical assistance.

> — *New York Times*, April 7, 1954

I am leaving for a brief stay in France, where we are negotiating a treaty that will define our position within the French Union . . . the hour of unanimity has come.

> — Emperor Bao Dai, statement on leaving for his mansion on French Riviera, never to return, April 10, 1954

Final success belongs to him who holds out to the last moment. I am convinced it will be the valorous soldiers of De Castries who will hold out to the last moment.

> — General Henri Eugène Navarre, commander in chief, French Union forces, Indochina, by radio to troops at Dienbienphu, quoted by *Time*, April 12, 1954

There is no reason why the French forces should not remain in Indo-China and win. They have greater manpower and a tremendous advantage over their adversaries, particularly air power. . . . What can be done? . . . More men are needed and the question is where to get them. They will not come from France, for France is tired of the war. . . . If this government cannot avoid it, the Administration must face up to the situation and dispatch forces.

> — Vice President Richard M. Nixon to American Society of Newspaper Editors; shocked reaction made President Eisenhower, Secretary Dulles, State Department, much of Congress disassociate themselves from speech; exception: Senator Hubert H. Humphrey, who praised it; April 16, 1954

First of all, you have the specific value of a locality in its production of materials that the world needs. . . . Finally, you have broader considerations that you might follow, what you would call the "falling domino" principle. You have a row of dominoes set up, you knock over the first one, and what will happen to the last one is the certainty that it will go over very quickly. So you could have a beginning of a disintegration that would have the most profound influences. Now, with respect to the first one, two of the items from this particular area that the world uses are tin and tungsten. They are very important. There are others, of course, the rubber plantations and so on. . . . But when we come to the possible sequence of events, the loss of Indochina, of Burma, of Thailand, of the Peninsula, and Indonesia following, now you begin to talk about areas that not only multiply the disadvantages that you would suffer through loss of materials, sources of materials, but now you are talking really about millions and millions and millions of people. . . . So, the possible consequences of the loss are just incalculable to the world.

> — President Dwight D. Eisenhower,
> April 17, 1954

Certain remarks with regard to United States policy toward Indo-China have been attributed to a high Government official. . . . The speech referred to, and the questions and answers which followed, were off the record. . . . The speech enunciated no new United States policy in regard to Indo-China.

> — State Department statement, April 17, 1954

RIÈN A SIGNALER [Nothing to report].

> — Radio message from Dienbienphu to French
> GHQ, April 18, 1954

The gallant defenders of Dien Bien Phu have done their part. . . . The attackers already lost more than they could win . . . learning again that the will of the free is not broken. . . . The violent battles now being waged in Vietnam . . . are not creating any spirit of defeatism. On the contrary, they are rousing the free nations. I leave for Geneva confident.

> — Secretary of State John Foster Dulles,
> Augusta, Ga., April 19, 1954

The French Union forces at Dien Bien Phu are fighting a modern Thermopylae.

> — Under Secretary of State Walter Bedell Smith,
> April 19, 1954

Back at Hanoi, French GHQ optimistically noted that Giap's fourth counteroffensive showed "definite lack of conviction," and the tired, outnumbered French garrison is still given a 50-50 chance to hold Dienbienphu.

> — *Time*, April 19, 1954

I'm going to kick General Giap's teeth in, one by one.

> — Brigadier General Christian de Castries,
> April 20, 1954

Vice President Nixon's "not for attribution" speech to the visiting editors . . . was by all odds the most lucid and comprehensive presentation that has been made by the Administration.

— Editorial, *Washington Post*, April 20, 1954

[The U.S. must act in Indochina] by putting our boys in . . . regardless of allied support. . . . The aim of the United States is to hold Indochina without war involving the United States if we can. . . . The United States would have to replace [the French] if necessary. . . . The United States will . . . oppose outright surrender to the Communists.

— Vice President Richard M. Nixon,
Cincinnati, Ohio, April 20, 1954

We have intervened in that war. They might just as well say we are in the war now.

— Congressman Usher L. Burdick,
Democrat of North Dakota, April 21, 1954

The U.S. should continue to supply money and equipment to the Franco-Vietnamese forces and establish U.S.–operated training centers for native troops of all three kingdoms—Vietnam, Laos, and Cambodia.

— Major General Claire L. Chennault, former
commander, "Flying Tigers," head of Civil Air
Transport, private CIA-financed Far Eastern
airline supplying French at Dienbienphu and
elsewhere, *Newsweek*, April 26, 1954

France must go beyond her previous efforts in granting unequivocal independence to Vietnam, Laos and Cambodia so that American entry into Indo-China would not have the taint of colonialism.

— President Dwight D. Eisenhower, message to
Prime Minister Winston Churchill, proposing
"united action," early April 1954

I am determined to prolong resistance of Dien Bien Phu as long as possible.

— General Henri Eugène Navarre,
April 26, 1954

As I reported to London at the time, the Americans seemed clearly apprehensive of reaching any agreement, however innocuous.

— Foreign Secretary Anthony Eden of Britain,
Full Circle

Above all, the Red River and Mekong deltas must be held, in order to prepare for the coming counterattack in two years' time.

> — Secretary of State John Foster Dulles, Geneva, departing conference, to chief, French delegation, Jean Chauvel, May 3, 1954, quoted by Devillers and Lacouture, *End of a War: Indochina 1954*

The Americans can only accept the Geneva agreements provisionally. They have reconciled themselves to "respecting" them during the stated two-year period until the elections are held. . . . As far as they are concerned, the general elections must be prevented by means of any excuse whatsoever. The only purpose of the Geneva agreements, as they see them, is to provide a cover for the political, economic, and military preparations for the conquest. In May, Dulles thought the preparations would take two years. This re-conquest must be achieved, if not through war, then at least by the threat of war.

> — Jean Chauvel, chief, French delegation, Geneva

This may finish us.

> — Brigadier General Christian de Castries to General René Cogny, GHQ, 1900 hours, May 6, 1954

We can keep on fighting for only ten more minutes. Shall we surrender?

> — Outpost commander to General de Castries, Dienbienphu, 0900 hours, May 7, 1954

Keep on fighting for ten more minutes.

> — General de Castries to outpost commander, 0900 hours, May 7, 1954

The violent barrage from mortars and artillery continues. The Viets are infiltrating massively through the strongpoints on the west.

> — General de Castries, Dienbienphu, to GHQ, 1600 hours, May 7, 1954

The central redoubt is about to be fully overrun. Further resistance is becoming hopeless.

> — General de Castries to GHQ, 1645 hours, May 7, 1954

The Viets are everywhere. The situation is very grave. The combat is confused and goes on all about. I feel the end is approaching, but we will fight to the finish.

> — General de Castries to General Cogny, GHQ,
> 1700 hours, May 7, 1954

Well understood. You will fight to the end. It is out of the question to run up the white flag after your heroic resistance.

> — General Cogny, GHQ, to General de Castries,
> Dienbienphu, 1700 hours, May 7, 1954

Well understood. We will destroy the guns and radio equipment. The radiotelephone link will be destroyed at 1730 hours. We will fight to the end. *Au revoir, mon general. Au revoir, mes camarades. Vive la France!*

> — General de Castries, Dienbienphu, to General
> Cogny, GHQ, 1700 hours, May 7, 1954

After 20 hours of ceaseless combat, just now man-to-man, the enemy has infiltrated right through our central bastion. Munitions are short. Our resistance is about to be overwhelmed. The Vietminh are now within a few meters from the radio transmitter where I am speaking. In five minutes everything will be blowing up here. I have given orders for maximum demolitions. The ammo depots are going up already. *Au revoir.*

> — General de Castries, Dienbiephu, to General
> Cogny, GHQ, 1730 hours, May 7, 1954

There is fighting around the door. The general has ordered me to destroy this equipment. Everything is blowing up here. Say hello to Paris for me. *Au revoir.*

> — Radio operator, Dienbienphu, last message
> from fortress, 1735 hours, May 7, 1954

It is like hearing the tap on the hull of a submarine that lies helpless at the bottom of the sea.

> — Staff officer, GHQ, hearing last message from
> Dienbienphu, May 7, 1954

Dienbienphu has fulfilled the mission assigned to it by the High Command.

> — Spokesman for General Henri Eugène
> Navarre, Hanoi, 1900 hours, May 7, 1954

On May 7, 1954, the struggle for Indochina was almost over for France. . . .

"You're not going to shoot any more?" asked the Vietminh in French.

"No, I'm not going to shoot anymore," said the colonel.

"*C'est fini?*" said the Vietminh.

"*Oui, c'est fini,*" said the colonel.

And all around them, as on some gruesome Judgment Day, soldiers, French and enemy alike, began to crawl out of their trenches and stand erect for the first time in 54 days, as firing ceased everywhere.

The sudden silence was deafening.

> — Bernard B. Fall, *Dienbienphu: A Battle to Remember*

We have a clean base there now without a taint of colonialism. Dienbienphu was a blessing in disguise.

> — John Foster Dulles, remark to Emmet John Hughes, quoted by Hughes in *Ordeal of Power*

Now, Dienbienphu has fallen. Its defense, of 57 days and nights, will go down in history as one of the most heroic of all time. The defenders . . . inflicted staggering losses on the enemy. The French soldiers showed that they have not lost either the will or the skill to fight. . . . It shows that Viet Nam produces soldiers who have the qualities to enable them to defend their country. An epic battle has ended. But great causes have, before now, been won out of lost battles. . . . Such a tragic event as the fall of Dienbienphu will harden, not weaken, our purpose. . . . It must be recognized that difficulties have been encountered, but this was expected. The complexity of the problem is great. . . . Under all the circumstances, I believe that good progress is being made. I feel confident. . . . In making commitments which might involve the use of armed force, the Congress is a full partner. Only Congress can declare war. President Eisenhower has repeatedly emphasized that he would not take military action in Indo-China without the support of Congress. . . . That is the spirit that animates us. If we remain true to that spirit, we can face the future with confidence.

> — Secretary of State John Foster Dulles, "The Issues at Geneva," radio-TV address to nation, May 7, 1954

Your Majesty: On behalf of the American people, I should like to express to you and the people of Viet-Nam our admiration for the gallant men of the Vietnamese forces who, together with their comrades of the French Union, for two months so heroically defended Dien Bien Phu against insuperable odds. It is sad indeed that the Fortress and its brave defenders have fallen to the enemy, but we can be heartened that their sacrifice has not been in vain. . . . With expressions of my personal regard,

> — President Dwight D. Eisenhower to Bao Dai, Chief of State of Vietnam, May 7, 1954

There is, of course, no military or logical reason why the loss of Dien Bien Phu should lead to collapse of French will. . . . Dien Bien Phu has become a symbol out of all proportion to its military importance.

> — Secretary of State John Foster Dulles to President Dwight D. Eisenhower, quoted in Eisenhower, *Mandate for Change*

Pentagon experts agree today that Allied military assistance is the only way to save Indochina. . . . Pentagon sources say the battle can still be waged.

> — *New York Journal-American*, May 8, 1954

The Viet Minh's battle corps is broken.

> — French High Command, Hanoi, May 10, 1954

What we are trying to do is create a situation in Southeast Asia where the Domino Theory will not apply.

> — Secretary of State John Foster Dulles, May 11, 1954

The situation in the delta is serious, but far from hopeless.

> — General Pierre Louis Bodet, chief aide to General Henri Eugène Navarre, news conference, Hanoi, May 12, 1954

TOP SECRET

The United States is not prepared to give its express or implied approval to any cease-fire, armistice, or other settlement which would have the effect of subverting the existing lawful governments . . . or of placing in jeopardy the forces of the French Union in Indochina. . . . You should, insofar as is compatible with these instructions, cooperate with the Delegation of France.

> — Secretary of State John Foster Dulles, cablegram to Under Secretary Walter Bedell Smith, May 12, 1954

Again, I forget whether it was before this body, I talked about the cork in the bottle. Well, it is very important, and the great idea of setting up an organism is so as to defeat the domino result. When, each standing alone, one falls, it has the effect on the next, and finally the whole row is down. You are trying, through a unifying influence, to build that row of dominoes so they can stand the fall of one, if necessary. Now, so far as I

am concerned, I don't think the free world ought to write off Indo-China.
I think we ought to all look at this thing with some optimism and some
determination. I repeat that long faces and defeatism don't win battles.

> — President Dwight D. Eisenhower,
> news conference, May 12, 1954

To the President of the United States: I have received with deep
emotion the noble message of May 8 in which you have wished
expressed . . . admiration for the valiant soldiers . . . who have
defended heroically Dien Bien Phu. . . . I think as you that their
sacrifices have not been in vain. . . . We can draw a great comfort in the
determination of the American people and in your personal will of
aiding the free forces. . . . Please accept, Mr. President, the expression of
my personal feeling of sincere affection,

> — Bao Dai, Chief of State of Vietnam,
> reply to President Eisenhower, released by
> White House, May 13, 1954

The Vietminh radio said today troops which captured French
headquarters at Dien Bien Phu found its commander, Brig. Gen.
Christian de Castries, sitting behind his desk in full military dress,
including medals.

> — *Washington Post*, AP dispatch from Hong
> Kong, May 13, 1954

France, who . . . has always risen above her reverses, can now once
again surmount a trial so painful and so glorious with all her energy.

> — President René Coty of France, message to
> President Eisenhower, May 13, 1954

The State Department is covertly "planting" stories with hand-picked
newsmen to stir up public support for American intervention in the
Indo-China war, an investigation disclosed today. State Secretary Dulles'
department, it was learned, put out intelligence information designed to
create the impression that Red China and Soviet Russia have numerous
"volunteers" helping the Viet Minh rebels fight the French in Indo-
China . . . as the basis for urging American intervention. . . . Newsmen
were asked not to identify the State Department as the source . . . but to
use some other source, such as "diplomatic circles." A Pentagon
spokesman, asked about the State Department story charging that
Chinese Reds and Soviet agents were helping the rebels in Indo-China,
said military intelligence could not confirm such charges.

> — *Chicago Tribune*, May 14, 1954

We have every expectation that increased military operation by the French and by the Associated States would defeat the Communist military forces.

> — Admiral Arthur W. Radford, chairman,
> Joint Chiefs of Staff, May 21, 1954

There is no military reason why the free world cannot regain the initiative against the Reds.

> — General René Cogny, commanding general,
> Red River Delta, quoted by Marguerite
> Higgins, *New York Herald Tribune*,
> May 24, 1954

Despite all the gloom radiating from rear headquarters of Paris, London and Washington, the will to fight is here. . . . I had been given so many pessimistic reports about the situation in the Hanoi delta that I had begun to wonder whether all was hopeless. The answer is certainly not. . . . The Hanoi-Haiphong area . . . is the richest and most populous area of Indo-China. . . . Life goes on as usual. The restaurants are full and the good champagne abundant. The town's night clubs . . . are jammed.

> — Marguerite Higgins, by wireless to *New York
> Herald Tribune*, May 24, 1954

The U.S. has handed France a plan to install an American commander in chief in Indo-China. . . . The plan also provides for throwing U.S. naval and air forces into France's war against the Viet Minh. . . . The plan . . . is now in the hands of Premier Joseph Laniel. In addition, the U.S. plan calls for bringing the armies of the Philippines and of Thailand into the conflict.

> — *Chicago Tribune*,
> Reuters dispatch from Paris, May 24, 1954

In Vietnam . . . the conditions . . . have been stable and unchanging over a considerable period of time.

> — Secretary of State John Foster Dulles,
> news conference, May 25, 1954

When are the Americans coming?

> — General Christian de Castries, by telephone to
> superiors, just before fall of Dienbienphu,
> quoted by Marguerite Higgins, *New York
> Herald Tribune*, May 25, 1954

TOP SECRET

The Joint Chiefs of Staff desire to point out their belief that, from the point of view of the United States, with reference to the Far East as a whole, *Indochina is devoid of decisive military objectives and the allocation of more than token* U.S. armed forces *in Indochina would be a serious diversion of* limited U.S. capabilities.

> — Admiral Arthur W. Radford to Secretary of
>   Defense Charles E. Wilson, May 26, 1954

We are approaching a fork in the road. . . . Do we want to turn into the smooth dead-end or take the rougher road that offers us a good destination.

> — Admiral Richard B. Carney, Chief of Naval
>   Operations, New York City, May 27, 1954

There has been no shortening of French Union defense lines within the Delta. There will be none. The whole Delta will be defended.

> — French High Command, Hanoi, quoted by
>   AP, May 30, 1954

I love troops and guns and maneuvers. . . . We must be enterprising and aggressive. We must be vigorous and young in action. We are going to win the battle of the Delta. Let someone else worry about the grand strategy. Let's keep up the fight. There's nothing wrong with us when we fight.

> — General René Cogny, address to French
>   Foreign Legionnaires in Delta, May 30, 1954

An effective job can be done in Indo-China against the threat of communism by aircraft carriers without the use of ground troops or without the Air Force.

> — Admiral Arthur W. Radford, May 30, 1954

The fact that America will join in training our troops gives a great lift to our people and our soldiers.

> — Governor Nguyen Huu Tri, chief, delta area,
>   Indochina, Hanoi, May 31, 1954

I frequently get to questioning myself about—we used to talk a lot about our sacrifices and so on—about what those sacrifices brought us. Of course they brought us—and bought us—an immediate safety from the danger then threatening. What did they bring us in the long run? We know they brought us the opportunity to do something, but what did these sacrifices mean? I have never been able—and probably never will be able—to write down something, myself, to satisfy me. But I do know this: . . . I believe these people that talk about peace academically, but who never had to dive in a ditch when a Messerschmitt 109 came over—they really don't know what it is.

> — President Dwight D. Eisenhower to corre-
> spondents leaving for France, June 1, 1954

Before the end of the year, progress and development of our National Army will hold many surprises for you. . . . You will see on the field of battle numerous divisions. . . .

> — General Nguyen Van Hinh, chief of staff,
> Vietnamese National Army, Saigon,
> June 2, 1954

The situation is grave, but by no means hopeless.

> — Secretary of State John Foster Dulles to
> Senate Foreign Relations Committee,
> June 4, 1954

The United States should face up to the fact that it may have to fight in Indo-China.

> — Senator William F. Knowland, Republican of
> California, Senate Majority Leader,
> June 5, 1954

Gen. Henri Eugène Navarre, retiring French Commander-in-Chief in Indo-China, declared tonight . . . he was an optimist about the ability of French Union forces to hold against Red attacks this summer. . . . He explained that recent reinforcements have created a situation . . . no more serious "than last November."

> — *New York Herald Tribune*, dispatch from
> Saigon, June 8, 1954

Mr. Dulles said that we will not give up; no matter what happens down there, we will never give up even if these three [Associated States of Indochina] should fall. . . . Naturally, all of us want to save them because of their importance, but it has to be done on their invitation. . . . No nation can be saved to the free world unless it itself wants to be saved. . . . The French Union forces have had a most difficult task, one that would have been made much easier could they have won the true allegiance and loyalty of the Vietnamese with whom they were working. . . . I understand the French are succeeding . . . no longer are they isolated by great areas of jungle. . . . So the situation in that respect is possibly better than it was. . . . The United States cannot alone by its military might achieve the policies that we must pursue. . . . Merely to go wage a battle somewhere is perfectly useless. Costly and useless.

> — President Dwight D. Eisenhower,
> June 10, 1954

We shall stay in the Far East; let our allies and our opponents make no mistake about it.

> — President Pierre Mendés-France of France,
> June 17, 1954

FRENCH COULD STILL WIN. . . . As Allied military experts see it, the gamble put before General Ely for decision is . . . that seizing the initiative from the Communists immediately might pay off in tremendous dividends. . . . Can it be done? These officers say yes, emphatically. . . . These officers contend that a sudden, bold strike against the Communists would far outweigh the cost. Militarily, it would upset the Viet Minh timetable and throw it completely off balance.

> — *U.S. News & World Report*, June 18, 1954

In the Eisenhower Administration, the tide of official thinking has turned against direct military intervention in Southeast Asia.

> — Ernest K. Lindley, column, *Newsweek*,
> June 21, 1954

President Ngo Dinh Diem . . . received an enthusiastic welcome from his Roman Catholic supporters. However, the great mass of the Saigon population stayed home.

> — *New York Times*, June 25, 1954

I do not exaggerate when I say that your friends everywhere have derived great inspiration from the successes which have marked the first two years of President Ngo Dinh Diem's administration.

> — Vice President Richard M. Nixon,
> Saigon, July 6, 1954

The Vietnamese have ample manpower and even today outnumber the enemy by 100,000, with superior firepower at least in a ratio of two to one and probably more. We are ready to assist them. . . . [The war can be won] without bringing in one single American soldier to fight.

> — General John W. (Iron Mike) O'Daniel,
> chief, U.S. military mission, Saigon,
> July 7, 1954

The United States will not sign an Indo-China settlement, but will not do anything to upset any reasonable accord sought by France.

— Secretary of State John Foster Dulles,
July 19, 1954

Agreement on the Cessation of Hostilities in Viet-Nam, July 20, 1954

CHAPTER I—*Article 1*—A provisional military demarcation line shall be fixed, on either side of which the forces of the two parties shall be regrouped after their withdrawal. . . .

CHAPTER III—*Article 16*—With effect from the date of entry into force of the present agreement, the introduction into Viet-Nam of any troop reinforcements and additional military personnel is prohibited. . . .
    Article 17—(a) . . . The introduction into Viet-Nam of any reinforcements in the form of all types of arms, munitions and other war material, such as combat aircraft, naval craft, pieces of ordnance, jet engines and jet weapons and armoured vehicles, is prohibited. . . .
    Article 18— . . . The establishment of new military bases is prohibited throughout Viet-Nam territory.
    Article 19— . . . No military base under the control of a foreign State may be established in the regrouping zone of either party; the two parties shall ensure that the zones assigned to them do not adhere to any military alliance and are not used for the resumption of hostilities or to further an aggressive policy.

CHAPTER VI—*Article 20*— . . . 47. All the provisions of the present Agreement, save the second sub-paragraph of Article 11, shall enter into force at 2400 hours (Geneva time) on 22 July 1954. Done in Geneva at 2400 hours on the 20th of July 1954 in French and in Viet-Namese, both texts being equally authentic.

For the Commander-in-chief of   For the Commander-in-Chief
the People's Army of Viet-Nam   of the French Union Forces
                                       in Indo-China
    TA-QUANG BUU
Vice-Minister of National   BRIGADIER-GENERAL DELTEII
Defense

— From Geneva Agreement, July 20, 1954

Frankly, I have no plan as of this moment to ask for anything that is outside the normal traditional processes in the operation of our

Government. I am glad, of course, that agreement has been reached at Geneva to stop the bloodshed in Indochina.

— President Dwight D. Eisenhower,
July 21, 1954

The Indo-China war ended officially in North Vietnam this morning after nearly eight years of bitter, bloody fighting. The French high command announced the case-fire agreed at the Geneva conference became effective in the north at 8 a.m. (9 p.m. EDT Monday) . . . Total casualties in the long and bitter fighting approached the million mark. The war cost France and the United States some 10 billions of dollars.

— *Washington Post*, AP dispatch from Saigon,
July 27, 1954

I don't happen to believe that the doctrine of co-existence will work, any more than you could co-exist with a tiger in a tiger's cage. . . . If we have to wait for India to make up her mind as to whether or not she's going to supply forces . . . by the time she makes up her mind, we will have lost Thailand, Laos, Malaya and probably Burma as well.

— Senator William F. Knowland,
Meet the Press, NBC, August 1, 1954

The battle for the delta is a good battle.

— General René Cogny,
quoted in *Time*, August 2, 1954

Bao Dai himself was in the French spa of Vittel last week, taking the waters. He had no comment to make ("Sorry"). He would probably never return to Viet Nam.

— *Time*, August 2, 1954

After eight years and at a cost of 34,000 French and Vietnamese dead, a war had ended in defeat. However the U.S. tried to disassociate itself morally or politically, it was also a defeat for the U.S. . . . Historians might yet mark Geneva as the first date in a new era: the decline of the West.

— *Time*, August 2, 1954

France wants the $490 million which President Eisenhower promised, to keep her fighting in Indo-China. The war is over, but France needs the cash to keep the 1955 budget somewhere near balance.

— *Chicago Tribune*, dispatch from Paris,
August 6, 1954

The guns fell silent last week across the Red River Delta and Central Viet Nam. In defeat, some of the French commanders politely declined to receive visitors. "The colonel does not wish to be rude," said one bearded adjutant, "but he feels pain this morning for himself and for France. He would rather be alone." . . . French Union and Vietnamese troops (less about 300 Vietnamese deserters a day) were pulling back from outposts to the west of Hanoi; tricolors were falling, yellow-starred Viet Minh flags were rising. More than 2,000 Catholic refugees streamed into Hanoi last week on the way to safety in the south. . . . In the south, plucky nationalist Prime Minister Diem appealed to the 12 million Vietnamese north of the 17th parallel to join in a mass migration south . . . he set up a $20 million emergency program (with U.S. help) to move and resettle 700,000 evacuees.

— *Time*, August 9, 1954

Ho Chi Minh, the goat-bearded leader of the Viet Minh, has not been seen alive by any non-Communist for more than three years and there have been many rumors (some for a time accepted by U.S. intelligence) that he was seriously ill or dead. Last week he proved to be alive and kicking. . . . Bao Dai . . . last week announced from France that he would return "soon" to Viet Nam. This presumably indicated that the French expect Prime Minister Diem to fall in a few months, and are preparing to prop up Bao Dai again.

— *Time*, August 23, 1954

It would be an understatement to say that we do not like the terms of the cease-fire agreement just concluded.

— Assistant Secretary of State for Far Eastern
Affairs Walter S. Robertson,
August 23, 1954

[After the Geneva settlement] Admiral Radford was emphatically in favor of landing a force in the Haiphong-Hanoi area even if it meant risking war with Red China. In this he was fully supported by the Chief of Staff of the Air Force and the Chief of Naval Operations.

— General James Gavin, writing of post-Geneva
period (1954), in *Crisis Now*

In 1954, most of the 860,000 refugees who fled to the south were Catholics . . . led by their two bishops and their priests. . . . In the south a considerable part of the Cochin Chinese propertied class was Catholic. . . . They were strengthened by the influx from the north and the privileged position Catholics were unofficially accorded by their coreligionists, who occupied important positions in the regime of Ngo Dinh Diem, himself a Catholic.

— Ellen J. Hammer,
Vietnam: Yesterday and Today

If Geneva and what was agreed upon there means anything at all, it means . . . taps for the buried hopes of freedom in Southeast Asia! Taps for the newly betrayed millions of Indochinese who must now learn the awful facts of slavery from their eager Communist masters! Now the devilish techniques of brainwashing, forced confessions, and rigged trials have a new locale for their exercise. . . . We shall risk bartering our liberties for lunacies, betraying the sacred trust of our forefathers, becoming serfs and slaves to Red rulers' godless goons. America must not be lulled into sleep by indifference nor be beguiled by the prospect of peaceful existence with Communists. How can there be peaceful coexistence between two parties if one of them is continually clawing at the throat of the other? Do you peacefully coexist with men who thus would train the youth of their godless, Red world?

— Francis Cardinal Spellman, speech at
American Legion Convention, *New York
Times*, August 31, 1954

The Viet Minh Communists . . . handed over their highest-ranking captive: Brigadier General Christian de Castries, 52, the dauntless but defeated commander of Dienbienphu, who had spent four months in Red hands. He seemed years older, much thinner, and his hair was greyer. He refused a stretcher. . . . Only a naval officer and an army doctor met him at Viettri, the exchange point near the Red River. "Where is my staff?" said Christian de Castries. . . . To reporters, De Castries said that he had never run up a white flag, even when Dienbienphu was overrun.

— *Time*, September 13, 1954

Saturday morning [April 3, 1954] eight members of Congress, five Senators and three Representatives, got the scare of their lives. They had been called to a secret conference with John Foster Dulles. What was wanted, Dulles said, was a joint resolution by Congress to permit the President to use air and naval power in Indochina. Radford offered the plan he had in mind once·Congress passed the joint resolution. Some 200 planes from the 31,000-ton U.S. Navy carriers *Essex* and *Boxer* . . . plus land-based U.S. Air Force planes from . . . the Philippines, would be used for a single strike to save Dien Bien Phu. In the end, all eight members of Congress, Republicans and Democrats alike, were agreed that Dulles had better first go shopping for allies. . . . Dulles ran into one rock of opposition—Britain. Messages flashing back and forth between Washington and London failed to crack the rock. Some of those at the meeting came away with the feeling that if they had agreed that Saturday to the resolution, planes would have been winging toward Dien Bien Phu without waiting for a vote of Congress—or without a word in advance to the American people.

> — Chalmers M. Roberts, "The Day We Didn't
> Go to War," *The Reporter*, September 14, 1954

Have been talking intimately with American officials here, including Ambassador Heath. Conferred at length yesterday with Vietnamese Premier Ngo Dinh Diem. . . . Success of effort to hold Vietnam from Communists depends on whether non-Communist Vietnamese can unite for struggle. United States Embassy, strongly supporting Diem, views him as key to the whole situation. Political and financial instability. . . . Unless Vietnamese Government can organize important forces and U.S. continues pouring in substantial help and money. If free elections held today, all agree privately Communists would win. . . . Situation not hopeless. . . . Future depends on organizing all resources to resettle refugees, sustain new bankrupt government, give people something to fight for, and unite them to resist Communism. . . . West can't afford to lose from now on.

> — Leo Cherne, executive director, founder,
> Research Institute of America, chairman,
> International Rescue Committee, cable to
> 30,000 subscribers of Research Institute,
> September 1954

I have never talked or corresponded with a person knowledgeable in Indochinese affairs who did not agree that had elections been held at the time of the fighting, possibly 80 percent of the population would have voted for Communist Ho Chi Minh as their leader rather than Chief of State Bao Dai.

> — President Dwight D. Eisenhower,
> *Mandate for Change*

Ho Chi Minh is not followed by only Communists. He has succeeded in welding behind him a great lot of people, most of them nationalists. The Vietminh soldiers fought with a great faith, the faith of those who fight for the freedom and the sovereignty of their country.

> — General Christian de Castries, after defeat of
> French, Paris, September 16, 1954

France and the United States are assisting the government of Viet-Nam in the resettlement of the Vietnamese who have of their own free will moved to free Viet-Nam and who already number some

300,000. . . . The channel for . . . economic aid . . . will be direct aid to that state.

— Communiqué Regarding Franco-American
Conversations, Washington,
September 29, 1954

[Diem has] a reputation throughout Vietnam for intense nationalism and equally intense corruptibility [and has] a constructive program . . . based on . . . sound principles.

— Senator Mike Mansfield, Democrat of
Montana, October 15, 1954

Dear Mr. President:

I have been following with great interest the course of developments in Vietnam. . . . Your recent requests for aid . . . are being fulfilled. I am glad that the United States is able to assist in this humanitarian effort. . . . I am, accordingly, instructing the American Ambassador [Donald R. Heath] to examine with you in your capacity as Chief of Government, how an intelligent program of American aid given directly to your Government can serve to assist Vietnam in its present hour of trial, provided that your Government is prepared to give assurances as to the standards of performance it would be able to maintain in the event such aid were supplied. The Government of the United States expects that this aid will be met by performance on the part of the Government of Vietnam in undertaking needed reforms. . . . Such a Government would, I hope, be so responsive to the nationalist aspirations of its people, so enlightened in purpose and effective in performance, that it will be respected both at home and abroad and discourage any who might wish to impose a foreign ideology on your free people.

— President Dwight D. Eisenhower, letter to
President Ngo Dinh Diem offering aid with
conditions, October 23, 1954

The President on November 3 designated Gen. J. Lawton Collins as Special United States Representative in Viet-Nam with the personal rank of Ambassador, to undertake a diplomatic mission of limited duration. He will coordinate the operations of all U.S. agencies in that country. General Collins will proceed immediately to Saigon, where he will confer with Ambassador Donald R. Heath. . . . The U.S. has already played an important role in the evacuation of hundreds of thousands of refugees from . . . North Viet-Nam. . . . In executing his temporary mission, General Collins will maintain close liaison with the French Commissioner General, Gen. Paul Ely, for the purpose of exchanging views.

— White House statement, November 3, 1954

The American Mission will soon take charge of instructing the
Vietnam Army. . . . I have come out to Indo-China to take measures to
save this region from Communism. I have come to bring every possible
aid to the government of Ngo Dinh Diem. . . . 90% of the equipment
will be American [and] French instructors will have to work as closely as
possible with American personnel. . . . American training methods
proved to be efficient.

> — General J. Lawton Collins,
> special ambassador to Vietnam, Saigon,
> November 17, 1954

Under the terms of the Geneva truce, all-Vietnam elections are
scheduled to be held in 1956 with the winner to take the entire country.
As of today, the winner would be Ho Chi Minh.

> — *Time*, November 22, 1954

I still believe the country can be saved.

> — General John W. (Iron Mike) O'Daniel,
> chief, U.S. military mission, Saigon,
> December 16, 1954

I don't agree that all the experts say [Vietnam would vote for Ho Chi
Minh]. I think if a truly free election were held in Indochina today, the
country would throw the Communists out. . . . We are making progress.
. . . President Eisenhower sent one of the very ablest men in the country
out there a few weeks ago, Gen. Joe Collins, J. Lawton Collins, to go as
his representative on the ground to evaluate and pull these things
together.

> — Harold E. Stassen, director,
> Foreign Operations Administration,
> *Face the Nation*, CBS, December 26, 1954

I haven't even begun to think of writing off this country. Americans
don't walk out on a situation because of a few setbacks.

> — General John W. (Iron Mike) O'Daniel,
> Saigon, quoted by *Time*, December 27, 1954

A sacred respect is due the person of the sovereign. . . . He is the
mediator between the people and the Heaven as he celebrates the
national cult. The magistrate in his official capacity must conduct
himself as one participating in a religious rite.

> — President Ngo Dinh Diem, 1954

Things are more like they are now than they ever were before.

> — President Dwight D. Eisenhower, 1954

1955-1963

Indochina is a confused picture, but General Collins is doing a remarkable job there.

> — Admiral Arthur W. Radford, Honolulu,
> January 5, 1955

Francis Cardinal Spellman arrived here today on a flying visit to South Vietnam and announced he had brought with him a check for $100,000 to help the refugees.

> — *New York Times*, dispatch from Saigon,
> January 6, 1955

U.S. officials believe that reforms in South Vietnam could tip the scales in favor of the free world in the all-Vietnam elections due in July 1956.

> — *New York Times*, January 8, 1955

Prolonged maintenance of the French expeditionary corps is not desirable.

> — General Paul Ely,
> French high commissioner, Saigon,
> January 10, 1955

The American Government is now taking over from France the responsibility for maintaining independence in rump Indochina. . . . Directly traceable to U.S. influence [is] the establishment of an independent banking system. . . . Washington is gambling whole hog on the Ngo Dinh Diem program. . . . The little Catholic statesman . . . was extricated from a Belgian monastery and flown to Saigon. . . . Foreign observers report with uniformity that he is neither popular nor yet of apparent use to the course we advocate. Nevertheless, the U.S. has decided it must take a calculated risk in Indochina. . . . A transition had to be devised so that fiscal aid could be pumped directly to a new and independent bank. . . . An official of the Federal Reserve System flew to

Saigon to sponsor an arrangement which started functioning a fortnight ago. . . .

Paris has passed its hand in Southeast Asia to Washington. This is going to create bitterness as it is realized here [Paris]. Neither the U.S. nor Ngo Dinh Diem Government signed the Geneva agreements. Therefore, if they so desire, they may decide they are not bound when the time for all-Vietnam elections rolls around. Already French efforts to save commercial advantages in Ho Chi Minh's domain are frowned upon in Washington. While Jean Sainteny, France's agent in Hanoi, labors to keep an economic toehold, French business concerns here are threatened by us with blacklisting. Public opinion here regards with increasing distaste the shape of things to come in Indochina. If Washington and Saigon refuse to go along with the elections provided for in the Geneva accord, it is feared Ho Chi Minh may renew open warfare. . . . France wonders whether the correct course has been chosen.

— C. L. Sulzberger, dispatch from Paris, *New York Times*, January 16, 1955

Desperate efforts must be made during the intervening period to check Ho Chi Minh's advance. One of the Americans most responsible for this gamble says, "Our policy is simply that we cannot give up hope while there is one chance in 50. The situation is similar to that of the prisoner condemned to death by an Oriental Sultan. He begged a last favor: 'Before I die I would like to teach Your Majesty's favorite black horse how to speak.' The Sultan was intrigued. He asked how long this was likely to take. The prisoner said about a year. When he returned to his cell, astonished guards asked how he had managed to avoid the executioner's axe. He explained. 'But,' asked the guards, 'do you really think you can teach that horse to speak?' The condemned man answered: 'Anything can happen in a year. Perhaps I shall attain a peaceful death. Or perhaps the Sultan will die and I will be released. Or perhaps—and who knows—I may even teach the animal to talk.' "

— C. L. Sulzberger, dispatch from Paris, *New York Times*, January 17, 1955

Intelligence reports from South Vietnam indicate that Premier Ngo Dinh Diem is extending the area of his control. . . . If present trends continue, there is hope. . . . The Premier is a mystic, idealistic celibate who . . . lived for two and a half years at Maryknoll [Seminary]. . . . Before the turn of the year, there were a good many more pessimists than optimists among the Washington officials who read the confidential dispatches from Saigon. Now the optimists are gaining the upper hand. . . . The factor that appears to have turned the tide is the financial power that the Premier has acquired since the U.S. on Jan. 5 began routing its economic and military aid directly to the South Vietnamese Government. . . . This not only gives the Premier control of the army but is rapidly extending his power over the religious-political sects, the Binh Xuyen, the Hoa Hao and the Cao Dai.

> — *New York Times*, January 20, 1955

The day before I left I received a letter from President Ngo Dinh Diem requesting that we take over the training of the armed forces.

> — General J. Lawton Collins,
> arrival in Washington from Saigon,
> January 23, 1955

Indo-China of course is not in the Far East. You have to define what you are talking about really. Indo-China is in the Middle East. It's not in the Far East.

> — Secretary of the Treasury George M.
> Humphrey, *Meet the Press*,
> NBC, January 23, 1955

Paris "has secretly concluded an agreement with the Ho Chi Minh Government granting the equivalent of recognition." . . . We see here . . . the classic illusion [of] the French. . . . They believe it possible to do business with the Communists. . . . The French colonial interests would prefer the defeat of the Government of President Ngo Dinh Diem. . . . The French have done everything in their power to undermine Premier Diem's authority and to sabotage his efforts to establish a strong Government. . . . The objective of the French is identical with the Communists. . . . In their pessimistic evaluation of the stability of Premier Diem's Government . . . the French are obviously the victims of a common form of self-deception. . . . Our Government is aware of the realities and is taking the necessary measures.

> — Joseph Buttinger,
> adviser to President Ngo Dinh Diem, quoted
> in *New York Times*, January 24, 1955

Vietnam will fall under Red control if Communists win elections set for July 1956. . . . If elections were held today, the overwhelming majority of Vietnamese would vote Communist.

> — Leo Cherne, *Look*, January 25, 1955,
> promoting International Rescue Committee as
> conduit to find and install "leaders" among
> Catholic refugees from North to take over
> Vietnamese government in South

Gloom over the future of free Indochina is giving way to cautious optimism here. . . . According to official U.S. reports reaching the Administration, President Ngo Dinh Diem is emerging as a sound and tenacious leader. . . . His influence has been growing since he forced the former Army Chief of Staff, Gen. Nguyen Van Hinh, to leave the country. . . . Gen. J. Lawton Collins, the President's special ambassador . . . gave a . . . promising picture when he visited the White House this week. President Ngo Dinh Diem is believed by American officials to have as strong an appeal to the nationalist-minded people as any of the leaders of . . . North Vietnam.

— *New York Times*, January 28, 1955

President Diem . . . has made genuine progress . . . South Vietnam is of great importance to us. I take it for granted we have no intention of fighting there and I hope and feel that there is a very good chance that there will be no more fighting . . . General Ely, the French Commander-in-Chief there . . . happens to be an old friend of mine and we have worked together wonderfully well. . . . Our people would have the responsibility of conducting the training according to our standards and using the methods which have proved so successful. . . . We would give the orders. [French] instructors and our instructors alike will be under the Chief of MAG, who happens to be my good friend General "Iron Mike" O'Daniel. . . . In a few days we will iron out the last remaining little technical difficulties. . . . I don't think that independence means that all French have to leave Vietnam . . . Diem has begun to move. . . . In North Vietnam . . . things aren't going too well. . . . Ho Chi Minh is definitely a Communist; so is General Giap, their commander. . . . You've got a corking good Chief of Staff in Matt Ridgway . . . I am cautiously optimistic. I said it's a gamble worth taking to continue to support South Vietnam. . . . We are not definitely committed. I would say that we would have a certain moral obligation. . . . We have made no firm commitments. . . . If Vietnam is lost . . . its fall would very seriously threaten not only Cambodia and Laos, but Burma, Malaya and India.

— General J. Lawton Collins,
Meet the Press, NBC, January 30, 1955

General J. Lawton Collins expressed "cautious optimism" tonight that South Vietnam could be strengthened. General Collins appeared on . . . "Meet the Press." . . . He said he based his cautious optimism on the "good progress" made in the last month by President Ngo Dinh Diem of Vietnam.

— *New York Times*, January 31, 1955

Ho Chi Minh would not dare attempt anything now.

> — Dr. Thomas A. Dooley, Haiphong,
> February 25, 1955

The Roman Catholic Bishop of England and Wales ordered Sunday to be a special day of prayer for the Catholics of Vietnam. Collections will be taken for refugees.

> — *New York Times*, Reuters dispatch from
> London, February 27, 1955

Secretary of State Dulles assured Vietnam's President Ngo Dinh Diem in Saigon . . . that no responsible allied quarter today had doubts as to his ability to handle Vietnam's affairs.

> — *New York Times*,
> dispatch from Manila, March 2, 1955

I am very much impressed by Prime Minister Diem.

> — Secretary of State John Foster Dulles,
> March 9, 1955

Refugees from North Vietnam are still streaming into the south at a rate of 10,000 a week and the rate will probably be increased before the May 10 deadline. This was reported yesterday by Msgr. Joseph J. Hartnett, director of the War Relief Services in Vietnam for the National Catholic Welfare Conference. He was interviewed at the Empire State Club in the Empire State Building. Msgr. Hartnett, who returned here to report on his work, said his agency had helped feed and house 700,000 refugees, 95 percent of whom are Roman Catholic. . . . The May 10 deadline was set at the Geneva conference ending the conflict in Indochina.

> — *New York Times*, dispatch,
> March 10, 1955

The weapons which were used during the Korean war and World War II are obsolete. Our artillery and our tactical Air Force in the Pacific are now equipped with atomic explosives. . . . Tactical atomic explosives are now conventional and will be used against the military targets of any aggressive force.

> — Vice President Richard M. Nixon,
> speech before Executive Club, Chicago,
> March 17, 1955

The groups fighting Vietnam's Government warned tonight that continued U.S. support of Premier Ngo Dinh Diem might lead to civil war. . . . The opposition front warned that the Premier was far removed from the common people here and that he did not pay any attention to national sentiment. The opposition charged that Ngo Dinh Diem was bent on using force to defend his personal political opinions and for the U.S. to continue to support him would definitely compromise the U.S. in the eyes of the Vietnamese.

— *New York Times*, dispatch from Saigon, April 6, 1955

If President Ngo Dinh Diem of Vietnam should be overthrown by the combination of gangsters, cultists and French colonialists who have been gunning for him, the Communists will have won a significant victory. . . . The U.S. must not be blackmailed by the dissident sects or by anyone else out of its determination to give all possible support to President Ngo Dinh Diem. . . . The French are accused of . . . lending at least moral aid and comfort to the dissident sects. . . . Vietnam must be saved. . . . Leadership such as that provided by President Ngo Dinh Diem can do it.

— Editorial, *New York Times*, April 6, 1955

Diem was originally France's choice. After the Dienbienphu disaster he was dispatched to Saigon with Paris' blessing. But the French soon realized he did not have the competence required for success. They began to depict him as an American—specifically a C.I.A.—choice. And since the United States and General Collins for months bullheadedly insisted Diem was the only answer to South Vietnam's problems, our actions confirmed French propaganda. Both General Ely, France's High Commissioner, and General Collins now recommend Diem be replaced. It is remarkable in the case of Collins. . . . Now there is talk of finding a new Premier from among the few nationalist leaders available: a man like Quat, Thoai, Minh or Than Van Do. If such a substitution is decided it will represent humiliation for the U.S. Diem is now regarded as an American puppet throughout South Vietnam and much of Asia. . . .

The mess in South Vietnam has brought our relationship with France to a new phase of crisis. The State Department, the Pentagon and the C.I.A. are all furious with the French. Even General Ely, hitherto regarded as a loyal friend of this country's policies, is now suspected. . . . Any objective observer in South Vietnam has known for months that there was no effective government. Diem ruled Saigon when the Binh Xuyen gang which controls the police was with him. The rest of the country is parcelled out in feudal lots held by the Cao Dai, Hoa Hao, the Communist Viet Minh, or simply by chaos. We tried to insist Diem's popularity and strength were gaining. The only people we fooled were ourselves. The Premier has shown little capacity. He depends largely on his brothers who are detested. The fact that he is a Roman Catholic mitigated unfairly [*sic*] against him in a country where that religion is regarded by the armed sects as a dangerous rival. . . . Whatever happens, if disintegration encompasses South Vietnam, two things must be kept in mind as having priority importance. The first is the saving of the hundreds of thousands of refugees from the North who gave up everything to find freedom. They simply cannot be permitted to fall again beneath the Communist tide.

— *New York Times*, April 18, 1955

We are behind the legal Government of Vietnam.

— General J. Lawton Collins, April 22, 1955

Premier Diem is the Churchill of Asia . . . history may yet adjudge Diem as one of the great figures of the twentieth century.

— Senator Lyndon B. Johnson,
Democrat of Texas, April 30, 1955

The present head of the legal government of Free Vietnam which we are supporting is Diem and we acknowledge Bao Dai as Chief of State.

— Henry Suydam, Department of State press
officer, quoted in *New York Times*, April 30,
1955

South Vietnam's army was winning the battle of Saigon yesterday against rebel forces.

— *New York Times*, April 30, 1955

Ngo Dinh Diem's government stands for decency and honesty while those conspiring to bring him down represent corruption. . . . The power arrayed against President Ngo Dinh Diem is that of the Black Hand, the pirate, the racketeer and the witch doctor.

— Senator Mike Mansfield, April 30, 1955

Premier Diem is the best hope that we have in South Vietnam. He is the leader of his people. He deserves and must have the wholehearted support of the American Government and our foreign policy. This is no time for uncertainty or half-hearted measures. . . . He is the only man on the political horizon of Vietnam who can rally a substantial degree of support of his people. . . . If we have any comments to make about the leadership in Vietnam let it be directed against Bao Dai. It is time we broke our ties with him and not with Diem. If the Government of South Vietnam has not room for both of these men, it is Bao Dai who must go.

> — Senator Hubert H. Humphrey, Democrat of
> Minnesota, speech in Senate,
> May 2, 1955

The United States strongly reaffirmed today its support of Ngo Dinh Diem as Premier of South Vietnam. At the same time the State Department disavowed any intention of trying to save Bao Dai's position as Chief of State. . . . Ngo Dinh Nhu, brother and spokesman of Premier Ngo Dinh Diem said today . . . "It is obvious Bao Dai is finished."

> — *New York Times*, May 7, 1955

Show complete confidence in the patriot Ngo Dinh Diem, who has always fought for the right of peoples to dispose of themselves [*sic*].

> — Part of program, Vietnamese "revolutionary
> movement," quoted by *New York Times*,
> May 16, 1955

You will find no Vietnamese who believes that the elections will ever be held. . . . Ho Chi Minh['s] . . . majority in the North and in the South is assured. . . . Diem is separated from the people by cardinals and police cars with wailing sirens and foreign advisers when he should be walking in the rice fields unprotected, learning the hard way how to be loved and obeyed—the two cannot be separated. One pictured him sitting there in the Norodom Palace, sitting with his blank, brown gaze . . . obstinate, ill-advised, going to his weekly confession, bolstered up by his belief that God is always on the Catholic side, waiting for a miracle. . . .

> — Graham Greene, *New Republic*, May 9, 1955

Ngo Dinh Diem will be able to lead the people of free Vietnam to success.

> — Ambassador George Frederick Reinhardt,
> May 27, 1955

The government of Diem, which seemed to be almost on the ropes a few weeks ago, I think is re-established with strength.

> — Secretary of State John Foster Dulles, quoted
> in *Department of State Bulletin*, May 30, 1955

Diem . . . has the will to win. No one else capable of fighting Ho Chi Minh to a standstill is presently visible. Diem should be supported to the limit.

> — Ernest K. Lindley, column, *Newsweek*,
> June 6, 1955

Indochina is being nibbled away from us, and so I would like . . . strong, aggressive support for Diem. By everything we can think of, because Diem represents the real nationalism in Vietnam, and to beat Ho Chi Minh he'll have to out-nationalist Ho Chi Minh.

> — Ambassador Carlos P. Romulo, special envoy,
> president, Philippines, to U.S., *Face the Nation*,
> CBS, June 26, 1955

Diem's young army [is] proving more efficient than critics expected.

> — *Time*, June 27, 1955

The first anniversary of Ngo Dinh Diem Premiership was celebrated today with mass meetings, athletic events, fireworks, and a parade of lantern-bearing soldiers. The troops marched past the Premier and his guests in his floodlit Independence Palace. It was a gala day for the short, stocky Catholic Premier. . . . Premier Diem outlined his accomplishments. . . . In the military field, the Premier said, "We have taken back command of military zones all over the country." The Premier then spoke of progress in foreign affairs. . . . There can be no doubt that Premier Diem has become immeasurably stronger in the past year. However . . . peasants make up 80 or 90 percent of the population and it often appears that the Diem Government has few real roots among them.

> — *New York Times*,
> July 7 dispatch from Saigon, July 18, 1955

There can be no question of a conference, even less of negotiations.

> — President Ngo Dinh Diem to *London Times*
> reporter, September 21, 1955

Whoever commits or attempts to commit . . . crimes . . . infringing upon the security of the State . . . whoever belongs to organizations designed to help to prepare or to perpetrate [these] crimes . . . will be sentenced to death. . . . Anyone who intentionally proclaims or spreads by any means unauthorized news about prices or rumors contrary to truth or distorts the truth concerning the present or future situation in the country or abroad . . . will be sentenced to death.

> — Law 10/59, Ordinance No. 61, Laws of the
> Government of South Vietnam, October 3,
> 1955 and May 6, 1959

I've been accused of betraying my country. But it is not I who have betrayed my country. . . . It is the big powers—the men who signed the Geneva pact.

> — Chief of State Bao Dai, quoted by *Time*,
> October 17, 1955

Premier Diem, a Roman Catholic, is a small, chunky, dark-haired man of 54 who works at a desk in Saigon surrounded by crises and a few personal things—a wooden crucifix, a picture of the Virgin. . . .

> — *Time*, October 17, 1955

I promise you that by the end of this year we will have a democratic regime and a national assembly.

> — President Ngo Dinh Diem, quoted by *Time*,
> October 17, 1955

What happened on October 23 [1955] was a foregone conclusion: The [Diem] republic was swept into being by a vote of 98.2% in favor and 1.1% against. There is not the slightest doubt that this plebiscite was only a shade more fraudulent than most electoral tests under a dictatorship. In nearly all electoral areas, there were thousands more "Yes" votes than voters. In the Saigon-Cholon area, for example, 605,025 votes were cast by 450,000 registered voters, and mountain or deep-swamp areas patently not even under control of the government reported as heavy voter participation as the well-controlled urban areas. *Life* magazine, in a laudatory profile of South Viet-Nam published May 13, 1957, during Diem's visit to the United States, nevertheless noted that American advisers had told Diem that a 60% margin was quite sufficient and would look better, "but Diem insisted on 98%."

> — Bernard B. Fall, *The Two Viet-Nams*

We are glad to see the evolution of orderly and effective democratic processes in . . . Southeast Asia.

> — Ambassador George Frederick Reinhardt,
> October 28, 1955

In the North, the fall of the illegitimate regime is near.

> — *Viet-Nam Press*, November 9, 1955

Lieut. Gen. John W. O'Daniel headed home by air today after having received South Vietnam's Grand Cross in recognition of his work as head of the U.S. Military Mission here.

> — *New York Times*,
> UP dispatch from Saigon, November 19, 1955

Relations between France and the theoretically associated state of Vietnam have become more strained than ever in the last days. . . . The French want South Vietnam to live up to the provisions of the [Geneva] accords calling for country-wide elections next year. South Vietnam has always been reluctant to agree to such elections until it had at least consolidated its own position.

> — *New York Times*,
> dispatch from Paris, December 2, 1955

South Vietnam has very good chances for success. With a little more training the South Vietnamese Army will be the equal of any other army.

> — Secretary of the Army Wilbur Brucker,
> after 2-day visit to Vietnam,
> Saigon, December 17, 1955

South Vietnam has made remarkable progress. . . . President Ngo Dinh Diem now controls his own Army and police force. . . . The feudal sects that divided up the country are being eliminated [*sic*]. . . . Almost 1,000,000 refugees had streamed down into South Vietnam. . . . President Diem has emerged as a strong and forceful leader. . . . The refugees . . . are being resettled on land once held by the feudal sects. . . . The foreign diplomatic community now feels there is real hope. It no longer believes a miracle is needed to save the country. . . . Observers agree that an enormous stride forward has been taken.

> — *New York Times*,
> dispatch from Saigon, February 8, 1956

The pro-Western regime of President Ngo Dinh Diem has won a solid victory in the first National Assembly election in the young republic of South Vietnam. All the candidates closely connected with the Administration, including four cabinet ministers and the brother and sister-in-law of President Diem, were swept into office by wide margins.

> — *New York Times*,
> dispatch from Saigon, March 6, 1956

We do not consider ourselves bound by the Geneva Agreement, which has been signed against the will and in contempt of the interest of the Vietnamese people.

> — South Vietnamese National Assembly,
> Saigon, March 8, 1956

They [the Vietminh] were stopped finally in the northern part of Vietnam; and Diem, the leader of the Southern Vietnamese, is doing

splendidly and a much better figure in the field than anyone even dared
to hope.

> — President Dwight D. Eisenhower,
> April 21, 1956

[There is] the amazing success of President Diem. . . . Vietnam
represents the cornerstone of the Free World in Southeast Asia, the
keystone to the arch, the finger in the dike. . . . Vietnam is crucial to the
free world in fields other than the military. Her economy is essential to
the economy of Southeast Asia; and her political liberty is an inspiration.
. . . We must assist the inspiring growth of Vietnamese democracy and
economy.

> — Senator John F. Kennedy, speech to American
> Friends of Vietnam [Leo Cherne's
> organization], June 1, 1956

This past March I had the pleasure of accompanying the Secretary of
State on his visit to Saigon where we conversed with President Diem.
. . . I was struck, as so many other recent observers have been, at the
progress Free Viet-Nam has made. . . . President Diem seemed to reflect
this progress in his own person. On the occasion of our earlier visit some
15 months ago, he seemed tense and gravely concerned. . . . This time
he was reposed, poised, and appeared confident about the future of his
country.

Among the factors that explain the remarkable rise of Free Viet-Nam
. . . there is in the first place the dedication, courage, and resourceful-
ness of President Diem himself. In him, his country has found a truly
worthy leader whose integrity and devotion to his country's welfare have
become generally recognized among his people. Asia has given us in
President Diem another great figure, and the entire free world has
become the richer for his example of determination and moral fortitude.
. . . Viet-Nam today, in mid-1956, progressing rapidly . . . its people
resuming peaceful pursuits, its army growing in effectiveness, sense of
mission, and morale . . . the refugees well on the way to permanent
resettlement, the countryside generally orderly and calm, the predatory
sects eliminated. . . . No more eloquent testimony . . . could be cited
than the voice of the people . . . in their free election last March . . . an
overwhelming majority for President Diem. . . . The U.S. is proud to be
on the side of . . . President Diem. . . .

The United States wishes to continue to assist . . . first of all toward
helping to sustain the internal security forces . . . of about 150,000 men,
a mobile civil guard of some 45,000, and local defense units which are
being formed to give protection against subversion on the village level.
We are providing budgetary support and equipment for these forces. . . .

We are also helping to organize, train and equip the Vietnamese police force. The refugees who have fled to South Viet-Nam . . . are being resettled on productive lands with the assistance of funds made available by our aid program. . . . Our aid program also provides assistance to the Vietnamese Government . . . to strengthen the economy. . . . President Diem and the Government of Free Viet-Nam reaffirmed on April 6 . . . their desire to seek the reunification of Viet-Nam. . . . In this goal we support them fully. We hope and pray that the partition of Viet-Nam . . . will speedily come to an end. . . . May those leaders of the north . . . realize the futility of the Communist efforts to subvert Free Viet-Nam. . . . May they force the abandonment of those efforts and bring about the peaceful demobilization of the large standing armies of the Viet Minh. May they, above all, return to the just cause of all those who want to reunify their country.

> — Assistant Secretary of State for Far Eastern
> Affairs Walter S. Robertson, speech to
> American Friends of Vietnam, June 1, 1956

The Catholic Relief Services is increasing its program of relief for . . . refugees in South Vietnam . . . 650,000 of whom are Roman Catholic. . . . Msgr. Joseph J. Hartnett, resident director of the service in Vietnam, said here that 48,000,000 pounds of food and clothing will be shipped in the next three months. Since August 1954, the service has sent 36,000,000 pounds of food and clothing. . . . The program, financed by the contributions of Catholics in this country, also furnishes medical assistance . . . in an effort to re-settle the refugees permanently. Much progress has been made with the refugee program since the end of the Indo-China War, according to Msgr. Hartnett. He said he felt another three years of emergency relief would be required.

> — *New York Times*, June 10, 1956

Our Government has been wise in deciding that Vice President Nixon can enlarge the Far Eastern trip upon which he has now started . . . and include a visit to Vietnam. Happily, he can be in Saigon at the time that the Vietnamese celebrate the second anniversary of the coming into authority of President Ngo Dinh Diem. . . . Free Vietnam's economic difficulty has been increased also by the influx of almost 1,000,000 refugees from the North. The progress that has been made in the past two years has been astonishing and gratifying. President Diem has been able to establish a stable government. . . . He and his government are hard at work now. . . . The economic position is improving. Some problems are being solved. The outlook is brighter. . . . The assistance of the United States . . . must continue.

> — *New York Times*, July 6, 1956

The militant march of Communism has been halted.

> — Vice President Richard M. Nixon, Saigon,
> July 6, 1956

We, today, point with pride to the free nation of Vietnam.

> — President Dwight D. Eisenhower,
> September 20, 1956

When the day comes for me to face my Maker and account for my actions, the thing I would be most humbly proud of was the fact that I fought against . . . the carrying out of some harebrained tactical schemes which would have cost the lives of thousands of men. To that list of tragic accidents that fortunately never happened I would add the Indo-China intervention.

> — General Matthew B. Ridgway,
> *Soldier: The Memoirs of Matthew Ridgway*,
> 1956

History may yet adjudge Diem as one of the great figures of the Twentieth Century.

> — William Henderson, "South Vietnam Finds
> Itself," *Foreign Affairs*, January 1957

The Vietminh authorities have disintegrated and been rendered powerless. . . . The dying gasps of bandit remnants. . . .

> — President Ngo Dinh Diem, quoted by
> Republic of Vietnam, Department of
> Information, January 1957

President Diem, slowly and almost unnoticed by the outside world, has brought to South Viet Nam a peace and stability few would have dared predict when his country was dismembered at Geneva three years ago. Last week a traveler could journey from one end of the country to the other, by day or night, with never a worry about Viet Minh bandits. . . . Even the French have taken heart. . . . Outside Saigon, thriving new villages testify to Diem's success (with massive U.S. financial help) in the tremendous job of resettling 900,000 refugees. . . . Diem himself was a man of peace. On a recent inspection trip, he discovered that the mountain tribes of Annam have no calendar. . . . Diem decided that it was a shame, picked Feb. 22 for the inauguration of an annual mountain New Year's party that will last for three days. . . . Diplomats flown up from Saigon will hunt tigers and wild buffalo.

> — *Time*, February 11, 1957

Vietnam is enjoying full physical security.

— Nguyên Van Hanh, managing director,
National Bank of South Vietnam,
New York City, February 18, 1957

We had no policy at all. . . . At the end of seven years of war we had come to a complete imbroglio, and no one, from the common soldier to the commander-in-chief, knew exactly why the war was being fought.

— General Henri Eugène Navarre, March 1957

The Government of South Vietnam announced yesterday a set of incentives it hopes will lure substantial dollar investments.

— *New York Times*, March 16, 1957

President Ngo Dinh Diem arrived today on President Eisenhower's personal plane, Columbine III, en route to a state visit in Washington.

— *New York Times*,
AP dispatch from San Francisco, May 7, 1957

You have exemplified in your part of the world a patriotism of the highest order. . . . That accomplished the miracle of Vietnam.

— President Dwight D. Eisenhower to President
Ngo Dinh Diem, Washington National
Airport, May 8, 1957

President Diem's accomplishments in these past two years will assure him admiration and respect. . . . The measures that he has taken have been practical as well as imaginative. . . . It will be a mistake if this trip is interpreted as just another visit to obtain American aid. . . . We honor him.

— Editorial, *New York Times*,
"Welcome President Diem," May 8, 1957

President Ngo Dinh Diem of South Vietnam came back to Washington in triumph today. President Eisenhower greeted him on a red carpet. . . . Today only the best was good enough. President Eisenhower met his visitor at Washington National Airport and praised him without reservation. . . . President Diem has carved a deep niche in official esteem in Washington. This was evident in the character of the welcome. During the last four years President Eisenhower has met only one other foreign leader, King Saud of Saudi Arabia, on arrival.

— *New York Times*, May 8, 1957

In March, 1957, the [Diem] regime openly violated the last restraints placed upon it by the Geneva Agreements with regard to reprisals exercised against 'former resistance members'—that is, ex-guerrillas of the Viet-Minh who had fought against the French, and many of whom were not Communists.

> — Bernard B. Fall, "Viet-Cong—The Unseen Enemy in Viet-Nam" (*Viet-Nam Reader*, Raskin and Fall)

[Vietnamese now have] irresistible dynamism. . . . Vietnam has good reason for confidence and hope. . . . They also draw strength from the moral and material aid they receive from . . . the American people.

> — President Ngo Dinh Diem, address to joint session of U.S. Congress, May 9, 1957

We cannot let ourselves be lulled by the song of peaceful co-existence. . . . If we have more aid, this consolidation [of Vietnam] can be effected more rapidly.

> — President Ngo Dinh Diem to National Press Club, Washington, May 10, 1957

Ngo Dinh Diem's life—all of it—is devoted to his country and to his God. A Roman Catholic, at an early age he took a vow of chastity which he renews daily.

> — *New York Times*, May 10, 1957

President Ngo Dinh Diem of the Republic of Vietnam will arrive today in New York for a three-day visit. He will be welcomed tomorrow by a ticker-tape parade up Broadway to the City Hall. . . . President Diem will proceed immediately to St. Patrick's Cathedral to attend the 10:00 a.m. Mass.

> — *New York Times*, May 12, 1957

We are delighted and we are proud to see in the sanctuary of our Cathedral the President of the Republic of Vietnam, His Excellency Ngo Dinh Diem. The entire world acclaimed him when the God-fearing anti-Communist and courageous statesman saved Vietnam.

> — Most Reverend Joseph F. Flannelly, auxiliary bishop of New York, St. Patrick's Cathedral, New York City, May 12, 1957

The first thing the Roman Catholic leader of the predominantly Buddhist country did after his arrival from Washington was attend a High Mass at St. Patrick's Cathedral. But the high point of the day came when the President had a joyful reunion on the pleasant rolling campus of Maryknoll Seminary outside Ossining, N.Y. Mr. Diem lived at the Seminary and at the Maryknoll Junior Seminary at Lakewood, N.J., when he was in self-imposed exile during the years 1951 to 1953. . . . The students, dressed identically in their black cassocks, gave him a rousing welcome . . . a lusty three-fold "Hip, Hip, Hoorah" that echoed in the sunlit hills. . . . The motorcycle escort formed and President Diem sped toward St. Patrick's. The High Mass was delayed until the President arrived. . . .

— *New York Times*, May 13, 1957

President Diem is a man to whom freedom is the very breath of life itself. . . . What has occurred in Vietnam is a political miracle. Certainly the principal credit for this miracle should be given to President Ngo Dinh Diem, a man history may yet judge to be one of the great figures of the 20th century.

— Mayor Robert Wagner, New York City, May 13, 1957

President Diem is opening up vast areas for the peaceful progress of mankind.

— President Dwight D. Eisenhower, telegram to President Ngo Dinh Diem, May 13, 1957

Ngo Dinh Diem is respected in Vietnam today for the miracles he has wrought. Order has replaced chaos. Communism is being defeated. . . . Diem's [greatest] hurdle was the famous "Geneva elections," the plebiscite which, according to the 1954 Geneva Agreement, should have been held last July 20. It was supposed to let the people of North and South Vietnam decide whether a reunited country should be governed by anti-Communist Diem or Communist Ho Chi Minh. . . . [Diem] knew that it was not a question of who could win the projected plebiscite: It was a question of who the people would expect to win, and all too many of them would have hedged by voting on the assumption that the Viet Minh might win. Diem saved his people from this agonizing prospect simply by refusing to permit the plebiscite.

— *Life*, May 13, 1957

South Vietnam's President Ngo Dinh Diem received a warm and open-hearted reception from New Yorkers yesterday. . . . His welcoming parade moved up Lower Broadway toward City Hall. . . . One police official said there were 100,000 people along the route of march; another said there were 250,000. . . . They drove to the Waldorf-Astoria Hotel

where the Mayor gave a luncheon for the city's honored guest. . . .
Mayor Wagner presented Mr. Diem with the city's Medal of Honor and
a scroll for "Distinguished and Exceptional Service." In the evening . . .
President Diem received the first Admiral Richard E. Byrd Memorial
Award for "inspired leadership in the cause of the free world" . . .
presented by Angier Biddle Duke, President of the International Rescue
Committee, co-sponsor of the dinner with the Friends of Vietnam. . . .
Henry R. Luce, Editor-in-Chief of Time, Inc., presided at the dinner.
Today President Diem will attend a Mass at the residence of Cardinal
Spellman and take breakfast with him.

> — *New York Times*, May 14, 1957

No American taxpayer need regret these expenditures. . . . This
investment has been wisely made.

> — President Ngo Dinh Diem to Far
> East–American Council of Commerce and
> Industry, Waldorf-Astoria Hotel, New York
> City, May 14, 1957

South Vietnam today is proof of what an authentic patriot, resolute
and shrewd, can accomplish. . . . In two years South Vietnam has been
transformed. . . . The main Communist pockets have been wiped out.
Most of the countryside has been pacified and brought under control of
the central government. . . . Aid to South Vietnam has been costly to the
American taxpayer. . . . But it is the end result which counts.

> — Ernest K. Lindley, column, *Newsweek*,
> May 20, 1957

Thus Viet-Nam has been saved for freedom.

> — President Dwight D. Eisenhower,
> May 21, 1957

Dynamic President Diem has created a stable regime, emerged as one
of the East's strongest statesmen. . . . U.S. aid ($250 million this year)
keeps his army in the pink and his budget in the black.

> — *Time*, December 30, 1957

Communist efforts to dominate South Viet-Nam have entirely failed.

> — President Dwight D. Eisenhower,
> February 25, 1958

The Vietnamese people are doing their utmost to attain democracy.

> — President Ngo Dinh Diem, Manila,
> March 22, 1958

In . . . Vietnam, the wars are ended.

> — President Dwight D. Eisenhower,
> April 17, 1958

South Vietnam today can be classed as one of the most stable and peaceful countries of Asia today.

> — Professor Wesley Fishel, senior civilian
> adviser to Ngo Dinh Diem, August 1958

TOP SECRET

President Diem continues to be the undisputed ruler of South Vietnam; all important and many minor decisions are referred to him. Although he professes to believe in representative government and democracy, Diem is convinced that the Vietnamese are not ready for such a political system and that he must rule with a firm hand. . . . He also believes that the country cannot afford a political opposition which could obstruct or dilute the Government's efforts to establish a strong rule. He remains a somewhat austere and remote figure to most Vietnamese and has not generated widespread popular enthusiasm. Diem's regime reflects his ideas. A facade of representative government is maintained, but the Government is in fact essentially authoritarian. The legislative powers of the National Assembly are strictly circumscribed; the judiciary is undeveloped and subordinate to the executive; and the members of the executive branch are little more than the personal agents of Diem. No organized opposition, loyal or otherwise, is tolerated, and critics of the regime are often repressed.

> — American intelligence estimate, May 1959

[South Vietnam has] had more striking progress in more ways than any other nation I have visited so far.

> — Ernest K. Lindley, column, *Newsweek*,
> June 29, 1959

Once a well-ordered colonial city under French rule, Hanoi . . . has turned into a place where, says one frequent foreign visitor, "the only noise is the absence of noise. Nobody smiles. Not even the children laugh." Life in Hanoi today is no laughing matter . . . anything beyond the necessities, anything like oil, flour or sugar, is prohibitively expensive. The dong—North Viet Nam's unit of currency—has no standing whatsoever in international exchange.

> — *Time*, July 6, 1959

Five years ago today Ngo Dinh Diem took over as Chief of State of the Republic of Vietnam. . . . Now five years have passed. . . . There is unity and order. The refugees have been put on the land with increasing success. . . . With American help the country has been made less vulnerable from a military point of view. . . . A five-year miracle . . . has been carried out. Vietnam . . . is becoming stronger. . . . There is reason, today, to salute President Ngo Dinh Diem.

> — Editorial, *New York Times*, July 7, 1959

We have entered into a comparatively recent commitment for the development of the organization of the constabulary police force and its army, which may prove helpful.

> — Secretary of State Christian Herter,
> news conference, July 9, 1959

A small band of terrorists, using sub-machine guns and a "human bomb," attacked an American army billet just 20 miles from Saigon. . . . This crime was fashioned to coincide with the Vietnamese celebration of the fifth anniversary of the accession to power of President Ngo Dinh Diem. . . . These things are part of a global plan.

> — Editorial, *New York Times*, July 10, 1959

I am proud of this program.

> — Ambassador Elbridge Durbrow, July 30, 1959

The [Vietnamese aid] program as a whole—far from being a "fiasco" or a "scandal"—has been a tremendous success.

> — Ambassador Elbridge Durbrow, before House
> Foreign Affairs Subcommittee, August 3, 1959

U.S. aid is serving as a major stimulant to the Vietnamese Government. The country is positively on the advance in all areas. . . . The country . . . is headed in the right way.

> — Dr. Daniel Russell, International Voluntary
> Service, August 7, 1959

The American aid program in Vietnam has proved an enormous success, one of the major victories of American policy.

> — General John W. (Iron Mike) O'Daniel,
> September 7, 1959

The Communist capability in Vietnam, south of the 17th Parallel, has been reduced to one of sheer nuisance activity. . . . It is one of the Asian areas where Communism has been rolled back. . . . There is little likelihood of a revolution against the Diem regime.

— Professor Wesley Fishel,
Yale Review, Autumn, 1959

Vietnam does have the potentials for excellent economic progress.

— Robert R. Nathan, consulting economist,
October 3, 1959

President Diem and his government have not resorted to force, setting up class against class, or to any of the methods used by the Communists to impose their brand of agrarianism. Social peace has been used throughout.

— Wolf Ladjinsky, advisor to Ngo Dinh Diem,
News from Vietnam, November 1959

TOP SECRET

DEPARTMENT OF STATE
Bureau of Intelligence Research

TO: The Secretary   Research Memorandum
THROUGH: Secretary of State   RFE-59 (Grav)
FROM: INR—Roger Hilsman   Dec. 3, 1959

SUBJECT: The Situation and Short-Term Prospects in South Vietnam

ABSTRACT

President Ngo Dinh Diem and other leading Vietnamese as well as many U.S. officials in South Vietnam apparently believe that the tide is now turning in the struggle.

The United States aid program in South Vietnam is soundly conceived and soundly executed.

— Senator Gale McGee, Democrat of Wyoming,
December 16, 1959

[The insurgents are only] local Viet-Minh agents in remote areas.

— Wolf Ladjinsky, *The Reporter*,
December 24, 1959

Faced with a common enemy, our two peoples share not only common interests, but the same fate.

— Generalissimo Chiang Kai-shek, state dinner
in Taipei, Taiwan, January 15, 1960

President Ngo Dinh Diem of South Vietnam arrived here aboard a U.S. Air Force plane today.

> — *New York Times*, dispatch from Taipei
> (Taiwan), January 16, 1960

The aid received by the free Asian countries . . . should therefore not be reduced, but should be further strengthened. . . .

> — President Ngo Dinh Diem and Generalissimo
> Chiang Kai-shek, joint statement, Taiwan,
> January 29, 1960

On the basis of the assurance of the head of the military aid mission in Viet-Nam . . . at least the U.S. Military Aid [*sic*] Advisory Group (MAAG) can be phased out of Viet-Nam in the foreseeable future.

> — Mansfield Report: *Situation in Viet-Nam*,
> Senate Foreign Relations Committee,
> February 1960

I am pleased to note the very strenuous efforts of U.S. officials in Vietnam.

> — Senator Albert Gore,
> Democrat of Tennessee,
> February 8, 1960

By any measure Vietnam has made great progress under President Ngo Dinh Diem.

> — Senator Mike Mansfield,
> Democrat of Montana,
> February 26, 1960

A $615,000 grant to South Vietnam . . . was announced yesterday by the Ford Foundation and the Brookings Institute.

> — *New York Times*, August 30, 1960

Distinguished soldiers such as former Army Chiefs of Staff Generals Ridgway and Taylor, General James M. Gavin . . . and General Powell, present Chief of the Strategic Air Command; such distinguished journalists as Joseph Alsop . . . and such research organizations as the Rand Corporation and the Rockefeller Brothers Fund . . . Robert A. Lovett, a Wall Street banker . . . and a Secretary of Defense . . . Mr. Robert Sprague . . . an industrialist, Chairman of the Federal Reserve Bank of Boston, and consultant to the National Security Council.

These men believe that our survival is imperiled; that we are not doing enough to assure our security . . . that we should do more; and if it costs more to do more we ought to pay for it in the spirit of "damn the torpedoes, go ahead." . . . We must have a high degree of discipline at home. . . . The President is the only man who can bring this forcibly to the Nation. . . . These men are men of substance—of course, it is true that Mr. Lovett is a Wall Street banker.

I do not believe that he would give this testimony in the hope that he might make a few more dollars. . . . It never occurred to me that anyone would rise and insinuate that they were giving testimony in order to get a few Government contracts. . . . I am quite sure that the International Business Machines Corporation has, either directly or indirectly, substantial Government contracts. . . . I do not believe, however, that interest is sufficient or direct enough to motivate Mr. Watson to give testimony. . . .

I should say that if we question the motives of such people we are in trouble. . . . I am unwilling to question their motives even if they do have contracts. . . . I have no doubt that Brown Brothers, Harriman has banking relations with people who do have contracts. . . . A case might be made that they would profit by defense contracts. I am only saying that I am unwilling to question their motives.

> — Senator J. William Fulbright, Democrat of
> Arkansas, chairman, Senate Foreign Relations
> Committee, debate in Senate, March 5, 1960

Doughty little Diem . . . the father of his country . . . without him the whole nation would have fallen to the communist Viet-Minh.

> — *Time*, November 21, 1960

In what everyone thought was the hour of total Communist triumph, we saw a near miracle take place. . . . Today that brave little state is working . . . with the United States, whose economic and military aid has . . . proved effective.

> — Senator John F. Kennedy,
> *Strategy of Peace*, 1960

The Communists now realize they can never conquer free Vietnam.

> — General J. W. O'Daniel,
> official military aide to Vietnam,
> January 8, 1961

In view of the President's instruction that we make every possible effort to launch guerrilla operations in Vietminh territory at the earliest possible time, would you report to the President as soon as feasible your views on what actions might be undertaken in the near future and what steps might be taken to expand operations.

> — Presidential Adviser for National Security
> Affairs McGeorge Bundy, to Secretary of
> Defense Robert S. McNamara, March 9, 1961

South Vietnam . . . has become a testing ground for new United States guerrilla tactics designed for fighting in tropical jungles.

— *New York Times*, March 22, 1961

In South Vietnam . . . a real shooting war is going forward. . . . Why is South Vietnam so important . . . ? It is physically . . . the gateway to Southeast Asia's millions of square miles, which offer vast resources. . . . The agrovilles . . . are the most fruitful pioneering rural ventures since the Israeli cooperative farm.

— Leo Cherne,
New York Times Magazine, April 8, 1961

Prospects for effective resistance to the Communists are better in South Vietnam than in Laos. The Ngo regime is more capable and more determined than the government of Laos and commands tougher, better-led and better-trained forces. . . . Free world forces still stand a chance in South Vietnam, and every effort should be made.

— Editorial, *New York Times*, April 8, 1961

President Ngo Dinh Diem and Vice President Nguyen Ngoc Tho were returned to office with about 78 percent of the total vote. Early returns indicated that about 90 percent of more than 7,000,000 registered voters cast ballots.

— *New York Times*, April 10, 1961

The black-pajamaed Vietnamese ranger lieutenant saluted smartly after making his whispered report, and ran out into the night. There was a sharp rattle of gunfire, not too far away. The young colonel turned to his large table full of guests with a brilliant, mildly teasing smile. . . . "I'm afraid dinner may be a little noisy." . . .

— Joseph Alsop, syndicated column, from Ben Tre, Kien Hoa Province, South Vietnam, April 11, 1961

There . . . remains an urgent need to strengthen Vietnam's political institutions as well as to continue the kind of military assistance and training that will make guerrilla warfare unprofitable.

— Editorial, *Washington Post*, April 11, 1961

TOP SECRET

I believe we must turn to gearing up the whole Viet-Nam operation. Among the possible lines of action that might be considered at an early high level meeting are the following: . . . A possible visit to Viet-Nam in the near future by the Vice President. A possible visit to the U.S. of Mr. Thuan, acting Defense Minister. . . . The sending to Viet-Nam of a . . . military hardware team which would explore with General McGarr which of the various techniques and gadgets now available or being explored might be relevant and useful. . . . The raising of the MAAG ceiling, which involves some diplomacy, unless we can find an alternative way of introducing into Viet-Nam operation a substantial number of Special Forces types. . . . The question of the extra funds for Diem. . . .

> — Deputy Presidential Assistant for National
> Security Walt W. Rostow, to President John F.
> Kennedy, April 12, 1961

In all the years of his reign Ngo Dinh Diem found only one ally in the countryside, and that was the Catholics, most particularly the northern refugees. From the beginning he staffed his administration heavily with Catholics and favored the Catholic villages over all the rest. The Diemist officials, working closely with the priests, saw to it that the Catholic villages took the bulk of U.S. relief aid, the bulk of the agricultural credit. They gave the Catholics the right to take lumber from the national reserves and monopoly rights over the production of the new cash crops introduced by the American aid technicians. . . . Thousands of people, including in some cases whole villages, turned Catholic . . . to avoid resettlement—for the benefit of their Catholic neighbors—into some hardship zone of jungle or swamp.

> — Frances FitzGerald, *Fire in the Lake*

Nowadays when a Western reporter finds a corner of the world which positively inspires hope, the impulse to linger there is all but irresistible. . . . The good guys have been coming out on top for once.

> — Joseph Alsop, syndicated column, from Ben
> Tre, Kien Hoa Province, South Vietnam,
> April 14, 1961

Ho Chi Minh's people live in a state of regimented wretchedness. . . . All the evidence still suggests that the North Vietnamese masses are just as bitter, disillusioned and hostile to their Communist regime as are the masses, say, in Poland. North Viet-Nam, in other words, is a ripe target for precisely the kind of underground assault now being made on South Viet-Nam—if anyone had the guts to take the risk of sponsoring and supporting this kind of assault.

> — Joseph Alsop, syndicated column,
> April 19, 1961

Now there's been an election in Vietnam, in which 75 percent of the people, or 80 percent, endorse the government.

> — President John F. Kennedy,
> news conference, April 21, 1961

[The U.S. will furnish] every possible help, across the entire spectrum in which help is needed.

> — Secretary of State Dean Rusk, May 4, 1961

The problem of troops . . . and the matter of what we are going to do to assist Vietnam . . . is . . . still under consideration.

> — President John F. Kennedy, May 5, 1961

TOP SECRET

Instruct ICS, CINCPAC, and MAAG to undertake an assessment of the military utility of a further increase in the G.V.N. forces from 170,000 to 200,000. . . . Grant to ICA the authority and funds to move into a rural development–civic action program. . . . This might cost roughly $3 to $5 million. . . . In coordination with CIA and the appropriate G.V.N. Ministry, USIS will increase the flow of information about unfavorable conditions in North Vietnam to media representatives. Develop agricultural pilot-projects throughout the country, with a view toward exploiting their beneficial psychological effects . . . by combined teams of Vietnamese Civic Action personnel, Americans in the Peace Corps, Filipinos in Operation Brotherhood, and other[s]. . . . Exploit as a part of a planned psychological campaign . . . rehabilitation of Communist Viet Cong prisoners, stressing the errors of Communism . . . broadcast to North Vietnam to induce defections. This rehabilitation program would be assisted by a team of U.S. personnel including U.S. Army (Civil Affairs Psychological Warfare and Counter-Intelligence), USIS and USOM experts. Provide adequate funds for an impressive U.S. participation in the Saigon Trade Fair of 1962. COVERT ACTIONS: Expand present operations in the field of intelligence, unconventional warfare and political-psychological activities to support the U.S. objective as stated. Initiate the communications intelligence actions, CIA and ASA personnel increases and funding which were approved by the President at the NCS meeting of April 1961. . . . FUNDING: . . . The funding of the counter-insurgency plan and the other actions recommended in this program might necessitate increases in U.S. support of the G.V.N. budget for FY 61 of as much as $58 million, making up to a total of $192 million compared with $155 million for FY 60. The U.S. contribution for the G.V.N. defense budget in FY 62 as presently estimated would total $161 million plus any deficiency in that Budget which the G.V.N. might be unable to finance. U.S. military assistance to G.V.N., in order to provide the support contemplated by the proposed program would total $140 million. . . . Authorization should be given . . . for the use in North Vietnam operations of civilian air crews of American and other nationality . . . over-flights of North Vietnam for photographic intelligence coverage, using American or Chinese Nationalist crews and equipment. . . . U.S. Army Security Agency teams could be sent to Vietnam for direct operations coordinated in the same manner—approved by the president at the NSC meeting of 29 April 1961. . . . In Laos, infiltrate teams under light civilian cover to Southeast Laos to locate and attack Vietnamese Communist bases and lines of communications. . . . In North Vietnam, using the foundation established by intelligence operations, form networks of resistance, covert bases and teams for sabotage and light harassment. A capability should be created by MAAG . . . to conduct ranger raids and similar military actions in North Vietnam. . . . Conduct over-flights for dropping of leaflets to harass the Communists and to maintain morale of North Vietnamese population, and increase gray broadcasts to North Vietnam. . . . Effect operations to penetrate political forces, government, armed services and opposition elements to measure support of government, provide warning of any coup plans and identify individuals with potentiality of providing leadership in event of disappearance of President Diem. . . . The expanded program outlined above was estimated to require an additional 40 personnel for the CIA station and an increase in the CIA outlay for Vietnam of approximately $1.5 million for FY 62. . . . The U.S. Army Security Agency actions to supplement communications intelligence will require 78 personnel and approximately $1.2 million in equipment.

> — "A Program of Action," presented to President
>   John F. Kennedy by interdepartmental task
>   force from Departments of State and Defense,
>   CIA, ICA, USIA, and Office of the President,
>   May 8, 1961

TOP SECRET

The Joint Chiefs of Staff recommend that the decision be made now to deploy suitable U.S. forces to South Vietnam . . . to . . . indicate the firmness of our intent.

> — Joint Chiefs of Staff, Memorandum
>   JCSM-320-61, to Secretary of Defense Robert
>   S. McNamara, May 10, 1961

TOP SECRET

The President directs full examination by the Defense Department . . . of the size and composition of forces which would be desirable in the case of a possible commitment of U.S. forces to Vietnam. . . . The U.S. will seek to increase the confidence of President Diem and his Government in the United States by a series of actions and messages relating to the trip of Vice President Johnson. The U.S. will attempt to strengthen President Diem's popular support within Vietnam by reappraisal and negotiation, under the direction of Ambassador Nolting. Ambassador Nolting is also requested to recommend any necessary reorganization of the Country Team for these purposes. . . . The U.S. will strengthen its efforts in the psychological field. . . . These decisions will be supported by appropriate budgetary action. . . . Finally, the President approves the continuation of a special Task Force on Vietnam, established in and directed by the Department of State under Sterling J. Cottrell as Director, and Chalmers B. Wood as Executive Officer.
— Presidential Assistant McGeorge Bundy,
National Security Action Memorandum 52,
May 11, 1961

It's almost unbelievable and beyond any expectation that we have reached a complete meeting of minds on President Kennedy's ideas and President Diem's ideas. . . . I have never attended a conference of any kind in 30 years that was more productive or more cordial. . . . President Diem is the Churchill of the decade. . . . He will fight Communism in the streets and alleys, and when his hands are torn he will fight it with his feet. . . . President Ngo Dinh Diem . . . is in the vanguard of those leaders who stand for freedom.
— Vice President Lyndon B. Johnson,
Saigon, May 13, 1961

The enthusiastic welcome [Vice President Johnson] received in Viet-Nam reflected a deep sense of common cause . . . clear to both Governments that action must be strengthened and accelerated. . . . The U.S. . . . is conscious of . . . the dedicated leadership of President Ngo Dinh Diem . . . also conscious of its responsibility . . . to assist a brave country . . . President Ngo Dinh Diem, who was recently reelected to office by an overwhelming majority of his countrymen . . . is in the vanguard of those leaders who stand for freedom. . . . It is necessary to give high priority to . . . security. . . . The following measures agreed . . . represent an increase and acceleration of U.S. assistance. . . . These may be followed by more far-reaching measures. . . . It was agreed that regular armed forces of the Republic of Viet-Nam should be increased, and that the U.S. would extend its military assistance programs . . . [and] provide . . . support for the entire Vietnamese civil guard force.

. . . It was agreed that . . . a group of highly qualified economic and fiscal experts would meet in Viet-Nam to work out a financial plan. . . . The two Governments would work together toward . . . further progress. . . . President Ngo Dinh Diem and Vice President Lyndon B. Johnson, on behalf of President Kennedy, established a sense of mutual confidence.

> — Joint communiqué by Vice President Lyndon
> B. Johnson and President Ngo Dinh Diem,
> Saigon, May 13, 1961

President Kennedy may send American combat troops to bolster South Vietnam defenses against outright Communist attack.

> — *Newsweek*, May 15, 1961

Society functions through personal relations between men at the top. . . . I know what is best for Vietnam.

> — President Ngo Dinh Diem,
> quoted by *Newsweek*, May 22, 1961

The decision on May 14 to send in nearly 100 of the specialists in irregular warfare who have been trained at Fort Bragg may prove a most fateful one. . . . If these Americans are under fire, they will presumably have the freedom to shoot back, and, once there are even a few well-publicized casualties, the prestige of the United States will have been for all practical purposes committed irrevocably to the Diem cause. The choices will then be humiliating withdrawal, as the size of the challenge grows, or progressively deeper involvement in a stalemate which may not admit of a victory in anything less than a decade—some experts say even longer. . . . Vietnam's borders are wide open to sanctuaries which cannot be sealed off, not only the border with North Vietnam, but also the unpoliced Laos and Cambodian frontiers.

> — Editorial, *New Republic*, May 22, 1961

TOP SECRET

I have come away from the mission there with . . . convictions sharpened and deepened by what I saw and learned. I have . . . reached certain other conclusions . . . as follows: The battle against Communism must be joined in Southeast Asia with strength and determination to achieve success. . . . The struggle is far from lost in Southeast Asia and it is by no means inevitable that it must be lost. . . . The will to resist . . . is there. The key . . . is confidence. . . . There is no alternative to United States leadership in Southeast Asia. . . . SEATO is not now and probably never will be the answer because of British and French unwillingness to support decisive action. . . . I recommend that we move forward promptly with a major effort. . . . In Vietnam and in Thailand we must move forward together. In Vietnam, Diem is a complex figure beset by many problems. He has admirable qualities. . . . The country can be saved—if we move quickly and wisely. . . . I believe that the mission—as you conceived it—was a success.

> — Vice President Lyndon B. Johnson, memorandum to President John F. Kennedy on Far Eastern tour, May 23, 1961

We are making an extensive effort in the training of indigenous forces in South Vietnam. . . . The Vietnamese are now . . . doing extremely well.

> — General George H. Decker, chief of staff, U.S. Army, interview, *U.S. News & World Report*, May 29, 1961

For you, intervention in this region will be an entanglement without end. From the moment that nations have awakened, no foreign authority, whatever its means, has any chance of imposing itself on them . . . although you find officials who, by interest, agree to obey you, the people will not consent. . . . The ideology that you invoke will not change anything. Even more, the masses will confuse it with your will to exert power. That is why the more you commit yourself there against communism, the more communists will appear to be champions of national independence. . . . We French have experienced this. You Americans wanted, yesterday, to take our places in Indochina. You want to assume a succession to rekindle a war that we ended. I predict to you that you will, step by step, be sucked into a bottomless military and political quagmire despite the losses and expenditures that you may squander. What you, we and others should do in this unfortunate Asia is not to substitute ourselves for states on their own soil but to give them what they need to get out of poverty and humiliation, which are, there as elsewhere, the causes of totalitarian regimes. I say this to you in the name of our West.

> — President Charles de Gaulle to President John F. Kennedy, Paris, May 31, 1961

TOP SECRET

Bob:

We must think of the kind of forces and missions for Thailand now, Vietnam later.

We need a guerrilla *deterrence* operation in Thailand's northeast.

We shall need forces to support a counterguerrilla war in Vietnam:
    aircraft
    helicopters
    communications men
    special forces
    military teachers
    etc.

                                                              WWR

> — Walt W. Rostow, handwritten memorandum
>   to Secretary of Defense Robert S. McNamara
>   during meeting of June 5, 1961

I believe we are going to bring this threat to the independence of Vietnam under control.

> — Walt W. Rostow, speech to U.S. Army Special
>   Warfare School, Fort Bragg, N.C., June 1961

The regime . . . can point to a record of steady accomplishment . . . the accomplishments of this regime are overlooked by many observers and commentators, who all too frequently have accepted uncritically the most abusive gossip and propaganda about President Diem and his administration.

> — Senator J. William Fulbright, speech in Senate,
>   June 1961

TOP SECRET

This is a Special Forces type of unit, with the mission of operating in denied (enemy) areas. It currently has some limited operations in North Vietnam and some shallow penetrations into Laos. . . . They have been trained for guerrilla operations at the Group's training center at Nha Trang. The unit is MAP-supported, as a TO&E unit of the RVNAF (Republic of Vietnam Armed Forces). It receives special equipment and training from CIA and U.S. control is by CIA/MAAG. The Group and its activities are highly classified by the Government of Vietnam.

The Group was organized in 1956. . . . The additional volunteers were reported as: (1) 60 Mois (Montagnard tribesmen) recruited, being security screened, to receive Special Forces training. (2) 400 military (RVNAF), to receive Special Forces training. . . . (3) 70 civilians, being organized and trained for stay-behind operations, penetration teams, and communicators. Other special units of the RVNAF, now committed to operations against the Viet Cong and with Special Forces/Ranger training are: 9,096 Rangers, in 65 companies. 2,772 more Rangers being activated, part of 20,000-man increase. 4,786 paratroopers. 2,300 Marines. 673 men in Psychological Warfare Bn. In addition, cadres from all other combat elements of the RVNAF have received Special Forces/ Ranger training. . . . THAILAND: The PARU [Police Aerial Resupply Unit] has a mission of undertaking clandestine operations in denied areas. 99 PARU personnel have been introduced covertly to assist the Meos in operations in Laos, where their combat performance has been outstanding. This is a special police unit, supported by CIA (CIA control in the Meo operations has been reported as excellent), with a current strength of 300 being increased to 550 as rapidly as possible. All personnel are specially selected and screened and have been rated as of high quality.

According to CINCPAC, there are two special commando companies in the Laos Armed Forces (FAL), with a total strength of 256. The commandos have received Special Forces training. About 9,000 Meo tribesmen have been equipped for guerrilla operations, which they are now conducting with considerable effectiveness . . . in Laos. . . . Political leadership of the Meos is in the hands of Touby Lyfoung, who now operates mostly out of Vientiane. The military leader is Lt-Col Vang Pao, who is the field commander. Command control of Meo operations is exercised by the Chief CIA Vientiane with the advice of Chief MAAG Laos.

The same CIA paramilitary and U.S. military teamwork is in existence for advisory activities . . . and aerial resupply. . . . National Directorate of Coordination . . . is the Intelligence arm of the RLG [Royal Laotian Government] . . . under the command of Lt-Col Siho, a FAL officer. In addition to intelligence operations this force has a capability for sabotage, kidnapping, commando-type raids, etc. There is also a local veteran's organization and a grass-roots political organization in Laos, both of which are subject to CIA direction and control and are capable of carrying out propaganda, sabotage and harassment operations.

> — Brigadier General Edward G. Lansdale,
> Pentagon guerrilla war expert, memorandum
> to General Maxwell D. Taylor, President
> Kennedy's military adviser, Secretary
> McNamara, Deputy Secretary Roswell
> Gilpatrick, Secretary Rusk, CIA Director
> Allen Dulles, and General C. P. Cabell deputy
> director, CIA, July 1961

TOP SECRET

Eastern Construction Company . . . is a private, Filipino-run public service organization, similar to an employment agency, with an almost untapped potential for unconventional warfare (which was its original mission). It now furnishes about 500 trained, experienced Filipino technicians to the Governments of Vietnam and Laos. . . . MAAG Chiefs . . . have rated this service as highly effective. CIA has influence and some continuing interest with individuals. The head of Eastern Construction is "Frisco" Johnny San Juan, former National Commander, Philippines Veterans Legion. . . . Eastern Construction was started in 1954 as Freedom Company of the Philippines . . . "to serve the cause of freedom." It actually was a mechanism to permit the deployment of Filipino personnel in other Asian countries, for unconventional operations, under cover of a public service organization having a contract with the host government. Philippine Armed Forces and government personnel were "sheep-dipped" and served abroad.

Its personnel helped write the Constitution of the Republic of Vietnam, trained Vietnam's Presidential Guard Battalion, and were instrumental in founding and organizing the Vietnamese Veterans Legion. . . . There is another private Filipino public-service organization, capable of considerable expansion in socio-economic-medical operations to support counter-guerrilla actions. It is now operating teams in Laos, under ICA auspices. It has a measure of CIA control. Operation Brotherhood (OB) was started in 1954 by the International Jaycees. . . . The concept was to provide medical service to refugees and provincial farmers in South Vietnam. . . . Their work was closely coordinated with Vietnamese Army operations which cleaned up Vietminh stay-behinds. . . . The Security Training Center . . . is a counter-subversion, counter-guerrilla and psychological warfare school overtly operated by the Philippine Government and covertly sponsored by the U.S. Government through CIA as the instrument of the Country Team. . . .

Civil Air Transport (Chinese Nationalist): CAT is a commercial airline engaged in scheduled and non-scheduled air operations throughout the Far East, with headquarters and large maintenance facilities located in Taiwan. CAT, a CIA proprietary, provides air logistical support under commercial cover to most CIA and other U.S. Government agencies' requirements. CAT supports covert and clandestine air operations by . . . aircraft under both Chinat and U.S. registry. CAT has demonstrated its capability on numerous occasions . . . it has had some notable achievements, including . . . air drop support to the French at Dien Bien Phu . . . air lifts of refugees from North Vietnam . . . and extensive air support in Laos.

> — Brigadier General Edward G. Lansdale,
> memorandum to General Maxwell D. Taylor,
> July 1961

The war between Government troops and communist-led guerrillas in South Vietnam is considered a test of the new United States Army tactics for jungle fighting.

> — *New York Times*, July 17, 1961

There is one card the Communists do not hold—time.

> — E. W. Kenworthy, *New York Times*,
> July 31, 1961

There lies the biggest trap of all for our conventional warriors, a quicksand which could absorb a major share of our youth in endless "limited" war.

> — *I. F. Stone's Newsletter*, July 31, 1961

The United States is determined that the Republic of Vietnam shall not be lost.

> — President John F. Kennedy, after meetings
> with Vice President Chen Cheng, Nationalist
> Republic of China, August 2, 1961

If the U.S. cannot or will not save South Vietnam from Communist assault, no Asian nation can ever again feel safe in putting its faith in the U.S.

> — *Time*, August 4, 1961

We are now in 97 of the 110 nations of the world with this [foreign aid] program. . . . In Vietnam . . . a highway planned to cost $18 million, 300 thousand. . . . But we finish it for $18 million, 300 thousand? No. It actually cost us $129 million, 900 thousand. . . . It has gotten out of control.

> — Congressman Otto E. Passman, chairman,
> House Appropriations Subcommittee on
> Foreign Operations, *Meet the Press*, NBC,
> August 6, 1961

Filtering into the Pentagon last week were encouraging reports from far-off Saigon. . . . Military sources were downright enthusiastic about the gains being made in Vietnam. "We're really making hay for the first time in a hell of a long while," one veteran officer said confidently. "The Communists are really going to have their hands full." . . . Major reason for the growing confidence . . . : New U.S. equipment (to go along with new combat tactics) especially designed for guerrilla warfare. . . . As one official put it: " . . . We have decided for the first time to use some of our newest weapons and best equipment. . . . We've got some wild ideas we're working on. Nothing is too fantastic for us." . . . The U.S. emphasis . . . represents a "revolution" in Pentagon thinking, said one military source. "The real secret," he went on, "is the boldness of approach."

> — *Newsweek*, August 21, 1961

Somewhere in South Vietnam there is a considerable supply of Metrecal supplied by American taxpayers. Sen. John J. Williams, Republican of Delaware, told the Senate today the United States foreign aid program recently had shipped 48,000 cans of the dietary drink to the Communist-threatened Asian nation.

> — *New York Times,*
> UPI dispatch from Washington,
> September 27, 1961

We are pressing ahead.

> — Joseph Reap, Department of State spokesman,
> October 2, 1961

A basic decision to send troops, including combat units as well as training personnel, has been made . . . dispatching to key points highly mobile regimental combat teams.

> — *New York Times*, October 8, 1961

Maybe it is a sign that the United States has attained a remarkable maturity. . . . It is an extraordinary . . . fact that neither the country nor the capital seems to be particularly excited because the President is seriously considering sending combat units of the U.S. Army and Marines to Southeast Asia. It has been on the public records for at least 10 days that the dispatch of combat troops to South Vietnam was under grave and urgent consideration. When first published in this space on Friday, October 6, the report was confirmed by the State Department on the same day. . . . Additional combat units may be sent to Thailand. . . . The national decision now being mulled over is vastly more interesting than most people as yet seem to think.

> — Joseph Alsop, syndicated column,
> October 11, 1961

General Taylor's expert appraisal should be of great usefulness in reaching the fateful decisions that are looming.

> — Editorial, *New York Times*,
> October 12, 1961

It's no longer a guerrilla war, but a real war.

> — President Ngo Dinh Diem,
> quoted in *Life*, October 13, 1961

Instead of helping the government forces against the Viet Cong, many villagers spy on the army for the Reds. Considerable skepticism exists here that all villagers assist the Viet Cong through fear of terroristic reprisal.

> — *New York Times*, October 18, 1961

Reports . . . that the United States is about to plunge into the guerrilla warfare of Southeast Asia . . . should be taken with considerable skepticism. . . . General Taylor is not only a soldier but a philosopher . . . he is not likely to favor plunging blithely into a jungle war 7,000 miles from home.

> — James Reston,
> column, *New York Times*, October 19, 1961

The human material I have seen looks very encouraging and augurs well for future leadership. The very special problem in guerrilla warfare here in South Vietnam offers no great task for generals.

> — General Maxwell D. Taylor, special military
> adviser to President John F. Kennedy, Nha
> Trang, South Vietnam, October 22, 1961

Guerrilla warfare is not new—after all, we did engage in a type of guerrilla warfare in the Mexican-border incident and also in Nicaragua earlier in this century. . . . You have substantial swampland in Southeast Asia . . . jungles and large areas of rice paddies. Parts of the Seventh Fleet are capable of operating successfully against guerrillas. . . . The problems of guerrilla warfare are recognized. . . . I think we have many very wonderful and fine friends out here. . . . We hold training exercises with all of these nations. . . . These people are very fine friends. . . . One of the important jobs the Seventh Fleet has to do out here . . . is to conduct what we call the people-to-people program. In the past year, Navy and Marine personnel have gone ashore on liberty nearly 4 million times. When our people go ashore they have an opportunity to meet the local people. . . . They take ashore a little bit of the United States. This contributes to a better understanding.

> — Vice Admiral Charles D. Griffin, commander
> in chief, U.S. 7th Fleet, interview aboard
> U.S.S. *St. Paul, U.S. News & World Report*,
> October 23, 1961

Let me assure you again the United States is determined to help Viet-Nam. . . . I am awaiting with great interest the report of General Maxwell Taylor. . . . I will then be in a better position to consider with you additional measures we might take. . . . We are confident of the success of the Vietnamese nation.

> — President John F. Kennedy, letter to President
> Ngo Dinh Diem on 6th anniversary, Vietnam,
> October 24, 1961

I have great confidence in the military capability of South Vietnam to cope with anything within its borders.

> — General Maxwell D. Taylor, farewell
> statement before enplaning for Bangkok,
> Saigon, October 25, 1961

The Taylor-Rostow mission was completed in early November. . . . General Taylor recommended the dispatch of combat support forces . . . and a greatly expanded Military Assistance Advisory Group. In addition he urged that the United States send ground forces that would directly engage the Viet Cong. A 6–8,000 man task force could be introduced into South Vietnam under the guise of performing flood relief work. These logistical troops, with the combat troops needed to protect their operations, would necessarily become involved in defensive operations and, in General Taylor's words, "expect to take casualties."

> — Senate Foreign Relations Committee Staff
> Study, "Vietnam Commitments, 1961"

TOP SECRET

My reasons for recommending the introduction of a U.S. military force into SVN. . . . As an area for the operations of U.S. troops, SVN is not an excessively difficult or unpleasant place to operate . . . where U.S. forces would probably be stationed . . . jungle-forest conditions do not exist to any great extent. . . . The High Plateau offers no particular obstacle to the stationing of U.S. troops. . . . The risks of backing into a major Asian war by way of SVN are present but are not impressive. NVN is extremely vulnerable to conventional bombing, a weakness which should be exploited diplomatically in convincing Hanoi to lay off SVN. . . . The DRV [North Vietnam] would face severe logistical difficulties in trying to maintain strong forces in the field in Southeast Asia. . . . By the foregoing line of reasoning, I have reached the conclusion that the introduction of [word illegible] military Task Force without delay offers definitely more advantage than it creates risks and difficulties.

> — General Maxwell D. Taylor, Top Secret
> memorandum from Baguio, Philippines, to
> President John F. Kennedy, November 1, 1961

TOP SECRET

General Lansdale has been requested by Diem; and it may be wise to envisage a limited number of Americans acceptable to Diem as well as to us—in key ministries. . . . Intimate liaison with the Vietnamese Central Intelligence Organizations (C.I.O.) . . . Jungle Jim [aerial commando operations] . . . counter infiltration operations in Laos (such operations are to some degree under way). . . . Increased covert offensive operations in North as well as in Laos and South Vietnam (to some degree under way). . . . The introduction, under MAAG operational control, of three helicopter squadrons—one for each corps area—and the provision of more light aircraft. . . . A radical increase in U.S. trainers at every level. . . . A radical increase in U.S. special force teams. . . . Increase the MAAG support for the Vietnamese Navy. . . . Introduction of U.S. Naval and/or Coast Guard personnel. . . . Reconsideration of the role of air power. . . . To execute this program of limited partnership requires a change in . . . MAAG. . . . It must be shifted from an advisory group to something nearer—but not quite—an operational headquarters in a theater of war. . . . Such a transition from advice to partnership has been made, in recent months, on a smaller scale, by the MAAG in Laos . . . the rapid build-up of an intelligence capability both to identify operational targets for the Vietnamese and to assist Washington in making a sensitive and reliable assessment of the progress of the war . . . must be quickly expanded. . . . In Washington, as well, intelligence and back-up operations must be put on a quasi-wartime footing.

> — General Maxwell D. Taylor, Top Secret report
> to President John F. Kennedy on mission to
> South Vietnam, November 3, 1961

On his return from a three-week mission to Southeast Asia, General Taylor said that President Ngo Dinh Diem had the "assets" available to prevail against the Communist threat. The General declined to comment on whether he would recommend sending United States combat troops to stiffen the Vietnamese forces in their fight against the Viet Cong.

> — *New York Times*, November 4, 1961

It is my contention that for the existing requirements of American foreign policy we have hobbled the President by too niggardly a grant of power.

> — Senator J. William Fulbright, lecture at
> Cornell University, later printed in *Cornell
> Law Quarterly*, 1961

Why count them [Viet Cong infiltrators]? Why not shoot them?

> — General Maxwell D. Taylor,
> quoted by *U.S. News & World Report*,
> November 6, 1961

The battle is not yet lost in South Vietnam; and, indeed, it can still be won.

— Editorial, *New York Times*, November 7, 1961

TOP SECRET

MEMORANDUM FOR THE PRESIDENT   November 8, 1961
. . . We accept General Taylor's judgment. . . . The introduction of a U.S. force of an initial 8,000 men in a flood relief context will be of great help to Diem. . . . The other side can be convinced we mean business only if we accompany the initial force introduction by a clear commitment. . . . If we act in this way, the ultimate possible extent of our military commitment must be faced. . . . In view of the logistic difficulties faced by the other side, I believe we can assume that the maximum U.S. forces required on the ground in Southeast Asia will not exceed 6 divisions, or about 250,000 men (CINCPAC Plan 32–59, Phase IV). . . . The domestic political implications of accepting the objective are also grave, although it is our feeling that the country will respond better to a firm initial position than to courses of action that lead us in only gradually. . . . In sum: . . . We are inclined to recommend that we do commit the U.S. and that we support this commitment by the necessary military actions. . . . If such a commitment is agreed upon, we support the recommendations of General Taylor as the first steps toward its fulfillment.

Signed: ROBERT S. McNAMARA
— From *Pentagon Papers*, Gravel Edition

TOP SECRET

The commitment of United States forces to South Viet-Nam . . . for the direct support of South Viet-Namese military effort . . . *should be introduced as speedily as possible.* . . . It is the view of the Secretary of Defense and the Joint Chiefs of Staff that, in the light of the logistic difficulties faced by the other side, we can assume that the maximum United States forces required on the ground in Southeast Asia would not exceed six divisions, or about 250,000 men (CINCPAC Plan 32/59, PHASE IV).

— Secretary of State Dean Rusk and Secretary of Defense Robert S. McNamara, memorandum to President John F. Kennedy, November 11, 1961

Mr. Kennedy endorsed Taylor's strategic judgment: Vietnam not only *must* be held; it *can* be if the U.S. wills it.

— *Newsweek*, November 13, 1961

U.S. aid to South Vietnam may be stepped up. *But no U.S. combat troops* are going into the jungle to engage in shooting war with *Communist guerrillas.*

> — *U.S. News & World Report*, November 13, 1961

The President and General Taylor are agreed . . . that the South Vietnamese Government is capable of meeting and turning back the . . . threat.

> — *New York Times*, November 16, 1961

In South Viet Nam, Madame Ngo Dinh Nhu is much more than bachelor President Ngo Dinh Diem's sister-in-law and a Christian first lady in a Buddhist land. . . . In an interview with a Western reporter, Madame Ngo . . . would like Western correspondents to establish a committee to decide on a common line to follow. Her choice for chairman: Syndicated Columnist Joseph Alsop. . . . "He fully understands the situation here," said Madame Ngo.

> — *Time*, December 1, 1961

North Vietnam is falling so far behind.

> — Deputy Under Secretary of State U. Alexis
> Johnson, December 5, 1961

I think there has been very welcome headway. . . . We have been very encouraged.

> — Secretary of State Dean Rusk,
> December 8, 1961

With the arrival yesterday of the Core, a former escort carrier bearing helicopters, four single-engine training planes and about 400 men, the United States military personnel here are now believed to total about 1,500. Many more are expected.

> — *New York Times*, December 13, 1961

DEAR MR. PRESIDENT:
I have received your recent letter. . . . In response to your request . . . we shall promptly increase our assistance to your defense effort as well as help relieve the destruction of the floods. . . . I have already given the orders to get these programs underway. . . . We are confident that the Vietnamese people will preserve their independence.

> — President John F. Kennedy,
> letter to President Ngo Dinh Diem,
> December 14, 1961

The years 1956 to 1960 produced something close to an economic miracle in South Vietnam. . . . It is a record of progress over a few brief years equalled by few young countries.

— "A Threat to the Peace," State Department
White Paper, December 1961

The Communists are really having trouble trying to arouse much enthusiasm. . . . People are either too hungry or too overworked to care. . . . People are either apathetic or hopeless. . . . There is still a desperate shortage of clothing. . . . Peasants wear more patches than original clothing. . . . Women work in the fields naked from the waist up to save on cloth. . . . Men go barefoot or wear sandals made from old automobile tires. Women wear wooden clogs. There are no cosmetics. . . . Hanoi, once known as "the Paris of the Orient," has become a drab and listless city. All but three of the numerous traffic lights have been turned off. Draft animals have disappeared. Barrows and carts are pulled along the streets and in the fields by men and women. The city folds up at 9 p.m., when the lights go off because of the shortage of electric power.

— "Tokyo report," reprinted in *U.S. News &
World Report*, December 18, 1961

By February 1962 Diem's government was so agitated by American and Western representations of the insurgency as a civil war that it called on foreign correspondents to cease labeling the Viet Cong "rebels" and "insurgents" and urged them instead to "use the following terms: Viet Cong, Communists, Hanoi's agents and aggressors from the North." Wedded to the idea that social and political reform should await the prior establishment of full security, Diem, like Washington, did not perceive that the war was first of all a political problem and could only be solved through primarily political means.

— George McT. Kahin and John W. Lewis,
The United States in Vietnam

The great idea of the family reign, of Mr. Nhu especially, was the creation of strategic hamlets in 1961. The idea is familiar to French observers for it is the same that led to the construction of regroupment camps in Algeria two years earlier. It involved the bringing together of the rural population into fortified or protected enclosures in order to withdraw the source of popular support from the rebellion, to take away from the renowned "revolutionary fish" the water in which it lives and flourishes. The same causes produced the same effects: a growing hostility of the peasant masses towards those regrouping them. . . .

By tampering with the village, Mr. Nhu and his supporters attacked the very foundations of Vietnamese peasant civilization . . . the very root of private life. The village, more than man himself, was a unity. . . . Everything went out from this unity, and returned to it. It expressed that "harmony under heaven" that each member of a society impregnated with Confucianism considers essential.

In attacking this unity, Mr. Nhu was, from the mechanical point of view, more revolutionary than the Vietminh who never dared to tamper with the basic cellular unit. But this so-called revolution, although it turned a society upside down, brought no solutions for the problems it had created. It was an end in itself . . . to play a strategic role . . . in . . . the struggle against the guerrillas who appeared to the poor people of the Vietnamese countryside as . . . brothers rather than enemies.

— Jean Lacouture,
Le Viet Nam Entre Deux Paix

Behind President Diem's stubborn opposition to suggested reform . . . are his younger brother Ngo Dinh Nhu, and Nhu's wife. . . . Nhu himself is the government's theoretician, who hopes to transform South Vietnam into a "Christian cooperative" state. But he has no use for democracy and has never been an admirer of the U.S. Nhu has used his powerful position to destroy every potential rival. Most opposition leaders were either scared, blackmailed, or forced into exile; some, like Dr. Phan Quang Dan, were thrown into "re-education camps."

— *Newsweek*, December 18, 1961

Without the Americans we could win the war in two or three years. With the Americans, who knows? Perhaps never.

— Ngo Dinh Nhu, quoted by John Mecklin in
Mission in Torment

United States military men were understood today to be operating in battle areas with South Vietnamese forces that are fighting communist guerrillas.

— Jack Raymond, *New York Times*,
December 20, 1961

If we have the common will to hold together and go on with the job, the struggle in Vietnam might be the last great confrontation of the postwar era.

— Walt W. Rostow, University of Leeds, 1961

QUESTION: Mr. President, are American troops in combat in Vietnam?
ANSWER: No.

— President John F. Kennedy,
news conference, January 15, 1962

Actions taken there [in Vietnam] have proved effective and will prove more effective as time goes on.

> — Secretary of Defense Robert S. McNamara,
> January 17, 1962

TOP SECRET

Any war in the Southeast Asian Mainland will be a peninsula and island-type of campaign—a mode of warfare in which all elements of the Armed Forces of the United States have gained a wealth of experience and in which we have excelled. . . . Study of the problem clearly indicates that the Communists are limited in the forces they can sustain in war in that area because of natural logistic and transportation problems. Our present world military posture is such that we now have effective forces capable of implementing existing contingency plans for Southeast Asia without affecting . . . Europe. . . . The Joint Chiefs of Staff recommend that . . . you again consider the recommendation provided you by JCSM-320-61, dated 10 May 1961, that a decision be made to deploy suitable U.S. forces to South Vietnam suitable to . . . indicate the firmness of our intent.

> — Joint Chiefs of Staff, memorandum to
> Secretary of Defense Robert S. McNamara,
> January 13, 1962; McNamara forwarded
> memorandum to President John F. Kennedy
> with covering letter stating, "I am not
> prepared to endorse . . ." on January 27, 1962

TOP SECRET

AMBASSADOR HAS OVER-ALL AUTHORITY FOR HANDLING OF NEWSMEN, IN SO FAR AS U.S. IS CONCERNED. HE WILL MAKE DECISIONS AS TO WHEN NEWSMEN PERMITTED TO GO ON ANY MISSIONS WITH U.S. PERSONNEL. . . . CORRESPONDENTS SHOULD NOT BE TAKEN ON MISSION WHOSE NATURE SUCH THAT UNDESIRABLE DISPATCHES WOULD BE HIGHLY PROBABLE. IT IS NOT REPEAT NOT IN OUR INTEREST TO HAVE STORIES INDICATING THAT AMERICANS ARE LEADING AND DIRECTING COMBAT OPERATIONS AGAINST VIET CONG. . . . SENSATIONAL STORIES ABOUT CHILDREN OR CIVILIANS WHO BECOME UNFORTUNATE VICTIMS OF MILITARY OPERATIONS ARE CLEARLY INIMICABLE TO NATIONAL INTEREST. U.S. MILITARY AND CIVILIAN PERSONNEL MUST SEE THAT [THESE INSTRUCTIONS] ARE ADHERED TO SCRUPULOUSLY AND THAT AMBASSADOR GIVEN COMPLETE COOPERATION IF WE ARE TO AVOID HARMFUL PRESS REPERCUSSIONS BOTH ON DOMESTIC AND INTERNATIONAL SCENE.

> — Top Secret State Department cablegram to
> U.S. Commanders in Vietnam, 1962

Officials in Washington . . . feel that there is a mounting danger that more United States servicemen will be killed in what are now openly described as United States military operations. . . . The United States is said to be determined to put in what it takes to win.

> — Jack Raymond, *New York Times*,
> February 12, 1962

I don't agree at all with any partisan or other criticism of the United States build-up in Vietnam. My only question is whether it may be too little and too late. It is essential that the United States commit all the resources of which it is capable. . . . I support President Kennedy to the hilt and I only hope he will step up the build-up and under no circumstances curtail it because of possible criticism.

> — Richard M. Nixon,
> Sacramento, Calif., February 15, 1962

The Vietnamese Government, under the devoted and courageous leadership of President Ngo Dinh Diem, attempts to realize, under difficult conditions, political, social, and economic progress for the people, with the help of the United States. . . . What a marvelous transformation would take place in this country if all those who criticize their government would decide to work with it and for it.

> — Ambassador Frederick E. Nolting, Jr.,
> speech at Saigon Rotary Club,
> February 15, 1962

We are going to win in Vietnam. We will remain here until we do win. I think the American people understand and fully support this struggle. . . . We have full confidence in President Diem.

> — Attorney General Robert F. Kennedy,
> Saigon, February 18, 1962

RESTRICTIONS IMPOSED BY THE U.S. EMBASSY MAKE IT IMPOSSIBLE TO REPORT FULLY ON THE EXTENT OF AMERICAN PARTICIPATION IN THE WAR EFFORT HERE. . . . VIETNAMESE GOVERNMENT AND ARMY ARE NOT INVOLVED IN THE RESTRICTIONS. . . . CURTAIN OF SECRECY LOOKS LIKE U.S. EMBASSY EFFORT TO CONFUSE AND DISGUISE THE SITUATION.

> — Cablegram from correspondent in Saigon,
> quoted in *U.S. News & World Report*,
> February 19, 1962

Massive U.S. effort is beginning to pay small dividends. Morale in the Vietnamese Army is higher. . . . Army is moving with more surprise. It should bring greater effectiveness. . . . Disaster in Vietnam . . . no longer appears inevitable. There is a feeling that not only can something be done, but it is being done.

> — *U.S. News & World Report*,
> February 19, 1962

It is a struggle this country cannot shirk.

> — Editorial, *New York Times*,
> February 23, 1962

I think we are trying to help out the government of South Vietnam, and I think that is what we should be doing. . . . Who can say the point at which we have another Korea? . . . We have to stand up and help our friends.

> — Senator Thomas J. Dodd, Democrat of
> Connecticut, *Meet the Press*, NBC,
> February 25, 1962

I am delighted with the progress made since my last trip, January 15.

> — Secretary of Defense Robert S. McNamara,
> on arrival from Honolulu, February 27, 1962

I came back optimistic.

> — Assistant Secretary of State for Far Eastern
> Affairs W. Averell Harriman, on arrival from
> Honolulu, February 27, 1962

In early 1962 when he [President Diem] came to visit the agricultural center in Doc Hue district . . . the people in several villages had spent almost two months preparing his walk way. Just imagine! Many people had to work day and night to cut all the bamboo trees in the villages to put on a ten-kilometer muddy road for the President to walk during his one-hour visit to the center. . . . All of the villagers disliked Ngo Dinh Diem, but no one dared say anything against him.

> — "Interviews," RAND Corporation File FD1A

The United States cannot now withdraw. . . . It is a situation which the American people must understand and face up to.

> — Editorial, *New York Times*, March 1, 1962

I use money in the most artistic way when I have it.

> — Madame Ngo Dinh Nhu,
> quoted by Time, March 23, 1962

The U.S. will provide whatever is needed.

> — General Lyman Lemnitzer, chairman,
> Joint Chiefs of Staff, Saigon, quoted by Time,
> April 6, 1962

The United States in short has passed the point of no return—short of victory.

> — François Sully, Newsweek, April 23, 1962

If we can use our heavy weapons and still get mobility, we can get at the Viet Cong where we can lick 'em.

> — Major General Robert E. Cushman,
> 3d Marine Divison,
> quoted by *Time*, April 30, 1962

There is no plan for introducing American combat forces in South Vietnam.

> — Secretary of Defense Robert S. McNamara,
> Saigon, May 9, 1962

Every quantitative measurement we have shows we are winning the war. . . . After 48 hours in South Vietnam, I was tremendously encouraged by developments. . . . I found nothing but progress and hope for the future. . . . U.S. aid to South Vietnam has reached a peak and will start to level off. . . . I doubt if U.S. military personnel assigned to South Vietnam will be increased above the present strength. . . . I am tremendously impressed.

> — Secretary of Defense Robert S. McNamara,
> remarks in Saigon after less than 48 hours in
> Vietnam, May 11, 1962

U.S. aid supports a pay scale of $1,049 a year per man for the Vietnamese Army. . . . A Defense spokesman told a Senate committee hearing that soldiering is "just about the best-paying job available in Vietnam."

> — *U.S. News & World Report*,
> dispatch from Washington, May 14, 1962

The French fought nine years in Vietnam and were kicked out. The Americans may fight fifteen years if they want but it will not help.

> — Premier Nikita Khrushchev,
> Sofia, Bulgaria, May 18, 1962

Since President Diem assumed office in 1955 he has taken dictatorial control, either directly or through a small group of intimates, many of whom are members of his family. It is estimated some 30,000 South Vietnamese nationalists are in concentration camps.

> — House Foreign Affairs Committee Special
> Study Mission to Far East, conclusions by
> Reps. Pilcher, Johnson, and Adair,
> May 22, 1962

It is forbidden to dance anywhere at all.

> — Article 4, Morality Law, Laws of the Republic
> of South Vietnam, May 24, 1962

President Ngo Dinh Diem . . . last week . . . acted in one area that was not considered exactly crucial by U.S. advisers: public morals. Diem, encouraged by his beautiful, puritanical sister-in-law Mme. Ngo Dinh Nhu, signed an austerity law aimed at protecting "the traditional virtue of Viet Nam" by banning beauty contests, cockfighting, abortions, contraceptives and boxing matches. Under the law, public or private dancing is punishable by fines ranging from $2.75 to $685, and up to three months' imprisonment.

> — *Time*, June 1, 1962

The United States Information Agency sponsored a contest "for a new name for the Vietcong guerrillas," admitting that it didn't think "communist is the type of a name to inspire hatred among the country's illiterate masses." It offered a cash prize for a "colloquial peasant term implying disgust or ridicule." In South Vietnam, the only names which meet that test are "French" and "American." . . . Seven leprosy clinics were wiped out by mistake in bombing raids last fall.

> — *New York Times*, June 5, 1962

Dancing with death is sufficient.

> — Madame Ngo Dinh Nhu, commenting on her
> new legal ban on public and private dancing,
> quoted by *Time*, June 22, 1962

Tactical air support is used extensively. It is difficult to ascertain whether the people who are being killed by napalm and fragmentation bombs are guerrillas or merely farmers.

> — *New York Times*, July 7, 1962

The South Vietnamese are beginning to hit the Viet Cong insurgents where it hurts most—in winning the people to the side of the Government.

> — Secretary of Defense Robert S. McNamara,
> Honolulu, July 24, 1962

Victory is remote. The issue remains in doubt because the Vietnamese President seems incapable of winning the loyalty of his people . . . visions of ultimate victory are obscured by the image of a secretive, suspicious, dictatorial regime. . . . Should the situation deteriorate further, Washington may face the alternative of ditching Ngo Dinh Diem for a military junta or sending combat troops to bolster the regime.

> — Homer Bigart, *New York Times*, July 25, 1962

Our military assistance to Vietnam is paying off. I continue to be encouraged. There are many signs of progress.

> — Secretary of Defense Robert S. McNamara,
> July 25, 1962

We are strong in Vietnam.

> — Senator Hugh Scott,
> Republican of Pennsylvania,
> *Issues & Answers*, ABC, August 29, 1962

I believe the emphasis will shift from military more to economic and social activities.

> — General Maxwell D. Taylor, chairman,
> Joint Chiefs of Staff,
> Saigon, September 13, 1962

A U.S. official put it more bluntly. "We're going to win this war, with this government, and as it is."

> — *Newsweek*, September 24, 1962

Ngo Dinh Diem's personal brand of nationalism has one aim: To identify the country exclusively with the Ngo family and with the mandarin class into which they were born. Lately, Ngo Dinh Nhu has been making increasing public appearances throughout the country. He travels like a viceroy, and often confuses the southern peasants with his aristocratic, low-keyed Annamese royal-court accent. One village notable told me recently: "If the effect of all this were not so disastrous, it would be hilariously funny."

> — François Sully, *Newsweek*, September 24, 1962

There is an incontestable turn for the better. . . . Government forces [have] taken the initiative . . . passing to the offensive . . . sowing insecurity in the Communists' reputedly impregnable strongholds, smashing their units one after another. . . . We are recovering the initiative, even during the rainy season, which heretofore the enemy has considered favorable to him. Victory is not only sure but imminent.

> — President Ngo Dinh Diem, address to
> National Assembly, Saigon, October 1, 1962;
> on October 26 National Assembly voted to
> extend for another year Diem's power to rule
> by decree

The news from South Vietnam recently has been encouraging.

> — *New York Times*, October 6, 1962

Viet Nam is going a great deal better than a year ago.

> — *Time*, October 12, 1962

I have unwavering faith in the future.

> — President Ngo Dinh Diem, at 7th annual
> National Day, quoted by *Time*,
> November 2, 1962

The fight against the Communists is going better than it was a year ago. . . . The armed forces of Vietnam now are larger, better equipped and more highly trained.

> — *U.S. News & World Report*, November 5, 1962

It is fashionable in some quarters to say that the problems in Southeast Asia are primarily political and economic. I do not agree. The essence of the problem in Vietnam is military.

> — General Earle K. Wheeler, November 1962

South Vietnam looks no better than it did, but no worse either.

> — *U.S. News & World Report*, December 3, 1962

TOP SECRET

The war in South Vietnam is clearly going better than it was a year ago. . . . The program to arm and train the Montagnards, which should go forward choking off the infiltration routes, has also made progress. . . . The areas through which one can travel without escort have been enlarged. . . . As of December 1, the Vietnamese government controlled 951 villages controlling about 51% of the rural population—a gain of 92 villages and 500,000 people in about six months. . . . U.S. aid programs . . . have given the Vietnamese military new confidence which they are

showing by increased aggressiveness. For the first time since the war
began in 1959, for example, the government forces began in September
to capture more weapons than they lost. . . . Finally, there is considerably more optimism among Vietnamese officials than there was a year
ago. . . . The Viet Cong, in sum, are being hurt.

> — Michael V. Forrestal, December 3, 1962

TOP SECRET

President Ngo Dinh Diem and other leading Vietnamese as well as
many U.S. officials in South Vietnam apparently believe that the tide is
now turning in the struggle. . . . Effective GVN control of the
countryside has been extended . . . peasant attitudes toward the
government appear also to have improved.

> — Roger Hilsman, director, State Department
> Bureau of Intelligence and Research,
> memorandum to Secretary of State Dean
> Rusk, December 3, 1962

It's the inherent right of the Government to lie to save itself.

> — Assistant Secretary of Defense for Public
> Affairs Arthur D. Sylvester, address at dinner
> of Sigma Delta Chi journalism fraternity, New
> York City, December 6, 1962

Up to now the Vietcong have operated with a collection of handmade
and homemade weapons and arms taken from Government troops.

> — *New York Times*, December 6, 1962

There are evidences that the villagers are responding to Diem's
program. In the opinion of Diem's responsible American advisers, his
strategy is right and he has made a promising start. . . . Madame Nhu,
the beautiful, strong-willed sister-in-law of the President and a member
of the national legislature, has sponsored and passed a morality code
which outlaws polygamy, prostitution and contraceptives. . . . Like the
President and 10 per cent of the population, Madame Nhu is a Roman
Catholic. . . . She considers American correspondents "worse than
Communists." . . . Diem's jails hold several thousand political prisoners,
many of them non-Communists. . . . Whatever his shortcomings,
confidence in his ability to hold out against Hanoi is growing. His
well-wishers, whatever their feeling about the President and his family,
see no preferable alternative.

> — Kenneth Crawford,
> special report from Saigon, *Newsweek*,
> December 10, 1962

We don't see the end of the tunnel, but I must say I don't think it is darker than it was a year ago, and in some ways [it is] lighter.

> — President John F. Kennedy,
> December 12, 1962

There is no connection, absolutely none, between the Peace Corps and the Central Intelligence Agency. They're most assuredly free of such entanglements.

> — R. Sargent Shriver, Director, Peace Corps,
> *Meet the Press*, NBC, December 23, 1962

The guerrillas . . . are poorly trained and equipped and not motivated by deep conviction. Rather, they are merely unsophisticated villagers or peasants who have been conscripted by terror or treachery. In such a case they are likely to have had only rudimentary training in weapon handling and tactics. Their equipment may be makeshift, often just what they can capture or fabricate themselves.

> — Under Secretary of State George W. Ball,
> *Vietnam Free-World Challenge in Southeast
> Asia*, Department of State, 1962

The cultural level of North Vietnam is undoubtedly one of the lowest imaginable. Eighty percent of the population is illiterate, ignorant to an incredible degree, and subject to the most extraordinary superstitions.

> — Gerard Tongas, French historian, 1962

The South Vietnamese should achieve victory in three years. . . . The Viet Cong face inevitable defeat. I am confident the Vietnamese are going to win the war.

> — Admiral Harry D. Felt, commander in chief,
> Pacific, after conference with General Paul D.
> Harkins, U.S. commander, South Vietnam,
> before departure from Saigon,
> January 11, 1963

The President's pre-eminent task is to educate and lead public opinion. . . . Accordingly, I think that we must contemplate the further enhancement of presidential authority in foreign affairs . . . the alternative is . . . the paralysis of national policy in a revolutionary world.

> — Senator J. William Fulbright, Democrat of
> Arkansas, chairman, Senate Foreign Relations
> Committee, speech in Senate, January 21, 1963

If the war here is not yet won, at least it is not yet lost. . . . There are

some reasonable grounds for hope as this troubled country begins, under its lunar calendar, "the Year of the Cat."
— *Life*, January 25, 1963

The South Vietnamese Army of President Ngo Dinh Diem has suffered reverses. . . . But to conclude from this experience that all is lost in Vietnam, as some have, is to be more darkly defeatist than a reasoned appraisal justifies. . . . American counter-insurgency experts . . . are not pessimistic. . . . Their charts show that Communist casualties over the last year averaged roughly three times government losses. . . . The Vietnamese are now capturing more weapons than the enemy . . . the government desertion rate is down and Communist defections are up . . . the government is gaining in the countryside. . . . Officials who deal with Diem . . . think that national security can be won eventually. And President Kennedy's recent comments about Vietnam, the latest of them in his State of the Union Message, suggest that he agrees.
— Kenneth Crawford, column, *Newsweek*,
January 28, 1963

They [the North Vietnamese] don't want to fight the United States because they know how strong we are.
— Admiral Harry D. Felt, January 30, 1963

There is a new feeling of confidence that victory is possible in South Vietnam.
— Secretary of Defense Robert S. McNamara,
January 31, 1963

There are some definitely encouraging elements. The ratio of casualties between Government and Viet Cong forces, the ratio of arms captured . . . the steady extension of the strategic-hamlet program, the increasingly effective work of the montagnards along the border areas—all those indicate some turning in the situation.
— Secretary of State Dean Rusk,
February 1, 1963

By every quantitative measure we are winning the war in Vietnam. . . . There is a new feeling of confidence.
— Secretary of Defense Robert S. McNamara,
February 5, 1963

Real progress is being made in the struggle. Vietcong morale is deteriorating.
— General Victor H. Krulak, U.S. Marine Corps,
official Top Secret minutes, Special Counter-
insurgency Group, February 7, 1963

I hope for a gradual strengthening of the control of the Government over the activities of the nation, and a gradual weakening of the influence of the Viet Cong. I think this will go on for a substantial period in the future. I can't really put a number on the years involved, but I think it would be maybe three or four years.

> — Secretary of Defense Robert S. McNamara,
> February 19, 1963

The South Vietnamese armed forces have now attained the experience, training and necessary equipment required for victory. . . . Victory is in sight.

> — General Paul D. Harkins, March 5, 1963

Since the army finds sullen villagers and does not know which are pro-Communist and which are merely dissatisfied with Saigon, and since the army must do its job, it shoots anyone seen running or looking dangerous. It often shoots the wrong peasants. They are in the records of battle listed as Communists. Anyone killed is automatically a Vietcong.

> — *Christian Science Monitor*, March 8, 1963

The corner has definitely been turned toward victory in South Vietnam.

> — Assistant Secretary of Defense for Public
> Affairs Arthur D. Sylvester, March 8, 1963

[The war] is turning an important corner . . . government forces clearly have the initiative in most areas of the country.

> — Secretary of State Dean Rusk,
> March 9, 1963

The stakes are sizable. Americans have given their solemn word that they will stay to win here: if they fail, the word will be out throughout this region that Americans are paper tigers.

> — David Halberstam,
> *New York Times*, March 11, 1963

Vietcong activity is at a level 50 percent below last year.

> — General Victor H. Krulak, official Top Secret
> minutes, Special Counterinsurgency Group,
> March 14, 1963

Virtually all of the fighting is done by U.S. troops.

> — *Saturday Evening Post*, March 23, 1963

My 10-day tour of United States installations from Japan to Vietnam
. . . encouraged me. . . . The authorities I talked to . . . believed we
have made a start at turning the tide.

> — James E. Powers, national commander,
> American Legion, *American Legion Magazine*,
> March 1963

United States policy planners believe that the Communist guerrilla
attack has been blunted. . . . [There is] a greater sense of progress.

> — *New York Times*, April 4, 1963

By Christmas it will all be over.

> — General Paul D. Harkins,
> Honolulu, April 1963, quoted by Roger
> Hilsman, *To Move a Nation*

I don't object to a dictatorship as violently as some people do.

> — Senator Barry Goldwater, Republican of
> Arizona, *Issues & Answers*, ABC, April 7, 1963

Kennedy's treatment of Chester Bowles reveals a great deal about
Kennedy the man and President. Bowles was one of Kennedy's earliest
and most loyal supporters for the Presidency, and a leading adviser on
foreign affairs. After the election, Kennedy named him as Dean Rusk's
first deputy in the State Department. He was instrumental in recruiting
superior men for ambassadorships and in stimulating some new thinking
in the department. . . . Bowles was right on the Bay of Pigs, and in the
fall of 1961, when the administration was moving toward its first big
decisions to intervene in Vietnam, he suggested that the entire area be
neutralized. Roger Hilsman writes: "As far as I know, President
Kennedy did not make any specific comment on this suggestion, but my
sense of his attitude is that he accepted the concept as a far-seeing
expression of the ultimate goal for Southeast Asia toward which we
should work, but that its time had not yet come."

Since neutralism was just what the National Liberation Front was
calling for in South Vietnam, a Kennedy decision to explore this
possibility could well have meant avoidance of the entire Vietnam
tragedy. Although a good case can be made that Bowles was a most
valuable man in the State Department, Kennedy soon decided that he
had to go. He liked Bowles, admired his thoughtful and imaginative
suggestions, but saw no other way to shake up a department whose lack
of responsiveness had distressed him. To remove Rusk would, as
Schlesinger put it, "constitute too severe a comment on his original
judgment." The conclusion was that Bowles had not succeeded in

running the department, although he had not been given the authority to do it.

> — Richard J. Walton, *Cold War and Counter-Revolution: The Foreign Policy of John F. Kennedy*

We are trying to fight this problem as if it were a tournament of roses. I think it is time for the dirty-tricks department to take over there. We are dealing with a bunch of scoundrels, and it seems to me we ought to catch them as if we were trying to run down Jesse James—$10,000, dead or alive. We might promise them a couple of water buffalo, or a new wife, or some money, or three or four acres of rice land—almost anything would be cheaper than what we are doing.

> — Senator Richard B. Russell, Democrat of Georgia, chairman, Senate Armed Services Committee, quoted by *Time*, April 12, 1963

I am very pleased with the progress we are making. In the past seventeen or eighteen months the Communist drive to subvert South Vietnam has been blunted. I anticipate further progress.

> — Secretary of Defense Robert S. McNamara, Honolulu, May 7, 1963

If Asian communists . . . eventually gain their demands in Vietnam— not necessarily a military victory—then the implications are immense, not only for this country's 15 million people. Equally important would be the psychological victory over . . . the Americans in an area where the Americans have staked out a line.

> — David Halberstam, *New York Times*, June 16, 1963

TOP SECRET

We believe that Communist progress has been blunted and that the situation is improving . . . the Viet Cong can be contained militarily and . . . further progress can be made.

> — Intelligence Report, April 17, 1963

I can't do it [withdraw from Vietnam] until 1965—after I'm reelected.

> — President John F. Kennedy to Senator Mike Mansfield, spring 1963, quoted by Kenneth O'Donnell

After Mansfield left the office, the President told me that he had made up his mind that after his reelection he would take the risk of unpopularity and make a complete withdrawal of American forces from Vietnam. "In 1965, I'll be damned everywhere as a Communist appeaser. But I don't care. If I tried to pull out completely now, we would have another Joe McCarthy red scare on our hands, but I can do it after I'm reelected. So we had better make damned sure that I *am* reelected."

> — Kenneth O'Donnell, "LBJ and the Kennedys,"
> *Life*

The South Vietnamese themselves are fighting their own battle, fighting well.

> — Secretary of State Dean Rusk,
> April 18, 1963

There is a steady movement toward a constitutional system. . . . The Government forces are able to maintain the initiative. . . . The strategic hamlet program is producing excellent results. . . . The villagers are fighting when attacked. . . . Morale in the countryside has begun to rise. . . . To the Vietnamese peasant [the Viet Cong] look less and less like winners. . . . Rice production is up. . . . Defections from the Viet Cong have risen. . . . The Viet Cong is losing more weapons than are the Government forces. . . . The Viet Cong has been unable to carry out its plan. . . . There is a good basis for encouragement. The Vietnamese are on their way to success.

> — Secretary of State Dean Rusk,
> April 22, 1963

When President Kennedy came in, South Vietnam was going very badly. . . . The South Vietnam government is beginning to get the initiative again and has stopped this Viet Cong attempt to take the country over. . . . In South Vietnam there is a vigorous government. There is a vigorous and determined people who are ready to fight. . . . They are beginning to succeed. I think the President has very sound policies, he has very sound advisors.

> — Under Secretary of State for Political Affairs
> W. Averell Harriman, *Issues & Answers*, ABC,
> May 5, 1963

Now, in March 1963, I can say, and in this I am supported by all members of the mission, that the Government is beginning to win the shooting war against the Viet Cong.

> — Sir Robert Thompson, British
> counterinsurgency expert in Malaya, chief,
> British advisory mission, Saigon, May 6, 1963

TOP SECRET

The over-all situation in Vietnam is improving. In the military sector of the counterinsurgency, we are winning. Evidences of improvement are clearly visible, as the combined impact of the programs . . . begin to have effect on the Viet Cong.

> — Secretary of Defense Robert S. McNamara,
> briefing paper for Honolulu Conference,
> May 6, 1963

A Pentagon spokesman said today . . . Defense Department officials are hopeful that the 12,000 forces [*sic*] can be reduced in one to three years.

> — *New York Times*, May 7, 1963

All trends are favorable.

> — General Victor H. Krulak, back from meeting
> with General Paul D. Harkins in Honolulu,
> official Top Secret minutes, Special
> Counterinsurgency Group, May 9, 1963

The Government on May 7 forbade Buddhist flags to be flown on May 8, which is traditionally celebrated as the birthday of the Buddha, although the Vatican flags were still being displayed, and Radio Hué was ordered on May 8 not to broadcast the day's religious ceremonies. An orderly crowd of about 20,000 Buddhists, including many women and children, gathered outside the radio station to protest, whereupon the local military commander called out troops which threw tear-gas grenades and finally opened fire with machine-guns. Nine people were killed, seven of them children, and about 20 wounded.

> — *Keesing's Research Report: South Vietnam, A
> Political History*

I don't think the Americans are able to advise us on subversive warfare. I am afraid the Americans don't know as much as we do.

> — Ngo Dinh Nhu, May 13, 1963

Part of the problem [of creating a broad political base in the South] has been that those who have collaborated in the war days and immediate postwar days with Ho Chi Minh were pretty much ruled out of consideration in Vietnam, and properly so.

> — Secretary of State Dean Rusk,
> testimony before Senate, 1963

We are hopeful that the situation in Viet-nam would permit some withdrawal in any case by the end of the year.

> — President John F. Kennedy, May 22, 1963

South Vietnam is on its way to victory. . . . We are winning.

> — Ambassador Frederick E. Nolting, Jr.,
> June 12, 1963

South Viet Nam's Buddhists, who comprise 80% of the country's 15 million people, are bitter over alleged favoritism by Diem and his Catholic ruling family toward the nation's 1,500,000 Catholics. The Buddhists have long complained that the government gives Catholics the best civil service jobs and that Diem, because he feels that Catholics are more solidly anti-Communist, promotes them to higher positions in the army. Many young Vietnamese army officers, claim Buddhist leaders, have become converts to Catholicism to win official favor. . . .

Buddhists feel that Diem's government is trying to make Catholicism the official state religion, point to the morality crusade of Diem's militantly Catholic sister-in-law, Mme. Ngo Dinh Nhu. In sharp variance with the easy social mores of most South Vietnamese, Mme. Nhu has banned abortion, adultery, polygamy, concubinage, divorce (except by presidential dispensation), and the sale of contraceptives.

> — *Time*, June 14, 1963

Vietnam is not a Buddhist country as . . . others in south-east Asia are.

> — *London Economist*, June 15, 1963

Buddhism in Viet Nam finds its fundamental safeguards in the constitution, of which I personally am the guardian.

> — Ngo Dinh Diem, quoted by *Time*,
> June 21, 1963

If you were defeated, you were defeated by yourselves.

> — General Giap to French journalist Jules Roy,
> as Roy was leaving for visit to old battlefield at
> Dienbienphu, 1963

TOP SECRET

The English-language "Times" of Viet-Nam, which is dominated by the Nhus . . . contained a veiled attack on the U.S. and on the Buddhists. . . . Recently we had urged Diem to make a speech which would include announcements that he intended to meet with Buddhist leaders, permit Buddhist chaplains in the army and so on. . . . The President's initial view was that Ambassador Nolting should return immediately and that Ambassador Lodge should assume his duties as soon thereafter as possible. The President volunteered that Ambassador Nolting had done an outstanding job, that it was almost miraculous the way he had succeeded in turning the war around . . . from the low point . . . when Ambassador Nolting took over. . . . The President said he hoped a way could be found to commend Ambassador Nolting publicly so as to make clear the fine job he had done and that he hoped an appropriate position could be found in Washington.

> — Assistant Secretary of State for Far Eastern
> Affairs Roger Hilsman, memorandum on
> White House meeting of President, Hilsman,
> Under Secretary Ball, Under Secretary
> Harriman, Presidential Assistant McGeorge
> Bundy, and White House Asia specialist
> Michael V. Forrestal, July 4, 1963

If our present military successes continue, we can win this war in three years.

> — Admiral Harry D. Felt,
> quoted by *Newsweek*, July 15, 1963

I think it is unfortunate that this dispute [between the Catholics and the Buddhists] has arisen at the very time when the military situation has been going better. I would hope that some solution could be reached for this dispute, which certainly began as a religious dispute, and because we have invested a tremendous amount of effort and it is going quite well. . . . We want to see a stable government there, carrying on a struggle. . . . We believe strongly in that. We are not going to withdraw from that effort. In my opinion, for us to withdraw from that effort would mean a collapse not only of South Vietnam, but Southeast Asia. So we are going to stay.

> — President John F. Kennedy,
> news conference, July 17, 1963

Kennedy told Rostow that Eisenhower could stand the political consequences of Dien Bien Phu and the expulsion of the West from Vietnam in 1954 because the blame fell on the French. "I can't take a 1954 defeat today."

> — Arthur Schlesinger, Jr., *A Thousand Days*

The trouble about this damn thing is that everybody focuses on a tiny aspect of it. The military effort against the Viet Cong has picked up enormously in the past half year. . . . The government has the support of the people, particularly in the rural areas, and it is winning more support.

. . . These people are getting schools . . . farmer credits and seeds and pigs . . . These are the important things. . . . These things are taking hold here.

> — Ambassador Frederick E. Nolting, Jr., Saigon, July 27, 1963

I myself . . . after almost two and a half years, have never seen any evidence of religious persecution.

> — Ambassador Frederick E. Nolting, Jr., quoted by *New York Times*, August 1, 1963

The government of Ngo Dinh Diem is popular with a silent majority and is criticized only by a noisy minority of the population.

> — Madame Ngo Dinh Nhu, sister-in-law of President Ngo Dinh Diem, Saigon, August 7, 1963

We hear that in his [Ambassador Henry Cabot Lodge's] family, they talk only to God. In that case, I hope we will walk together, with God in the middle.

> — Madame Ngo Dinh Nhu, quoted by *Time*, August 9, 1963

The more bullish predictions emanate from Saigon. General Paul Harkins, commander of the U.S. forces in South Viet Nam, says that the war will be over in December; statistics show that the Viet Cong launched an average of 120 attacks weekly last year, and for the first seven months this year the average was down to 74. . . . There are some reasons for optimism. Substantial progress has been made in the central highlands.

> — *Time*, August 9, 1963

I think the military campaign . . . by the North Vietnamese Army, which is being advised by the Americans, is going well, and I believe that in the next 12 months you are going to see some very impressive victories. . . . Last year there were 4400 of the VC . . . killed in this war and the casualties go up at about 300 a week. . . . We have a very ably-led and effective army group in Vietnam. . . . I think it is quite likely that the Vietnamese Army will have a very great success and that the country will be able to stand on its own two feet. . . . I think that is quite likely.

> — Ambassador Henry Cabot Lodge, *Issues & Answers*, ABC, August 11, 1963

Those Buddhist leaders are actually crypto-Communists. . . . We know exactly who the troublemakers are. . . . Once this affair is finished, it will be finished for good. Buddhism will die in this country. These people dare to claim they are leaders of 80% of the population. As long as I have any breath in my body, I shall make them swallow that pretense. They behave as though we were all stupid idiots. I am furious.

> — Madame Ngo Dinh Nhu, interview with
> Milton Orshefsky, *Life*, August 16, 1963

All they've done is barbecue a bonze. . . . Let them burn . . . and we shall go ahead and clap our hands. . . . I would beat the bonzes ten more times.

> — Madame Ngo Dinh Nhu,
> quoted by *Newsweek*, August 19, 1963

The Chief C.I.A. agent, Colonel Edward G. Lansdale, threw his support behind Ngo Dinh Diem, opposing the United States Ambassador, General Lawton Collins, who recommended that the United States withhold support from the Saigon Government. Allen W. Dulles, then Director of the Intelligence Agency, persuaded his brother, Secretary of State John Foster Dulles, that Colonel Lansdale was right.

> — *New York Times*, August 22, 1963

I am extremely pleased with the progress made. . . . In January this year, Admiral Felt, Commander in Chief Pacific, ventured an opinion that the rebel Viet Cong could be defeated in three years. That target date is indeed realistic. However, if the current momentum and rate of progress are maintained, it is my considered opinion that victory over the Viet Cong could be achieved sooner.

> — General Paul D. Harkins,
> letter to *Time*, August 23, 1963

TOP SECRET

U.S. Government cannot tolerate situation in which power lies in Nhu's hands. Diem must be given chance to rid himself of Nhu and his coterie and replace them with best military and political personalities available. If, in spite of all your efforts, Diem remains obdurate and refuses, then we must face the possibility that Diem himself cannot be preserved.

> — Joint Chiefs of Staff, cablegram to
> Ambassador Henry Cabot Lodge, drafted by
> Roger Hilsman, Averell Harriman, George W.
> Ball, and Michael V. Forrestal, and approved
> by President Kennedy, Secretary Rusk,
> Roswell Gilpatrick, and General Taylor; the
> date: August 24, 1963

TOP SECRET

It is now clear that whether military proposed martial law or whether Nhu tricked them into it, Nhu took advantage of its imposition to smash pagodas with police. . . . We recognize the necessity of removing taint on military for pagoda raids and placing blame squarely on Nhu. . . . Needless to say we have held knowledge of this telegram to minimum essential people and assume you will take similar precautions to prevent premature leaks.

> — State Department, cablegram to Ambassador Henry Cabot Lodge in Saigon, August 24, 1963

TOP SECRET

Believe that chances of Diem's meeting our demands are virtually nil. . . . Therefore, propose we go straight to Generals with our demands, without informing Diem. Would tell them we prepared to have Diem without Nhus but it is in effect up to them whether to keep him. . . . Harkins concurs. I present credentials President Diem tomorrow 11 A.M.

> — Ambassador Henry Cabot Lodge, cablegram to Secretary of State Dean Rusk and Assistant Secretary of State Roger Hilsman, replying to State Department cablegrams, August 24, 25, 1963

TOP SECRET

During meeting with Harkins, Trueheart, Mecklin, and COS [Chief of Station] on morning 26 Aug Lodge made decision that American official hand should not show. . . . We in agreement Nhus must go.

> — John Richardson, CIA station chief, Saigon, cablegram to John A. McCone, director, CIA, August 26, 1963

Some officials now believe that the only plausible solution may be to remove Mr. Nhu or both brothers through a *coup d'état.*

> — Tad Szulc, *New York Times*, August 28, 1963

TOP SECRET

Situation here has reached point of no return. Saigon is armed camp. Current indications are that Ngo family have dug in for last ditch battle. It is our considered estimate that General officers cannot retreat now. . . . We all understand that the effort must succeed and that whatever needs to be done on our part must be done. If this attempt by the generals does not take place or if it fails, we believe it no exaggeration to say that VN runs serious risk of being lost over the course of time.

> — John Richardson, CIA station chief, Saigon,
> cablegram to John A. McCone, director, CIA,
> August 28, 1963

TOP SECRET

We are launched on a course from which there is no respectable turning back: the overthrow of the Diem government. . . . There is no turning back because there is no possibility, in my view, that the war can be won under a Diem administration, still less that Diem or any member of the family can govern the country in a way to gain the support of the people who count, i.e., the educated class in and out of government service, civil and military—not to mention the American people.

> — Ambassador Henry Cabot Lodge,
> cablegram to Secretary of State Dean Rusk,
> August 29, 1963

TOP SECRET

Highest level meeting noon today. . . . General Harkins is hereby authorized to repeat to such Generals as you indicate the messages previously transmitted. . . . He should stress that the USG supports the movement to eliminate the Nhus from the government, but that . . . General Harkins must know who are involved, resources available to them and overall plan for coup. The USG will support a coup which has a good chance of succeeding but plans no direct involvement of U.S. armed forces. Harkins should state that he is prepared to establish liaison with the coup planners and to review plans . . . you should consider the importance of timing and managing announcement so as to minimize appearance of collusion with Generals and also to minimize danger of unpredictable and disruptive reaction by existing government.

> — Secretary of State Dean Rusk, cablegram to
> Ambassador Henry Cabot Lodge, following
> National Security Council meeting,
> August 29, 1963

TOP SECRET

We fully understand enormous stakes at issue and the heavy responsibilities which you and Harkins will be carrying in the days ahead. . . . We had indicated earlier to the Generals that if the Nhus were removed the question of retaining Diem would be up to them. My own personal assessment is (and this is not an instruction) that the Nhus are by all odds the greater part of the problem in Vietnam, internally, internationally and for American public opinion. Perhaps it is inconceivable that the Nhus could be removed without taking Diem with them. . . . Good luck.

> — Secretary of State Dean Rusk,
> cablegram to Ambassador Henry Cabot
> Lodge, August 29, 1963

TOP SECRET

I agree that the Nhus out is the prime objective and that they are "the greater part." This surely cannot be done by working through Diem. In fact Diem will oppose it. He wishes he had more Nhus, not less. The best chance of doing it is by the Generals taking over the government lock, stock and barrel. . . . If I call on Diem to demand the removal of the Nhus, he will surely not agree. But before turning me down, he will pretend to consider it and involve us in prolonged delays. This will make the Generals suspicious of us and add to the inertia. . . . It is possible, as you suggested, for the Generals when, as and if their operation gets rolling to demand the removal of the Nhus before bringing their operation to fruition. But I am afraid they will get talked out of their operation which will then disintegrate, still leaving the Nhus in office. If the Generals' operation does get rolling, I would not want to stop it until they were in full control. They could then get rid of the Nhus and decide whether they wanted to keep Diem. It is better for them and for us for them to throw out the Nhus. . . . I am sure that the best way to handle this matter is by a truly VNese movement even if it puts me rather in the position of pushing a piece of spaghetti. I am contemplating no further talks with Diem at this time.

> — Ambassador Henry Cabot Lodge,
> cablegram to Secretary of State Dean Rusk,
> August 30, 1963

The United States appears to be moving deliberately toward a confrontation with the Ngo family government. . . . The United States is ready to initiate action that might lead to the overthrow of the government. Most observers here believe that Americans will give a signal to key elements of the military. . . . Americans are known to have been contacting key people in the military recently.

> — David Halberstam, *New York Times*,
> August 31, 1963

TOP SECRET

Mr. Hilsman undertook to present . . . factors which bear directly on the problem confronting the U.S. now. They are, in his view: (A) The mood of the people, particularly the middle level officers, noncommissioned officers and middle level bureaucrats who are most restive. Mr. McNamara interrupted to state that he had seen no evidence of this and General Taylor commented that he had seen none either. . . . [In] the matter of U.S. and world opinion, Hilsman stated that . . . part of the problem . . . is the press. . . .

Mr. Murrow added that this problem of press condemnation is now worldwide. Mr. Kattenburg stated that as recently as last Thursday it was the belief of Ambassador Lodge that, if we undertake to live with this repressive regime, with its bayonets at every street corner . . . we are going to be thrown out of the country in six months. . . . General Taylor asked what Kattenburg meant when he said that we would be thrown out of the country in six months. Kattenburg replied that in from six months to a year, as the people see we are losing the war, they will gradually go to the other side and we will be obliged to leave. . . .

Mr. Rusk then said that we should present questions to Lodge which fall within these parameters. He added that he believes we have good proof that we have been winning the war. . . . The Vice President stated that he agreed with Secretary Rusk's conclusions completely. . . . He had never really seen a genuine alternative to Diem. He stated that from both a practical and political viewpoint it would be a disaster to pull out; that we should stop playing cops and robbers and get back to talking straight to the GVN, and that we should once again go about winning the war. . . .

> — General Victor H. Krulak, special assistant,
> Joint Chiefs of Staff, counterinsurgency and
> special activities, memorandum on meeting at
> State Department between Krulak, Vice
> President Johnson, Secretaries Rusk and
> McNamara, Deputy Secretary of Defense
> Roswell Gilpatric, McGeorge Bundy, General
> Maxwell Taylor, USIA Director Edward R.
> Murrow, Lieut. Gen. Marshall S. Carter,
> Deputy Director of CIA Richard Helms and
> William E. Colby of CIA, former Ambassador
> Frederick E. Nolting, Jr., Assistant Secretary
> Hilsman and Paul M. Kattenburg of State
> Department, head, Interdepartmental
> Working Group on Vietnam; the meeting took
> place on August 31, 1963

We are satisfied that we have a sound strategy; progress is being made.

> — Deputy Under Secretary of State U. Alexis
> Johnson, *Department of State Bulletin*,
> September 2, 1963

I don't agree with those who say we should withdraw. That would be a great mistake. I know people don't like Americans to be engaged in this kind of effort. 47 Americans have been killed in combat with the enemy, but this is a very important struggle even though it is far away. . . . We . . . have to participate—we may not like it—in the defense of Asia.

— President John F. Kennedy, television
interview with Walter Cronkite, CBS,
September 2, 1963

The numbers of incidents have been dropping rapidly from last year. Such elements as sabotage, propaganda incidents [sic], the larger sized attacks, those were dropping. Additional areas of the country were coming under Government control. The strategic-hamlet program had been moving forward. I think it is still moving forward.

— Secretary of State Dean Rusk,
Department of State Bulletin,
September 2, 1963

I have proof people are with us. . . . It is unfair to claim we cannot win politically and militarily because of a stupid Buddhist plot against us. All the facts are to the contrary. . . . People talk about a more representative Government here, but this Government wants only people who will fight Communists, not dubious elements. . . . Also, there are too many American civilians here. I don't know what they are all doing. . . . Some of the civilians may be agents. Why should you pay money to them to stab us in the back? . . . Ambassador Lodge is a statesman. We expect him to have a firm hand. . . . You will win here with us. That is why I am so angry when people sabotage this effort and instead believe a noisy minority, such as the so-called Buddhists, that has proved itself absolutely untrustworthy. . . . Are the pagodas to be untouchable when they harbor Reds wearing yellow robes?

— Madame Ngo Dinh Nhu, Saigon,
September 4, 1963

The lessons of the present crisis are plain. One is that the anti-communist war in South Vietnam, which has produced the best fighting force in Indochina, is not only, as President Kennedy declared, "their war" but our war—a war from which we cannot retreat and which we dare not lose.

— Editorial, *New York Times*, September 6, 1963

I believe it [the Domino Theory]. I believe it. I think that the struggle is close enough. . . . If South Vietnam went, it would . . . give the impression that the wave of the future in Southeast Asia was China and the communists. So I believe it. . . . What I am concerned about is that Americans will get impatient and say because they don't like events in Southeast Asia or they don't like the government in Saigon, that we should withdraw. . . . I think we should stay. . . . We should not withdraw. . . . We must be patient. We must persist.

> — President John F. Kennedy,
> interview on Huntley-Brinkley Report, NBC,
> September 9, 1963

TOP SECRET

The shooting war is still going ahead at an impressive pace. . . . The Viet Cong war will be won if the current U.S. military and sociological programs are pursued, irrespective of the grave defects of the ruling regime.

> — General Victor H. Krulak
> to National Security Council,
> September 10, 1963

I am operating on the basis of, really, the unanimous views and opinions expressed by the most experienced Americans there [in Vietnam]—in the military, diplomatic, AID agency, the Voice of America. . . . We are not there to see a war lost.

> — President John F. Kennedy,
> September 12, 1963

We're winning the war in the Mekong Delta.

> — General Paul D. Harkins, September 12, 1963

Confidential reports from high American authorities in Saigon say that the war can be won in nine months. . . . The border with North Vietnam has been 90% closed. . . . The V-C guerrillas are being starved out.

> — Marquis Childs, *Washington Post*,
> September 13, 1963

A withdrawal of our forces at this time would . . . be unacceptable.

> — Senator J. William Fulbright,
> *Face the Nation*, CBS, September 15, 1963

Everything that tends to help win the war . . . we are in favor of. . . . The Laotians are very interesting people. They don't like to kill each other.

> — Secretary of State Dean Rusk,
> *Issues & Answers*, ABC, September 15, 1963

TOP SECRET

We see no good opportunity for action to remove present government in immediate future. . . .

> — White House, cablegram to Ambassador
> Henry Cabot Lodge, following National
> Security Council meeting, September 17, 1963

TOP SECRET

Agree that no good opportunity for action to remove present government in immediate future is apparent. . . . Situation . . . seems particularly grave to me, notably in the light of General Big Minh's opinion expressed very privately yesterday that the Viet Cong are steadily gaining in strength; have more of the population on their side than has the GVN; that arrests are continuing and that the prisons are full; that more and more students are going over to the Viet Cong; that there is great graft and corruption in the Vietnamese administration of our aid; and that the "Heart of the Army is *not* in the war." All this by Vietnamese No. 1 General is now echoed by Secretary of Defense Thuan who wants to leave the country. . . . I believe that we should pursue contact with Big Minh and urge him along if he looks like acting. I particularly think that the idea of supporting a Vietnamese Army independent of the government should be energetically studied. . . . I have talked . . . to Diem and to Nhu last night. They have scant comprehension of what it is to appeal to public opinion as they have really no interest in any other opinion than their own.

> — Ambassador Henry Cabot Lodge, cablegram
> to State Department, "For President Only,"
> September 19, 1963

The anti-Communist struggle has been making progress.

> — South Vietnamese government press agency,
> September 22, 1963

The junior officers of the U.S. military mission are acting like little soldiers of fortune. They don't know what is going on. With their irresponsible behavior, they have forced the senior officers into following a confused policy.

> — Madame Ngo Dinh Nhu, interview at South
> Vietnamese Embassy, Rome, while on world
> tour, September 22, 1963

The war . . . could be won inside a year—perhaps six months. . . . The Vietnamese soldier I have the highest respect for—and the junior officers. There is no question on that. . . . They have the will and the necessary desire to go out and to defeat the enemy. They're fighters, all right.

> — Lieutenant Colonel John Paul Vann (ret.),
> senior U.S. military adviser, "pacification,"
> Mekong Delta, in charge of 200 other advisers,
> interview, *U.S. News & World Report,*
> September 22, 1963

Surely we are here only to win the war. And the most annoying feature of the whole situation is that we actually were winning the war this spring, until the Diem government went right around the bend with considerable help from the high-minded crusaders.

> — Joseph Alsop, syndicated column,
> September 22, 1963

As President Kennedy has stated, the stakes in Southeast Asia are too high for us to see the war lost.

> — Editorial, *New York Times,* September 22, 1963

Even today, the Diem government is at least far better than that in the North. . . . Look at the facts! No more clichés! Down with twaddle-think! These should be the new slogans.

> — Joseph Alsop, syndicated column,
> September 25, 1963

Madame Nhu's statement is shocking. These men should be thanked and not insulted.

> — Ambassador Henry Cabot Lodge,
> Saigon, September 27, 1963, referring to Mme.
> Nhu's statement of September 22

I was misinterpreted.

> — Madame Ngo Dinh Nhu, September 28, 1963

Even if you Americans pull out, I will still win the war at the head of [my] great guerrilla movement.

> — Madame Ngo Dinh Nhu, interview with
> Joseph Alsop, quoted in *Newsweek,*
> September 30, 1963

I feel we shall achieve victory in 1964.

> — Major General Than Van Dong,
> South Vietnamese Army, Ben Cat,
> October 1, 1963

TOP SECRET

The military indicators are still generally favorable and can be much more so. . . . In closing, Mr. President, may I give you my most important impression? Up to now the battle against the Viet Cong has seemed to be endless. . . . After talking to scores of officers, Vietnamese and American, I am convinced that the Viet Cong insurgency in the North and Center can be reduced to little more than sporadic incidents by the end of 1964. The Delta will take longer but should be completed by the end of 1965.

> — General Maxwell D. Taylor,
> chairman, Joint Chiefs of Staff,
> October 1, 1963

The military campaign has made great progress and continues to progress. . . . There is no solid evidence of the possibility of a successful coup. . . . We recommend that: General Harkins review with Diem . . . An increase in the military tempo in all corps areas . . . Emphasis on "clear and hold operations" . . . A consolidation of the strategic hamlet program . . . A program be established to train Vietnamese so that essential functions now performed by U.S. military personnel can be carried out by Vietnamese by the end of 1965. It should be possible to withdraw the bulk of U.S. personnel by that time. . . . We believe the U.S. part of the task can be completed by the end of 1965, the terminal date which we are taking as the time objective of our counterinsurgency programs. The military program in Vietnam has made progress and is sound in principle.

> — Secretary of Defense Robert S. McNamara
> and General Maxwell D. Taylor, joint
> memorandum to President John F. Kennedy,
> October 2, 1963

Secretary McNamara and General Taylor reported to the President this morning and to the National Security Council this afternoon. Their report included a number of classified findings and recommendations. . . . The military program in South Vietnam has made progress and is sound in principle. . . . Secretary McNamara and General Taylor reported their judgment that the major part of the U.S. military task can be completed by the end of 1965.

> — President John F. Kennedy, October 2, 1963

The military program in South Viet-Nam has made progress and is sound in principle. . . . Secretary McNamara and General Taylor reported their judgment that the major part of the U.S. military task can be completed by the end of 1965. . . . By the end of this year . . . 1,000 U.S. military personnel assigned to South Vietnam can be withdrawn.

— White House statement, October 3, 1963

TOP SECRET

Reference Big Minh–Conein meeting. While neither General Harkins nor I have great faith in Big Minh, we need instructions on his approach. My recommendation, in which General Harkins concurs, is that Conein, when next approached by Minh should: (1) Assure him that U.S. will not attempt to thwart his plans. (2) Offer to review his plans, other than assassination plans. (3) Assure Minh that U.S. aid will be continued. . . . (Conein should press Minh for details his thinking Re composition future Government.) I suggest the above be discussed with Secretary McNamara and General Taylor who contacted Minh in recent visit.

— Ambassador Henry Cabot Lodge,
cablegram to Secretary of State Dean Rusk,
October 5, 1963

TOP SECRET

Lt. Col. Conein met with Gen. Duong Van Minh at Gen. Minh's Headquarters on Le Van Duvet for one hour and ten minutes morning of 5 Oct 63. This meeting was at the initiative of Gen. Minh and had been specifically cleared in advance by Ambassador Lodge. No other persons were present. The conversation was in French. Gen. Minh stated that he must know American Government's position with respect to a change in the Government of Vietnam within the very near future. Gen. Minh added the Generals were aware the situation is deteriorating rapidly and that action to change the Government must be taken or the war will be lost to the Viet Cong because the Government no longer has the support of the people. Gen. Minh identified the other Generals participating with him in this plan. Maj. Gen. Tran Van Don, Brig. Gen. Tran Thien Khiem, Maj. Gen. Tran Van Kim. Gen. Minh made it clear . . . he does need American assurances that the USG will not rpt not attempt to thwart this plan. Gen. Minh also stated that he himself has no political ambitions. . . . Gen. Minh outlined three possible plans . . . : (a) Assassination of Ngo Dinh Nhu and Ngo Dinh Can keeping President Diem in Office. Gen. Minh said this was the easiest plan to accomplish. (b) The encirclement of Saigon by various military units . . . (c) Direct confrontation between military units involved in the coup and loyalist military units in Saigon. In effect, dividing the city of Saigon into sectors and cleaning it out pocket by pocket. Gen. Minh claims under the circumstances Diem and Nhu could count on the loyalty of 5,000 troops within the city of Saigon. . . . Gen. Minh stated "if I get rid of Nhu, Can and Hieu, Col. Tung will be on his knees before me." . . . Minh further stated that one of the reasons they are having to act quickly was the fact that many regimental, battalion and company commanders are working on coup plans of their own which could be abortive and a "catastrophe." . . . No specific date was given for this next meeting.

> — Ambassador Henry Cabot Lodge,
>   cablegram to State Department,
>   October 5, 1963

TOP SECRET

President today approved . . . urgent covert effort with closest security, under broad guidance of Ambassador to identify and build contacts with possible alternative leadership as and when it appears. Essential that this effort be totally secure and fully deniable and separated entirely from normal political analysis and reporting and other activities of country team. . . . In order to provide plausibility to denial suggest you and no one else in Embassy issue these instructions orally to Acting Station Chief and hold him responsible to you alone for making appropriate contacts and reporting to you alone. All reports to Washington on this subject should be on this channel.

> — White House, cablegram to Ambassador
>   Henry Cabot Lodge in Saigon, transmitted on
>   Central Intelligence Agency channel; message
>   followed National Security Council meeting,
>   October 5, 1963

TOP SECRET

We have following additional general thoughts which have been discussed with President. While we do not wish to stimulate coup, we also do not wish to leave impression that U.S. would thwart a change of government or deny economic and military assistance to a new regime if it appeared capable of increasing effectiveness of military effort, ensuring popular support to win war and improving working relations with U.S. . . . You should also consider with Acting Station Chief [of C.I.A.] whether it would be desirable in order to preserve security and deniability . . . for follow-up contacts by individuals brought in especially from outside Vietnam. As we indicated in CAP63560 we are most concerned about security problem and we are confining knowledge these sensitive matters in Washington to extremely limited group, high officials in White House, State, Defense and CIA with whom this message cleared.

> — White House, cablegram to Ambassador
>   Henry Cabot Lodge in Saigon, transmitted on
>   CIA channel, October 6, 1963

You said that the Buddhists were clubbed. . . . When you stop the traffic in the street, what can you do? . . . Those so-called Buddhists, they are just hooligans, dressed as saffron monks. . . . The Americans in Vietnam do not take seriously enough their—yes, their role as ally. . . . They consider themselves as just spectators of a show. They do not give us the impression that they are actually fighting with us. It is just that, the problem. Really, we have the impression that they feel exactly as they are at a show watching us, just as spectators. . . . We have absolutely the impression they do not participate. Yes, we feel it. . . . When you speak of reforms we say but why do you speak as if you should reform yourselves, etcetera? . . . We are winning the war. . . . I think that so far nobody has ever said that I am stupid. . . . Maybe I am a good girl. . . . Oh, I shall talk with the Communists when I have vanquished them, beat them.

> — Madame Ngo Dinh Nhu,
> interview, Paris, *Issues & Answers*, ABC,
> October 6, 1963

Victory will be achieved in 1964.

> — Joint General Staff,
> Vietnamese Armed Forces, October 1963

Our policy henceforth will be to interfere in Vietnamese politics. . . . Vietnam must be held.

> — Editorial, *Life*, October 11, 1963

My instructions were that I was to inform General Minh that the United States Government would not thwart their coup. And I conveyed this. You could liken it to a football team. Ambassador Lodge was the quarterback, the coaching was being conducted by Washington, D.C. and I was the eyes and ears and the mouthpiece of Henry Cabot Lodge to the junta. It was quite obvious that if at one point that this American hand had shown that the whole thing would blow up and therefore it would be an extreme embarrassment. Therefore, Ambassador Lodge made it very clear to me that if something went wrong that he would have to be able to have deniability that I even existed.

> — Lieutenant Colonel Lucien Conein, CIA,
> interviewed on "The Death of Diem," NBC

I prefer not to comment on my daughter at all. . . . There is no possibility at all of victory . . . under the present regime in Vietnam. In order to achieve victory we have first to remove or change completely the present regime, which has become unwittingly the greatest asset to the Communists and the greatest obstacle to victory. . . . It is a war to win

the hearts and minds of the people and there is not a possibility of
winning that war with a government which, in fact, is simply pushing the
people into the arms of the Communists. . . . The Buddhists were, above
all, involved in a revolt against injustice and oppression.

> — Tran Van Chuong, former South Vietnamese
> ambassador to U. S. and father of Madame
> Nhu; on August 22, 1963, day after Saigon
> government began crackdown on Buddhists,
> ambassador resigned, saying he could no
> longer represent such a government; *Face the
> Nation*, CBS, October 13, 1963

I do not know why you dislike us. . . . The world is under a spell, the
Communist-inspired spell, which is called now liberalism. . . . Your own
public in America . . . are not so strongly anti-Communist as we. . . .
You know in my country your people act very openly, and they speak
. . . are you anti-coup or are you pro-coup? They do not hide it. . . .
Your government . . . follows what we call the new fashion in the
political field now which is to liberalism. That means, which stands much
more towards Communism, and I can assure you that the American
government in the Vietnamese' eyes looks much less anti-Communist
than the Vietnamese government, that is sure. . . . It is absolutely untrue
that we are dictatorial. . . . Nobody is perfect. . . . Every day we try to
improve ourselves. . . .

So far we have not received any official advice. The only unofficial
advice was this, and now I can tell you publicly, and I find it absolutely
unreasonable. It is just that my husband and myself, we must leave the
country. And we ask why? Why should we leave the country? Because if
we leave the country, the whole country may be demoralized. . . .
Unofficially it has been requested that my husband and myself, we leave
the country. . . . We say that if we leave the country, we demoralize the
people. . . . To say that 70 percent of my country is Buddhist is
absolutely wrong, absolutely wrong. . . . I wonder on what basis people
can say that the Buddhists are a majority. . . . My father is against me
from childhood. For me it is a family tragedy. . . . There is a kind of
incompatibility. . . . We must remember one thing: It is that we are
winning. We are absolutely winning. And I cannot understand why it is
not repeated enough. . . . We have accepted that we are winning. . . .
When there are errors . . . it is my duty to tell it. Do you not think that
you should thank me. . . . I see only now that we are in the last minutes
. . . in the last 15 minutes of the last battle.

> — Madame Ngo Dinh Nhu, sister-in-law of
> President Ngo Dinh Diem, *Meet the Press*,
> NBC, October 13, 1963

TOP SECRET

CAS [CIA Chief, Acting Station] has been punctilious in carrying out my instructions. I have personally approved each meeting between Gen. Don and [Col.] Conein who has carried out my orders in each instance explicitly. While I share your concern about the continued involvement of Conein in this matter, a suitable substitute for Conein as the principal contact is not presently available. Conein, as you know, is a friend of some 18 years' standing with Gen. Don, and Gen. Don has expressed extreme reluctance to deal with anyone else. . . . As a precautionary measure, however, I of course refused to see Gen. Don. . . . In the event that the coup aborts, or in the event that Nhu has masterminded a provocation, I believe that our involvement to date through Conein is still within the realm of plausible denial. CAS [CIA] is perfectly prepared to have me disavow Conein at any time it may serve the national interest. . . . We should not thwart a coup for two reasons. First, it seems at least an even bet that the next government would not bungle and stumble as much as the present one has. Secondly, it is extremely unwise in the long range for us to pour cold water on attempts at a coup, particularly when they are just in their beginning stages. . . . The war effort has been interfered with already by the incompetence of the present government. . . . Gen. Don's intention to have no religious discrimination in a future government is commendable. . . . But I do not think his promise of a democratic election is realistic. This country simply is not ready for that procedure.

> — Ambassador Henry Cabot Lodge,
> cablegram to McGeorge Bundy,
> October 25, 1963

TOP SECRET

We are particularly concerned about hazard that an unsuccessful coup, however carefully we avoid direct engagement, will be laid at our door by public opinion almost everywhere. Therefore while sharing your view that we should not be in position of thwarting coup, we would like to have option of judging and warning on any plan with poor prospects of success. We recognize that this is a large order, but President wants you to know of our concern.

> — McGeorge Bundy, cablegram to Ambassador
> Henry Cabot Lodge in Saigon,
> October 25, 1963

Madame Nhu is proving that she has beauty and brass. . . . In her speeches . . . she [says] that the Buddhist uprising in her country was inspired more by political fanaticism than by religious zeal. . . . The

lady has something. . . . The most that can be demonstrated is that the
Catholics have enjoyed advantages denied the Buddhists.

> — Kenneth Crawford, column, *Newsweek*,
> October 28, 1963

TOP SECRET

View of Vice Pres Tho that there are only 15 to 20 all-around hamlets
in the area south of Saigon which are really good is ridiculous and
indicates need for him to get out of Saigon and visit countryside so as to
really know of progress which is being made. In the past two weeks I
have visited nine Delta provinces . . . and I do not find the province
chiefs or sector advisors to hold the same views as Vice Pres Tho. . . . I
am unable to concur in statement that quote one cannot drive as much
around the country as one could two years ago end of quote. . . . I am
unable to concur in statement that VC is quote in fact, reckoned at a
higher figure than it was two years ago end quote. I have not observed
the signs that hatred of the government has tended to diminish the
Army's vigor, enthusiasm and enterprise. . . . I feel we have made and
are making significant strides.

> — General Paul D. Harkins,
> cablegram to General Maxwell D. Taylor,
> October 30, 1963

TOP SECRET

My general view is that the U.S. is trying to bring this medieval
country into the 20th Century and that we have made considerable
progress. . . . We do not believe it wise to ask that "Big Minh" pass his
plans to Gen. Stilwell. The Vietnamese believe that there are members of
the U.S. military who leak to the Government of Vietnam. . . . I much
appreciate your furnishing the berth-equipped military aircraft which I
trust is a jet. I intend to tell Pan American that a jet has been diverted for
my use and therefore I will no longer need their services. This will
undoubtedly leak to the newspapers and the GVN may study this move
with some suspicion. . . . To allay suspicions further, I will offer space
on the aircraft to MACV. . . . I wish to reserve comment on my actual
time of departure until I have some additional information. . . .

Your para 7 [regarding consultation with Harkins] somewhat per-
plexes me. It does not seem sensible to have the military in charge of a
matter which is so profoundly political as a change of government. In
fact, I would say to do this would probably be the end of any hope for a
change of government here. This is said impersonally as a general
proposition, since Gen. Harkins is a splendid General. . . . We
anticipate at the outset of the coup . . . the GVN will request me or Gen.

Harkins to use our influence to call it off . . . we would certainly be unable to do so. . . . The Generals . . . may well have need of funds at the last moment with which to buy off political opposition. To the extent that these funds can be passed discreetly, I believe we should furnish them, provided we are convinced that the proposed coup is sufficiently well organized to have a good chance of success. . . . Heartily agree that a miscalculation could jeopardize position in Southeast Asia. We also run tremendous risks by doing nothing. If we were convinced that the coup was going to fail, we would, of course, do everything we could to stop it. Gen. Harkins has read this and does not concur.

— Ambassador Henry Cabot Lodge, cablegram
to McGeorge Bundy, October 30, 1963

TOP SECRET

We do not accept as a basis for U.S. policy that we have no power to delay or discourage a coup. . . . You should take action to persuade coup leaders to stop or delay any operation which in your best judgment does not clearly give high prospect of success. . . . Therefore, if you should not conclude that there is not clearly a high prospect of success, you should communicate this doubt to generals in a way calculated to persuade them to desist at least until chances are better. . . . But once a coup under responsible leadership has begun . . . it is in the interest of the U.S. Government that it should succeed. We have your message about return to Washington and we suggest that all public comment be kept as low-key and quiet as possible, and we also urge that if possible you keep open the exact time of your departure.

— McGeorge Bundy, cablegram to Ambassador
Henry Cabot Lodge in Saigon,
October 30, 1963

TOP SECRET

Our attitude to coup group can still have decisive effect on its decisions. We believe that what we say to coup group can produce delay of coup and that betrayal of coup plans to Diem is not repeat not our only way of stopping coup. . . . We badly need some corroborative evidence whether Minh and others directly and completely involved. In view Don's claim he doesn't handle "military planning" could not Conein tell Don that we need better military picture and that Big Minh could communicate this most naturally and easily to Stilwell? We recognize desirability involving MACV to minimum, but believe Stilwell far more desirable this purpose than using Conein. . . . Concur you and other U.S. elements should take no action that could indicate U.S. awareness coup possibility. However, DOD is sending berth-equipped military aircraft that will arrive Saigon Thursday and could take you out thereafter as late as Saturday afternoon in time to meet your presently proposed arrival Washington Sunday. . . . Whether you leave Thursday or later, believe it essential that prior your departure there be fullest consultation Harkins and CAS [CIA]. . . . We are now examining post-coup contingencies here and request your immediate recommendations on positions to be adopted . . . if coup (A) succeeds, (B) fails, (C) is indecisive. . . . We reiterate burden of proof must be on coup group to show a substantial possibility of quick success.

> — McGeorge Bundy, cablegram to Ambassador
> Henry Cabot Lodge in Saigon,
> October 30, 1963

TOP SECRET

On balance we are gaining in the contest with the VC. There will continue to be minor ups and downs but the general trend has been and continues upward. . . . The general trend continues to be favorable. The tempo of the RVN-initiated operations is increasing and recently the tempo of VC-initiated activity has fallen off.

> — General Paul D. Harkins,
> cablegram to General Maxwell D. Taylor,
> October 30, 1963

TOP SECRET

. . . Believe our attitude to coup group can still have decisive effect on its decisions. We believe that what we say to coup group can produce delay of coup and that betrayal of coup plans to Diem is not repeat not our only way of stopping coup. . . . We reiterate burden of proof must be on coup group to show a substantial possibility of quick success; otherwise we should discourage them from proceeding since a miscalculation could result in jeopardizing U.S. position in Southeast Asia.

> — McGeorge Bundy, cablegram to
> Ambassador Henry Cabot Lodge,
> October 30, 1963

TOP SECRET

FROM: Lodge   30 October 1963

CAS 2063

TO: State Department

We must, of course, get best possible estimate of chances of coup's success and this estimate must color our thinking. . . . If we were convinced that the coup was going to fail, we would, of course, do everything we could to stop it. Gen. Harkins has read this and does not concur.

We have completed the job of training South Vietnam's armed forces. The Vietnamese armed forces are just as professional as you can get . . . under ideal conditions, if all this equipment is used properly and barring any political upheavals, I feel we could wrap this thing up by the end of next dry season . . . we will have driven the Viet-Cong sufficiently underground by the end of next year that they will no longer be a national threat.

> — Major General Charles J. Timmes,
> Commander of M.A.A.G., South Vietnam;
> interview in Tokyo quoted by *Stars and Stripes*, October 31, 1963

I can tell you categorically that we are winning the war in the Mekong Delta. Victory . . . is just months away, and the reduction of American advisers can begin any time now. . . . I can safely say the end of the war is in sight.

> — General Paul D. Harkins, commander, U.S.
> Military Assistance Command, Saigon;
> interview in Tokyo quoted by *Stars and Stripes*, October 31, 1963

When Secretary McNamara and General Taylor came back from Viet Nam, they announced that we could expect to withdraw a thousand men from South Viet Nam by the end of the year and there has been some reference to that by General Harkins. If we are able to do that, that would be our schedule. . . . It would be our hope to lessen the number of Americans there by 1,000.

> — President John F. Kennedy, October 31, 1963

A cautiously optimistic report on the war came last week from Brigadier General Frank A. Osmanski, a U.S. logistics expert in South Viet Nam, who estimated that government forces have stepped up their "intensity of operations" to $2\frac{1}{2}$ times what it was a year ago, now launch ten attacks to every one by the Viet Cong. . . . They are still outkilling the Viet Cong 4 to 1. What all the statistics add up to, according to the best estimates in Saigon, is that the South Vietnamese are holding their own.

> — *Time*, November 1, 1963

TOP SECRET

DIEM: Some units have made a rebellion and I want to know what is the attitude of the U.S.?

LODGE: I do not feel well enough informed to be able to tell you. I have heard the shooting, but am not acquainted with all the facts. Also it is 4:30 A.M. in Washington and the U.S. Government cannot possibly have a view.

DIEM: But you must have some general ideas. After all, I am a Chief of State. I have tried to do my duty. I want to do now what duty and good sense require. I believe in duty above all.

LODGE: You have certainly done your duty. As I told you only this morning, I admire your courage and your great contributions to your country. No one can take away from you the credit for all you have done. Now I am worried about your physical safety. I have a report that those in charge of the current activity offer you and your brother safe conduct out of the country. Had you heard this?

DIEM: No.(*and then after a pause*) You have my telephone number.

LODGE: Yes. If I can do anything for your physical safety, please call me.

DIEM: I am trying to re-establish order.

> — Ambassador Henry Cabot Lodge, excerpt
> from Top Secret cablegram to State
> Department containing last telephone
> conversation with President Ngo Dinh Diem,
> November 1, 1963

I believe all the devils of hell are against us, but we will triumph eventually.

> — Madame Ngo Dinh Nhu, suite 843, Beverly
> Wilshire Hotel, Beverly Hills, Calif., on
> hearing of coup, 7:50 A.M. PST,
> November 1, 1963

The army has swung into action . . . the army will certainly be victorious.

> — South Vietnamese Council of Generals,
> proclamation after *coup d'état,*
> November 1, 1963

The Administration welcomes the coup-d'état in South Vietnam . . . and is confident of greater success now in the war.

> — Max Frankel, *New York Times,*
> November 2, 1963

The war can be won.

> — Joseph Alsop, syndicated column,
> November 4, 1963

We believe the present regime has moved promptly to . . . resolve
some of the internal difficulties. . . . The people of that country will
move in greater units on behalf of the total effort.

> — Secretary of State Dean Rusk,
> November 8, 1963

We are going to bring back several hundred before the end of the
year. . . .

I have great confidence in General Harkins. There may be some who
would like to see General Harkins go, but I plan to keep him there
because we do have a new situation there, and a new government, we
hope, an increased effort in the war. The purpose of the meeting in
Honolulu—Ambassador Lodge will be there, General Harkins will be
there, Secretary McNamara and others, and then, as you know, later
Ambassador Lodge will come here—is to attempt to assess the situation
. . . and . . . how we can intensify the struggle.

> — President John F. Kennedy,
> News conference, November 14, 1963

In the view of the United States Embassy, General Duong Van Minh
has the potential to become a national leader. Americans are impressed
by his simplicity and his bluntness.

> — *New York Times*, November 15, 1963

The Devil is exasperated to see that he is still unable to make a dent in
my immortal spirit. . . . I cannot stay in a country [the U.S.] whose
Government stabbed me in the back. . . . If really my family has been
treacherously killed with either the official or unofficial blessing of the
American Government, I can predict to you all that the story of South
Vietnam is only at its beginning.

> — Madame Ngo Dinh Nhu, before leaving for
> Rome, Los Angeles, November 15, 1963

Small numbers of the U.S. personnel will be able to return by the end
of this year.

> — Secretary of Defense Robert S. McNamara,
> November 19, 1963

[There is] an encouraging outlook for the principal objective . . . the
successful prosecution of the war [and] excellent working relations
between U.S. officials and the members of the new Vietnamese
government.

> — Ambassador Henry Cabot Lodge,
> Honolulu, November 20, 1963

The administration's top military and diplomatic officials decided today that the war against the Vietcong in South Vietnam has taken a decided turn for the better since the coup d'état that overthrew the Diem régime November 1.

— *New York Times*, November 21, 1963

The U.S. has . . . good reason to welcome the new regime in Vietnam . . . the assassination of Ngo Dinh Diem . . . the evil genius of what had become a nepotic despotism. . . . What about his successors? The three generals, led by Duong Van Minh, now running Vietnam have shown every sign of being more able and willing to pursue the war against the Viet Cong. . . . In their new optimism some officers are talking about an end to the war in 1964. . . . The change in government means, above all, a greatly improved chance of victory. . . . But that chance will dwindle unless it is seized and backed at once by a stronger American commitment. . . . Now is the time to pour on more coal. . . . Even when the Viet Cong guerrillas are beaten . . . the U.S. commitment and presence there will be vital.

— Editorial, *Life*, November 22, 1963

For the first time this year there is cautious optimism.

— *U.S. News & World Report*, November 25, 1963

TOP SECRET

The President expects that all senior officers of the government will move energetically to insure the full unity of support for established U.S. policy in South Vietnam. Both in Washington and in the field, it is essential that the government be unified. . . . We should concentrate our efforts, and insofar as possible we should . . . turn the tide not only of battle but of belief.

— Excerpts from National Security Action Memorandum 273, 4 days after assassination of President John F. Kennedy, November 26, 1963

For the 9-hour conference, Secretary of State Dean Rusk, Defense Secretary Robert McNamara and Joint Chiefs of Staff Chairman Maxwell Taylor had flown in from Washington; from Saigon came Ambassador Henry Cabot Lodge and General Paul Harkins. The Honolulu meeting exuded almost relentless optimism about the war.

— *Time*, November 29, 1963

I am not going to be the President who saw Southeast Asia go the way China went.

> — President Lyndon B. Johnson, November
> 1963, quoted by Tom Wicker,
> *JFK and LBJ*

We have every reason to believe that plans will be successful in 1964.

> — Secretary of Defense Robert S. McNamara,
> December 12, 1963

I am optimistic as to the progress that can be made in the coming year.

> — Secretary of Defense Robert S. McNamara,
> Saigon, December 20, 1963

The plans of the South Vietnamese and the plans of our own military advisers for operations during 1964 . . . will be successful. We are determined that they shall be.

> — Secretary of Defense Robert S. McNamara,
> White House statement, December 21, 1963

TOP SECRET

In accordance with your request this morning, this is a summary of my conclusions after my visit to Vietnam on December 19–20. . . . The situation is very disturbing. Current trends, unless reversed in the next 2–3 months, will lead to neutralization at best and more likely to a Communist-controlled state. The new government is the greatest source of concern. Although Minh states that he, rather than the Committee of Generals, is making decisions, it is not clear that this is actually so. In any event, neither he nor the Committee is experienced in political administration and so far they show little talent for it. . . .

The Country Team is the second major weakness. It lacks leadership, has been poorly informed. . . . A recent example of confusion has been conflicting USOM and military recommendations. . . . Above all, Lodge has virtually no official contact with Harkins. Lodge sends in reports with major military implications without showing them to Harkins and does not show Harkins important incoming traffic. My impression is that Lodge simply does not know how to conduct a coordinated administration. This has of course been stressed to him both by Dean Rusk and myself (and also by John McCone) . . . he has just operated as a loner all his life and cannot readily change now. . . .

Viet Cong progress has been great during the period since the coup, with my best guess being that the situation has in fact been deteriorating in the countryside since July to a far greater extent than we realized because of our undue dependence on distorted Vietnamese reporting. The Viet Cong now control very high proportions of the people in certain key provinces, particularly those directly south and west of Saigon. The Strategic Hamlet Program was seriously over-extended in those provinces and the Viet Cong has been able to destroy many hamlets, while others have been abandoned or in some cases betrayed or pillaged by the government's own Self Defense Corps. In these key provinces, the Viet Cong have destroyed almost all major roads and are collecting taxes at will. . . . This gloomy picture prevails predominantly in the provinces and around the capital and in the Delta. . . .

> — Secretary of Defense Robert S. McNamara,
> memorandum to President Lyndon B.
> Johnson, December 21, 1963

Now let's be real tough.

> — Secretary of Defense Robert S. McNamara,
> quoted by *Time*, December 27, 1963

Created, financed, and defended by Americans, the Saigon regime was less a government than an act of the American will—an artificial military bureaucracy that since the beginning of the Diem regime had governed no one and represented no one except on occasion the northern Catholics. The U.S. attempt to polarize the Vietnamese between Communists and non-Communists made as much sense as an attempt to polarize the American people between Southerners and Catholics. . . . The period from 1963 to the spring of 1965 demonstrated clearly enough that American-supported governments corresponded to no internal political forces. After a dozen coups and counter-coups, the Ky junta was not even the leadership of the army, but a group of officers who happened to be occupying the Armed Forces Headquarters at the time of the American military intervention.

> — Frances FitzGerald, *Fire in the Lake*

The U.S. . . . is committed . . . to win out there. This is an unshakeable commitment. . . . The Vietnamese . . . have shown that they want to reject these Communists, they want nothing of neutralism. And we are absolutely firm in that commitment to stand by this. Neutralism is something that will not [work] for South Vietnam. Our intention is to support the Vietnamese to a victory against the Viet Cong. The war—we have had a lot of progress here. . . . In the coastal provinces, in the mountain regions, it has gone very well. The security is much improved. In fact, it has gone better than we dared hope. It is a . . . problem that I certainly think we can deal with. . . . It has been amazing, the wave of popular support for the revolutionary military committee. In fact, I would think that the danger is that the people are so enthusiastic in their support that it is going to be hard for anyone to fulfill all the expectations. . . . They certainly have been moving in the right direction, they certainly have the support of the people. . . . I am hopeful. . . . I think we are making encouraging progress. . . . A victory . . . I am confident that it will come about.

> — Assistant Secretary of State for Far Eastern Affairs Roger Hilsman, Jr., *Face the Nation*, CBS, December 29, 1963

DEAR GENERAL MINH:

. . . I want to wish you . . . success. . . . The United States will continue to furnish you . . . the fullest measure of support. . . . We shall maintain in Viet-Nam American personnel and material as needed to assist you in achieving victory. . . . The United States Government shares the view of your government that "neutralization" of South Viet-Nam is unacceptable. . . . Under your leadership your people may win a victory. . . .

> Sincerely,
> LYNDON B. JOHNSON

> — President Lyndon B. Johnson, message to General Duong Van Minh, chairman, Military Revolutionary Council, Vietnam, December 31, 1963

1964–1968

Neutralization of South Vietnam would only be another name for a Communist takeover. . . . We shall maintain in Vietnam American personnel and material as needed to assist you in achieving victory. . . . As the forces of your government become increasingly capable of dealing with this aggression, American military personnel . . . can be progressively withdrawn.

> — President Lyndon B. Johnson, New Year's
> message to General Duong Van Minh, chief of
> state, South Vietnam, January 1, 1964

Most defeatist voices will no doubt find their echoes on Capitol Hill, as soon as Congress reconvenes.

> — Joseph Alsop, syndicated column,
> January 3, 1964

I've got on my watch the Golden Rule: "Do unto others as you would have them do unto you."

> — President Lyndon B. Johnson,
> quoted by *U.S. News & World Report*,
> January 6, 1964

TOP SECRET

National Security Action Memorandum No. 273 makes clear the resolve of the President to ensure victory. . . . In order to achieve that victory, the Joint Chiefs of Staff are of the opinion that the United States must . . . commit additional U.S. forces, as necessary, in support of the combat action within South Vietnam [and] commit U.S. forces as necessary in direct actions against North Vietnam . . . to enhance our position in Southeast Asia. The past few months have disclosed that considerably higher levels of effort are demanded of us if U.S. objectives are to be attained.

> — General Maxwell D. Taylor, chairman,
> Joint Chiefs of Staff, to Secretary of
> Defense Robert S. McNamara, January 22,
> 1964

We continue to be hopeful that we will be able to complete the training responsibilities of many of the United States personnel now in Vietnam and gradually withdraw them over the period between now and the end of 1965.

> — Secretary of Defense Robert S. McNamara, testimony before House Armed Services Committee, January 27, 1964

I have attended your General Staff College at Ft. Leavenworth, Kansas. . . . I have no personal ambitions. I am a soldier. But if the people ask me to serve, I will obey—not for myself, for them. I only want to serve, as I served Diem. I was sorry that we had to kill him. I cried.

> — General Ton That Dinn, minister of security, South Vietnam, general who led raids against Buddhists, former military governor of Saigon when President Ngo Dinh Diem declared martial law, *Look*, January 28, 1964

A start could be made in reducing the number of U.S. military personnel in Vietnam as their training missions were completed.

> — Secretary of Defense Robert S. McNamara, January 30, 1964

The armed forces . . . are determined to sweep away the Communists and the Vietnamese traitors who advocate neutrality . . . to achieve the final victory quickly.

> — Major General Nguyen Khanh, at time of his military *coup d'état,* January 30, 1964

I think that the present course we are conducting is the only answer . . . and I think that the operations should be stepped up there.

> — President Lyndon B. Johnson, February 1, 1964

Obviously we cannot retreat from our position in Vietnam. . . . It is a difficult situation, to say the least. But we are in to the tune of some $350 million. I think the last figure I have seen indicates that we have over 15,500 military out there, ostensibly as advisors and that sort of thing. We are not supposed to have combatant troops. . . . But we are going to have to muddle through for awhile and see what we do, even though it costs us $1.5 million a day. . . . There is some hope that the new military leaders, who are allegedly at least very much in our corner and definitely pro-American, will give a better account of themselves than we got from the coup. . . . If they don't, then of course we will have to take another tack in the matter, but we can not certainly let it go down the drain. . . . If Vietnam went down the drain, it could conceivably cost us all of Southeast Asia.

> — Senator Everett M. Dirksen, Republican of
> Illinois, Senate Minority Leader, *Meet the
> Press*, NBC, February 2, 1964

General Khanh boasted he had ten million dollars and could flee to lead a life of ease if he wanted to.

> — *New York Herald Tribune*, February 3, 1964

I am hopeful we can bring back additional numbers of men. . . . This is a war the Vietnamese must fight. . . . I don't believe we can take on that combat task for them.

> — Secretary of Defense Robert S. McNamara,
> February 3, 1964

The U.S. still hopes to withdraw most of its troops from South Vietnam before the end of 1965.

> — Secretary of Defense Robert S. McNamara,
> February 19, 1964

Our men in Vietnam are there . . . to keep a promise that was made 12 years ago.

> — President Lyndon B. Johnson,
> February 23, 1964

The New Year will bring the mobilization of all our forces to foil the Viet Cong.

> — Lieutenant General Nguyen Khanh,
> quoted by *Newsweek*, February 24, 1964

The resources and the capabilities are there to get this job done.

> — Secretary of State Dean Rusk,
> February 24, 1964

I do not think that the speculation that has been made that we should enter into a neutralization of that area, or that we are losing the fight in that area, or that things have gone to pot out there, are at all justified. I think that they do our cause a disservice, but we are keeping in close touch with it daily. . . . We feel that we are following the proper course.

> — President Lyndon B. Johnson,
> news conference, International Treaty Room,
> State Department, February 29, 1964

In testimony released last week by the House Armed Services Committee, Gen. Maxwell D. Taylor, chairman of the Joint Chiefs of Staff, attacked "defeatists" in the U.S. press and insisted that the war "can be and will be won." Secretary of Defense Robert S. McNamara agreed, adding that the U.S. still hopes to have its training mission in South Vietnam accomplished and most of its 15,500 military advisers withdrawn by 1965. . . . "No matter what happens," said one State Department official last week, "we will not be cowed."

> — *Newsweek*, March 2, 1964

On February 18, Secretary of Defense McNamara's views came to light. He was quoted as telling Congressmen most U.S. forces could be withdrawn from Vietnam by the end of '65.

> — *U.S. News & World Report*, March 2, 1964

From South Vietnam . . . we have called back approximately 1,000 people. . . . From time to time, as our training mission is completed, other people will be withdrawn.

> — President Lyndon B. Johnson,
> March 7, 1964

There is no question of the United States' abandoning Vietnam. . . . We shall stay for as long as it takes . . . to win the battle.

> — Secretary of Defense Robert S. McNamara,
> on arrival in Saigon, March 8, 1964

CBS CORRESPONDENT DAVE DUGAN: This morning Secretary McNamara said in Saigon that we will stay in Vietnam as long as necessary to defeat the Communist guerrillas.
GOVERNOR NELSON ROCKEFELLER: Well, now this is excellent. This is a new position.

> — Governor Nelson Rockefeller, Republican of
> New York, *Face the Nation*, CBS, March 8,
> 1964

General Khanh and his government are acting vigorously and effectively. They have produced a sound central plan for the prosecution of the war.

> — White House statement, based on report of
> Secretary of Defense McNamara and JCS
> Chairman Taylor after March 13 return from
> 5-day inspection trip to Vietnam, released
> March 17, 1964

I did not talk to a single official who was unable to agree that, if the proper effort is made, the war can be won.

> — Secretary of Defense Robert S. McNamara,
>   reporting on visit to South Vietnam,
>   March 13, 1964

TOP SECRET

Substantial reductions in the number of U.S. military training personnel should be possible before the end of 1965. However . . . the situation has unquestionably been growing worse. . . . Large groups of the population are now showing signs of apathy and indifference, and there are some signs of frustration within the U.S. contingent. . . . The ARVN and paramilitary desertion rates . . . are high and increasing. Draft dodging is high while the Viet Cong are recruiting energetically and effectively. The morale of the hamlet militia and the Self Defense Corps . . . is poor and failing. In the last 90 days the weakening of the government's position has been particularly noticeable. . . . The greatest weakness in the present situation is the uncertain viability of the Khanh government. Khanh . . . does not yet have wide political appeal and his control of the army itself is uncertain. . . . On the positive side, we have found many reasons for encouragement in the performance of the Khanh Government to date.

> — Secretary of Defense Robert S. McNamara,
>   memorandum to President Lyndon B.
>   Johnson, March 16, 1964

General Khanh and his government are acting vigorously and effectively. They have produced a sound central plan for the prosecution of the war. . . . General Khanh has informed us that he proposes in the near future to put into effect a National Mobilization Plan. . . . Steps are required to bring up . . . the pay and status of the paramilitary forces and to create a highly trained guerrilla force that can beat the Viet Cong on its own ground. . . . Significant additional equipment is proposed for the air forces, the river navy, and the mobile forces. . . . This program will involve substantial increases in cost. . . . The policy should continue of withdrawing U.S. personnel where their roles can be assumed by South Vietnamese. . . . Secretary McNamara and General Taylor reported their overall conclusion that with continued vigorous leadership from General Khanh and his government . . . the situation can be significantly improved in the coming months.

> — White House statement, based on
>   McNamara-Taylor report to President Lyndon
>   B. Johnson and National Security Council,
>   March 17, 1964

TOP SECRET

I am asking State to have Bill Bundy make sure that you get our latest planning documents on ways of applying pressure against the North. . . . On dealing with de Gaulle, I continue to think it may be valuable for you to go to Paris after Bohlen has made his first try. . . . Your mission is precisely for the purpose of knocking down the idea of neutralization wherever it rears its ugly head and on this point I think that nothing is more important than to stop neutralist talk wherever we can by whatever means we can. I have made this point myself to Mansfield and Lippmann and I expect you to use every public opportunity to restate our position firmly. You may want to convey our concern on this point to General Khanh and get his ideas on the best possible joint program to stop such talk in Saigon, in Washington, and in Paris.

> — President Lyndon B. Johnson, cablegram
> to Ambassador Henry Cabot Lodge in Saigon,
> March 20, 1964

Speaking from a platform hard by the storied Perfume River [in Hué], Defense Secretary McNamara vowed continued U.S. military aid to South Viet Nam "now and forever."

> — *Time*, March 20, 1964

We have reaffirmed U.S. support . . . for as long as it takes. . . . Prime Minister Khanh intends . . . to mobilize. . . . We intend to leave an independent and stable South Vietnam, rich with resources and bright prospects.

> — Secretary of Defense Robert S. McNamara,
> March 26, 1964

We are confident these plans point the way to victory.

> — Secretary of Defense Robert S. McNamara,
> March 1964

The United States cannot afford any more compromises with the Communists, whether called neutralization or something else.

> — Richard M. Nixon, Phu My, South Vietnam,
> April 2, 1964

Vietnam is now, I think, actually emerging from the twilight. . . . There are today good reasons for faith. . . . The downward spiral . . . has been arrested. . . . The back of the snake will have been broken. . . . There are able province chiefs. . . . The new Prime Minister, Nguyen Khanh, appears to be a man of impressive ability. . . . The government is strengthening the militia. . . . We have organized for military success. . . . We must not be easily discouraged. . . . If we and the Vietnamese persist . . . we will win. . . . We oppose neutralism for Vietnam. . . . I would not be surprised to see the Mekong Delta totally cleared of Communist guerrilla forces by the end of 1965. . . . If we in America are persistent, the outlook is good. . . . There is no substitute for force and the will to use it.

> — Ambassador Henry Cabot Lodge,
> quoted by *Life*, April 17, 1964

We have got to take some action that will actually force the Viet Cong to give up the fight.

> — Senator Barry Goldwater, Republican of
> Arizona, April 18, 1964

In Viet-Nam the Communists today try . . . guerrilla warfare. . . . This, too, will prove futile. . . . The fighting spirit of South Viet-Nam is a reality. . . . There is an old American saying that "when the going gets tough, the tough get going." . . . No negotiated settlement in Viet-Nam is possible, as long as the Communists hope to achieve victory by force. Once war seems hopeless, then peace may be possible. . . . We have entered a new arena. The door has closed behind us, and the old stage has passed into history. . . . There is no turning.

> — President Lyndon B. Johnson, address to AP,
> New York City, April 20, 1964, published by
> State Department

In Saigon . . . I was encouraged . . . pacification is moving ahead . . . good progress is being made. . . . I must say the overwhelming impression I got in South Viet-Nam was that that country could be a gleaming country if only it had peace. . . . General Khanh himself is an impressive man. He shows great vigor and understanding. . . . He is on the right track, and he is making good progress. We believe that the prospect there is that there can be steady improvement . . . we can go ahead now. . . . So I came back encouraged from my trip.

> — Secretary of State Dean Rusk,
> April 20, 1964

Given time and the support he must have, General Khanh seems likely to make a real effort.

> — *Atlantic Monthly*, April 1964

2 percent of the landowners hold 45 percent of the land, and 72 percent hold 15 percent.

> — Bernard B. Fall,
> *The Two Vietnams*, 1964

I'd drop a low-yield atomic bomb on the Chinese supply lines in North Vietnam.

> — Senator Barry Goldwater,
> quoted in *Look*, April 21, 1964

General Khanh is on the right track and the situation has shown steady improvement.

> — Secretary of State Dean Rusk,
> April 21, 1964

KHANH QUITTING

> — Headline, *New York Times*, April 21, 1964

If Khanh goes, the President is going to have to get another Secretary of Defense.

> — Secretary of Defense Robert S. McNamara,
> Washington cocktail party, quoted by *Time*,
> April 24, 1964

It is inconceivable that the Vietcong could ever defeat the armed forces of South Vietnam.

> — General William C. Westmoreland,
> U.S. commander, Vietnam, April 25, 1964

In Viet-Nam, I talked at length with General Khanh and his colleagues, as well as with Ambassador Lodge, General Harkins, and other members of our American team. These talks reinforced my confidence in the will and the ability of the Government of the Republic of Viet-Nam to lead the people of that country to victory. . . . South Viet-Nam made great economic and social progress. . . . I saw at first hand that progress. . . . The Viet Cong have scored some gains in the last few months. . . . General Khanh's objective is not only to "clear" but to "hold." With American assistance, he is moving ahead. . . . I believe his efforts are beginning to show results. We can all take deep pride in the performance of the American military men. . . . We should also take pride in our civilian officials and their families.

> — Secretary of State Dean Rusk, address,
> Valparaiso, Ind., April 25, 1964, as published
> by State Department

I frankly don't think they have gained in the Delta. . . . You have the Government forces giving a really good account of themselves in two or three fights down there. . . . The Government forces fought extraordinarily well. . . . We have studied this very carefully and we are

continuing to do so. . . . It will be better to win the war on present lines
which we still believe can be done. . . . I would say that we have
certainly arrested the downward trend. . . . It has levelled out. . . . The
present advisory relationship works remarkably well. The strategic
hamlets . . . will produce lasting results.

> — Assistant Secretary of State for Far Eastern
> Affairs William P. Bundy, *Issues & Answers*,
> ABC, May 3, 1964

My solution? Tell the Vietnamese they've got to draw in their horns
. . . or we're going to bomb them back into the Stone Age.

> — General Curtis E. LeMay, chief of staff,
> U.S. Air Force, May 6, 1964

Now things are going to be settled one way or the other in Viet Nam;
Westy won't let things drift along. He won't mope around about it.

> — General James Gavin, former deputy chief of
> staff, U.S. Army, quoted by *Time*, May 8, 1964

We have a promising policy. . . . The biggest asset on our side, I
think, is the demonstrated will of the South Vietnamese people to fight.
. . . We are trying . . . to help them to carry on that fight. I think we are
going to succeed. . . .

> — Under Secretary of State George W. Ball,
> *Issues & Answers*, ABC, May 10, 1964

We have brought two million back under control already. We have
raised the army's pay and the civil guard's pay, and the self-defense
force's. We are making progress. First we must restore stability and
confidence; then we shall go forward.

> — General Nguyen Khanh, quoted by Joseph
> Alsop,
> syndicated column, May 11, 1964

The plans which the Government of Vietnam has developed . . . will
lead to success. . . . The number [of U.S. personnel] is not likely to
increase.

> — Secretary of Defense Robert S. McNamara,
> May 14, 1964

Minh actually had been doing pretty well. We had a couple of good
days out in the provinces, and people were beginning to respond to him.
I actually thought I could see daylight ahead.

> — Ambassador Henry Cabot Lodge, referring to
> coup overthrowing Duong Van Minh, quoted
> in *Time*, May 15, 1964

A new government under Prime Minister Khanh has come to power, bringing new energy and leadership and new hope for effective action. I share with Ambassador Lodge the conviction that this new government can mount a successful campaign. . . . In March, Prime Minister Khanh declared his intention to mobilize his nation. This intention has now been confirmed by . . . expanding the Vietnamese army, civil guard, civil defense corps, and police forces. . . . These and other measures . . . will require an increase of about 40 percent in Viet Nam's domestic budget. . . . We must share the increased costs. . . . I strongly urge the Congress to provide the additional $125 million to Viet Nam, and to appropriate the full $3,517 million now required.

> — President Lyndon B. Johnson,
> Message to Congress, May 18, 1964

There is no hope for mankind if we continue to use jungle law of military might which the United States is using in South Viet Nam to try to win a peace, where no longer in history can you win a peace through war.

> — Senator Wayne Morse, Democrat of Oregon,
> *Face the Nation*, CBS, May 24, 1964

South Vietnam, in my opinion, lacks decision and the decision has to be made sooner or later, or we are not going to win down there. . . . Defoliation of the forests by low-yield atomic weapons could well be done.

> — Senator Barry Goldwater, Republican of
> Arizona, *Issues & Answers*, ABC, May 24, 1964

The President . . . told me in May 1965 that he had made the decision to bomb . . . four months before Pleiku.

> — Charles Roberts, *LBJ's Inner Circle*

America keeps her word. We are steadfast in a policy which has been followed for 10 years in three administrations. . . . Our commitment today is just the same as the commitment made by President Eisenhower to President Diem in 1954.

> — President Lyndon B. Johnson,
> news conference, June 2, 1964

A unit of Vietnamese soldiers, sent to take a Vietcong-controlled village near the Cambodian border, landed by helicopter. The village had been bombarded from the air and the soldiers met no resistance. They found no men except old men helping the women put out the fires. . . .

They flushed 43 guerrillas hiding in dugouts, dragged them out and set about learning where their weapons were hidden. The Vietnamese commander whipped the captives with a bamboo cane and booted them as they lay trussed on the ground. The women and children watched the torture of their husbands and fathers with steady faces. The guerrillas were jackknifed into position of agony. They were held under the river's surface and tortured with water that was forced into their noses. Rags were put over their faces and then water was poured over the rags. . . . Photographer Okamura protested: this seemed needless and cruel. A soldier replied, "but this is my duty." Still the prisoners would not talk.

— *Life*, June 12, 1964

Here is what we see . . . with respect to South Vietnam. . . . The United States . . . actually is, I believe, acting on behalf not only of the morality and conscience of the world, but also consonant with our own concepts of security and peace in that area. . . . It is a matter of principle.

— Ambassador Adlai E. Stevenson, U.S.
representative to UN, *Face the Nation*, CBS,
June 14, 1964

I am an optimist. I guess I was born one, and I continue to be an optimist about Vietnam.

— General Paul D. Harkins, receiving
Distinguished Service Medal at White House
ceremony as outgoing commander, Military
Assistance Command, Saigon, June 22, 1964

The United States . . . seeks no wider war.

— President Lyndon B. Johnson,
June 23, 1964

The Secretary of Defense has gone to South Vietnam four times now within recent months. And each time he has come back with a different report. Once he reported the American boys would be out of there in 1965. The next report was that we would be there for a long, long time. The next report was that we did not need to step up our military commitments. The next report was that he requested $200,000,000 additional to step up the fighting in South Vietnam. We were a party, under this Administration, to a coup which overthrew the Diem government and was handled so very badly that the President and his brother were murdered and now, after poor Madame Nhu has lost her husband and brother-in-law, they were afraid to let her have a visa here because she herself would be a danger to the security of the United

States. . . . It is incredible. . . . I think it is time the American people were told what is going on in South Vietnam. We have not been so far.

> — Congressman William E. Miller, Republican of New York, chairman, Republican National Committee, *Face the Nation*, CBS, June 28, 1964

The war is being properly managed and the Vietnamese Army is in a much better position to meet the Communist insurgency than when I came here in 1962. We must keep doing what we are doing. Keep the pressure on and we can win.

> — General Paul D. Harkins, quoted by *Newsweek*, June 29, 1964

We are not in Southeast Asia for the primary purpose of keeping a treaty or helping "our friends and allies." . . . We are there to stop Communist China from obtaining the rice and other resources it must have if it is ever to become a world power.

> — General Thomas D. White, USAF (ret.), contributing editor, *Newsweek*, June 29, 1964

We're trying to get this area so that it can stand on its own two feet. . . . General Khanh . . . is a bright, able soldier . . . he recognizes the importance of politics . . . of finance, economics, he studies, he works. . . . He's in a great hurry. . . . We're defoliating every day. We're doing a lot of defoliation. . . . It's a military measure. . . . You kill the bushes and the trees and it broadens out and you can't be ambushed. . . . We ought to step up the status of our military. Well, the United States was not involved in the overthrow of the Diem regime. . . . Now, the overthrow was—of the Diem regime—was a purely Vietnamese affair. We never participated in the planning. We never gave any advice. We had nothing whatever to do with it. . . . We never did.

> — Ambassador Henry Cabot Lodge, interview, *New York Times*, June 30, 1964

1. The United States Government, through its Ambassador and CIA personnel in Saigon, maintained regular contact with the coup plotters from August 23 to 31 and from October 2 through the coup.

2. In these contacts, the United States told the plotting generals that we were prepared to withdraw support from Diem if he did not rid himself of Nhu and that we would provide direct support to the generals during any "interim" government.

3. The United States repeatedly asked to review coup plans in order to comment on them and to advise as to the probability of their success.

4. The United States engaged in a series of public actions that . . .

were also intended to encourage the plotters to act; . . . exonerated the
Vietnamese military from complicity in [Buddhist pagoda] raids . . . and
suspended aid programs that were vital to the Diem government.

5. Throughout the coup, Colonel Conein, the CIA contact man, was at
rebel headquarters with full authorization to report on the progress of the
coup to the Ambassador.

6. Diem and Nhu . . . the U.S. did little to protect, the reaction of U.S.
officials to the coup was one of extreme satisfaction. Recognition of and
cooperation with the new government began immediately after the coup.

> — Senate Foreign Relations Committee, staff
> study based on *Pentagon Papers*: "U.S.
> Involvement in the Overthrow of Diem, 1963"

I think they [the Viet Cong] have very serious problems . . . in terms
of losses . . . in terms of morale. So I am not pessimistic about the
situation. . . . I don't feel any sense of despair whatever.

> — Secretary of State Dean Rusk,
> July 1, 1964

If we in America are persistent, the outlook is good.

> — Ambassador Henry Cabot Lodge, National
> Press Club, July 1, 1964

Look for . . . a steadily increasing push for long-term gains. . . .
Now, the Red chiefs in Peiping and Hanoi may believe it when the U.S.
announces it has no intention of being pushed out of Southeast Asia.
. . . As one observer close to the Administration put it, "It's unthinkable
that the U.S. is bluffing this time."

> — *U.S. News & World Report*, July 6, 1964

They are swinging wildly. They are suffering substantial losses in their
sneak attacks.

> — President Lyndon B. Johnson,
> July 9, 1964

One thing we're going to have to do is to make up our minds that we
are going to win. . . . We should win as easily as possible, and with the
best tactics available. I don't think it would take large numbers of troops.
We could use small detachments. . . . Our people who go in there should
fight like hell. . . . If we make up our mind that our troops are really
going to fight . . . we will win. . . . We have never had a war that
couldn't be forecast years ahead.

> — Admiral Arleigh Burke (ret.), former Chief of
> Naval Operations, director, Center for
> Strategic Studies, Georgetown University,
> interview, *U.S. News & World Report*,
> July 13, 1964

The U.S. Air Force decided that by using some of its transports to drop flares on hamlets under attack it might be able to turn night into day in Vietnam. . . . Kicked out of the aircraft two at a time by the paratroopers, the flares floated gently down on their nylon parachutes, then suddenly burst into a blaze of 750,000 candlepower light. . . . That month we dropped 7,000 flares, and dispatched 225 T-28s, B-26s, and Skyraiders to defend attacked outposts. . . . Since then, significant Viet Cong attacks have dropped to an average of only two or three a night. . . . The flareships have destroyed the myth of Viet Cong in vulnerability at night.

> — *Newsweek*, July 13, 1964

Yesterday it was Korea; tonight it is Vietnam. Make no bones of this. Don't try to sweep this under the rug. We are at war in Vietnam . . . extremism in the defense of liberty is no vice . . . moderation in the pursuit of justice is no virtue.

> — Senator Barry Goldwater,
> San Francisco, July 16, 1964

We're already aiding the Vietnamese in a thousand and one ways. But let's not be satisfied when it might prove that the thousand and second way is the decisive one.

> — General Maxwell D. Taylor,
> Danang, quoted in *Time*, July 17, 1964

We are ready. We could go this afternoon. I cannot assure that all of North Vietnam would be destroyed, but Hanoi would certainly be destroyed.

> — Vice Marshal Nguyen Cao Ky, commander,
> South Vietnamese Air Force,
> *New York Times*, July 20, 1964

We do not believe in conferences called to ratify terror, so our policy is unchanged.

> — President Lyndon B. Johnson,
> news conference, July 24, 1964

Events of the last few weeks indicate that the Viet-Cong guerrillas have lost the initiative. . . . A final decision may be expected in the next six to twelve months.

> — *Los Angeles Times*, July 26, 1964

The Americans arrived [in Indochina] with their aid, their policy. . . . I believe that one can add, without hurting our American friends, that

their sense of vocation, and also their aversion to all colonial activity
which was not theirs, led them to take the place of France in Indochina.

— General Charles de Gaulle, press conference,
Elysée Palace, Paris, quoted in *Time*,
July 31, 1964

The other side got a sting out of this [the Tonkin Gulf incident]. If they
do it again they'll get another sting.

— Secretary of State Dean Rusk,
August 2, 1964

On the fate of South Vietnam depends the fate of all Asia. For South
Vietnam is the dam in the river. A Communist victory there would mean,
inevitably and soon, that the flood would begin; next would come the
loss of Laos, Cambodia, Thailand, Malaysia and Indonesia. . . . All that
is needed, in short, is the will to win—and the courage to use our
power—now.

— Former Vice President Richard M. Nixon,
Reader's Digest, August 1964

In Tonkin Bay . . . our Navy defended itself in this unprovoked
attack and did it in a very admirable and creditable manner. That's
about all, Mr. Niven, that I learned about it. . . . I believe that our
government is being very frank with the American people. The President
is deeply concerned with the situation in South Vietnam. . . . We have a
commitment there. . . . We have a commitment that we are going to
sustain. We are not going to withdraw; we are not going to let this part of
the world be overrun. . . . Mr. Niven, my briefing was so limited, as you
know, just prior to the program, that I have had very little opportunity to
get more information than is on the ticker. But let me say this: a great
world power such as the United States . . . is . . . able to meet these
crises. . . . I believe that we have that capability.

— Senator Hubert H. Humphrey,
Vice-Presidential candidate,
Face the Nation, CBS, August 2, 1964

I have asked for this urgent meeting to bring to the attention of the
Security Council acts of deliberate aggression by the Hanoi regime
against naval units of the United States . . . in the Gulf of Tonkin. . . .
As President Johnson said last night, "We still seek no wider war." . . .
The mission of the United States is peace. Under the explicit instructions
of President Johnson, I want to repeat that assurance in the Security
Council this afternoon: Our mission is peace. . . . We are dealing here

with a regime that has not yet learned the lesson that aggression does not pay.

> — Ambassador Adlai E. Stevenson, U.S.
> representative to UN, August 5, 1964

These latest actions of the North Vietnamese regime [in Tonkin Gulf] have given a new and grave turn to the already serious situation. . . . Our policy in Southeast Asia has been consistent and unchanged since 1954. . . . America keeps her word. . . . The United States intends no rashness, and seeks no wider war. . . . I recommend a resolution expressing the support of the Congress for all necessary action to protect our Armed Forces and to assist all nations covered by the SEATO Treaty. . . . I urge the Congress to enact such a resolution promptly and thus to give convincing evidence . . . that our policy in Southeast Asia will be carried forward.

> — President Lyndon B. Johnson,
> Message to Congress, August 5, 1964

I do not think there is any substance to the fear that the South Vietnamese may lead us down a road that we do not wish to travel.

> — Senator J. William Fulbright, chairman,
> Senate Foreign Relations Committee,
> speech in U.S. Senate, August 7, 1964

In the case of Vietnam, it [President Johnson's ordering the North Vietnam mainland bombed] was a matter of responding to a direct attack on our ships. The escalation came from the enemy. . . . It is difficult for me to see how they [the North Vietnamese] could possibly gain anything from it. . . . It may be that they were bored. Sometimes, they say, this is what moves people.

> — Senator Eugene J. McCarthy, Democrat of
> Minnesota, *Face the Nation*, CBS,
> August 9, 1964

Whereas naval units of the Communist regime in Vietnam, in violation of the principles of the Charter of the United Nations and of international law, have deliberately and repeatedly attacked United States naval vessels lawfully present in international waters, and have thereby created a serious threat to international peace; and . . .

Whereas the United States is assisting the peoples of Southeast Asia to protect their freedom. . . . Now, therefore, be it

Resolved by the Senate and the House of Representatives of the United States of America in Congress assembled, That the Congress approves and supports the determination of the President, as Commander in Chief, to take all necessary measures to repel any armed attack against the forces of the United States and to prevent further aggression . . . the United States is, therefore, prepared, as the President determines, to take all necessary steps, including the use of armed force, to assist any member or protocol state of the Southeast Asia Collective Defense Treaty requesting assistance in defense of its freedom.

> — Southeast Asia Resolution (Gulf of Tonkin Resolution), August 10, 1964

TOP SECRET

The basis of this report [is] the results of a country-wide canvass of responsible U.S. advisors and observers. . . . In broad terms, the canvass results are surprisingly optimistic. . . . In terms of equipment and training, the VC are better armed and led today than ever in the past. VC infiltration continues from Laos and Cambodia. No indication that the VC are experiencing any difficulty in replacing their losses in men and equipment. . . . For the present, the Khanh government has the necessary military support to stay in power. It is estimated that Khanh has a 50/50 chance of lasting out the year. The government is ineffective, beset by inexperienced ministers who are jealous and suspicious of each other. Khanh does not have confidence or trust in most of his ministers and is not able to form them into a group with a common loyalty and purpose. There is no one in sight to replace Khanh. . . . The population is confused and apathetic. Khanh has not succeeded in building active popular support in Saigon. . . . Extensive intelligence programs are underway to improve our intelligence capability by the end of the year. . . . U.S. MISSION OBJECTIVES: Do everything possible to bolster the Khanh Government. Improve the in-country pacification campaign against the VC. . . . Undertake "show-window" social and economic projects in secure urban and rural areas. Be prepared to implement contingency plans against North Vietnam with optimum readiness by January 1, 1965.

> — Ambassador Maxwell D. Taylor, first mission report from Saigon, transmitted by Col. A. R. Brownfield to Secretary McNamara, General Wheeler, chairman, JCS, and Deputy Defense Secretary Cyrus R. Vance, August 10, 1964

In Viet-Nam, too, we work for world order. . . . Let no one doubt for a moment that we have the resources and the will to follow this course as long as it may take. No one should think for a moment that we will be worn down, nor will we be driven out, and we will not be provoked into rashness.

> — President Lyndon B. Johnson,
> August 12, 1964

"Business as usual" was the word passed by several U.S. firms operating in South Vietnam in early August. . . . "Our man in Saigon has shown no worry so far," according to one American company.

> — *U.S. News & World Report*, August 17, 1964

China is not a nuclear power and will not be an effective one for years, if not decades. . . . Let the Chinese Communists beware.

> — Major General Max S. Johnson (ret.), former
> planner, Joint Chiefs of Staff, now with *U.S.
> News & World Report*, interview there, August
> 17, 1964

The crucial hour has struck. The coming weeks will decide the destiny of our country.

> — Premier Nguyen Khanh, first formal
> appearance, Dien Hong Palace, Saigon,
> announcing state of emergency and imposition
> of martial law, *Newsweek*, August 17, 1964

TOP SECRET

The present in-country pacification plan is not enough in itself to maintain national morale or to offer reasonable hope of eventual success. Something must be added in the coming months. . . . A second objective in this period is the maintenance of morale in South Viet Nam particularly within the Khanh Government. . . . We should express our willingness to Khanh to engage in planning and eventually to exert intense pressure on North Viet Nam.

> — U.S. Mission, Saigon, cablegram to State
> Department, August 18, 1964

TOP SECRET

The Joint Chiefs of Staff . . . consider . . . an accelerated program of actions with respect to the DRV is essential to prevent a complete collapse of the U.S. position in Southeast Asia. Additionally, they do not agree that we should be slow to get deeply involved. . . . The U.S. is already deeply involved. The Joint Chiefs of Staff consider that only significantly stronger military measures on the DRV are likely to provide the relief and psychological boost necessary. . . .

> — Joint Chiefs of Staff, memorandum to
> Secretary of Defense Robert S. McNamara,
> August 26, 1964

The strength of your country . . . is greater than any adversary's. . . . It is greater than the combined might of all the nations in all the wars in all the history of this planet. And . . . our superiority is growing.

> — President Lyndon B. Johnson, Address to
> Nation, August 27, 1964

Last week General Nguyen Khanh promoted himself from Premier to President and took over virtually absolute power. . . . Asked whether he was now a dictator, Khanh replied quizzically: "For six months I have been head of a totalitarian regime without being totalitarian. I can head a dictatorial regime without being a dictator."

> — *Time*, August 28, 1964

Peasant attitudes appear to be turning against the Viet Cong. . . . The South Vietnamese will support their Government. . . . The military situation . . . appears to have stabilized. . . . Government forces have shown particular improvement. . . . It is not true that Viet Cong morale and motivation are always high. There are many reports of low morale. . . . Many Viet Cong in the lower ranks undoubtedly serve because of fear.

> — State Department, *Viet-Nam: The Struggle for
> Freedom*, August 1964

TOP SECRET

The situation in South Vietnam is deteriorating. . . . The government sank into confusion last week. . . . War weariness was apparent. . . . The objective of the United States is to reverse the downward trend. Failing that, the alternative objective is to emerge from the situation with as good an image as possible. . . . We must in any event keep hard at work . . . to press the presently visible leaders to get a real government in action. . . . New initiatives might include action: to establish a U.S. naval base, perhaps at Danang; to embark on a major project to pacify one province adjacent to Saigon . . . to enlarge significantly the U.S. military role in the pacification program inside South Vietnam—e.g., large numbers of U.S. special forces, divisions of regular combat troops, U.S. air, etc., to "interlard" with or take over functions of geographical areas from the South Vietnamese armed forces. . . . There is a chance that the downward trend can be reversed . . . if [there are] actions outside the borders of South Vietnam but [not] the kind of military action which would be difficult to justify to the American public. . . . While the above course of action is being pursued, we should watch for other DRV actions which would justify [words illegible]. Among such DRV actions might be the following: . . . VC attacks (e.g., by mortars) on, or take-over of, air fields on which U.S. aircraft are deployed (likely). Some barbaric act of terrorism which inflames U.S. and world opinion (unlikely). . . . Throughout the scenario, we should be alert to chances to . . . back the DRV down, so South Vietnam can be pacified. . . . If worst comes and South Vietnam disintegrates . . . to "disown" South Vietnam, hopefully leaving the image of "a patient who died despite the extraordinary efforts of a good doctor." . . . The relevant "audiences" of U.S. actions are the Communists . . . our allies . . . and the U.S. public (who must support our risk-taking with lives and prestige).

> — Assistant Secretary of Defense John T.
> McNaughton, memorandum,
> September 3, 1964

We seek no wider war. . . . We would, therefore, prefer to pursue the policy we are pursuing of maximum assistance in South Viet-Nam.

> — Assistant Secretary of State for Far Eastern
> Affairs William P. Bundy, *Department of State
> Bulletin*, September 7, 1964

All across the war-torn country, Buddhists and Roman Catholics attacked each other with machetes, knives, iron bars, wooden clubs, and flaming torches. . . . Buddhist leaders dislike him [Premier Major General Nguyen Khanh] because they feel he has shown too much favor to the Catholics. . . . Khanh seemed on his way out. . . . Taking over as active Premier was a new face altogether, Nguyen Xuan Oanh, 43 . . . Harvard-educated. . . .

> — *Newsweek*, September 7, 1964

TOP SECRET

This memorandum records the consensus reached in discussions between Ambassador Taylor and Secretary Rusk, Secretary McNamara and General Wheeler. . . . The GVN over the next 2–3 months will be too weak for us to take any major deliberate risks of escalation that would involve a major role for, or threat to, South Vietnam. However, escalation arising from and directed against U.S. action would tend to lift GVN morale at least temporarily. . . . The main further question is the extent to which we should add elements to the above actions that would tend deliberately to provoke a DRV reaction, and consequent retaliation by us. Example of actions to be considered would be running U.S. naval patrols increasingly close to the North Vietnamese coast. . . . We believe such deliberately provocative elements should not be added in the immediate future while the GVN is still struggling to its feet. By early October, however, we may recommend such actions depending on GVN progress. . . . The aim of the above actions, external to South Vietnam, would be to assist morale in SVN and show the Communists we still mean business. . . . There are a number of immediate-impact actions we can take, such as pay raises for the police and civil administrators.

> — Assistant Secretary of State for Far Eastern
> Affairs William P. Bundy, memorandum to
> President Lyndon B. Johnson,
> September 8, 1964

The Ambassador [Maxwell Taylor] was able to report continued progress in the field in the Vietnamese Army's fight.

> — President Lyndon B. Johnson,
> September 9, 1964

TOP SECRET

The President emphasizes again that no activity of this kind [economic programs and covert political action in Vietnam] should be delayed in any way by any feeling that our resources for these purposes are restricted. We can find the money.

> — National Security Council, top secret action
> memorandum, September 10, 1964, quoted in
> *Pentagon Papers*

TOP SECRET

The President reemphasizes the importance of economic and political actions having immediate impact in South Vietnam, such as pay raises for civilian personnel. . . . The President emphasizes again that no activity of this kind should be delayed in any way by any feeling that our resources for these purposes are restricted. We can find the money. . . . He expects that Ambassador Taylor and the country team will take most prompt and energetic action in this field. . . . The first order of business at present is to take actions which will help to strengthen the fabric of the Government of South Vietnam.

> — Presidential Adviser on National Security
> McGeorge Bundy to Secretaries McNamara
> and Rusk, September 10, 1964

I am not mentally ill. I have hemorrhoids.

> — Premier Nguyen Khanh, Dalat, South
> Vietnam, quoted by *Time*, September 11, 1964

I am sick of having Buddhists run my country.

> — General Tran Thien Khiem,
> minister of defense, South Vietnam,
> quoted by *Newsweek*, September 14, 1964

We have no intention of pulling out of South Vietnam. . . . We are carrying out the same policy. . . . This is a commitment. . . . If there is any part of the world that has been fully discussed here before the American public . . . it is South Vietnam and Southeast Asia. Fully and frankly discussed . . . I think the Administration has done that.

> — Senator Hubert H. Humphrey,
> vice-presidential candidate, *Face the Nation*,
> CBS, September 16, 1964

There is an upward trend.

> — General Maxwell D. Taylor,
> quoted by *Time*, September 18, 1964

To see freedom sent around the world, this is our mission. . . . It was God's charge to us.

> — Senator Barry Goldwater,
> quoted by *Newsweek*, September 21, 1964

We have not lost yet.

> — Roger Hilsman, quoted by *Newsweek*,
> September 21, 1964

America's military strength alone or in combination with that of our allies today adds up to the greatest aggregation of force in human history. It has been harnessed into flexible, usable power which can be controlled with remarkable precision. It is a triumph of strategy, science and human ingenuity.

> — Secretary of Defense Robert S. McNamara,
> September 22, 1964

We don't want our American boys to do the fighting for Asian boys. We don't want to get . . . tied down to a land war in Asia.

> — President Lyndon B. Johnson,
> September 25, 1964

We are not going North and drop bombs at this stage of the game, and we are not going South and run out. . . . We still have our problems in Vietnam. Every day some one jumps up and says, "Tell us what is happening in Vietnam and why are we in Vietnam, and how did you get us into Vietnam?" Well, I didn't get you into Vietnam. You have been in Vietnam 10 years. . . . And we have now had four or five governments [in Vietnam] in the last year. I can't tell you who runs the Government here, much less who runs it in Vietnam. . . . Well, I wish we never did have a crisis. I would like to play with my radio or go to a football game, or go out in my speedboat. There are a lot of things I would like to do. . . . Now we have lost 190 American lives. . . . I welcome this involvement. It may bring danger but it brings an added dimension to the prospects for freedom.

> — President Lyndon B. Johnson,
> Manchester, N.H., September 28, 1964

Once the Vietcong and Hanoi have been convinced that their attempt at aggression is doomed to failure, they will stop.

> — Ambassador Henry Cabot Lodge,
> USIS television interview,
> Saigon, September 1964

If South Vietnam falls, the rest of Southeast Asia will be in grave danger of progressively disappearing behind the Bamboo Curtain.

> — Assistant Secretary of State for Far Eastern
> Affairs William P. Bundy, Tokyo,
> September 29, 1964

The land spreads out flat and open, but the villages are usually built about 30 yards inside treelines. These are the Asian equivalent of Normandy hedgerows; they offer excellent protection, and camouflage is one of the military arts that the Vietcong practice to perfection. When they arrive in a hamlet for the night, they will immediately prepare perfect defensive positions along the treeline. "You can never tell our Air Force that," one Vietnamese colonel said. "The Air Force always wants to bomb the hamlet. You tell them, 'Bomb the treeline, the VC are always in the treeline,' and they pay no attention at all. The French were the same way; they always bombed the hamlet, too."

> — David Halberstam, *The Making of a Quagmire*

At first they felt sick and had some diarrhea, then they began to feel it hard to breathe and they had low blood pressure; some serious cases had trouble with their optic nerves and went blind. Pregnant women gave birth to stillborn or premature children. Most of the affected cattle died . . . river fish floated on the surface of the water belly up, soon after the chemicals were spread.

> — Cao Van Nguyen, M.D., report following U.S.
> chemical attack on area of 2,500 acres with
> approximately 1,000 inhabitants, near Saigon,
> October 3, 1964

Crisis in North Vietnam is as bad, if not worse, as in the South. Economic collapse is close. . . . Food shortages are critical. . . . People are starving to death. . . . Industry is sagging, short of parts, raw materials. Morale is low.

> — *U.S. News & World Report*, October 5, 1964

If Southeast Asia is allowed to fall, it will trigger a big war to save the Philippines.

> — Former Vice President Richard M. Nixon,
> Salisbury, N.C., October 10, 1964

With our help, the people of South Vietnam can defeat Communist aggression.

> — President Lyndon B. Johnson,
> Mall Shopping Center, Bergen, N.J.,
> October 14, 1964

The most valuable and realistic gift that Americans can give Vietnam is to concentrate above everything else on helping the Vietnamese leadership.

> — Major General Edward G. Lansdale,
> *Foreign Affairs*, October 1964

General Khanh now has only two weeks more in which to turn his disparate coalition of Buddhists and young army officers into a workable civilian government. If he fails, there are several power groups waiting in the wings—most notably a band of militant, mainly Roman Catholic army officers led by General Khiem and Col. Pham Ngoc Thao. . . . This group, which strongly opposes Khanh's concessions to the Buddhists, was all set to unseat the Premier a month ago.

> — *Newsweek*, October 19, 1964

The Communist offensive in the underdeveloped areas will fail.

> — Presidential Assistant for National Security,
> Walt W. Rostow, 1964

We are not about to send American boys nine or ten thousand miles away from home to do what Asian boys ought to be doing for themselves.

> — President Lyndon B. Johnson,
> Akron, Ohio, October 21, 1964

Adding up the recent news from Vietnam, one is tempted to conclude that our side is at last winning the war there. . . . The incoming tide seems to have reached full flood but has not yet started to recede.

> — Kenneth Crawford, column, *Newsweek*,
> October 25, 1965

TOP SECRET

Bien Hoa may be repeated at any time. This would tend to force our hand, but would also give us a good springboard for any decision for stronger action. The President is clearly thinking in terms of maximum use of a Gulf of Tonkin rationale . . . an action that would show toughness. . . . We probably do not need additional Congressional authority, even if we decide on very strong action. . . . A Presidential statement with the rationale for action is high on any check list. . . . To prepare a climate for an action statement is probably indicated. . . . We should probably consult with the U.K., Australia, New Zealand, and possibly Thailand. . . . We would hope for firm moral support from the U.K. and for participation in at least token form from the others. . . . We should consult the Philippines a day or so before such action but not necessarily before we have made up our minds. . . . For negative reasons, France probably deserves VIP treatment. . . . World-wide, we should select reasonably friendly chiefs of state for special treatment seeking their sympathy and support, and should arm all our representatives with the rationale and defense of our action whether individual reprisal or broader. USIA must be brought into the planning process not later than early next week, so that it is getting the right kind of materials ready for all our information media, on a contingency basis. The same [word illegible] true of CIA's outlets.

> — William P. Bundy, Assistant Secretary of State
> for Far Eastern Affairs, November 5, 1964

TOP SECRET

The situation in South Vietnam is deteriorating. Unless new actions are taken, the new government will probably be unstable and ineffectual, and the VC will probably continue to extend high hold over the population and territory. It can be expected that soon (6 months? two years?), (a) government officials at all levels will adjust their behavior to an eventual VC take-over, (b) defections of significant military forces will take place, (c) whole integrated regions of the country will be totally denied to the GVN, (d) neutral and/or left-wing elements will enter the government, (e) a popular front regime will emerge which will invite the dummy

U.S. out, and (f) fundamental concessions to the VC and accommodations to the DRV will put South Vietnam behind the Curtain.

— John T. McNaughton, Assistant Secretary of Defense for International Security Affairs, memorandum, "Action for South Vietnam," November 6, 1964

Our present tendency is to adopt a tougher program both privately and publicly against them. . . . We should start in January a slowly graduating military action on Hanoi.

— Secretary of State Dean Rusk, cablegram to General Maxwell D. Taylor in Saigon, November 8, 1964

It is time to stand firm . . . in Vietnam.

— Richard M. Nixon, *Reader's Digest*, November 1964

We have no plans at present to send combat troops to South Vietnam.

— Secretary of Defense Robert S. McNamara, Austin, Texas, November 10, 1964

TOP SECRET

Following our conversation of last night I am concerned that too much thought is being given to the actual damage we do in the North, not enough thought to the signal we wish to send. The signal consists of . . . we are ready and able to go much further . . . we are ready and able to meet any level of escalation they might mount in response . . . I am convinced we should not go forward into the next stage without a U.S. ground commitment of some kind. . . . They should feel they now confront an LBJ who has made up his mind.

— Walt W. Rostow, chairman, Department of State Policy Planning Council, personal letter to Secretary of Defense Robert S. McNamara, November 16, 1964

We made a big mistake in going in there, but I can't figure out any way to get out.

— Senator Richard B. Russell, quoted in *New York Times*, November 27, 1964

The ability of the Viet Cong continuously to rebuild their units and to make good their losses is one of the mysteries of this guerrilla war. . . .

We still find no plausible explanation of the continued strength of the Viet Cong if our data on the Viet Cong losses are even approximately correct. Not only do the Viet Cong units have the recuperative powers of the phoenix, but they have an amazing ability to maintain morale.

> — General Maxwell D. Taylor,
> top secret memorandum from *Pentagon Papers*, Thanksgiving 1964

We have stopped losing the war.

> — Secretary of Defense Robert S. McNamara,
> November 29, 1964

The President today reviewed the situation in South Vietnam with Ambassador Taylor and with the Secretaries of State and Defense, the Director of Central Intelligence and the Chairman of the Joint Chiefs of Staff. Ambassador Taylor reported . . . that the new government under Prime Minister Huong was making a determined effort to strengthen national unity, to maintain law and order, and to press forward with the security program . . . to defeat the Viet Cong insurgency. The Ambassador also reported that . . . the strength of the armed forces of the government was being increased. . . . The government forces continue to inflict heavy losses on the Viet Cong. On the economic front, Ambassador Taylor noted that agricultural output was continuing to increase, with U.S. assistance in fertilizers and pesticides playing an important role.

> — White House statement, December 1, 1964

U.S. ambassador to Saigon Maxwell D. Taylor could well reflect that what once had been dubbed "McNamara's War" was now very much "Taylor's War." . . . Three years ago . . . the former four-star general presented a Taylor-made plan to the late President Kennedy urging a firm U.S. commitment to the defeat of the Viet Cong. Kennedy accepted Taylor's reasoning. . . . In little more than a year, South Vietnam has had four different governments and last week the four-week-old regime of Premier Tran Van Huong was tottering ominously. Meantime, the Viet Cong have steadily increased their strength until now they fully or partly control nearly half the country. . . . Taylor . . . made it plain that he would call for a drastic remedy: escalation of the Vietnamese fighting. . . . This was a policy which Taylor himself had opposed when he was head of the Joint Chiefs of Staff. But where he once argued that escalation made no sense unless there was a stable government in Saigon . . . he was now expected to maintain that escalation was the only way to raise the morale of Saigon's war-weary people. . . . No less ironic was the fact that, in common with the rest of Washington officialdom, Taylor presumably regarded escalation not as a means of winning the war but rather as a way to pave the ground for a negotiated settlement of it. . . . Behind Taylor on the side of escalation are Secretary of Defense Robert McNamara and McGeorge Bundy's brother William, the Assistant Secretary of State for the Far East. Even the "hawks" are not unanimous, however. John McCone, director of the Central Intelligence Agency and normally a hawk, has made it plain that he will not vote for escalation until he is shown a sound plan with reasonable chances for success. "We cannot go to war," he has told intimates, "just to release somebody's frustrations."

— *Newsweek*, December 7, 1964

The U.S. Government has offered additional military and economic assistance. . . . The Government of Viet-Nam has accepted this offer. . . . Together the Government of Viet-Nam and the U.S. Mission are making joint plans to achieve greater effectiveness. . . . The U.S. representatives expressed full support for . . . Prime Minister Huong.

— Joint communiqué, December 11, 1964

There is no evidence that a Buddhist-controlled government would press the war against the Viet Cong. There is a great deal of evidence that instead it would try to negotiate with the Reds to bring about the "neutralization" of South Vietnam. . . . [Buddhist leader Thich] Tri Quang is guilty of the classic, fatal error: he seems to believe that he and his fellow Buddhists could "handle" the Communists.

— *Time*, December 11, 1964

The President's judgment has been right, as President Kennedy's judgment was, and as President Eisenhower's judgment was, that the center of the problem is in South Vietnam.

— McGeorge Bundy, Presidential Assistant for
National Security Affairs, *Issues & Answers*,
ABC, December 13, 1964

[North Vietnam is a] raggedy-ass little fourth-rate country.

— President Lyndon B. Johnson, during great
debates on bombing North, December 1964,
quoted by David Halberstam

TOP SECRET

AMBASSADOR TAYLOR: Do all of you understand English? I told you all clearly at General Westmoreland's dinner we Americans were tired of coups. Apparently I wasted my words. Maybe this is because something is wrong with my French because you evidently didn't understand. . . . Now you have made a real mess. We cannot carry you forever if you do things like this. Who speaks for the group? Do you have a spokesman?

GENERAL KY: I am not the spokesman for the group but I do speak English. I will explain why the Armed Forces took this action last night. We understand English very well. We are aware of our responsibilities. . . . We know that you want stability, but you cannot have stability until you have unity . . . the HNC [High National Council] does not want unity. It does not want to fight the Communists. It has been rumored that our action of last night was an intrigue of Khanh against Minh, who must be retired. Why do we seek to retire these generals? Because they had their chance and did badly. . . . Yesterday we met, 20 of us, from 1430 to 2030. We reached agreement that we must take some action. We decided to arrest the bad members of the HNC, bad politicians, bad student leaders, and the leaders of the Committee of National Salvation, which is a Communist organization. We must put the trouble-making organizations out of action. . . . We have no political ambitions. . . . We did what we thought was good for this country. . . .

ADMIRAL CANG: It seems that we are being treated as though we were guilty. What we did was good and we did it only for the good of the country. . . .

AMBASSADOR TAYLOR: This is a military coup that has destroyed the government-making process that, to the admiration of the whole world, was set up last fall. . . . You cannot go back to your units, General Ky. You military are now back in power. You are up to your neck in politics. Your statement makes it clear that you have constituted yourselves as a Military Revolutionary Committee. The dissolution of the HNC was totally illegal. . . . This will be interpreted as a return of the military to power. . . . Who commands the Armed Forces? General Khanh?

GENERAL KY: Yes, sir. . . .

GENERAL THIEU: After all, we did not arrest all the members of the HNC. Of nine members, we detained only five. These people are not under arrest. They are simply under controlled residence. . . .

AMBASSADOR TAYLOR: Our problem now, gentlemen, is to organize our work for the rest of the day. For one thing, the government will have to issue a communiqué.

GENERAL THIEU: We will still have a press conference this afternoon but only to say why we acted as we did.

AMBASSADOR TAYLOR: I have real troubles on the U.S. side. I don't know whether we will continue to support you after this. Why don't you tell your friends before you act? I regret the need for my blunt talk today but we have lots at stake. . . . Was it really all that necessary to carry out the arrests that very night? Couldn't this have been put off a day or two?

. . . You people have broken a lot of dishes and now we have to see how we can straighten out this mess.

> — Transcript sent State Department of
> Ambassador Maxwell D. Taylor's
> confrontation with "Young Turks" who
> dissolved High National Council, seized
> several members, and made large number of
> political arrests by night, December 20, 1964

It seems to me that we have no choice but to support the South Vietnamese Government and Army by the most effective means available. . . . It should be clear to all concerned that the United States will continue to meet its obligations and fulfill its commitments with respect to Vietnam.

> — Senator J. William Fulbright,
> speech in Senate, 1964

There are, of course, many Buddhists staunchly fighting the Viet Cong . . . but the Catholics as a group have always seemed to be tougher anti-Communists.

> — *Time*, December 25, 1964

I expect 1965 to be a better year for United States interests in South Vietnam.

> — General Maxwell D. Taylor, January 2, 1965

I fully support what the President has done and is doing, because I feel that we cannot withdraw. . . . We are in Vietnam to help the legal government. . . . The Administration is telling the truth. . . . I think that the President has been most frank in his discussions with the American people. . . . We are not at all certain what the position of General Khanh is at the moment and what we are doing now I think is paying for the mistake of getting rid of Diem when we did.

> — Senator Mike Mansfield, Democrat of
> Montana, January 3, 1965

The South Vietnamese have got plenty of trained troops to fight this war. . . . We are the coaches. . . . The Skyraider, the old Douglas A1-H, the last of the prop dive-bombers that were used on carriers, lifts its own weight in napalm, high-fragmentation bombs and rockets. . . . The Vietnamese love them, our guys love them. . . . You have trouble with certain Buddhist priests. . . . These are exhibitionists. . . . They are not important to the country. The people in the villages couldn't care less. . . . I flew over the Viet Cong lines [*sic*]. You are safer at 2,000 feet over

Vietnam than you are over Washington, because there is no anti-aircraft fire.

> — Senator A. S. (Mike) Monroney,
> Democrat of Oklahoma, *Issues & Answers*,
> ABC, January 3, 1965

Ernest Gruening of Alaska calls a Vietcong victory "ultimately inevitable." . . . Besides despairing demands like Gruening's and Wayne Morse's for outright withdrawal, there are increasing suggestions (the latest by Senator Church) about negotiations toward a settlement along the lines of De Gaulle's proposed "neutralization" of the whole Indo-Chinese area. . . . This proposal is really a euphemism for U.S. withdrawal. . . . The Administration has repeatedly rejected it. . . . Our policy needs reappraisal. . . . Such a reappraisal would still, we believe, give the President ample reason for not quitting the war. . . . It might commit him to commit American troops to more active engagement with the enemy. . . . Our efforts . . . have borne some fruit. They are a reason for doing more in this line, not less; and for lengthening the term of our commitment.

> — Editorial, *Life*, January 8, 1965

I think the Vietnamians are a very tough people. . . . They were conquered by France. They put up gallant resistance in the 19th century, but they were outclassed in weapons. They got rid of the French and immediately there were the Americans and now they are divided. I think they are determined to be re-united and I think they won't stop fighting until they are. I imagine the Vietnamians who don't like Communism do wish for national re-union.

> — Professor Arnold J. Toynbee, historian,
> *Issues & Answers*, ABC, January 10, 1965

The Government in South Vietnam is not stable. . . . Vietnam seems to be far away from Japan. . . . Japan is not obligated to help the U.S. in Vietnam.

> — Prime Minister Eisaku Sato of Japan,
> interview, *U.S. News & World Report*,
> January 11, 1965

We ought to carry on and never give up because we are frustrated and discouraged.

> — General Maxwell D. Taylor, quoted in *Le Monde*, January 11, 1965

We can plainly say we are not escalating the war.

> — Senator John A. Sparkman, Democrat of
> Alabama, January 15, 1965

We should do what we are doing, but do it even better.

> — Senator Mike Monroney, after trip to
> Vietnam, quoted by *Time*, January 15, 1965

They also do a disservice who deny that much has been achieved; [our] programs have all accomplished much, have indeed built the springboards of victory.

> — Former Ambassador Henry Cabot Lodge,
> January 17, 1965

Fulbright opposes any attempt to negotiate now and declares that "neutrality talk only feeds the disease." One of his more arresting views on Viet Nam, which may shock many of his liberal admirers, is that the U.S. decision to get rid of Diem was a mistake . . . that the nation needed a leader. . . . The U.S. may be willing to carry on the war for another decade—its financial cost of $2,000,000 a day is tolerable and so are the U.S. casualties.

> — *Time*, January 22, 1965

The real problem is not overextension but nonassertion of leadership by America. The U.S. is still the No. 1 power. As such, it can't turn away from the responsibilities of its power.

> — Professor Zbigniew Brzezinski, Columbia
> University, quoted by *Time*, January 22, 1965

The Vietnamese military forces continue to fight well. . . . We have shown in the Gulf of Tonkin that we can act, and North Vietnam knows it and knows its own weaknesses. But we seek no wider war.

> — Assistant Secretary of State for Far Eastern
> Affairs William P. Bundy, January 23, 1965

If we pulled out of Vietnam . . . all of the trusteed islands in the Pacific as well as the Philippines are in danger.

> — Senator Everett M. Dirksen, Republican of
> Illinois, Senate Minority Leader, *Meet the
> Press*, NBC, January 24, 1965

I was in Vietnam three or four months ago and it is . . . a complicated thing. . . . It is complex, and so on and so on. So I will give a simple answer to that question . . . making it clear to the rulers of North Vietnam that we will not tolerate any sort of aid sent to South Vietnam. . . . Insofar as we see this aid coming, we will . . . "punish" by specific destruction of oil tanks or bridges and so on. In other words, we will say

"you have got to stop it and until you stop it we are going to punish."
. . . Having announced the aim, we have got to go until it is
accomplished. . . . To take up the attitude at this point of isolationism
. . . just because it seems too difficult to work out anything in Asia, I
think is deplorable.

> — Henry R. Luce, editorial chairman, *Time*, *Life*,
> and *Fortune*, *Issues & Answers*, ABC, January
> 24, 1965

Current trend is toward a deal with Communists to end war in
Vietnam.

> — *U.S. News & World Report*, January 25, 1965

Until last week . . . air operations in Laos were directed from the
office of White House aide McGeorge Bundy.

> — *Newsweek*, January 25, 1965

This is going to be one of those guerrilla stand-offs, of which we have
several on record.

> — Dr. Bernard B. Fall, *Meet the Press*, NBC,
> January 31, 1965

General Nguyen Khanh was back in power in South Viet Nam last
week. . . . The civilian regime of Premier Tran Van Huong folded
without a sound. . . . The week began with the Buddhists pressing their
riots against Huong and the U.S. . . . In Saigon, Khanh and his "Young
Turk" officers—notably pistol-packing Air Force Chief Nguyen Cao
Ky—decided that the time had come to dump Huong. After hearing of
Khanh's plans [Ambassador Maxwell] Taylor decided that he and
Washington had no choice but to go along, and he flew off on a
previously arranged "orientation visit" to Laos and Thailand. Next day,
Khanh advised Deputy U.S. Ambassador U. Alexis Johnson that
Huong's ouster would be announced in half an hour over Radio Saigon.
Thoughtfully, Johnson suggested that the Premier should be informed
too, so he would not have to learn of his downfall via radio. Khanh
telephoned Huong, notified him that he was through. Khanh re-
appointed Harvard-educated Economist Nguyen Xuan Oanh ("Jack
Owen") as acting Premier—a post Jack held for a full six days last year.

> — *Time*, February 5, 1965

On February 7, U.S. and South Vietnamese air elements were directed
to launch retaliatory attacks against barracks and staging areas in the
southern area of North Viet-Nam. . . . Results of the attack . . . will be

announced as soon as they are reported from the field. . . . As the U.S. Government has frequently stated, we seek no wider war.
> — White House statement, February 7, 1965

TOP SECRET

We believe that the best available way of increasing our chance of success in Vietnam is the development and execution of a policy of *sustained reprisal* against North Vietnam. . . . While we believe that the risks of such a policy are acceptable, we emphasize that its costs are real. It implies significant U.S. air losses . . . it seems likely that it would eventually require an extensive and costly effort against the whole air defense system of North Vietnam. U.S. casualties would be higher—and more visible to American feelings. . . . Yet measured against the costs of defeat in Vietnam, this program seems cheap. And even if it fails to turn the tide—as it may—the value of the effort seems to us to exceed its cost. . . . It seems very clear that if the United States and the Government of Vietnam join in a policy of reprisal, there will be a sharp immediate increase in optimism in the South. . . . We have the whip hand in reprisals. . . . We think it plausible that effective and sustained reprisals . . . would have a substantial depressing effect upon the morale of Viet Cong cadres in South Vietnam. This is the strong opinion of CIA Saigon. . . . Even if it fails, the policy will be worth it. . . . A reprisal policy . . . will set a high price for the future upon all adventures of guerrilla warfare, and it should therefore somewhat increase our ability to deter such adventures. We must recognize, however, that our ability will be gravely weakened if there is a failure for any reason in Vietnam.
> — McGeorge Bundy, annex to memorandum
> to President Lyndon B. Johnson,
> February 7, 1965

I've gone far enough. I've had enough of this.
> — President Lyndon B. Johnson to members of
> National Security Council in Cabinet Room,
> White House, when informed of VC attacks, as
> he gave orders sending U.S. and Vietnamese
> warplanes bombing north of 17th parallel,
> February 7, 1965

The risk involved in winning the war is not as great as that involved in losing it.
> — Richard M. Nixon, speech to Sales Executive
> Club of New York, quoted by *U.S. News &
> World Report*, February 8, 1965

What would you negotiate now? . . . This is no time to negotiate. . . . What do you talk about? . . . I think the South Vietnamese are . . . well able to take care of themselves. . . . I think very highly of Ambassador Taylor. I think he is a wonderful man. He has a wonderful mind. He has great good judgment. I am a Taylor fan, if you want to put it that way, so I think very highly of him. I have had an opportunity to observe him, and I think he is one of the best men we have got anywhere in the world. . . . General Taylor, Ambassador Taylor, as he is properly called, is a man who knows war.

> — Senator Thomas J. Dodd, Democrat of Connecticut, *Face the Nation*, CBS, February 14, 1965

I don't think the outlook in Vietnam is hopeless. . . . Should the war be continued as it is being fought now? That's better than pulling out. We should keep on fighting until we find a way to make things turn for the better.

> — Senator Thomas J. Dodd, quoted by *U.S. News & World Report*, February 15, 1965

I don't think the situation is hopeless. . . . There is a fair prospect of mounting an indigenous effort. . . . I don't think we should try to negotiate at present.

> — Senator George A. Smathers, Democrat of Florida, quoted by *U.S. News & World Report*, February 15, 1965

Nothing, in my opinion, is ever hopeless in a situation of this kind.

> — Senator Karl E. Mundt, Republican of South Dakota, quoted by *U.S. News & World Report*, February 15, 1965

Every operation that the U.S. troops have been engaged in to date . . . has been a success, a military success. . . . I, myself, have no doubt that, in the long term, we can achieve military victory. . . . The objective is to kill as many Viet Cong as we possibly could. . . . These actions are going to pay off in the long term.

> — General Earle G. Wheeler, chairman, Joint Chiefs of Staff, testimony before Senate Armed Services Committee, released February 15, 1965

We have lost 133 crew members over there. . . . We have lost a total of 210 aircraft to hostile action. . . . They are acceptable casualties. They are about what we would expect. . . . I have asked my staff and all my commanders to put on their thinking caps. I asked them about three months ago to come up with any idea, even if it looked like it was completely preposterous, as to what we might do to get this war over earlier. We are not able to come up with any solution to it except by just fighting.

> — General John P. McConnell, chief of staff,
> U.S. Air Force, testimony before Senate
> Armed Services Committee, released February
> 15, 1965

I think a conference now would be disastrous. . . . It would be fine if South Vietnam were strong enough to sit down at the table and negotiate—but she isn't strong enough yet. . . . I think this struggle can be won. Certainly there is no quick solution. . . . Now, I like victory as much as anybody does, but I say that a stalemate is better than a defeat. And we are bringing about a stalemate there right now. And that's not to be sneezed at. I mean the smoldering deadlock you have there now. . . . If we are successful in Vietnam . . . it will start the whole free world off on an upward course.

> — Former Ambassador Henry Cabot Lodge,
> interview, *U.S. News & World Report*,
> February 15, 1965

We should make an increased effort to win the war. And I think it could be won. . . . I think you could suppress the guerrillas to a great extent. . . . I would have no faith in a negotiated peace.

> — Senator Bourke B. Hickenlooper, Republican
> of Iowa, quoted by *U.S. News & World Report*,
> February 15, 1965

The Vietnam situation is not hopeless. . . . This is not the time for negotiation. You don't deal from weakness; you deal from strength. We should continue in Vietnam, but with a stronger effort.

> — Senator Howard W. Cannon, Democrat of
> Nevada, quoted by *U.S. News & World Report*,
> February 15, 1965

The situation in Vietnam is bad, but I certainly would not say it is hopeless. . . . I believe things can be done. . . . My feeling is that a great deal can be done toward drying up the Ho Chi Minh Trail. . . . I do not think the time has come to seek a settlement. I certainly would not want to withdraw. I should like to see a stepped-up effort.

> — Senator John J. Sparkman, Democrat of
> Alabama, quoted by *U.S. News & World
> Report*, February 15, 1965

This is the poorest time for any such move as seeking a settlement. If you are winning, you can work out arrangements and settlements. We certainly are not winning.

> — Senator Frank Carlson, Republican of Kansas, quoted by *U.S. News & World Report*, February 15, 1965

A coalition government in South Viet Nam will not work out.

> — Senator Frank J. Lausche, Democrat of Ohio, quoted by *U.S. News & World Report*, February 15, 1965

We should take such action as is recommended by our military advisers.

> — Senator Jack Miller, Republican of Iowa, quoted by *U.S. News & World Report*, February 15, 1965

I doubt if now is the time to seek a negotiated settlement.

> — Senator Leverett M. Saltonstall, Republican of Massachusetts, quoted by *U.S. News & World Report*, February 15, 1965

I believe that neutralization of the entire area is not an unworthy goal.

> — Senator Joseph S. Clark, Democrat of Pennsylvania, quoted by *U.S. News & World Report*, February 15, 1965

Any negotiations should be from a position of strength. . . . Militarily, we're in good shape.

> — Senator Daniel K. Inouye, Democrat of Hawaii, quoted by *U.S. News & World Report*, February 15, 1965

I favor added effort by the U.S. on all fronts, including specialized combat troops to show how it can be done.

> — Senator Thomas J. McIntyre, Democrat of New Hampshire, quoted by *U.S. News & World Report*, February 15, 1965

As to whether the time has come to seek a settlement with Ho Chi Minh, my answer is: No. Should the war be continued as now? I can't see any alternative at the moment.

> — Senator Robert C. Byrd, Democrat of West Virginia, quoted by *U.S. News & World Report*, February 25, 1965

Our policy is clear. . . . We seek no wider war. . . . Our goal is peace.
> — Vice President Hubert H. Humphrey, speech
> to U.N. General Assembly, New York City,
> February 17, 1965

That empire in Southeast Asia is the last major resource area outside of the control of any one of the major powers on the globe. . . . I believe that the condition of the Vietnamese people, and the direction in which their future may be going, are at this stage secondary, not primary.
> — Senator Gale McGee, Democrat of Wyoming,
> speech in Senate, February 17, 1965

TOP SECRET

Intensified pacification within South Vietnam . . . might include a significant increase in present U.S. force strength.
> — Assistant Secretary of State William P. Bundy,
> draft paper entitled "Where Are We
> Heading?", February 18, 1965

TOP SECRET

Policy on Viet-Nam adopted today calls for the following: (1) Joint program with GVN of continuing air and naval action. . . . Air strikes will be jointly planned and agreed with GVN. . . . (2) Intensification by all available means of pacification program within South Viet-Nam, including every possible step to find and attack VC concentrations and headquarters within SVN by all conventional means available to GVN and U.S. (3) Early detailed presentation to nations of the world and to public of documented case against DRV as aggressor.
> — State Department, cablegram to heads of nine
> U.S. diplomatic missions, Far East, February
> 18, 1965

The regular South Vietnamese forces have been considerably strengthened by the continuing flow of equipment. . . . The combat performance of regular troops continues to inspire confidence.
> — Secretary of Denfese Robert S. McNamara,
> statement before House Armed Services
> Committee, February 19, 1965

Our decision to begin a program of punitive bombing attacks has served to recommit us deeply in Vietnam, and it is a commitment that must be carried through without hesitation or confusion of purpose. . . . Air strikes . . . can help force North Vietnam out of the military equation, and at the same time give new spirit to our friends in the South.
> — Editorial, *Life*, February 19, 1965

This is not a coup d'état but it is a military operation. . . . We want to get rid of Khanh and restore order.

> — Colonel Pham Ngoc Thao, head of coup
> overthrowing General Khanh, Saigon,
> February 19, 1965

South Vietnam . . . is worth any kind of a risk. . . . If South Vietnam falls, then Laos will fall, Cambodia will fall. . . .

> — Senator Barry Goldwater, Republican of
> Arizona, *Issues & Answers*, ABC,
> February 21, 1965

Neo-isolationists and the "Doves" who believe we must cut our losses and get out . . . represent the voices of defeat and despair, caution and fear. . . . You cannot win a war without spilling blood. We must pay the price of power.

> — Hanson W. Baldwin, military editor, *New York
> Times*, in *New York Times Magazine*, February
> 21, 1965

It is imperative to force a showdown.

> — Senator Gale McGee, radio interview,
> February 22, 1965

If the ultimate question is raised about pulling out, Mr. President, I want you to know that my answer is a large, resonant, and emphatic no.

> — Senator Everett M. Dirksen,
> quoted by *Time*, February 22, 1965

I think the pacification of the country would be easy if the external aggression were stopped.

> — Secretary of State Dean Rusk,
> February 25, 1965

We should provide whatever aid is necessary to win it. . . . We propose to resort to whatever methods are necessary and to use whatever weapons are necessary to win that battle. . . . We are going to win this thing. . . . We don't propose to stop. . . . Guerrilla warfare . . . can be won here. . . . We may have to use stronger methods.

> — Senator Russell Long, Democrat of Louisiana,
> Senate Majority Whip, *Meet the Press*, NBC,
> February 28, 1965

Geographically, Vietnam stands at the hub of a vast area of the world—Southeast Asia—an area with a population of 249 million

persons. . . . He who holds or has influence in Vietnam can affect the
future of the Philippines and Formosa to the east, Thailand and Burma
with their huge rice surpluses to the west, and Malaysia and Indonesia
with their rubber, ore and tin to the south. . . . Vietnam thus does not
exist in a geographical vacuum—from it large storehouses of wealth and
population can be influenced and undermined [sic].

> — Ambassador Henry Cabot Lodge, address
> before Middlesex Club of Cambridge, Mass.,
> reported by *Boston Sunday Globe*,
> February 28, 1965

American commanders in Saigon were instructed to prepare for a
continuing aerial offensive, but publicly and with announcements.
Ambassador Maxwell D. Taylor argued for silence, but was overruled by
the argument that clandestine raids would be politically unpopular in the
United States.

> — Dispatch from Saigon, *New York Times*,
> March 1, 1965

I think the period of time required to counter effectively a substantially guerrilla effort . . . whether it is one year, two years or more, I
really can't say.

> — Secretary of Defense Robert S. McNamara,
> March 2, 1965

A U.S. pilot back from a raid said: "I killed 40 Viet Cong today.
That's the number they told me were in the village, anyway, and I leveled
it."

> — AP dispatch from Qui Nhon, South Vietnam,
> *Washington Evening Star*, March 4, 1965

You generals have all been educated at the taxpayers' expense, and
you're not giving me any ideas and any solutions for this damn little
piss-ant country. . . . I want some solutions. I want some answers.

> — President Lyndon B. Johnson, March 4, 1965,
> to General Harold K. Johnson and others
> before General Johnson's departure for
> Vietnam March 5, quoted by David
> Halberstam

The South Vietnamese . . . are fighting with effectiveness and
gallantry. . . . HAPTAK programs are moving ahead. . . . We . . .
make it quite clear to the other side that their attempt to solve this
problem by military means . . . will not work. . . . If you talk about
negotiations, it takes more than one to negotiate.

> — Secretary of State Dean Rusk,
> *Face the Nation*, CBS, March 7, 1965

Unceremoniously dumped by South Vietnam's military junta as Commander in Chief of the Armed Forces, Lt. Gen. Nguyen Khanh last week ceremoniously turned over command to his successor, Maj. Gen. Tran Van (Little) Minh. . . . That, in effect, meant exile for the 37-year-old strong man who had dominated South Vietnamese politics for the past year. He had beaten off a coup attempt by disaffected officers—mainly Roman Catholics—on February 19. . . . At least one American diplomat in Saigon professed to find cause for optimism in Khanh's exile. "Now we're hoping for a period of stability," he said. . . . "His departure is a gain."

> — *Newsweek*, March 8, 1965

We can win in Southeast Asia.

> — *National Review*, March 9, 1965

President Johnson has shown admirable toughness and skill. More of the same could very well change the complexion of that war from galloping disaster to creeping hope. . . . U Thant tactlessly suggested that the American people were misled about the "true facts" and that "further bloodshed is unnecessary." . . . Johnson has properly refused to bow to the premature pressure to negotiate and has pursued his air strikes. . . . Johnson's determination has given the cause of free Vietnam another chance. New openings on the political front would make that chance brighter.

> — Editorial, *Life*, March 12, 1965

The President, so far as I can see, is trying to keep the lid on a dangerous volcano in Southeast Asia. . . . The President has a policy in Vietnam.

> — Senator Mike Mansfield, quoted by *Newsweek*, March 15, 1965

Odds are on eventual success for the U.S. side.

> — *U.S. News & World Report*, March 15, 1965

I think it would be catastrophic to pull out of South Vietnam. . . . The President has made it clear that we intend to stay. . . . What we are doing now is, we are upping the price, upping the heat, trying to convince them that we do mean it. . . . I would keep increasing the pressure.

> — General Thomas S. Powers, U.S. Air Force (Ret.), former commander in chief, Strategic Air Command, *Meet the Press*, NBC, March 21, 1965

TOP SECRET

Events in March were encouraging. . . . VC activity was considerably below the norm. . . . In summary, March has given rise to some cautious optimism. The current government appears to be taking control of the situation and . . . should be able to counter VC offensives successfully. . . . Friendly forces retained the initiative during April and a review of events reimposes the feeling of optimism generated last month. . . . In summary, current trends are highly encouraging and the GVN may have actually turned the tide at long last.

> — COMUSMACV Monthly Evaluation, March
> 1965 [Military Assistance Command, Vietnam]

There is a little light showing at the end of the tunnel. . . . Such is the case for a modest additional commitment of U.S. ground forces.

> — Joseph Alsop, syndicated column,
> March 22, 1965

TOP SECRET

1. *U.S. aims:*
    70%—To avoid a humiliating defeat (to our reputation as a guarantor).
    20%—To keep SVN (and the adjacent territory) from Chinese hands.
    10%—To permit the people of SVN to enjoy a better, freer way of life.
    ALSO—To emerge from crisis without unacceptable taint from methods used.
    NOT—to "help a friend," although it would be hard to stay in if asked out.

2. *The situation:* The situation in general is bad and deteriorating. The VC have the initiative. Defeatism is gaining among the rural population, somewhat in the cities, and even among the soldiers. . . . The Hop Tac area around Saigon is making little progress; the Delta stays bad; the country has been severed in the North. GVN control is shrinking to the enclaves, some burdened with refugees. In Saigon we have a remission: Quat is giving hope on the civilian side, the Buddhists have calmed, and the split generals are in uneasy equilibrium. . . .

Progress inside SVN is our main aim. . . . With the physical situation and the trends as they are the fear is overwhelming that an exit negotiated now would result in humiliation for the U.S. It is essential . . . that U.S. emerge as a "good doctor." We must have kept promises, been tough, taken risks, gotten bloodied, and hurt the enemy very badly.

> — Assistant Secretary of Defense for
> International Security Affairs John T.
> McNaughton, memorandum to Secretary of
> Defense Robert S. McNamara, March 24,
> 1965

The United States still seeks no wider war.

— President Lyndon B. Johnson,
March 25, 1965

Weapons used by American and Vietnamese forces also have become controversial. One of these weapons is the .223-caliber Armalite rifle, introduced in combat for the first time in Viet-Nam. The rifle has a muzzle velocity so high that its metal-jacketed bullet virtually explodes when it hits a human being, causing a huge jagged wound. The effect is similar to the Dum-Dum expanding bullet outlawed by the Geneva Convention.

— AP dispatch from Saigon,
March 25, 1965

We just goddamn well can't let them [the South Vietnamese] down.

— Stewart Alsop, *Saturday Evening Post*,
March 27, 1965

The situation in South Vietnam has generally improved since the end of last year.

— General Maxwell D. Taylor, March 28, 1965

Well, the South Korean personnel that are going into South Viet-Nam are not going there for combat purposes. They will be primarily engaged, I understand, on engineering tasks here and there.

— Secretary of State Dean Rusk,
Department of State Bulletin, March 29, 1965

Fortunately we are not doing all the fighting. . . . There is a Korean division which is fighting there.

— David E. Bell, former administrator, Agency
for International Development, quoted in U.S.
Senate, *Supplemental Foreign Assistance Fiscal
Year 1966—Vietnam*

Johnson . . . in April 1965 . . . offered the North Vietnamese the opportunity to participate in a billion-dollar American development project for Southeast Asia, centering on a vast TVA-like development of the Mekong River. It would have been the greatest piece of pork-barrel legislation in history—except that the Mekong River does not run through North Vietnam. But perhaps that could be fixed, too.

— Frances FitzGerald, *Fire in the Lake*

We seek no wider war.

> — President Lyndon B. Johnson, April 1, 1965

What has been done thus far is public knowledge. What will be done in the future is something for Hanoi to worry about.

> — General Maxwell D. Taylor, speech at Saigon
> Lions Club, quoted by *Time*, April 2, 1965

TOP SECRET

I have reported that the strikes to date have not caused a change in the North Vietnamese policy of directing Viet Cong insurgency, infiltrating cadres and supplying material. If anything, the strikes to date have hardened their attitude. . . . With . . . a program of slowly ascending tempo of air strikes . . . we can expect increasing pressure to stop the bombing. This will come from various elements of the American public, from the press, the United Nations and world opinion.

> — John A. McCone, director, CIA,
> memorandum to Secretaries Rusk and
> McNamara, McGeorge Bundy and
> Ambassador Taylor, April 2, 1965

TOP SECRET

On Thursday, April 1, the President made the following decisions with respect to Vietnam. . . . The President approved the urgent exploration of the 12 suggestions for covert and other actions submitted by the Director of Central Intelligence. . . . The President repeated his earlier approval of the 21-point program of military actions submitted by General Harold K. Johnson . . . and re-emphasized his desire that aircraft and helicopter reinforcements under this program be accelerated. The President approved an 18–20,000 man increase in U.S. military support forces. . . . The President approved a change of mission for all Marine Battalions deployed to Vietnam. . . . We should continue roughly the present slowly ascending tempo of ROLLING THUNDER operations being prepared to add strikes in response to a higher rate of VC operations. . . . Leaflet operations should be expanded to obtain maximum practicable psychological effect on North Vietnam population. . . . Air operation in Laos . . . should be stepped up to the maximum remunerative rate.

> — National Security Action Memorandum 328,
> signed by McGeorge Bundy, addressed to
> Secretaries of State and Defense and Director
> of CIA, April 6, 1965

Why must we take this painful road? . . . We do this to convince the leaders of North Vietnam. . . . We will not be defeated. We will not grow tired. . . . We now find it necessary to say with guns and planes: Armed hostility is futile. . . . This war, like most wars, is filled with terrible irony. . . . Every night before I turn out the lights to sleep, I ask myself this question: Have I done everything that I can do . . . to try to bring peace and hope to all the peoples of the world? Have I done enough?

> — President Lyndon B. Johnson,
> Johns Hopkins University speech, Baltimore,
> April 7, 1965

I think that we are following a course of action that is calculated to best represent the interests of this nation.

> — President Lyndon B. Johnson,
> quoted by *Time*, April 9, 1965

We are simply going to stay on our program of doing what we did before. We've just got to do what we have been doing more effectively. . . . What I do see is a very notable increase in morale and confidence.

> — General Maxwell D. Taylor,
> quoted by *Time*, April 9, 1965

Government expenditure for the development of chemical and biological agents has grown by $175 million—to $275 million—in the last five years. Hottest area of research is psychochemical agents—e.g., compounds that induce temporary, partial disabilities (blindness, deafness, paralysis, amnesia).

> — *Chemical Week*, April 10, 1965

We continue what we're doing, we continue to respond in a measured but appropriate way, whatever that may mean. . . . In South Vietnam, the government has made a good start. . . . I don't think that we should look for too-quick results.

> — Under Secretary of State George W. Ball,
> *Face the Nation*, CBS, April 11, 1965

Negotiation now is not the answer.

> — Raymond Moley, *Newsweek*, April 12, 1965

If . . . national liberation . . . succeeds in South Viet-Nam, it can succeed anywhere in the world.

> — Secretary of State Dean Rusk,
> Department of State Publication #7921, 1965

TOP SECRET

Mac . . . we want to stay alive here because we think we're winning—and will continue to win unless helped to death.

> — General Maxwell D. Taylor to McGeorge
> Bundy, April 15, 1965

"The Viet Cong now fear defeat . . ." is a good summary of the total impression conveyed. . . . The Viet Cong [is] . . . seriously troubled by the war-weariness of some of their adherents.

> — Joseph Alsop, syndicated column,
> April 16, 1965

We will not withdraw, either openly or under the cloak of a meaningless agreement.

> — President Lyndon B. Johnson,
> April 17, 1965

One proof of the wisdom of President Johnson's Vietnamese policy is its marked success to date.

> — Joseph Alsop, syndicated column,
> April 21, 1965

This is the best job I've ever had. . . . The Vietnamese army is O.K. When they're getting killed, you know they're fighting.

> — Admiral U. S. Grant Sharp,
> U.S. commander in chief, Pacific,
> *Life*, April 23, 1965

I continue to see and hear nonsense about the nature of the struggle there. There is no evidence that the Vietcong has any significant popular following in South Vietnam.

> — Secretary of State Dean Rusk,
> April 23, 1965

The "unwinnable" war in South Vietnam can indeed be won. . . . The first category is always K.I.A.—Killed in Action. . . . The official K.I.A. statistics for the last year and the first three months of this year are:

> Americans: 223
> South Vietnamese Forces: 9,650
> Viet Cong: 22,580

This grim tabulation tells a lot. . . . In the first place, the K.I.A. totals mean that, on our side at least, the Vietnamese war is notably nonlethal in comparison with a conventional infantry war. And this comparatively undeadly nature of the war has meaning for all the participants. . . . No sensible man could suppose that 223 fatal casualties put any very terrible strain on a nation of some 192 million. Moreover, those who weep about "American boys" dying in the jungle overlook the fact that, almost without exception, the few thousand who have the really dangerous jobs out in the boondocks are professional soldiers. A man does not become a professional soldier, after all, in order to avoid all risk.

After chatting with some of them in the field, I scribbled in my notebook: "These guys seem so damned happy." This may sound fatuous, but it is true. . . . They are also happy because they are doing a job that needs doing, and doing it well. . . . Hope of victory is precisely what the third K.I.A. tabulation—more than 22,000 dead Viet Cong— *ought* to provide. American officers in the field swear that the figures are accurate—based largely on a count of dead bodies. And if the figures are accurate, the Viet Cong *ought* to be running out of live bodies . . . that represents about their maximum manpower available. . . . The North Vietnamese . . . may halt the aggression. In that case, the supposedly unwinnable war in Vietnam might be won, for all practical purposes, in rather short order.

> — Stewart Alsop, *Saturday Evening Post*, April 24, 1965

We still seek no wider war.

> — President Lyndon B. Johnson, April 25, 1965

One of the most infamous methods of torture used by the government is partial electrocution—or "frying" as one U.S. advisor called it. . . . Sometimes the wires are attached to the male genital organs, or to the breasts of a Vietcong woman prisoner. . . . Other techniques . . . involve cutting off the fingers, ears, fingernails or sexual organs of another prisoner. Sometimes a string of ears decorates the wall of a government military installation. . . .

The Viet Cong prisoners were interrogated on an airplane flying toward Saigon. The first refused to answer questions and was thrown out of the airplane at 3,000 feet. The second immediately answered all the questions. But he, too, was thrown out.

> — Beverly Deepe, dispatch from Vietnam, *New York Herald Tribune*, April 25, 1965

One must be thankful for the flawless timing and the brilliant sureness of foot that the President has shown in the period since the Pleiku incident.

> — Joseph Alsop, syndicated column, April 26, 1965

A turning point . . . lies ahead in the war in Vietnam. . . . War
. . . is starting to hurt Communist North Vietnam. The longer the war
. . . the greater the hurt becomes. It can become unbearable.
> — *U.S. News & World Report*, April 26, 1965

These spots are called free zones, meaning that . . . everything that
moves and lives, animals included, is considered as the enemy and is
killed. . . . Tayninh became a free zone . . . the American air force
unleashed an immense operation in the region. First 20 planes dropped
incendiary bombs. Then around 100 cargo planes dropped tons of
napalm. An immense fire broke out. The last week in the same area the
Americans had dropped 1,000 tons of bombs in 18 square kilometers of
forest where they suspected Vietcong troop concentrations.
> — Max Clos, "The Machine Against the
> Guerrilla," *Le Figaro*, April 27, 1965

Stonewall Jackson was wonderfully simple in his approach. Once an
officer came to him and said there were Union forces on all sides of him
and what should he do? Jackson said: "Kill them." I thought that was
pretty wonderful. "Kill them all." . . . Religion and military life are
wholly compatible in my mind. You can't go into this disciplined life
. . . without spiritual support. . . . If the Vietcong attacked us at Da
Nang, we would defeat them. We have the power to do it. . . . In the end
we would win.
> — Lieutenant General Victor H. (Brute) Krulak,
> commander, Fleet Marine Force, Pacific,
> quoted by *Life*, April 30, 1965

It is quite possible . . . to win a war against . . . guerrillas. . . . The
air raids . . . have had a marked effect. . . . News from the battlefield is
improving. . . . Apathy as well as fear compose the water in which the
Vietcong swim. . . . It can be dried up.
> — Editorial, *Life*, April 30, 1965

I continue to hear and see nonsense about the nature of the struggle in
Viet Nam. I sometimes wonder at the gullibility of educated men and the
stubborn disregard of plain facts by men who are supposed to be helping
our young to learn—especially to learn how to think.
> — Secretary of State Dean Rusk, to American
> Society of International Law, quoted in *Time*,
> April 30, 1965

We are beginning to win. We are winning more battles every day. . . .
> — Senator Thomas J. Dodd, Democrat of
> Connecticut, *Meet the Press*, NBC,
> May 2, 1965

Defense officials do not like the terminology, but they readily concede that Vietnam has given the U.S. armed forces a "laboratory for war." Tactical theories are being tried, men trained and weapons tested. . . . Among the gimmicks is the so-called Lazy Dog. This is a drum of steel pellets dropped from a plane that explodes at 6,000 feet. The pellets have a buckshot effect against men and equipment when they reach the ground. A similar but more powerful weapon is the CBU, for Cluster Bomblet Unit. Small fragmentation bombs are released from a drum against guerrilla units in the jungle.

> — Jack Raymond, *New York Times*, May 3, 1965

I ask the Congress to appropriate at the earliest possible moment an additional $700 million to meet mounting military requirements in Vietnam.

> — President Lyndon B. Johnson,
> Message to Congress, May 4, 1965

It is my opinion that the bombings will not have much effect one way or the other. I don't think we will gain much by it or lose much.

> — Senator Richard B. Russell, Democrat of
> Georgia, May 5, 1965

The strength of the Vietcong is overrated.

> — Foreign Minister Thanat Khoman of
> Thailand, May 6, 1965

Withdrawal . . . would involve a repudiation of commitments undertaken and confirmed by three administrations. . . . We must show Hanoi that it cannot win the war.

> — Senator Robert F. Kennedy, Democrat of
> New York, speech in Senate, May 6, 1965

There are many evidences of improved morale on the Government side. . . . The Government forces have in recent months tremendously strengthened their position and now have the Viet Cong on the run.

> — Senator Thomas J. Dodd, Democrat of
> Connecticut, member, Senate Foreign
> Relations Committee, Cleveland, May 6, 1965

The one job I want them to do is to find Viet Cong and kill them. We got one today and we're going to get more. Sure, we're suffering casualties, but we're going to be dealing out more. We're fighting a war here now.

> — General Wallace Greene, Jr., commandant,
> U.S. Marine Corps, Vietnam visit, quoted in
> *Time*, May 7, 1965

We are hopeful.

> — Deputy Secretary of Defense Cyrus R. Vance,
> *Issues & Answers*, ABC, May 9, 1965

I think it is perfectly clear that the situation in Vietnam has deteriorated during the past year.

> — Secretary of Defense Robert S. McNamara,
> May 9, 1965

I say categorically . . . the struggle can achieve success. . . . What can be negotiated? . . . I prefer to see victory.

> — Thanat Khoman, *Meet the Press*, NBC,
> May 9, 1965

I continue to hear and see nonsense about the nature of the struggle there. . . . There is no evidence that the Viet Cong has any significant popular following in South Viet-Nam.

> — Secretary of State Dean Rusk,
> *Department of State Bulletin*, May 10, 1965

TOP SECRET

I have learned from Bob McNamara that nearly all ROLLING THUNDER [code name for sustained bombing of North Vietnam] operations for this week can be completed by Wednesday noon, Washington time. This fact and the days of Buddha's birthday seem to me to provide an excellent opportunity for a pause in air attacks which might go into next week and which I could use to good effect with world opinion. . . . Could you see [Chief of State Phan Huy] Quat right away on Tuesday and see if you can persuade him to concur in this plan. I would like to associate him with me in this decision. . . . I think it important that he and I should get together in such matters, but I have no desire to embarrass him if it is politically difficult for him to join in a [bombing] pause over Buddha's birthday. . . . Do not yet have your appreciation of the political effect in Saigon of acting around Buddha's birthday. From my point of view it is a great advantage to use Buddha's birthday . . . in political terms. I assume we could undertake to enlist the Archbishop and the Nuncio in calming the Catholics. . . . I have kept this plan in the tightest possible circle here and wish you to inform no one but Alexis Johnson.

> — President Lyndon B. Johnson,
> cablegram to General Maxwell D. Taylor in
> Saigon, May 10, 1965

Some top U.S. officials are saying privately that the tide actually has been turned in the Vietnam war.

> — *U.S. News & World Report*, May 10, 1965

Only the Vietcong has committed atrocities in Vietnam.

> — Vice President Hubert H. Humphrey,
> Pittsburgh, May 13, 1965

Aggression . . . just will not work. . . . We combine unlimited patience with unlimited resources in pursuit of an unwavering purpose. We will not abandon our commitment to South Vietnam. . . . And I am continuing and I am increasing the search for every possible path to peace. . . . This year . . . a new variety of sweet potato . . . will be distributed to Vietnamese farmers. Corn output should rise. . . . Pig production has more than doubled. . . .

For most Americans this is an easy war. . . . The lives of most of us, at least most of us in this room . . . are untroubled. Prosperity rises, abundance increases, the nation flourishes. . . . I, therefore, hope that every person within the sound of my voice . . . will find ways to help progress in South Vietnam.

> — President Lyndon B. Johnson to Association
> of American Editorial Cartoonists, East
> Room, White House, May 13, 1965

I can't get out. I can't finish it with what I've got. So what the hell can I do.

> — President Lyndon B. Johnson, Spring 1965,
> quoted by Lady Bird Johnson, *A White House
> Diary*

The Vietnamese struggle is absolutely inescapable for the U.S. in the mid-60s—and in that sense, it is the right war in the right place at the right time.

> — *Time*, May 14, 1965

I support the Administration's objective and I support their means. . . . We are engaged and our interests are very important, very vital. . . . The objective of the strikes is to bring about a negotiation. . . . This is a sound policy. These air strikes on North Vietnam I think were reasonable to impress upon them the seriousness of the situation. . . . That it would be wise . . . to have a negotiation. . . . I wouldn't expect to lose this fight.

LAWRENCE SPIVAK: Senator, there was a report yesterday that the United States may send a division of ground forces to South Vietnam. If the President decides to do that, will you support the move?

SENATOR FULBRIGHT: The President is in this difficulty and we have to support him. When we are in this critical a matter, we have to support our President, you know that.

> — Senator J. William Fulbright, Democrat of
> Arkansas, chairman, Senate Foreign Relations
> Committee, *Meet the Press*, NBC,
> May 14, 1965

TOP SECRET

1. Historically, guerrilla wars have generally been lost or won cleanly: Greece, China mainland, North Viet-Nam, Malaya, Philippines. . . .

2. In all the cases won by Free World forces, there was a phase when the guerrillas commanded a good part of the countryside. . . . They failed to win because all the possible routes to guerrilla routes were closed, and, in failing to win, they lost. They finally gave up in discouragement. . . .

3. If we succeed in blocking . . . routes to victory . . . there is no reason we cannot win as clear a victory in South Viet-Nam as in Greece, Malaya, and the Philippines. . . . The most realistic hope of the VC should be avoidable. This . . . argues for more rather than less pressure on the North, while continuing the battle in the South in such a way as to make VC hopes of military and political progress wane.

4. The objective of the exercise is to convince Hanoi that its bargaining position is being reduced with the passage of time. . . . Hanoi . . . wants . . . to get some minimum face-saving formula for the VC.

5. I believe Hanoi understands its dilemma well. . . . It is now staring at quite clear-cut defeat, with the rising U.S. strength and GVN morale in the South and rising costs in the North. That readjustment in prospects is painful [for them]. . . .

6. . . . We will have to consolidate with the South Vietnamese a victory that is nearer our grasp than we . . . may think.

> — Walt W. Rostow, chairman, State
> Department's Policy Planning Council,
> memorandum to Secretary of State Dean
> Rusk, May 20, 1965

Negotiations would be disastrous, the equivalent of turning South Vietnam over to the wolves. . . .

> — Henry Cabot Lodge, former ambassador to
> South Vietnam, recently returned from Asian
> trip as President Lyndon Johnson's personal
> representative, *Meet the Press*, NBC,
> May 23, 1965

We do not believe that this Liberation Front has any strong political base among the South Vietnamese people.

> — Secretary of State Dean Rusk,
> *Meet the Press*, NBC, May 30, 1965

TOP SECRET

I was most grateful to you for asking Bob McNamara to arrange the very full briefing about the two oil targets near Hanoi and Haiphong that Col. Rogers gave me yesterday. . . . I know that you will not feel that I am either unsympathetic or uncomprehending . . . however . . . I am bound to say that, as seen from here, the possible military benefits that may result from this bombing do not appear to outweigh the political disadvantages. . . . The last thing I wish to do is add to your difficulties, but, as I warned you in my previous message, if this action is taken we shall have to disassociate ourselves from it. . . . Nevertheless I want to repeat . . . that our reservations about this operation will not affect our continuing support for your policy over Vietnam.

> — Prime Minister Harold Wilson,
> cablegram to President Lyndon B. Johnson,
> June 3, 1965

Nothing succeeds like success, and nothing fails like failure. . . . The best thing to do if it is possible is to win, and in some meaningful sense, I would guess it can be done. . . . In Vietnam, you find the leader of a local area and go and get him . . . put a price on his head. . . . But we do have people in this country who can do it. Many members of our police departments, or intelligence service, ought to be able to do it. . . .

On the whole, people in this country are not used to doing dirty tricks and playing rough. . . . It isn't pleasant. But, in this kind of war, one's standards are almost automatically going to be lower than in a normal set-piece battle. . . . I don't want to be on the side of saying, "Let's be rough." . . . But, in this kind of war, you must either drop your standards or get out. . . . Something between 10 and 20 U.S. divisions could probably occupy the entire country—North and South. . . .

QUESTION: How long before the U.S. can nail down victory in Vietnam?

ANSWER: At least in a couple more years.

> — Dr. Herman Kahn, "master strategist,"
> Department of Defense, Atomic Energy
> Commission, other agencies, physicist,
> mathematician, director, Hudson Institute,
> author, *On Escalation: Metaphors and
> Scenarios*, interview, *U.S. News & World
> Report*, June 7, 1965

If the United States is resolute, the prospects could be transformed in a year or two.

> — Sir Robert Thompson, British
> counterinsurgency expert, Malaya, former
> head, British Military Mission, Saigon,
> commercial consultant, antiguerrilla tactics,
> interview, *London Evening Standard*, quoted in
> *U.S. News & World Report*, June 7, 1965

American forces would be available for combat support with Vietnamese forces when and if necessary.

> — Robert J. McCloskey,
> State Department spokesman, June 8, 1965

There has been a noisy minority . . . clamoring for withdrawal from Vietnam. . . . They are their own worst enemies . . . the enemies of . . . decency.

> — Senator Thomas J. Dodd, Democrat of
> Connecticut, speech in Senate, June 10, 1965

I am opposed to unconditional withdrawal from Vietnam.

> — Senator J. William Fulbright, June 15, 1965

Whether or not the initial decision was a mistake is now moot. The United States does have a commitment in South Vietnam. The flag is there. United States honor and prestige are there. And, most important of all, United States soldiers are there.

> — Senator Richard B. Russell, Democrat of
> Georgia, chairman, Senate Armed Services
> Committee, remarks in Senate, June 15, 1965

They're fighting well. They're fighting hard. They're fighting effectively.

> — Secretary of Defense Robert S. McNamara,
> June 16, 1965

I do not believe it is hopeless . . . it is somewhat too soon for America to pull the plug. We have to stay with it.

> — McGeorge Bundy, speech on foreign policy in Lowell Lecture Hall, Harvard University, June 18, 1965

Many Americans do not understand the relationship between a war in Vietnam and their own lives. . . . If the United States gives up the fight and, as the most powerful nation in the world, withdraws from the contest, there will be more acts of aggression. Ultimately, Western Europe will be overrun.

> — David Lawrence, syndicated column, *New York Herald Tribune*, June 25, 1965

I think we have to hold the line somewhere. . . . This is . . . in the interests of the peace of the world.

> — Ambassador Adlai E. Stevenson, U.S. representative to UN, *Meet the Press*, NBC, June 27, 1965

TOP SECRET

The South Vietnamese are losing the war to the Viet Cong. No one can assure you that we can beat the Viet Cong or even force them to the conference table on our terms, no matter how many hundred thousand *white foreign* (U.S.) troops we employ. No one has demonstrated that a white ground force of whatever size can win a guerrilla war—which is at the same time a civil war between Asians—in jungle terrain in the midst of a population that refuses cooperation to the white forces (and the South Vietnamese). . . . So long as our forces are restricted to advising and assisting the South Vietnamese, the struggle will remain a civil war between Asian peoples. Once we deploy substantial numbers of troops in combat it will become a war between the U.S. and a large part of the population of South Vietnam. . . . The decision you face now, therefore, is critical. Once large numbers of U.S. troops are committed to direct combat, they will begin to take heavy casualties in a war they are ill-equipped to fight in a non-cooperative if not downright hostile countryside. Once we suffer large casualties, we will have started a well-nigh irreversible process. Our involvement will be so great that we cannot—without national humiliation—stop short of achieving our complete objectives. *Of the two possibilities I think humiliation would be more likely than the achievement of our objectives—even after we have paid terrible costs.* . . .

> — Under Secretary of State George W. Ball, memorandum to President Lyndon B. Johnson, July 1, 1965

TOP SECRET

Secretary McNamara this morning suggested that General Wheeler form a small group to address the question, "If we do everything we can, can we have assurance of winning in South Vietnam?" General Wheeler suggested that he would have you head up the group. . . . I would hope that the study could produce a clear articulation of what our strategy is for winning the war in South Vietnam.

> — Assistant Secretary of Defense John T.
> McNaughton, memorandum to Lieutenant
> General Andrew J. Goodpaster, assistant
> chairman, Joint Chiefs of Staff, July 2, 1965

It is absolutely essential that we back up the people of South Viet Nam. This isn't a question of if we can afford it or how far away it is.

> — Ambassador-at-large W. Averell Harriman,
> speech, New York City, quoted by *Time*,
> July 2, 1965

The political outlook in Vietnam should not be hopeless.

> — Eugene V. Rostow, former dean, Yale Law
> School, consultant to State Department and
> UN Secretariat, brother of Walt W. Rostow,
> quoted in *Life*, July 2, 1965

In the shock and disbelief of what is still an incredulous minute in American history, he became President. . . . In the cabin of Air Force One . . . the new President sat there, like a large grey stone mountain, untouched by fear or frenzy, from whom everyone began to draw strength. And suddenly, as though the darkness of the cave confided its fears to the trail of light growing larger as it banished the night, the nation's breath, held tightly in its breast, began to ease, and across the land the people began to move again. The President, thank the good Lord, has extra glands, I am persuaded, that give him energy that ordinary men simply don't have. . . . His mind is an alarm clock that silently nudges him about 4 in the morning whenever there is air action in Viet Nam. . . . Like Antaeus, whose mother was Earth . . . President Johnson . . . sought this renewal and found it . . . in the outpouring of love and affection, in the outstretched arms of mothers holding up their babies to see the President, in the tears and laughter of the people. I sleep each night a little better, a little more confidently because Lyndon Johnson is my President.

> — Special Assistant to President Jack Valenti, to
> Advertising Federation of America, Boston,
> July 2, 1965

People ask me who my heroes are. I have only one—Hitler. I admire
Hitler . . . We need four or five Hitlers in Vietnam.

> — Prime Minister Nguyen Cao Ky,
> interview with Brian Moynahan,
> London *Sunday Mirror*, July 4, 1965

If we can get the Vietcong to stand up and fight, we will blast him.

> — General William C. Westmoreland,
> July 5, 1965

I think that if the right things are done within Vietnam . . . then the
American combat role, which is comparatively small . . . should be
sufficient to halt them.

> — Sir Robert Thompson, former head, British
> Advisory Mission, South Vietnam, quoted in
> *Newsweek*, July 5, 1965

If Ho Chi Minh and the Communist leaders are smart enough they
will . . . stop fighting and continue in an underground fight. . . . That's
why we never [will] accept a cease-fire, a so-called—you know—a peace,
or this temporary peace.

> — Nguyen Cao Ky, television interview,
> July 1965

Last week, as the fighting reached a new peak and the economy
reached its nadir, Washington dispatched its top economic trouble-
shooter to Saigon: former World Bank boss Eugene Black, now Lyndon
Johnson's special envoy for Southeastern Asian development.

Black's mission is to expand and refine U.S. aid to South Viet Nam so
that the economy will not go under. . . . Speculators, profiteers and
black-market rings have fattened greedily on the cities. While banks will
give only 74 piasters to the U.S. dollar, the going black-market rate has
soared from 125 piasters four months ago to as much as 170 today. . . .

A huge, incalculable bite from Washington's $1 billion foreign-aid
program is taken each year by government and military officials. U.S.
refrigerators and air conditioners meant for hospitals end up in generals'
homes; troop commanders collect the "phantom pay" of soldiers whose
deaths in combat go unreported to Saigon. For $675, a well-to-do youth
can buy an Interior Ministry "diploma" that certifies him as a
government spy, thus exempting him from army service. A trick
currently in favor with provincial chiefs is to blow up a provincial bridge,
blame the Viet Cong, and win a fat construction contract from Saigon.

> — *Time*, July 9, 1965

Many of our political leaders are in a rained-in mood of "no-win"
gloom. . . . The scale of engagements is mounting. . . . Such news . . .

magnifies the new warnings of old defeatists. "You will never win," says
DeGaulle to Hubert Humphrey; and Britain's envoy Patrick Gordon
Walker tells Washington much the same. . . . Senate Minority Leader
Everett Dirksen continues to support the President. . . . The reasons for
U.S. involvement in Vietnam have been thoroughly debated and the case
for our staying there (it was spelled out by Eugene Rostow in last week's
Life) may be considered closed. . . . Johnson has shown wisdom in his
decisions on Vietnam. . . . Let him . . . ask for public support. He'll get
it.

> — Editorial, *Life*, July 9, 1965

Besides destroying the village, the paratroops captured one 50-caliber
machine gun.

> — Jack Langguth, *New York Times*,
> July 9, 1965

President Johnson suggested that the Vietcong were now "swinging
wildly."

> — *New York Times*, July 10, 1965

We committed our power and our honor and that has been reaffirmed
by three Presidents.

> — President Lyndon B. Johnson,
> news conference, July 10, 1965

Dan, it looks very good. The Vietcong are going to collapse within
weeks. Not months but weeks. What we hear is that they're already
coming apart under the bombing.

> — Walt W. Rostow to Daniel Ellsberg, July 1965,
> quoted by David Halberstam in *The Best and
> the Brightest*

MORLEY SAFER OF CBS: Surely, Arthur, you don't expect the American press to be the handmaidens of government.

ARTHUR SYLVESTER, ASSISTANT SECRETARY OF DEFENSE FOR PUBLIC
AFFAIRS: That's exactly what I expect. . . . Look, if you think any
American official is going to tell you the truth, then you're stupid. Did
you hear that?—Stupid.

> — Dialogue in Saigon, July 17, 1965, quoted by
> David Halberstam, *The Making of a Quagmire*

I am confident that we can convince . . . the Viet Cong that it is
foolhardy, it is too expensive for them to continue. . . . I am convinced

that if we expedite, if we intensify our air and sea power in South Vietnam, we can convince Ho Chi Minh that it is too costly.

> — Congressman Gerald Ford, Republican of
> Michigan, *Issues & Answers*, ABC,
> July 18, 1965

Concerning military operations, I think the situation is better now. . . . Until now we break all their offensives. . . . I think we need more American troops or Allied troops, so thus to allow the Vietnamese troops and the government of Vietnam to reorganize the rear. . . . If really a U.S. government wants to help us or give us everything we need . . . I think within one year the situation will be better. . . . Now we are short in many things. . . . The problem for the government to solve is how to get the participation of the population in the war effort. . . . I am not politician, but I am patriot and revolutionary man. . . . I want the people loyal . . . so, regardless of his groups, religions, if they agree with me, I always happy to have them helping me. . . . I think the morale of people in North Vietnam is affected very much by these air attacks. . . . I am a military man, so my job is fight, fight.

> — President Nguyen Cao Ky, interviewed in
> Saigon, *Face the Nation*, CBS, July 18, 1965

The situation is serious today. . . . It has deteriorated over the past 12 months. I do want to mention one thing about the future, however, that I think is very interesting. Within the last three or four weeks, Ho Chi Minh looked into the future and he said it might take 20 years for them to win.

> — Secretary of Defense Robert S. McNamara,
> July 21, 1965

President Johnson is on the verge of making the kind of ruinous historical mistake which . . . Hitler made when he attacked Russia. . . . At some point, the President and his advisers are going to have to ask themselves why everything goes wrong . . . why over the years all of our hopes have been dashed and one plan after another has failed. . . . It is, I believe, that we have set ourselves a task which, like squaring the circle or perpetual motion or living 200 years, is impossible to do. It is an impossible task for the United States to reach across the Pacific Ocean and . . . by force of American arms to assure a weak country that it will be non-Communist.

> — Walter Lippmann, 1965

The Viet Cong . . . are suffering increasingly heavy losses, and the

U.S. combat forces are adding substantially to the military power of the government.

> — Secretary of Defense Robert S. McNamara,
> Saigon, July 21, 1965

It is going to take some tears and some blood.

> — President Lyndon B. Johnson to White House
> associates, quoted by *Time*, July 23, 1965

I have asked the commanding general, General Westmoreland, what more he needs to meet this mounting aggression. He has told me. And we will meet his needs. . . . We cannot be defeated by force of arms. . . . We will stand in Vietnam.

> — President Lyndon B. Johnson,
> July 28, 1965

U.S. Air Force Skyraiders bombed a village 1,700 yards from a convoy of U.S. troops and destroyed a Buddhist monastery. Four monks were badly wounded and about 20 others were slightly hurt.

> — AP dispatch from Saigon, July 29, 1965

The Communists are pouring more men in all the time. They've suffered their greatest losses.

> — President Lyndon B. Johnson,
> quoted by *Time*, July 30, 1965

We are trying to put this little nation on its feet. . . . They have responded well to training. . . . We have to . . . strengthen our forces.

> — Senator John C. Stennis, Democrat of
> Mississippi, chairman, Senate Preparedness
> Subcommittee, *Meet the Press*, NBC,
> August 1, 1965

I was one of those who didn't think we should go in there. I have never been able to understand the attitude of those who are demanding an all-out war against Communists 10,000 miles away, when we have a terrible logistics problem in supplying our people . . . getting them there and bringing them back when they're wounded. . . . I don't think it has any value strategically. . . . We don't have to have South Vietnam to hold back the hordes of Communism. I am fairly familiar with the Domino Theory. . . . I don't think this is necessarily true. . . . But . . . South Vietnam is to show the world that when the United States pledges its honor and its word in any written document to carry out any treaty or agreement, even if we were mistaken in signing it, that we will do it. . . .

I still don't think that we have done enough. I think that we could do more. . . . I have great admiration for Senator Lodge. . . . I have great confidence in General Taylor. . . . General Taylor is a remarkable man. He is not only a great soldier, he is a great scholar, and I think a statesman. . . . It is going to cost a great deal of money . . . because we are 10,000 miles away from there. . . . It is going to run into fantastic figures. . . . It will be a highly expensive war. . . . We have very few planes that cost less than $2 million each, and many of them, with all their electronic equipment, cost nearer to $3 millions. And I am not talking about the large bombers now, I am talking about the fighter-bombers. . . .

I say to mobilize the Pennsylvania and New York National Guard Divisions. . . . It will take a great many of those boys to get out in the jungle and find one of those Viet Cong and you would lose a great many of them in the process. But if we train our men to the nth degree in this special type of guerrilla fighting, I don't know any reasons why our soldiers shouldn't equal those there. . . . I am an admirer of Secretary McNamara. He has more vitality and more drive and more energy than any man that I know and a great deal of ability. . . . Secretary McNamara . . . has done a great job. . . . I want to make it perfectly clear that the United States Army is equipped better than any other army on earth. There is no doubt about that. It has the finest equipment, it has the best equipment, it has the most equipment per man of any army on earth. . . . Probably 75 percent of all South Vietnamese would vote for Uncle Ho if given the chance.

> — Senator Richard B. Russell, Democrat of
> Georgia, chairman, Senate Armed Services
> Committee, *Face the Nation*, CBS,
> August 1, 1965

The real issue has to be joined in the South and this is where it is being joined. . . . The major burden will still be carried by the South Vietnamese forces, but we are going to help them in a larger manner. . . . The reason we are sending American forces in greater number to South Vietnam now is to assure that they don't have many local successes in the future. . . . The problem right now is to prevent the North Vietnamese from increasing their infiltration into the South. This is what we have been concentrating on and I think with a certain amount of success.

> — Under Secretary of State George W. Ball,
> *Issues & Answers*, ABC, August 1, 1965

My directive says that our policy is one of minimum candor.

> — Barry Zorthian, chief of public information,
> Saigon, quoted by *Time*, August 2, 1965

I think we've got more respect in the world than at any time in history.
. . . The polls on Vietnam run about 80–20 in favor of what we're doing.
. . . Somebody ought to do an article on you, on your damn profession,
your First Amendment. . . . I don't think things will look up until
they're convinced they cannot win. Power. Power on land, power in the
air, power wherever it's necessary. We've got to commit it, and this will
convince them that we mean it.

> — President Lyndon B. Johnson,
> interview, *Newsweek*, August 2, 1965

At the end of the village a woman lay gasping as blood poured from a
wound in her side. Around her were clustered terrified children, wailing
and alternately staring in fear at the Marines and turning to clutch the
dying woman. . . . The Marines burned down houses from which they
believed the Viet Cong had fired. . . . "Kill them, I don't want anyone
moving," a Marine said. . . .

> — *New York Herald Tribune* (Paris edition),
> August 3, 1965

"I got me a VC, man. I got at least two of them bastards." . . . The
Marines ordered a Vietnamese corporal to go down into the grenade-
blasted hole to pull out the victims. The victims were three children
between 11 and 14—two boys and a girl. . . . "Oh my God," a young
Marine exclaimed. "They're all kids."

> — *New York Herald Tribune*, UPI dispatch,
> August 3, 1965

This is no time for defeatism about Asia.

> — *Life*, August 6, 1965

I think we have made progress. . . . By far the most optimistic element
in the situation is the new broadened and deepened United States
commitment . . . indicated by the President's announcement of his
intention to send additional forces to South Vietnam. This gave an
enormous lift to all of us. . . . If one analyzes the experiences of past
history, there has always been a very large preponderance of force on the
side of the government which has won. . . .

We have resources and capabilities in South Vietnam no counter-
guerrilla force or government ever had in the past. I refer to our air
mobility, our helicopters, our fixed-wing aircraft, and all the devices and
techniques we have brought to that country. . . .

Bear in mind that we are really filling a gap in indigenous Vietnamese
forces by putting in our own combat ground troops. I am quite confident

that in the course of the next year, 1966, the Vietnamese can raise considerably more forces than in the past. . . . I would not agree that any figure like 300,000 to 400,000 is likely to be required. . . . We are trying to destroy an enemy, namely the Viet Cong. . . . We must fill in the manpower gap . . . to . . . blunt and defeat the monsoon offensive and remove from the minds of the leaders of Hanoi any hope that they may have of a successful military outcome. . . .

No one ever suggested that the air attacks are going to stop completely infiltration. They obviously will not. . . . These attacks have had a very clear, depressive effect upon infiltration. . . . We are fulfilling the pledge. . . . I would say that our strategy today is that which I have been recommending. . . . Our bombing program in North Vietnam was designed . . . to remind the leaders in Hanoi that they must pay an increasingly high price. . . . As we get greater forces we can always move toward some objective which is so valuable to the Viet Cong that they must stand and fight.

> — General Maxwell D. Taylor,
> *Meet the Press*, NBC, August 8, 1965

There is no way to get peace just by stopping the war.

> — David Lawrence, editor,
> *U.S. News & World Report*, August 9, 1965

The firm stand of the United States in the Vietnam war provides a ray of hope.

> — President Chiang Kai-shek, interview with
> *U.S. News & World Report*, Taipei,
> August 9, 1965

They have swung rather wildly and they have suffered some substantial reverses. . . . I think there are a good many things happening out there that would give you pride. . . .

> — President Lyndon B. Johnson,
> August 9, 1965

Intimates of President Johnson confide that he is more optimistic today about eventual success than at any time since the election.

> — *New York Herald Tribune*, August 11, 1965

Members of the 1st Battalion, the Royal Australian Regiment killed four Vietcong and destroyed five enemy villages in a five-day operation north of Saigon, the Australian Army Force headquarters reported today. About seven tons of rice, 100 lbs. of salt, a large quantity of peanuts, and weapons and clothing were destroyed. Australian casualties were reported to be "very light."

> — *London Times*, August 12, 1965

There isn't a way out just now. We are deeply committed, and it's been a growing commitment. We can't leave now without breaking our word.

> — Senator Richard B. Russell,
> quoted by *Time*, August 13, 1965

Within the Senate, there is solid support for standing firm in Viet Nam. Within the group, there are a great many regrets that we are in there. But we are in there. Our flag is committed. Our boys are committed. We've got to back them up. . . . We can't pull out.

> — Senator John C. Stennis,
> quoted by *Time*, August 13, 1965

I have misgivings because I can't see what the ultimate outcome will be. My problem is the same as it is for so many others. When I'm asked what to do, I am at a loss for answers.

> — Senator Frank Moss, Democrat of Utah,
> quoted by *Time*, August 13, 1965

We can't afford to clear out of Viet Nam.

> — Senator George Aiken, Republican of
> Vermont, quoted by *Time*, August 13, 1965

It can't be settled soon—because it can't be.

> — Senator Mike Mansfield, Democrat of
> Montana, Majority Leader, quoted by *Time*,
> August 13, 1965

It's not a question of how we got there or why. We're there.

> — Senator George Smathers, Democrat of
> Florida, quoted by *Time*, August 13, 1965

We can't predict that we will have the right results in Viet Nam, but our actions are rightly conceived. I know this is the only course we can follow. . . . President Johnson is doing his best to control events. There isn't anything to do but what the President is doing.

> — Senator Fred Harris, Democrat of Oklahoma,
> quoted by *Time*, August 13, 1965

We have to stand firm.

> — Senator Russell Long, Democrat of Louisiana,
> Majority Whip, quoted by *Time*,
> August 13, 1965

I don't have any alternative that I consider realistic or any more effective than what the President is doing. . . . I can't accept the idea of withdrawal. I feel unhappy about Viet Nam—but I'm not particularly rebellious.

> — Senator Edmund Muskie, Democrat of Maine, quoted by *Time*, August 13, 1965

I don't think that you can scuttle and run. I think that as you watch the President's position . . . it's just another indication of his political genius.

> — Senator Joe Clark, Democrat of Pennsylvania, quoted by *Time*, August 13, 1965

The situation that confronts us now is not debatable. We have a commitment. Our men are engaged. The Administration, with the backing of Congress, has stated the policy. It's firm. It's fixed. It does us all well to support it unequivocally. By and large, the great majority of the Senate—with very few, very, very few exceptions—supports the President in his position.

> — Senator John Pastore, Democrat of Rhode Island, quoted by *Time*, August 13, 1965

This insidious aggression, known as "wars of national liberation," stands on trial in Viet Nam. . . . If it fails, we can hope that aggression may be over forever.

> — Senator Gale McGee, Democrat of Wyoming, quoted by *Time*, August 13, 1965

Now our people are giving support in a broader and deeper sense than they were before. . . . The effort was deemed to be successful two years ago, and I was one of those who thought we had success in sight, after a careful analysis of the situation and a visit to Vietnam. But it was successful militarily. . . . Due to the sizeable increase in the Viet Cong forces in the past year, the situation has changed. . . .

I believe, then, that our U.S. forces in conjunction with the Vietnamese forces should be able to defeat the Viet Cong and to re-establish this favorable balance that we had a couple of years ago. . . . No, we are not turning it into an American war. Our forces are not there to replace the Vietnamese forces, they are there to supplement the Vietnamese forces. General Westmoreland understands this clearly.

> — General Earle G. Wheeler, chairman, Joint Chiefs of Staff, *Issues & Answers*, ABC, August 15, 1965

"There is little talk in Washington any more of winning over the Vietnamese people," reports *Newsweek*'s Lloyd Norman. "The new attitude is 'we're out to kill the Viet Cong and we're not worried about winning friends.'"

— *Newsweek*, August 16, 1965

We supported the French . . . after . . . they had surrendered. . . . Finally we had this treaty at Geneva and they made this division along the 17th parallel and we said then: 'All right, we will help that country.' Now, we were talking at that time not in terms of military support. . . . We were talking about economic and what we could call foreign aid. . . . We found a lone leader who seemed to meet the requirements of the situation—young Diem—and we supported him. Now, since that time he is gone and since he's gone we have had some 8 or 9 different Governments. But I think there was no commitment ever given in a military context that said we are going . . . to do anything in a military way.

— Dwight D. Eisenhower, press conference,
August 17, 1965, as recorded by NBC News

Last week the vast engine of military power that the U.S. has installed in South Viet Nam was finally warming to its task. A new air of confidence pervaded the week's decisions, a new professionalism was apparent. . . . The despair of earlier months was fading as the great war engine revved up.

— *Time*, August 20, 1965

I believe it to be true that military success of the kind which we have seen in recent days does help us bring nearer the day when there will be effective negotiation.

— Presidential Assistant for National Security
Affairs McGeorge Bundy, CBS-TV,
August 23, 1965

The fact that . . . we are not going to be pushed out . . . has made a big difference.

— Secretary of State Dean Rusk,
CBS-TV, August 23, 1965

We have to persevere. . . . Our message is loud and clear. . . .

— Ambassador Arthur Goldberg,
U.S. representative to UN, CBS-TV,
August 23, 1965

Richard Nixon, speaking from the West Branch, Ia., birthplace of the late President Herbert Hoover, had some advice for President Johnson on how to prosecute the war in Vietnam. . . . Mr. Johnson should "discipline" top Senate Democrats who do not believe in his Vietnam policy. Mr. Nixon said he meant Senators J. William Fulbright and Mike Mansfield when he spoke of "disciplining" dissident Democrats. . . .

In North Vietnam the steady U.S. air assault is starting to cause real damage. The economy is grinding down.

— *U.S. News & World Report*,
August 23, 1965

We seek to defend the right of people . . . in . . . South Vietnam. . . . I do not believe this right can be secured by retreat. Retreat leads to retreat. . . . America must use its wisdom.

— Adlai E. Stevenson, last article,
Look, August 24, 1965

Peace—peace, that simple little five-letter word—is the most important word in the English language.

— President Lyndon B. Johnson,
August 25, 1965

A new generation of Americans tasted major combat last week and passed the test. . . . Three battalions of the 3rd Marine Division attacked some 2,000 Viet Cong troops . . . at Chu Lai. By week's end the U.S. had fought its first large-scale battle since Korea and had won decisively. Smashed with the Viet Cong was the myth that the Red foe is invincible in the tangled underbrush of his homeland; smashed also was the myth that the U.S. can't fight on land in Asia. . . . "Operation Starlight" had begun. . . . Some 50 marines were killed in the battle for Van Tuong, and another 150 wounded . . . "nearly 75% of them were shot in the back." . . . The battle left the Americans with much to be encouraged about. . . . "Operation Starlight" proved . . . the U.S. can more than hold its own in Viet Nam.

— *Time*, August 27, 1965

BOB CLARK, ABC White House Correspondent: Do you make any criticism at all of President Johnson's conduct of the Vietnam war?

SENATOR KENNEDY: No, I don't. As a matter of fact, I myself believe that we have made a commitment in South Vietnam, that we have to stand by our commitment, that we have to take every means possible to see that it is realized. . . . I certainly support the effort that is being made. . . . I believe that there has been broad bipartisan support for the policy out in South Vietnam and I think that this will continue. . . . I know that President Kennedy had a very high regard for Secretary Rusk.

> — Senator Edward M. Kennedy, Democrat of
> Massachusetts, *Issues & Answers*, ABC,
> August 29, 1965

We must follow the President.

> — Former President Dwight D. Eisenhower, who
> commented "all rot" to reports of rift between
> him and President Lyndon B. Johnson,
> Gettysburg, Pa., quoted by *U.S. News & World
> Report*, August 30, 1965

Mr. Johnson ordered retaliation against North Vietnam by bomber attacks and now has commanded a buildup of American forces to 125,000. . . . The result in the last few weeks has been a marked improvement in South Vietnamese fortunes.

> — Kenneth Crawford, column, *Newsweek*,
> August 30, 1965

Both in Saigon and Washington last week smiling officials suddenly began to express "cautious optimism" over the course of the war in Vietnam.

> — *Newsweek*, August 30, 1965

U.S. Marines in South Vietnam have achieved what the U.S. high command has long hoped for—a big and dramatic victory in their first major engagement with the Viet Cong. . . . U.S. authorities hoped the battle would be an eye-opener for all of Southeast Asia. Points they expected to be made: The Communists are not "10 feet tall." American manpower plus superior American equipment can turn the war around. U.S. combat troops can set a victorious example for the Vietnamese forces. . . . Did it mean a turning point in the fighting? . . . Indicators . . . could point that way—The Viet Cong is having recruiting trouble. . . . The tide seemed to be turning in the Mekong Delta.

> — *U.S. News & World Report*, August 30, 1965

In the ground action, United States marines have killed 87 Viet Cong guerrillas, including 66 men killed in a tunnel with a charge of TNT, in two days of fighting on the Batangan Peninsula, it was reported today. . . . The 66 persons killed in a huge Viet Cong tunnel yesterday apparently died of concussion and blast after a Marine demolition team, covered by automatic-weapons fire, crept to the camouflaged entrance and placed a charge of explosives in it. "I was so proud of my marines I could hardly talk," said Maj. Gen. Lewis W. Walt, commander of the Third Marine Amphibious Force. "The victory is encouraging, but we will not rest until we search out and destroy all the Viet Cong."

— Charles Mohr, *New York Times*,
September 10, 1965

I think the term "turning the corner" is probably appropriate, compared with the situation I saw on my last visit to Vietnam in the spring of 1964. . . . When I left this time, I was convinced the Viet Cong would not win. . . . We are looking down the road toward two or three years more [when] the Vietnamese will be able to handle them without our help. . . . The guerrillas must be reduced in their power to the point where they recognize that they can't win and that they will lay down their arms. . . . I am against concessions. . . . Our goal must be . . . punishment for the aggressor, and certainly no concessions. . . . The war is going better than it was. . . . The number of 125,000 [troops] will meet the immediate commitment, but if resistance continues, we have to put in more so that we can break down their resistance. . . . What must happen first is a victory. . . . I think one thing we can be sure of—On the ideological front we have won. . . . It is to our interests to fight as much as possible on the sea [*sic*] and in the air. That is why I think we need to bring . . . additional sea power against North Vietnam.

— Richard M. Nixon, *Meet the Press*, NBC,
September 12, 1965

At last there is light at the end of the tunnel.

— Joseph Alsop, syndicated column,
September 13, 1965

I am cautiously optimistic about the war situation.

— Secretary of Defense Robert S. McNamara,
September 17, 1965

The Viet Cong is presumed to be in a state of retreat from South Vietnam.

— Admiral David L. McDonald,
Chief of Naval Operations,
Honolulu, September 17, 1965

I would say the war in South Vietnam changed irrevocably on Feb. 19, 1965. America began using its immense air power in a less-heralded way. U.S. jet pilots started to bomb South Vietnam. Secretary of State Dean Rusk often says that American policy in Vietnam seems to him very simple. But what the United States is now doing would make more sense, in a way, if one were to imagine South Vietnam as a hostile country.

American pilots fan out over the country each day on hundreds of missions. They bomb huts, afterward described as "structures," and they kill Vietnamese, afterward described as "Communists."

I was greeted by an officer with one of the helicopter units.

"Terror," he said pleasantly. "The Vietcong have terrorized the peasants to get their cooperation, or at least to stop their opposition. We must terrorize the villagers even more, so they see that their real self-interest lies with us. We've got to start bombing and strafing the villages that aren't friendly to the Government."

> — Jack Langguth, *New York Times Magazine*,
> September 19, 1965

Good results have already been achieved. . . . [Walter Lippmann] announced that the U.S. government has "recognized" that it is impossible to "impose a military solution in Viet-Nam" by "capturing and subduing Viet Cong rebels." But just that, in point of fact, is what the 1st Cavalry Division is here for.

> — Joseph Alsop, syndicated column,
> September 20, 1965

I cannot make any positive statement about Viet Nam that I cannot honestly contradict with another statement.

> — U. Alexis Johnson, deputy U.S. ambassador to
> Vietnam, quoted in *Quote, the Weekly Digest*,
> September 26, 1965

The President is a peace-loving man. I am a peace-loving man. The President said I have an obsession for peace. I do. I abhor violence. And I think American policy under his direction is aimed toward a peaceful solution.

> — Ambassador Arthur J. Goldberg, U.S.
> representative to UN, *Meet the Press*, NBC,
> September 26, 1965

There truly is a future here, that makes the war worth winning.

> — Joseph Alsop, syndicated column,
> September 27, 1965

There's been a big change in Asia's jungle war. Communists are . . . running for cover. . . . There are reasons for optimism. . . . Today the tide in this war is turning.

> — *U.S. News & World Report*,
> September 27, 1965

Vietnamese Army police and paramilitary organizations such as the national guard and the militia frequently shoot Vietcong captives out of hand, beat or brutally torture them or otherwise mistreat them. Many Vietcong are also non-uniformed partisans. . . . The favorite methods of torture used by Government troops are to slowly beat a captive, drag him behind a moving vehicle, apply electrodes to sensitive parts of his body or block his mouth while water spiced with hot pepper is poured down his nostrils. . . . The U.S. is in the unhappy position of asking humane treatment for American prisoners of Communists while it has declined to guarantee similar treatment to Vietcong taken prisoners by American ground combat units. Such prisoners, after a preliminary interrogation, are handed over to the Vietnamese authorities by whom of course they can be and frequently are subjected to brutality.

> — Neil Sheehan, *New York Times*,
> September 30, 1965

The V-C plans for winning the war this year have gone very badly wrong.

> — Joseph Alsop, syndicated column,
> October 4, 1965

Now Reds must fight—or run. U.S. military might is beginning to pay off in Vietnam. Communists are hurting, losing the initiative. Red hopes for a quick knockout are gone . . . clearly being hurt on the battlefield. Prisoners and captured documents are giving U.S. advisers a fresh new view of the enemy's problems. . . . U.S. combat troops are destroying guerrillas in large numbers.

> — *U.S. News & World Report*,
> October 4, 1965

In Asia over the last year, I have felt that there is an encouraging mood of new confidence. . . . The North Vietnamese and the Viet Cong monsoon offensive that gave us concern failed.

> — President Lyndon B. Johnson,
> news conference, October 13, 1966

The progress in the past 12 months has exceeded our expectations.

> — Secretary of Defense Robert S. McNamara,
> October 14, 1966

Victory in the end, by long, hard toil and courage and endurance, can certainly be hoped for. The means for winning in Viet-Nam are now in place. And that is the measure of the debt owing to Lyndon Johnson, for the courageous decisions that have wrought this vital change.

> — Joseph Alsop, syndicated column,
> October 15, 1965

In other air actions, American and South Vietnamese pilots flew 36 missions over North Vietnam and 324 over South Vietnam. River shipping was a prime target in the South, and 26 sampans were reported sunk.

> — R. W. Apple, Jr., *New York Times,*
> October 17, 1965

The U.S. Air Force flew 26,858 sorties against Vietnam in a single week.

> — *Newsweek,* October 18, 1965

The tide is turning—you might say that. . . . There's a more general sense of optimism on the military front. . . . The important thing at this moment is that we are no longer losing on the military front. . . . Our manpower build-up is still going on—probably will go to 200,000 men. . . . I think that increasingly the Viet Cong have lost sight of their revolution.

> — Lucian W. Pye, Professor of Political Science,
> M.I.T., senior staff member, Center for
> International Studies, lecturer, U.S. war
> colleges, expert on Southeast Asia, interview,
> *U.S. News & World Report,* October 18, 1965

We have stopped losing the war. . . . Today, the Vietnamese can see a possibility of winning, whereas they didn't a few months ago. There's no doubt we can stay in there until we've got it cleaned up.

> — Admiral U. S. Grant Sharp, commander in
> chief, Pacific, Honolulu, October 21, 1965,
> interview with Hanson W. Baldwin, *New York
> Times*

[Our 1,000 bombing sorties a month] should be enough to knock the hell out of them. We must be hitting the wrong targets.

> — General Curtis E. LeMay, former chief of staff,
> U.S. Air Force, speech, October 21, 1965

The only way we can lose this war now is in a political or moral way—not in a tactical way. So why should any of us talk of negotiation?

> — President Nguyen Cao Ky, quoted in *Time,*
> October 22, 1965

Today, South Vietnam throbs with a pride and power, above all an *esprit.* . . . The remarkable turnabout in the war. . . . The Viet Cong's

once-cocky hunters have become the cowering hunted. . . . As one
top-ranking U.S. officer put it: "We've stemmed the tide."

> — *Time*, October 22, 1965

The morale of the insurgents is sinking, while the whole character of
the Viet Cong is becoming progressively more northern, and alien to
South Vietnam.

> — P. J. Honey, British professor,
> consultant on Vietnam, October 1965

Presently the military operations appear to be going better. . . . There
have been some very favorable reports from a military point of view in
recent weeks. . . . We have also insisted on continuing the bombing as
we did in the spring. The President made some very impressive speeches
in that direction.

> — Senator J. William Fulbright,
> *Meet the Press*, NBC, October 24, 1965

Adding up the recent news from Vietnam, one is tempted to conclude
that our side is at last winning the war there. . . . The incoming tide
seems to have reached full flood but has not yet started to recede.

> — Kenneth Crawford, column, *Newsweek*,
> October 25, 1965

I think it is important to recognize that progress has been made during
the summer.

> — Secretary of Defense Robert S. McNamara,
> October 26, 1965

The Viet Cong will just peter out.

> — General Maxwell D. Taylor, October 27, 1965

I'm impressed. . . . There has been a distinct improvement over the
last six months.

> — Ambassador Henry Cabot Lodge,
> October 28, 1965

In August . . . the tide had turned. . . . McNamara's . . . strategy in Viet Nam may prove itself.

> — Charles Bartlett, *Washington Star*,
> October 28, 1965

48 civilians were killed and 55 were wounded in the strike in which the

planes dropped 260-pound fragmentation and phosphorus bombs, which cause deep, excruciating burns. Many of the victims were believed to be women and children. Both U.S. Embassy and military officials cleared all American personnel of any responsibility. The attack took place Saturday on De Duc, about 40 miles northwest of the U.S. disembarkation port of Qui Nhon.

— AP dispatch from Saigon, October 31, 1965

The initiative in the fighting has passed from the Communist insurgents to the United States and the South Vietnamese forces.

— McGeorge Bundy, October 1965

As soon as President Johnson took a very firm stand in Vietnam, you noticed the situation immediately became better. . . . There are enough troops in Vietnam, you have enough troops there—I think you have something like 160,000 and there are plenty of Vietnamese troops, so I do not think they need any more troops.

— Madame Chiang Kai-shek, *Meet the Press*, NBC, October 31, 1965

The Viet Cong . . . have paid an inordinate price. . . . According to Pentagon estimates, 25,000 Viet Cong have been killed so far this year—which is 8,000 more than were killed in all of 1964. The trouble seems to be, however, that every time a Viet Cong is killed, another Vietnamese is ready to step into his place. In fact, according to the same Pentagon figures, there are more Viet Cong soldiers in the field now than there were a year ago.

— *Newsweek*, November 1, 1965

In Southeast Asia the United States is now committed to a war which can only have one conclusion: victory. . . . The name of the game is war.

— Hanson W. Baldwin, military editor, *New York Times*, article in *Reader's Digest*, November 1965

It is clear now the Communists are losing the war. There is no longer any real prospect that North Vietnam . . . can get a victory.

— *U.S. News & World Report*, November 8, 1965

The tide has turned. The Viet Cong has been stopped. They cannot win.

— Vice President Hubert H. Humphrey, quoted by *Newsweek*, November 8, 1965

Were recent military victories . . . first harbingers of victory? . . . In recent weeks, a number of high U.S. political and military officials have begun to make some gingerly optimistic predictions. Professional military men are hopeful. . . . Former ambassador to Saigon Gen. Maxwell D. Taylor feels . . . that the enemy may just gradually cease his aggression in the face of growing U.S. power.

> — *Newsweek*, November 8, 1965

Neither the Chinese nor the North Vietnamese have reached the moment of truth. They have always assumed that they would win in South Vietnam. What they will do when faced, instead, with the prospect of defeat in South Vietnam will be somewhat uncertain until the moment comes.

> — Joseph Alsop, syndicated column,
> November 10, 1965

It will be necessary to add further to the strength of U.S. combat forces in Vietnam.

> — Secretary of Defense Robert S. McNamara,
> November 11, 1965

South Vietnamese torn from their homes by war may increase to a million over the next year, reports tonight indicated. This would be about one in 14 of all the troubled country's inhabitants. . . . There are now 720,000 displaced persons in South Viet Nam.

> — AP, November 12, 1965

Pacification is the thing that struck me most. . . . The American build-up there . . . is tremendous. . . . Our policy of bombing the villages in South Vietnam . . . I don't get the impression from talking with people that this has cost us the friendship of the South Vietnamese people. We are only doing it where we have to do it. . . . Pacification . . . will succeed. . . . In certain areas clearly it has advanced. . . . I think there is a good deal of confidence in this particular regime and certainly I must say that I was impressed with General Ky, what I saw of him. . . . Morale was . . . just unbelievable, really. A spirit of dedication the likes of which I haven't seen for a long time. I was tremendously impressed with this. . . . I hope to go back [to Vermont] and give my people and my state a feel of what is going on over there.

> — Governor Philip H. Hoff, Democrat of
> Vermont, *Meet the Press*, NBC,
> November 14, 1965

Development of the farms, aid with the fertilizers and all these things, don't have much appeal to the press, and therefore aren't reported. They are interested more in how many Viet Cong were killed and not in how much fertilizer has been distributed. . . . The decision at home has to be made between guns and butter. At least for the present apparently we can have both. I don't know how long this can keep up, but certainly if the decision has to be made, it has clearly got to be guns abroad. . . . I think that we are on the way up over there in South Vietnam, and I don't think it is a bottomless pit. I think that the steps we are taking are the correct ones, and I base this on the fact that we are getting control of more areas. . . . We are getting the upper edge. . . . It is the fault of the press. . . . You can't just run out in the countryside and distribute fertilizer. You have got to get the people security first. . . . The A.I.D. and the military people, they couldn't have been more helpful and more enthusiastic.

> — Governor John H. Chafee, Republican of
> Rhode Island, *Meet the Press*, NBC,
> November 14, 1965

The Communists will be worn out . . . they will run downhill toward military ineffectiveness and defeat.

> — Lieutenant General B. E. Spivey, top military
> planner, Joint Chiefs of Staff,
> November 15, 1965

The South Vietnamese, with our help, have blunted and defeated the Viet Cong monsoon offensive, and the Viet Cong have paid a very high price indeed.

> — Secretary of Defense Robert S. McNamara,
> quoted by *Time*, November 19, 1965

Statistics cannot adequately describe the increasing intensity of American air attacks and the damage they are doing to the South Vietnamese countryside. . . . The number of strike sorties rose . . . to about 7,500 in July. In the past month alone, there have been about 12,000 strike sorties—more than in all 1964—and about 11,000 buildings were destroyed or damaged. . . . To wipe out villages remote from any specific combat area on the strength of reports—often ill-founded—that the Vietcong have been sheltered there . . . more is involved than the deaths, the carnage and the alienation of peasant loyalty. The bombs that destroy South Vietnam's villages are smashing the social structure of the countryside.

> — *New York Times*, November 21, 1965

I consider this an unprecedented victory.

> — General William C. Westmoreland, referring
> to battle of Ia Drang, succeeding Chu Pouy as
> costliest battle of war in U.S. lives, quoted by
> *Time*, November 26, 1965

I think we are . . . determined. . . . This question of Viet Cong participation . . . is really what the war is about. . . . We are going to do what is necessary. . . . I don't call that necessarily escalation. . . . Secretary McNamara is surprised, as I think many of us are surprised, that the Viet Cong and North Vietnamese units have chosen to stand and fight. There was some thinking that . . . they would refuse battle. . . . Why they did I can only speculate. I am not sure what the answer is. . . . They got a very bloody nose and as we know their monsoon offensive was not successful. . . . The loss ratio . . . doesn't indicate that we are just reaching a stalemate. It raises the question as to whether or not they will be able to maintain the intensity of the effort they are mounting. I personally don't think they can. . . . Our problem is to convince Hanoi that this is no go, that they can have no hope of success, and I think once this is accomplished, I think we could hope for a relatively quick solution. . . . We can . . . persuade Hanoi that . . . its interest is to call it off. . . . I think we can continue . . . to make a maximum effort. . . . It is hard for me to read the mind of Hanoi. . . . I think our best chance of obtaining settlement is, as the President said, to go ahead and do what is necessary on the military front.

> — Deputy Under Secretary of State for Political
> Affairs U. Alexis Johnson, *Face the Nation*,
> CBS, November 28, 1965

Anyone who has spent much time with Government units in the field has seen the heads of prisoners held under water and bayonet blades pressed against their throats. Photographs of such incidents were common until the Government decided the publicity was not improving Saigon's public relations. In more extreme cases, victims have had bamboo slivers run under their fingernails or wires from a field telephone connected to arms, nipples, or testicles. Another rumored technique is known as "the long step." The idea is to take several prisoners up in a helicopter and toss one out in order to loosen the tongues of the others.

> — William Tuohy, *New York Times Magazine*,
> November 28, 1965

We have stopped losing the war.

> — Secretary of Defense Robert S. McNamara,
> November 29, 1965

The war is progressing well.

> — Secretary of State Dean Rusk,
> Saigon, November 29, 1965

We'll lick them.

> — Secretary of State Dean Rusk,
> quoted by *Newsweek*, November 29, 1965

For the first time since we spun into the Vietnam mess, there is hope for the United States. . . . The credit justly belongs to President Lyndon B. Johnson. He has made the war "unlosable." . . . Every day, we must stalk through villages, warily and with weapons cocked, and some innocents are inevitably hurt.

If such casualties do not endear foreigners to the Vietnamese, neither does their habit of harboring guerrilla snipers make us love them. So there is mutual terrorism, as there is in every war. Both sides have been guilty of abuse, torture and mutilation of prisoners. A kind of nameless rage builds up in most men at the dirt and heat and terrifying suspense of this struggle in which there is no front line, no real way of knowing who is with you and who is against you. Rage ebbs into hunger for revenge, then more rage piles upon it, and men begin devising ingenious, hideous ways of giving their enemy the jitters.

— Sam Castan, *Look* senior editor,
November 30, 1965

The International Committee of the Red Cross in Geneva . . . complained again that the United States was violating an international accord on the treatment of prisoners.

— *New York Times*, December 1, 1965

The Communists . . . have thus far suffered disastrous defeats. . . . The South Vietnamese . . . fought with immense courage. . . . The stern application of American power in Viet-Nam, meanwhile, dealt a far heavier blow. . . . What is happening inside South Vietnam must therefore be regarded as downright encouraging, despite the heavy price being paid. . . . The pressure we are exerting must eventually cause a crack somewhere, and the war will be close to won. . . . [For] the North Vietnamese . . . the war is close to being lost.

— Joseph Alsop, syndicated column,
December 3, 1965

I would like to see him [Robert S. McNamara] go back to making Edsels.

— Senator Barry Goldwater,
quoted by *Time*, December 3, 1965

The U.S. is beginning to turn the corner in Viet Nam.

— *Time*, December 3, 1965

The presence of the American troops has had a tonic effect on the

Vietnamese. They are more aggressive and fighting better than ever before.

> — General William C. Westmoreland,
> quoted by *Time*, December 3, 1965

I basically support the Administration's policy.

> — Senator Robert F. Kennedy, Democrat of
> New York, *Meet the Press*, NBC,
> December 5, 1965

Air power in Vietnam is accomplishing and will accomplish every task assigned to it.

> — General John O. McConnell, chief of staff,
> U.S. Air Force, address, Detroit,
> December 6, 1965

TOP SECRET

We believe that . . . the U.S. must send a substantial number of additional forces to VN if we are to avoid being defeated there. . . . Deployments of the kind we have recommended will not guarantee success. . . . We expect them, upon learning of any U.S. intentions to augment its forces, to boost their own commitment and to test U.S. capabilities and will to persevere at the higher level of conflict and casualties (U.S. KIA [killed in action] with the recommended deployments can be expected to reach 1000 a month. . . .

> — Secretary of Defense Robert S. McNamara,
> memorandum to President Lyndon B.
> Johnson, December 7, 1965

We believe that we're going to win this war. Afterwards you'll have a major job of reconstruction on your hands. That will take financing and financing means banks. . . . It would be illogical to permit the English and French to monopolize the banking business because South Vietnam's economy is becoming more and more United States oriented.

> — Henry M. Sperry, vice president,
> First National City Bank of New York,
> quoted by *New York Times*, December 9, 1965

I would say that the Communists had the offensive at the start of the monsoon offensive and gave it up. . . . I would say that we have the offensive. . . . I would say that we rather clearly have the offensive. . . . I would say our whole purpose is to get the Hanoi leadership to mend their ways. . . . We have to create a very clear, unmistakable picture to them that they can't possibly win this thing. . . .

> — General Maxwell D. Taylor, special consultant
> to President, *Issues & Answers*, ABC,
> December 12, 1965

Manpower drain of war in South Vietnam is a worry for Hanoi's Reds.

> — *U.S. News & World Report*,
> December 13, 1965

Now there is a curious rebirth of interest in investing in South Vietnam with the risks appearing to be reduced. More and more U.S. businessmen are combining business with Far East vacations by booking stopovers in Saigon. . . . More than 50 million dollars has been put into industry in the Saigon area since 1961. Most of this has gone into light manufacturing plants.

> — *U.S. News & World Report*,
> December 13, 1965

Although the war in Vietnam is going to cost a lot more money than was anticipated, this country is rich enough to wage a war against poverty at home and a successful war in Vietnam at the same time.

> — Sargent Shriver, director, Office of
> Economic Opportunity and Peace Corps,
> *Meet the Press*, NBC, December 19, 1965

From the moment the U.S. dropped its first bomb on North Vietnam, it welded the nation together unshakably.

> — James Cameron, British correspondent,
> *New York Times*, December 20, 1965

A wartime building boom in South Vietnam has attracted some two dozen American construction and engineering firms. More are believed ready to enter the scene. Military and civil contracts are the lure. They range from building ports and airfields to . . . electric-power and water systems. . . . Builders also eye postwar possibilities, hope to nudge out established French competitors on reconstruction work.

> — "What U.S. Companies Are Doing Abroad,"
> *U.S. News & World Report*, December 20, 1965

Our object in Vietnam is not war but peace.

> — President Lyndon B. Johnson,
> toast to Chancellor Ludwig Erhardt,
> Washington, December 20, 1965

Pressure on the enemy is already beginning to get the kind of result that is desired.

> — Joseph Alsop, syndicated column,
> December 20, 1965

Your belief in the disastrous trend in American foreign policy . . . I do not share with you. . . . Its purposes and directions are sound. I do not believe [in] the policy of retreat in Asia or anywhere else. . . . This is the point of the conflict in Viet-Nam.

> — Ambassador Adlai E. Stevenson, U.S.
> representative to UN, last letter, written 3 days
> before death, released posthumously by
> Adlai III, quoted in *Time*, December 24, 1965

I think the intellectual community of the Free World is rather sharply divided on . . . Vietnam, and we are, in essence, trying to be as persuasive as we can. . . . To those people who are not supporting us in this conflict, I think there is a misconception that the intellectual community is totally against us.

> — John Chancellor, director, Voice of America,
> *Issues & Answers*, ABC, December 26, 1965

Evidence is growing that the Russian antiaircraft missiles installed in North Vietnam are not so effective after all.

> — *U.S. News & World Report*,
> December 27, 1965

Many a news correspondent or U.S. Army military adviser has seen the hands whacked off prisoners with machetes. Prisoners are sometimes castrated or blinded. In more than one case a Viet Cong suspect has been towed after interrogation behind an armored personnel carrier across the rice fields. This always results in death in one of its most painful forms.

> — Malcolm Browne, AP correspondent, Pulitzer
> Prize winner for news reporting from Vietnam,
> *The New Face of War*

The fighting is going on on four fronts: the government versus the generals, the Buddhists versus the government, the generals versus the ambassador, and, I hope, the generals versus the VC.

> — General Maxwell D. Taylor to American
> newsmen, Saigon, 1965

Westmoreland was trying to play chess while his enemy was playing Go.

> — Frances FitzGerald, *Fire in the Lake*

All of Viet Nam is one great big goddam booby trap.

> — G.I. at Bien Hoa to author,
> December 1965

The enemy is no longer close to victory. . . . The thrust of the aggression has been blunted. . . . Victory cannot come to the Communists. . . . We shall continue to resist and to pacify the area. . . . We move prudently. . . . What we have tried to do is to escalate the peace. . . . Hanoi . . . ought to know, as many nations have already told it, that it is impossible for them to gain a victory. [Senator Mansfield's report on Vietnam] was too gloomy. . . . I think its conclusion was too gloomy. . . . The Viet Cong and the North Vietnamese have suffered many military reverses. . . .

It is also a fact that the thrust of the aggression . . . has been turned back and, as the President pointed out, the possibility of Viet Cong success militarily is no longer present. The Viet Cong cannot win militarily. And the aims of the enemy, as the President put it, have been put out of reach. . . . The Mansfield Report . . . conclusions, I believe, are just a little bit pessimistic. . . . I do not think the dissenters . . . will be right, nor are they correct. . . . There is an overwhelming support in this Nation for the President and his policy in Vietnam. . . .

I would suggest that we have forbearance and patience. . . . Much of the opposition . . . to our efforts in Vietnam . . . is rather foolish . . . I would say doctrinaire.

> — Vice President Hubert H. Humphrey,
> *Face the Nation*, CBS, January 16, 1966

TOP SECRET

The ARVN is tired, passive and accommodation-prone. . . . The PAVN/VC are effectively matching our deployments. . . . The bombing of the North . . . may or may not be able effectively to interdict infiltration (partly because the PAVN/VC can simply refuse to do battle if supplies are short). . . . Pacification is stalled despite efforts and hopes. The GVN political infrastructure is moribund and weaker than the VC infrastructure among most of the rural population. . . . South Vietnam is near the edge of serious inflation and economic chaos. . . . [But] . . . attrition . . . may push the DRV [North Vietnam] 'against the stops' by the end of 1966. . . . The Ky government is coming along . . . making progress slowly and gaining experience and stature each week. . . . There is no doubt that the cost of infiltration . . . can be made very high and that the flow of supplies can be *reduced* substantially below what it would otherwise be. . . .

The present U.S. objective in Vietnam is to avoid humiliation. The reasons why we *went into* Vietnam to the present depth are varied; but they are now largely academic. Why we have *not withdrawn* from Vietnam is, by all odds, *one* reason: (1) to preserve our reputation as a guarantor, and thus to preserve our effectiveness in the rest of the world.

We have not hung on (2) to save a friend, or (3) to deny the Communists the added acres and heads (because the dominoes don't fall for that reason in this case), or even (4) to prove that "wars of national liberation" won't work (except as our reputation is involved). At each decision point we have gambled; at each point . . . we have upped the ante. . . .

The ante (and commitment) is now very high. It is important that we behave so as to protect our reputation. At the same time, since it is our *reputation* that is at stake, it is important that we do not construe our obligation to be more than the countries whose opinion of us *are* our reputation. *We are in an escalating military stalemate.* There is an honest difference of judgment as to the success of the present military efforts in the South. . . . There is a serious question whether we are now defeating the VC/PAVC main forces and whether planned U.S. deployments will more than hold our position in the country. . . . As stated above, the U.S. end is solely to preserve our reputation as a guarantor . . . it could take us months (and could involve lopping some white as well as brown heads) to get us in position to go for a compromise. We should not expect the enemy's molasses to pour any faster than ours. And we should "tip the pitchers" now if we want them to "pour" a year from now. . . .

We are in a dilemma . . . while going for victory we have the strength for compromise, but if we go for compromise we have the strength only for defeat. . . . The situation therefore requires . . . great care in what is said and done. It also requires a willingness to escalate the war. . . . The risk is that it may be that the "coin must come up heads or tails, not on edge."

> — Assistant Secretary of Defense John T.
> McNaughton, Pentagon memorandum,
> January 19, 1966

South Vietnam . . . is a country . . . with substantial resources; it is potentially a very rich country. . . . Vietnam . . . is not going to be surrendered. We have a very important commitment there. . . . We would welcome assistance in any form from any government. . . . We here very much appreciate the very strong political support that we have had from Britain on this problem in Vietnam.

> — Secretary of State Dean Rusk,
> *Meet the Press*, NBC, January 23, 1966

TOP SECRET

JCS believe the evaluation [of the McNamara memorandum of December 7, 1965] is on the pessimistic side in view of the constant and heavy military pressure which our forces in SEA [Southeast Asia] will be capable of employing. . . . Greater weight should be given to . . . the constancy of will of the Hanoi leaders to continue a war which they realize they cannot win in the face of progressively greater destruction of their country.

> — Pentagon memorandum, January 24, 1966

We must commit substantial numbers of American fighting men. . . . "Great Society" programs with the billions they are gulping down should be relegated to the rear. . . . They should be secondary to war. . . . Our purpose is to win. . . . We can bring to bear sufficient military might to . . . defeat them on the field of battle. Only the last alternative offers us the chance of peace with honor.

> — Senator John C. Stennis, chairman, Senate
> Preparedness Investigating Subcommittee,
> January 27, 1966

If the Vietcong come to the conference table as full partners, they will in a sense have been victorious.

> — Secretary of State Dean Rusk,
> January 29, 1966

TOP SECRET

There is no evidence that bombings have made it more likely the DRV [North Vietnam] will decide to back out of the war. . . . Knowing that if they are not influenced we cannot stop them, the DRV will remain difficult to influence. With continuing DRV support, victory in the South may remain forever beyond our reach. [Therefore it is proposed] that the U.S. and GVN adopt the concept of physically cutting off DRV support to the VC by an on-the-ground barrier across the Ho Chi Minh Trail in the general vicinity of the 17th Parallel and Route 9 . . . from the sea across Vietnam and Laos to the Mekong, a straightline distance of about 160 miles. . . . That a major military and engineering effort be directed toward constructing a physical barrier of minefields, barbed wire, walls, ditches and military strong points flanked by a defoliated strip on each side.

> — Assistant Secretary of Defense John T.
> McNaughton, memorandum to Secretary of
> Defense Robert S. McNamara,
> January 30, 1966

The war in South Viet-Nam has few of the attributes of an indigenous revolt. . . . This point is at the heart of our determination to stay the course in the bloody contest now under way. . . . We do have a sense of history.

> — Under Secretary of State George W. Ball,
> address to Northwestern University Alumni
> Association, Evanston, Ill., January 30, 1966

It was not the proper place to make an all-out fight. But it is too late for us to back down.

> — Senator A. Willis Robertson, Democrat of
> Virginia, quoted by *U.S. News & World Report*,
> January 31, 1966

I think the time will soon come when we should—we must—fight the war to win. To get out now would be surrender.

> — Senator John L. McClellan, Democrat of
> Arkansas, quoted by *U.S. News & World
> Report*, January 31, 1966

We have become so much involved in South Vietnam that a voluntary withdrawal at this time would do us much harm. . . . Unless we fight it out and obtain some kind of victory . . . we will be inviting more trouble.

> — Senator Allen J. Ellender, Democrat of
> Louisiana, quoted by *U.S. News & World
> Report*, January 31, 1966

Our proud United States forces—we have no doubt at all of their ability to cope with the Viet Cong.

> — General Maxwell D. Taylor, former
> ambassador to South Vietnam, former
> chairman, Joint Chiefs of Staff, special
> consultant to President, address to Rotary
> Club of New York, February 3, 1966

Total military construction in Vietnam is in the order of $450 million in fiscal year 1966 . . . the present intention is that the military construction will rise to a monthly rate of $40 million a month. . . . $1.2 billion is the total military construction supplemental budget request of the Defense Department for Southeast Asia.

> — Rutherford M. Poats, assistant administrator,
> Far East, Agency for International
> Development, testimony before Senate
> Foreign Relations Committee,
> February 4, 1966

It seems to me quite possible for major military units to beat back, to destroy, to overcome the Vietcong and North Vietnamese troops; to clear steadily larger areas. . . . We know enough about how to do it to widen steadily the areas within which there is very substantial security, and economic and social progress. . . . There will be a gradually enlarging area of normal security and peaceful activities. . . . We are taking the initiative within South Vietnam, both in a military and in a non-military sense . . . there has been some improvement in tax administration . . . teams which will be working in the villages are much larger, better trained . . . there is a greater chance of success now than in the past. . . . We have plans. We think they are good plans.

> — David E. Bell, Agency for International
> Development, testimony before Senate
> Foreign Relations Committee,
> February 4, 1966

. . . Some estimates have said that it is costing a million and two or three hundred thousand dollars for every Viet Cong killed, I ought to know what the facts are about the long-range plans. . . . We are a strong country. We have nothing to fear. . . . We have the manpower, the machinery and everything else to accomplish a victory.

> — Senator Vance Hartke, Democrat of Indiana,
> *Issues & Answers*, ABC, February 6, 1966

Those who counsel retreat belong to a group that has always been blind to experience and deaf to hope.

> — President Lyndon B. Johnson,
> on arrival at Honolulu,
> February 6, 1966

I believe that if we are going to be successful over there, we have got to resume the bombing. . . . We have 191,000 men over there. . . . I think one reason for not making a declaration of war is to help it from expanding unnecessarily.

> — Senator Leverett Saltonstall, Republican of
> Massachusetts, *Face the Nation*, CBS,
> February 6, 1966

For us to go in a weakened condition to the peace table . . . would be courting suicide. We can only deal . . . when we have an indestructible position . . . and our position in Vietnam, I admit freely, still has many weaknesses.

> — President Nguyen Cao Ky to 1st plenary
> session of conference, Honolulu,
> February 7, 1966

Never before have U.S. businessmen followed their troops [*sic*] on such a scale.

> — "Saigon: Boomtown for U.S. Businessmen,"
> *Newsweek*, January 1, 1966

If Vietnam goes, it's entirely logical to assume that Thailand, Laos, ultimately the Philippines, will be involved in similar struggles.

> — Congressman Hale Boggs, Democrat of
> Louisiana, Majority Whip, House of
> Representatives, recently returned from
> Vietnam, quoted by *U.S. News & World
> Report*, January 3, 1966

There is a feeling on the part of the South Vietnamese people now that the war is going to be won. I think that we cannot back out, and I completely support President Johnson's policy. . . . I think that the President's popularity will certainly be high if we appear to be really winning the war. On the other hand, if we suffer great casualties and appear to be losing the war, then I think it's going to help the party that is out of power.

> — Congressman John V. Tunney, Democrat of
> California, recently returned from Vietnam,
> quoted by *U.S. News & World Report*, January
> 3, 1966

I would hope that certainly by November of 1966 we will have achieved a stalemate.

> — Senator Daniel B. Brewster, Democrat of
> Maryland, member, Senate Armed Services
> Committee, recently returned from Vietnam,
> quoted by *U.S. News & World Report*, January
> 3, 1966

I think I've modified my views to the extent that—with increased inputs of military power—I now feel that a military victory of sorts might be possible. A year ago I didn't think even a military decision could be won.

> — Senator George McGovern, Democrat of
> South Dakota, recently returned from
> Vietnam, quoted by *U.S. News & World report*,
> January 3, 1966

By spring, the allies should outnumber the enemy 4 to 1. . . . Once that happens, said a U.S. official, "we can begin pacification and the tide will begin to turn."

> — *Time*, cover story naming General William C.
> Westmoreland "Man of the Year,"
> January 7, 1966

Hold on a little longer and pretty soon we will have them on their knees at the bargaining table.

— Senator Everett M. Dirksen, Republican of
Illinois, *Issues & Answers*, ABC,
January 9, 1966

I study the world press. The world press is overwhelmingly gratified by the peace offensive taken by this Administration. . . . We certainly do a great deal of polling. We do a great deal of research. . . . You would be very gratified if you could see the reports that come in from our field representatives whose job it is to go to the villages, the remote areas of Vietnam, and explain what is being done . . . to resist the Viet Cong. They do understand. . . . I personally am confident that . . . informing the people of Vietnam has been successful. I also want to tell you that the work that is being done to try to get the Viet Cong to defect has been successful.

— Leonard H. Marks, director, U.S. Information
Agency, *Face the Nation*, CBS, January 9, 1966

TOP SECRET

Bombing . . . will bring the enemy to the conference table or cause the insurgency to wither from lack of support.

— Admiral U. S. Grant Sharp, message to Joint
Chiefs of Staff, January 12, 1966

Tonight the cup of peril is full in Vietnam. . . . We will stay until aggression is stopped. . . . The aims of the enemy have been put out of reach. . . . The enemy is no longer close to victory. Time is no longer on his side. There is no cause to doubt the American commitment. . . . We must stand or see the promise of two centuries tremble. I believe tonight that you do not want me to try that risk. And from that belief your President summons his strength. . . . With whatever guidance God may offer us, we must nevertheless and alone with our mortality strive to ennoble the life of man on earth.

— President Lyndon B. Johnson,
State of the Union Address, January 12, 1966

We must have capitulation before there is peace.

— Senator Everett M. Dirksen,
quoted in *Time*, January 14, 1966

I am not, myself, worried about the level of public understanding and public support for the course of the United States in Vietnam.

— McGeorge Bundy, *Issues & Answers*, ABC,
January 16, 1966

Vietnam is but one aspect of the world role we are playing. . . . The war in South Vietnam has few of the attributes of an indigenous revolt. It is a cynical and systematic aggression by the North Vietnamese. . . . To recognize the National Liberation Front would do violence to the truth. . . . The National Liberation Front is not a political entity expressing the will of . . . any substantial element of the South Vietnamese population. . . . We do have a sense of history, and it is that which enables us to view the war in South Vietnam for what it is. . . . We are confident.

— Under Secretary of State George W. Ball,
speech, Evanston, Ill., January 30, 1966

North Vietnam is a backward, underdeveloped country with a primitive "rice and fish" economy. . . . Some rather interesting and possibly very effective alternatives . . . open up if we recognize it as a land where gods, devils and animistic spirits . . . lurk [at] night. . . . Example: North Vietnam's Red River Delta is the nation's rice bowl. Flooding is controlled by damming upstream and subsequent release of water to rice paddies. . . . Many tons of harmless soluble dye might be dropped upstream. A single B-52 is capable of delivering in excess of 27 tons of dye. Consider adding an ingredient which also is harmless but creates an obnoxiously offensive odor. The dye and the odor will be picked up by the growing rice. North Vietnamese eat rice every day at every meal. The need to eat this kind of unsightly, unappetizing but harmless and nutritious mess day after day could become a dear price to pay for Hanoi's transgressions. . . .

To an oriental there is nothing lower than a running dog. Cheap plastic toy models of Ho Chi Minh and Mao Tse-tung joined in the shape of running dogs could be airdropped in large quantity. In Vietnam the ace of spades is considered as deadly an omen as it is in Sicily. Hundreds of thousands of plastic ace of spades playing cards could be dropped throughout the country. . . . Seeing a woman on first leaving one's dwelling in the morning is a certain sign in Vietnam the day will be one of misfortune, therefore rain plastic models of women from the sky during the night to be found as a morning greeting.

On hearing an owl cry "thrice in the night" North Vietnamese flatly expect death in the immediate family. The experience generally results in the strongest sense of dread. Cheap air drop devices which simulate three hoots of an owl should be easy to design. . . . The use of plastic for these objectionable symbols rather than paper is desirable because they are just that much harder to get rid of. Air drops of good-luck symbols bearing identification with the Republic of South Vietnam should occasionally be made both for the obvious reason and because they might induce a Pavlovian reaction. It is to be recalled that the Russian psychologist, Pavlov, induced in dogs a state of total disorganization by alternating acts of ill-usage and kindness. . . . On hillsides visible while marching southward defoliate the shape of the unlucky ace of spades. . . .

I have a few words for so-called defense intellectuals and assorted sophisticates who deride and ridicule these suggestions. . . . This is not a conventional war; it is an unconventional war.

> — Congressman Craig Hosmer, Republican of
> California, speech in House of
> Representatives, February 7, 1966

Congressman Craig Hosmer is nobody's nut. . . . Hosmer's latest suggestion—to prey upon primitive oriental superstitions in waging the Vietnam war—should not be dismissed too readily. He makes it seriously and it deserves consideration. . . .

> — Editorial, *Pasadena Independent*,
> February 8, 1966

"Only We Can Prevent Forests."

> — Sign above "Operation Ranch Hand"
> Headquarters for defoliation, Tonsannhuet
> Airbase, Saigon

I come back to the mainland refreshed and confident. . . . We shall fight the battle against aggression in Viet Nam; we shall fight the battle for social construction; and throughout the world we shall fight the battle for peace. And we shall prevail.

> — Vice President Hubert H. Humphrey,
> on return from Asia, Los Angeles,
> February 8, 1966

TOP SECRET

Mr. McNamara said that it was mandatory that the situation be brought under better control. For example, the Southeast Asia construction program was $1.2 billion in the FY 66 Supplement; yesterday at Honolulu the figure of $2.5 billion was raised. Yet there is only the vaguest information as to how these funds will be spent, where, on what, and by whom. . . . McGeorge Bundy is to help organize the country team to deal with this problem.

> — Richard C. Steadman, special assistant to
> Secretary of Defense Robert S. McNamara,
> memorandum summarizing Pentagon meeting,
> February 9, 1966

TOP SECRET

Preserve this communiqué, because it is one we don't want to forget. It will be a kind of bible that we are going to follow. When we come back here 90 days from now or six months from now, we are going to start out and make reference to the announcements that the President, the Chief of State and the Prime Minister made in paragraph 1, and what the leaders and advisors reviewed in paragraph 2. . . . We are going to give you an examination and the finals will be on just what you have done. . . . Give us dates, times, numbers. . . . We don't want to talk about it; we want to do something about it. . . . Next is refugees. That is just as hot as a pistol in my country. You don't want me to raise a white flag and surrender so we have to do something about that. . . . We haven't gone into the details of growing military effectiveness. . . . This is not the place, with 100 people sitting around, to build a military effectiveness [and] I want to put it off as long as I can, having to make these crucial decisions. I enjoy this agony.

> — President Lyndon B. Johnson, from minutes of
> remarks to senior U.S. and Vietnamese
> officials after issuance of joint communiqué at
> Honolulu conference; those present included
> Ambassador Lodge, Admiral Sharp, General
> Wheeler, Ambassador Harriman, Leonard
> Marks; February 9, 1966

Last Monday I mentioned in the House a number of psychological actions that might be productive in North Vietnam. Many of these might be put to productive use against the Viet Cong in the south. By strumming on the myths, superstitions and ignorance of the Viet Cong their morale and will to fight can be damaged severely. Already we have in South Vietnam an intelligent and dedicated group of U.S. Information Agency and military experts trained and wise in the ways of psychological war. . . . The Viet Cong do not wear uniforms. They never have. They never will. They wear the same "black pajama" costume all Vietnamese wear. . . . Our soldiers on land and sailors patrolling the inland waterways have no way to join battle with them. . . . The unrecognized Vietnamese walking past you in a village by day may be the Viet Cong guerrilla attacking you by night. . . . It makes no sense whatever to neglect the use of any effective and civilized means there may be to identify the Viet Cong. . . . The Viet Cong cannot be seen beneath a cover of tropical growth. . . .

If instead of dropping TNT bombs over an area, an equal tonnage of dye were dropped, it would not be possible for the Viet Cong to move without getting stained. . . . None of these people have any spare clothing to replace that stained. Their skin discoloration would last as long as a suntan. . . . Inescapably a number of Vietnamese who are not guerrillas would be stained. This is not a serious objection from the military security standpoint since already there exists a monumental problem in separating even unstained Vietnamese between VC and non-VC. . . . Dye could be dropped in as simple a container as a wax paper milk carton. . . .

Even the addition of fluorescent chemicals such as used in household detergents to produce "whiter than white" laundry would not greatly increase cost. . . . It is well to anticipate the bleeding hearts who will throw up their hands and raise their voices in wretched screams over the alleged inhumanity of dyeing people yellow, even if they are killing America's sons.

> — Congressman Craig Hosmer,
> speech in House of Representatives,
> February 9, 1966

There can be no doubt of our ultimate success.

> — Vice President Hubert H. Humphrey,
> Saigon, February 10, 1966

A precipitate and disorderly withdrawal would represent in present circumstances a disservice to our own interests. . . . We must dig in and wait. . . . They cannot dislodge us.

> — George F. Kennan, diplomat and foreign
> policy expert, before Senate Foreign Relations
> Committee, February 10, 1966

Every free country in the world should be making a contribution. I have no hesitancy in asking the governments I will visit to do just that. . . . Tremendous progress has been made against the Viet Cong. They are suffering severe reverses and severe punishment.

> — Vice President Hubert H. Humphrey,
> news conference, Saigon, February 12, 1966

Can the war be won? I will answer unequivocally: Yes. The war to defeat the aggressor can be won. . . . I am sure victory will be won. It is a real delight to discover the fine leadership here. . . . I have received encouraging reports.

> — Vice President Hubert H. Humphrey, at
> Tonsannhuet Airport, near Saigon, before
> departing for Bangkok, February 13, 1966

We are not changing our objective in South Vietnam. We have adhered to it since 1954 and I hope we will continue to adhere to it to the end. North Vietnam knows exactly what we are doing, why we are bombing. . . . We are a leader of the Western World. . . . It is really as simple as that. . . . It is very curious, as I read the comments on the situation in South Vietnam, that in some quarters the word "victory" has acquired an evil connotation. It is something that one shouldn't strive for. Well, I hope we are striving for victory . . . victory is just accomplishing what we set out to do. . . . That's victory. . . .

The reason we have more men in Vietnam today than we had last year is that the threat has increased, the requirement has increased. And in spite of the great growth of the forces in South Vietnam they have not grown fast enough. Today there is almost 700,000 [sic] men under arms in South Vietnam. South Vietnam is the strongest military ally we have in the world. . . .

The guerrillas . . . are pure ethnic North Vietnamese, confirming the foreign character, the support of the war. . . . They can't support combat on an enlarged scale. . . . What we are trying to do is to convince Hanoi that they are on a losing gambit. They better change it. And I think we can do that. . . . Fortunately, in spite of what is said about South Vietnam as being the wrong place to have a war . . . I would say the logistic problems are comparatively simple. . . . It is the most supportable war . . . without great resources I would say we can lay a logistic base there in time for almost any force we wanted. . . .

I would not say 400,000 [men will be needed]. I would say more than 200,000. I am not sure where the ceiling will be. What we are trying to do is simply break the back of his resistance in the South so that the people in Hanoi see clearly they have no chance of a military victory. That is our objective. Whenever that comes, everything comes to a happy ending.

> — General Maxwell D. Taylor, former
> superintendant, U.S. Military Academy; chief
> of staff, U.S. forces, Europe; commander,
> American Military Government and Army
> forces in Berlin; commander, 8th Army,
> Korea; commander, U.S. Army, Far East;
> commander, UN forces, Korea; chairman of
> the board, chief executive officer, director,
> Mexican Light & Power Co.; president,
> Lincoln Center; military representative, U.S.
> President; chairman, Joint Chiefs of Staff;
> U.S. Ambassador to South Vietnam; special
> consultant to President; president, Institute of
> Defense Analyses; chairman, President's
> Foreign Intelligence Advisory Board; *Face the
> Nation*, CBS, February 13, 1966

I am not prepared to say I favor pulling out of Vietnam. . . . I don't know how we can pull out of Vietnam. . . . I would like to see an honorable peace.

> — Edward W. Brooke, attorney general of
> Massachusetts, candidate for Senate, *Meet the*
> *Press*, NBC, February 13, 1966

I bring friendly greetings and good wishes from the people of the United States. . . . You have some fine country here—it looks like Minnesota.

> — Vice President Hubert H. Humphrey,
> addressing, in English, audience of peasants at
> Nong Khai, on Laotian border, flying there by
> helicopter from Vientiane, Laos,
> February 14, 1966

I don't believe that the bombing up to the present has significantly reduced, nor any bombing that I could contemplate in the future would significantly reduce, actual flow of men and materiel to the South.

> — Secretary of Defense Robert S. McNamara to
> executive joint session, Senate Armed Services
> and Appropriations Committees, released
> February 14, 1966

I myself have no doubt that, in the long term, we can achieve military victory.

> — General Earle G. Wheeler, chairman, Joint
> Chiefs of Staff, secret testimony before Senate
> Armed Services Committee and Senate
> Appropriations Subcommittee on Defense,
> January 20–25 and February 2, 1966, released
> February 15, 1966

Terrorism, deliberately planned and coldly carried out, continues to be the chief instrument of Viet Cong aggression in South Vietnam. . . . It is the way they hope to win the war. Who—and what—are their targets? School teachers and school administrators.

> — President Lyndon B. Johnson to convention of
> school superintendents, Convention Hall,
> Atlantic City, N.J., February 16, 1966

The state of agriculture in Vietnam is amazingly good, and much better than reasonably could have been expected. . . . The Administration plans to ship more fertilizer to Vietnam.

> — Secretary of Agriculture Orville L. Freeman,
> February 17, 1966

I swell with pride when I see Old Glory flying from the Capitol. I swell with pride when I see the flags around the Washington Monument. I swell with pride when I see the American flag flying from the Senate Office Building. . . . My prayer is that there may never be a white flag of surrender up there. . . . Every time a Senator suggests that we retreat and accept defeat or surrender, that word goes back to Ho Chi Minh. . . . It would be a great humiliation for this nation to be defeated by a small nation of 16 million people. . . . To be defeated and run out and downgraded to a second-class power by that little nation.

> — Senator Russell Long, Democrat of Louisiana, outburst before Senate Foreign Relations Committee, February 17, 1966

If the Senate shilly-shallies with this supplemental bill, it will be much harder to convince those opposing us of our determination to see this commitment through, and our adversaries are much more likely to be intransigent and contemptuous toward our efforts to find peace.

> — Senator Richard B. Russell, Democrat of Georgia, on supplemental appropriation authorizing $4.8 billion additional emergency funds for war, February 17, 1966

We want peace. We do not want to throw our weight around. We need your prayers and not your imprecations. . . . We have to establish law.

> — Secretary of State Dean Rusk to National Rural Electric Cooperative Association, February 17, 1966

I think there is some rationality on the other side. [They] will decide that it is too costly, that it doesn't make sense for them to persist. . . . There is just too much power immediately available in the area. . . . The principal problem is to find the enemy. . . . Defections from the Viet Cong are multiplying rapidly. They are having very considerable difficulties. . . . Toughness is absolutely essential for peace. If we don't make clear where we stand, then the prospect for peace disappears.

> — Secretary of State Dean Rusk before Senate Foreign Relations Committee, February 18, 1966

. . . like men watching a dance from outside through heavy plate glass windows. They see the motions but they can't hear the music. They put the mechanical gestures down on paper with pedantic fidelity. But what rarely comes through to them are the injured racial feelings, the

misery, the rankling slights, the hatred, the devotion, the inspiration and
the desperation. . . . So they do not really understand what leads men to
abandon wife, children, home, career, friends; to take to the bush and
live gun in hand like a hunted animal; to challenge overwhelming
military odds rather than acquiesce any longer in humiliation, injustice
or poverty.

— I. F. Stone, *In a Time of Torment*, 1966

Ho Chi Minh's legions of guerrillas should learn they cannot defeat
the might and power of the United States of America and South
Vietnamese [*sic*].

— *San Diego Union*, February 18, 1966

General Maxwell D. Taylor brought out in public today what other
officials here have made increasingly plain in private—namely that the
United States terms for peace in Vietnam are much stiffer than the offer
of "unconditional negotiations has implied. . . ." General Taylor . . .
said the U.S. could, should and would achieve military and political
successes of sufficient magnitude to force the Communists to accept an
independent and non-Communist South Vietnam. The Johnson Administration . . . has never said anything to contradict the retired General's
assertion that his personal testimony was wholly consistent with official
policy. Many observers and diplomats here and abroad, however, have
misinterpreted the Administration's offer to negotiate as an offer to
compromise with the Viet Cong in South Vietnam. General Taylor's
testimony should have made it clear that such a compromise is not
anticipated here.

— Max Frankel, *New York Times*,
February 18, 1966

A vast Allied offensive on the central coast of South Vietnam
appeared to be drawing slowly to a close today. Qualified military
officials considered the results disappointing in view of the effort, size
and expense. The offensive, now 24 days old, has been the largest
coordinated military effort in the history of the Vietnam war and has cost
$500,000 to $1 million a day. . . .
The offensive involved about 25,000 U.S., South Vietnamese and
South Korean troops, including helicopter, artillery, armor and support
units. . . . Military spokesmen in Saigon assert that the Allied force has
killed 1,536 enemy soldiers and has captured 372, and has seized 293
weapons. Some high-ranking American military officers privately voiced
doubt about these casualty claims, but it is certain that more than 500

enemy soldiers have been killed. . . . Allied casualties . . . have climbed above 600. . . .

In the opinion of military officials, the disappointing results of the offensive have once more called into question the wisdom of large-scale military operations against an elusive enemy. They have again demonstrated, these officers say, the enormous difficulties a conventional army faces when it tries to maneuver a guerrilla opponent into fighting under conditions he does not deem advantageous.

> — Neil Sheehan, dispatch from Saigon,
> *New York Times*, February 18, 1966

A Congressman from California suggests that we bomb North Vietnam with . . . ace of spades playing cards, gadgets that hoot like an owl, and plastic models of girls and running dogs. . . . Craig Hosmer, a Republican . . . suggest dropping a foul-smelling . . . dye into irrigation ditches around rice paddies. The water would change the color of the rice. A good dosage of such incidents would, Hosmer is convinced, prompt the North Vietnamese to lose interest in pursuing the war. . . . Vietnam is a strange country of strange people with many strange customs and practices. . . . Fighting the Viet Cong is largely an effort of search and destroy. It might be worth an exploratory attempt to see if this method could be trumped by an ace of spades.

> — *New Haven Register*, February 19, 1966

The Communist juggernaut will be halted. . . . So to the doubters—and we have plenty—to those who feel that this struggle in Vietnam cannot be won, I say it *can*. I say—what's more important—it *must* be won.

> — Vice President Hubert H. Humphrey,
> Canberra, Australia, February 19, 1966

If negotiation is our aim, as we have so clearly said it is, we must seek a middle ground. A negotiated settlement means that each side must concede matters that are important in order to preserve positions that are essential. I believe there is a middle way. . . . Whatever the exact status of the National Liberation Front . . . any negotiated settlement must accept the fact that there are discontented elements in South Vietnam . . . who desire to change the existing political and economic system of the country. There are three things you can do with such groups: kill or repress them, turn the country over to them, or admit them to a share of power and responsibility. The first two are now possible only through force of arms. The last—to admit them to a share of the power and

responsibility—is at the heart of the hope for a negotiated settlement.
. . . We ourselves must look at our own cards.

> — Senator Robert F. Kennedy, proposing
> coalition government for Vietnam,
> February 19, 1966

The reason for [our] lack of success . . . is that we have been deluding ourselves that our weaknesses could not be remedied while we were fighting a war. . . . The people in the North are suffering. I know, I'm a Yankee. I'm from the North.

> — President Nguyen Cao Ky,
> quoted by *U.S. News & World Report*,
> February 21, 1966

I am very optimistic. . . . The Vietnamese are in good morale.

> — General William C. Westmoreland,
> quoted by *U.S. News & World Report*,
> February 21, 1966

If related properly to the military effort, this thing can work.

> — David E. Bell, quoted by *U.S. News & World Report*, February 21, 1966

"PHILANTHROPY" is defined by the dictionary as an act or service performed because of "love for mankind." What the United States is doing in Vietnam is the most significant example of philanthropy . . . that we have witnessed in our times. . . . The job to be done in Vietnam now is challenging. . . . The effect on other nations which are watching the Vietnam experiment is bound to be stimulating. . . . The mission we have undertaken in Vietnam is the essence of patriotism. May the other large nations of the world be inspired to follow our example. . . . Sacrifice for the cause of human betterment is the greatest philanthropy of all.

> — David Lawrence, Editorial,
> *U.S News & World Report*, February 21, 1966

When he flew into Saigon last week, Vice President Hubert H. Humphrey . . . took to his task with over-flowing enthusiasm. On a visit to an experimental animal-husbandry station established with American aid money, he spotted a brand-new pigpen full of Berkshire Blacks, cleared his throat and let out a Minnesota hog call. "Hooeee, hooeee," bellowed the Vice President of the United States. "That's the best call for a hog there is," he added. "Hooeee is a universal language." Then, in a more serious vein . . . "There's a social revolution taking place here. I'm really impressed with what they are doing."

> — *Newsweek*, February 21, 1966

[Allowing the Vietcong in a coalition government is] a prescription for the ills of South Vietnam which includes a dose of arsenic . . . it would be like putting a fox in a chickencoop. Soon there wouldn't be any chickens left.

> — Vice President Hubert H. Humphrey,
> press conference, Wellington, N.Z.,
> February 21, 1966

General Westmoreland ought to thank God he is not General Vo Nguyen Giap. . . . Now the intelligence pours in. . . . The payoff can be seen in the battle results. . . . In central Vietnam and one or two other areas, the reserves of manpower available to the VC has already shrunk almost to zero.

> — Joseph Alsop, syndicated column,
> February 21, 1966

I return with a deep sense of confidence in our cause and its ultimate triumph. I am confident because the tide of battle in Vietnam has turned in our favor.

> — Vice President Hubert H. Humphrey, on
> return from Asian trip, February 23, 1966

The high hopes of the aggressor have been dimmed and the tide of battle has been turned.

> — President Lyndon B. Johnson, address on
> receiving National Freedom Award,
> Waldorf-Astoria Hotel, New York City,
> February 23, 1966

About 96,000 men deserted from South Vietnam's armed forces last year.

> — Neil Sheehan, dispatch from Saigon,
> *New York Times*, February 24, 1966

There is nothing in modern international law which requires a state to declare war before engaging in hostilities against another state.

> — Secretary of Defense Robert S. McNamara,
> written statement to Senate explaining official
> view of Johnson Administration,
> February 24, 1966

I told President Johnson that we were winning in Vietnam.

> — Lieutenant General Lewis W. Walt,
> commanding general, 3d Marine Amphibious
> Force, Vietnam, February 25, 1966

We reaffirm our intention to sustain the struggle . . . of using military power of almost limitless quantity in measured, limited degree.

> — Vice President Hubert H. Humphrey to
> theologians, Riverside Church, New York
> City, February 25, 1966

Senator R. Kennedy proposes Communists be included in the Saigon Government. It would be more honest to suggest abandoning Viet Nam without even bothering to negotiate.

> — C. L. Sulzberger, *New York Times*,
> February 25, 1966

Economists predict that South Vietnam, which three years ago exported 300,000 tons of rice, may have to import 400,000 tons from the United States this year.

> — Neil Sheehan, dispatch from Saigon, *New York
> Times*, February 26, 1966

We faced the "hordes of Asia" in Korea and defeated them. If we cannot win the kind of war now being fought in Vietnam, then God help us, for we are undone throughout the world! . . . Our military leaders believe we can win. . . . Escalation in Vietnam accompanied by mobilization actually will help to *strengthen* our global posture. . . . The Korean war tremendously increased the U.S. military potential. . . . Indeed, there is a very strong belief among our strategists that if, once again, we must fight Chinese manpower on the ground, South Vietnam and Southeast Asia is, from our point of view, a good place to do it. . . . We scare ourselves with shadows.

> — Hanson W. Baldwin, military editor, *New York
> Times*, in *New York Times Magazine*, February
> 27, 1966

The Viet Cong is not an Asian version of Americans for Democratic Action. . . . I can't for the life of me see why the United States of America would want to propose that such an outfit be made part of any government. . . . Remember, I was in Asia. . . . There is no legitimacy to the National Liberation Front. . . . I don't think the American people want to commit 200,000 of their sons to battle against the Viet Cong and then in the midst of the battle . . . you start offering them a little inducement like, say, "Why don't you come join us at the peace table." . . .

— Vice President Hubert H. Humphrey,
Issues and Answers, ABC, February 27, 1966

In his 14 years in Congress, Craig Hosmer (California Republican) has earned the reputation of being one of the most original members of the lower house. . . . The North Vietnamese, Hosmer points out, are superstitious. They regard the ace of spades as a deadly omen and believe a man will have bad luck all day if the first thing he sees upon leaving his house in the morning is a woman. The Hosmer plan, therefore, calls for U.S. planes to blanket North Vietnam with plastic replicas of women and aces of spades. As for the guerrillas in South Vietnam, what could be more practical than to drop an indelible yellow dye upon them. Last week Hosmer claimed that letters in praise of his ideas were pouring into his office from all over the United States.

— *Newsweek*, February 28, 1966

The situation is quite different [from 1954]. There is definitely not an analogy. . . . First, the French were losing in 1954. It was quite obvious that they were going down. . . . This time, our ally is not being defeated—we are certainly not being defeated, and we don't intend to be. . . . All these things add up to a situation that is entirely different.

— General Maxwell D. Taylor, White House consultant on Vietnam, interview, *U.S. News & World Report*, February 28, 1966

Whose side is God on in this weary war? Captain Jim Hutchens thinks ours. Definitely and without doubt, ours. Hutchens is a combat chaplain here . . . he feels the enemy's children have fallen from grace. "I think," he said recently, "God is on the GIs' side. . . . Because the enemy is largely atheistic . . . our goal is a Christian one. . . . God answers prayers," he says. "And since we are a Christian people and the Communists are not, it's logical to assume He will answer our prayers more often because we pray more often." . . . "But," the chaplain was interrupted, "many Christian soldiers die. . . . Can you give a reason?" "Only that it's God's will." . . . Thus, the GI here may die or he may live. But he does neither alone. Not with God on his side, anyway.

— Tom Tiede, in *Your Men at War*, February 1966

The year-end tally, prepared last month at headquarters of the 2d Air Division in Saigon, shows that during 1965 pilots flew almost 50,000 sorties. Of these, 10,570 were tactical strikes over North Vietnam and

37,940 over South Vietnam. . . . More than 1,000 B52 sorties were launched from Guam. . . . USAF tactical pilots dropped 80,290 tons of bombs. The B-52 tonnage has not been disclosed.

VNAF pilots flew more than 23,700 tactical strikes, most of them in South Vietnam. They used 26,600 tons of bombs. . . . In the South, all strikes were directed by the USAF Tactical Air Control Center (TACC) at Tan Son Nhut Air Base, near Saigon.

TACC directed all pilots of USAF, the Navy, Marines, and VNAF. Air Force Forward Air Controllers (FAC), flying O-1 spotter planes, logged 10,330 missions in 1965. They also flew most of the 22,200 USAF visual reconnaissance flights. USAF and VNAF strike pilots, hitting targets marked by the FAC, destroyed 80,330 Viet Cong buildings and damaged 44,390. They sank 2,756 sampans. It is estimated they killed more than 20,000 Viet Cong.

> — "The Air War," *Air Force*, February 1966

Unless the United States is prepared to oppose a coalition interim government at a peace conference, South Vietnam will go the way of the satellite nations of Eastern Europe and of Laos.

> — Congressman Melvin Laird, Republican of
> Wisconsin, chairman, Republican Conference,
> Congress, speech in House of Representatives,
> March 1, 1966

I want to infuse in our youth the same fanaticism, the same dedication, the same fighting spirit as Hitler infused in his people.

> — Prime Minister Nguyen Cao Ky, quoted by Vo
> Van Thai, South Vietnamese Ambassador to
> the U.S., Cornell University, Ithaca, N.Y.,
> March 3, 1966

We now have reached the stage where our military forces can sustain a planned, methodical forward movement.

> — Vice President Hubert H. Humphrey,
> day after addressing Congress, quoted by
> *Time*, March 4, 1966

More and more peasants are caught in the crossfire of war, losing their homes, property and lives. Refugees continue to stream out of the countryside to escape B-52 raids and ground fighting. There are now more than 800,000 of these refugees.

> — AP dispatch from Saigon, March 4, 1966

I hope . . . that they know they can't win. Once they know they can't win, they will sit down meaningfully at a conference table. . . . As soon as they know we mean it, they will change. . . . I think Secretary Rusk did an admirable job, really an outstanding job. I think that General Taylor did a very good job, too.

> — Senator Thurston B. Morton, Republican of
> Kentucky, *Face the Nation*, CBS,
> March 6, 1966

I would like to tell you what my position is on Vietnam. I support our fundamental commitment in Vietnam. We have some 235,000 American fighting men who are here to see that this commitment is fulfilled. I support our commitment. It was made some time ago, but I believe it is fundamental and it is sound. I believe that we have to utilize every resource in our power whether it is military or it is diplomatic to see that this commitment is fulfilled. I support the efforts which President Johnson has made and the statements which he has made. . . .

If a negotiated settlement is not going to be possible, it is possible that we will have to go to a military solution, but I think his objectives are sound. . . . I believe that President Johnson is doing just fine.

> — Senator Edward M. Kennedy, Democrat of
> Massachusetts, *Meet the Press*, NBC,
> March 6, 1966

War in Vietnam . . . is taking a noticeable turn for the better. . . . Optimism about the future is high, and rising. . . . "We are now doing something in the war that's never been done before," explains a Marine officer. "We are denying night to the Viet Cong. Until recently, night was their shield. But Americans are patrolling and ambushing at night."

> — *U.S. News & World Report*, March 7, 1966

Our purpose is . . . helping the people of South Vietnam to build a new social order. . . . Nor do I think you have any reason to believe that the Communists would win a genuinely free election in South Vietnam. . . . The Government of South Vietnam is really exerting itself now to gain the allegiance and the support of the peasantry. . . . I am happy to be able to tell you, sir, that out of every 100 wounded, 99 live. This is the highest rate of survival of the wounded ever in the history of warfare. That is eight times better than in World War I, four times better than in World War II, twice as good as in the Korean War. . . . The rate of casualties upon the enemy is something that they ought to be concerned about, because that rate is running five to one. . . . Most of their wounded, severely wounded, die. . . .

We are, in a sense, moving on a premeditated, preconceived plan, week by week and month by month. We are on the offensive. And that plan includes . . . areas that have been cleaned of the Viet Cong. . . .

The villagers are beginning to cooperate. . . . I think the most encouraging sign in South Vietnam right now is the fact that we are getting information from the villagers. . . . I went into the Mekong Valley, by the way. I made it my business to do so. . . . The leaders of government now know that we have the will, we have the determination, we have the resources to stick it out, as we say. . . .

General Williamson was with the President yesterday. . . . I was so pleased to hear what he had to say, because . . . I came back with the same conclusions . . . that things were better militarily, that we did have a plan of operation which we were following . . . that the villagers were now cooperating . . . that the rate of defection of the Viet Cong were running at over 2,000 a month, that we were being able to break into the military strongholds of the Viet Cong; we were defeating their main units. . . . If we stick with it, sir, we will have to do less of what some people think we might have to do because we have it coming with us now. . . . I have sat in on the councils of this Government, I have studied long and hard the situation in Southeast Asia, and I believe we are following the right course.

— Vice President Hubert H. Humphrey,
Meet the Press, NBC, March 13, 1966

I favor continuing our military commitment. . . . We can pull out, which would be catastrophic for American interests. That's so unacceptable that it hardly needs to be discussed.

— Senator Robert F. Kennedy,
interview, *U.S. News & World Report*,
March 14, 1966

Our Vietnamese allies are not only regaining their physical security but also getting on with the vital task of building a nation.

— General William C. Westmoreland,
quoted by *Time*, March 18, 1966

The year of the U.S. buildup has thus . . . turned the tide of war.

— *Time*, March 18, 1966

We have the lowest ratio of dead to wounded we've ever had. . . . The greatest efficiency in the history of the world. . . . We don't think Hanoi has yet realized how serious it is. They are looking at things through rose-colored glasses. . . . I want to leave the footprints of America there. . . . We can turn the Mekong into a Tennessee Valley. We can teach them to read and write.

— President Lyndon B. Johnson, statement to
Professor Henry F. Graff, Oval Room, White
House, in presence of Bill Moyers, quoted in
New York Times Magazine, March 20, 1966

I have no doubt at all that Buddhists, Catholics, and all the rest of them combine in rejecting Hanoi and the National Liberation Front.

> — Secretary of State Dean Rusk,
> *Face the Nation*, CBS, March 20, 1966

The other side is hurting. . . . On the present basis, they are not going to come out of it like they had hoped. . . . They may just let things peter out, the way the Greek guerrillas did.

> — Secretary of State Dean Rusk, statement to
> Professor Henry F. Graff, *New York Times
> Magazine*, March 20, 1966

Unlike President Johnson and Vice President Humphrey, Gen. Earle G. Wheeler, chairman of the Joint Chiefs of Staff, was not at all sure last week that the tide of war in Vietnam had turned. . . . Wheeler, however, did express confidence that the tide would eventually turn.

> — *Newsweek*, March 21, 1966

We can out-patience anybody if we want to.

> — Walt W. Rostow, quoted by *Time*,
> March 25, 1966

We have reports already that the VC are suffering from lack of food. We have captured thousands of tons of rice from the Viet Cong. . . . They can't keep up this pace forever. . . . As we get more troops in the country, more of them can go on the offensive. . . . We will really move out. There are some bright signs. Our intelligence is getting better. Our air power is used better. The South Vietnamese Army uses air much better now than it did a year ago. We have more air available. Our armed helicopters are being used with great effect. Artillery is doing a good job. . . . All of these things amount to a markedly increased efficiency of the whole operation. . . . As time goes on, there will be more and more pressure on the VC. Yes, as I have said, we can take the initiative and win in Vietnam. . . . Go out and get them. That's the way you win. . . . We've captured a lot of rice. . . . We're proving that the United States ground forces can fight antiguerrilla war. . . .

> — Admiral U. S. Grant Sharp,
> interview, *U.S. News & World Report*,
> March 28, 1966

I talked to our senior commander in Danang, General Lew Walt, and he told me that the situation was calm out there. . . . I think that the situation is well in hand in Danang. The present government . . . has been doing a good job. . . . Danang is pacified. . . . We can handle

ourselves during the so-called rainy season, the monsoon season, as well
as the Viet Cong can. For instance, in the last monsoon season they
weren't able to get off the ground. We, up in our area, own the night
now.

> — General Wallace M. Greene, Jr.,
> commandant, Marine Corps,
> *Issues & Answers*, ABC, April 3, 1966

It would be a great joy to me to return to the wind and the clouds. I
have no political ambition.

> — President Nguyen Cao Ky,
> quoted by *Newsweek*, April 4, 1966

We should give our full support to the President's determined efforts.
. . . We should then employ whatever force is needed. . . . We should
repose complete confidence in the capability of our military leaders in
Southeast Asia to accomplish any mission they may be assigned, for
these men are among the best that our nation has produced.

> — General Matthew B. Ridgway,
> commander, UN forces, Korea,
> *Look*, April 5, 1966

The country is more stable militarily.

> — Seymour Topping, *New York Times*,
> April 5, 1966

Napalm is one of the most effective tools of the Air Force. It burns
hotter, longer and covers more area than the variety used in Korea and
makes the World War II stuff "seem like a pocket lighter by comparison," one Air Force officer said.

> — AP dispatch from Saigon, April 6, 1966

This is the decisive battle when the survival of our country is at stake.

> — Nguyen Van Thieu, Saigon, April 6, 1966

I think that the tide has turned. . . . The Vietcong is no longer
winning.

> — William E. Griffith, director, International
> Communism Project, M.I.T. Center for
> International Studies; Professor of Soviet
> Diplomacy, Fletcher School of Law and
> Diplomacy, Tufts University; formerly
> political adviser to Radio Free Europe in
> Germany; *Reader's Digest*, April 1966

A mysterious layer of defeatism about the war in Vietnam has been increasingly evident in Washington. . . . This defeatism is mysterious, if only because the war in Vietnam is really a very small war for a very great power to have to fight. The strains the war imposes on this country are entirely bearable, and indeed not even very noticeable. . . . There are two measures of the strains of war—dollars and deaths. By both measures this is the most bearable war we have had to fight since the Spanish-American War, which cost a mere $250 million and took the lives of 385 Americans in battle. . . . The dollar side of the equation provides no excuse for hand wringing or defeatism. . . . In this war, the ratio is . . . weighted on the side of boredom. . . . This is the least deadly war the United States has fought in this century. As this is written, almost exactly 2,000 American soldiers have been killed in action since U.S. combat forces began to arrive in Vietnam early last summer.

> — Stewart Alsop, *Saturday Evening Post*,
> April 9, 1966

A fleet of U.S. B52 bombers . . . had each been modified to carry 60,000 pounds of explosives; the previous capacity was 37,500 pounds.

> — *New York Times*, dispatch from Saigon,
> April 10, 1966

What we are supporting is the government in South Vietnam. . . . General Dinh has been set up to represent the Saigon government in getting hold of the 1st Corps Command, which is based in Danang. He is a man who has very good credentials for that. . . . He is doing a very good job of asserting the authority of the Saigon government in that area. . . . The present government . . . is going forward. . . . The social and economic and political base in South Vietnam has been going forward—as have the military operations.

> — Under Secretary of State George W. Ball,
> *Face the Nation*, CBS, April 10, 1966

Those who have been saying that only the worst can happen in Saigon . . . may well be wrong. The way is beginning to open to avoid the worst and possibly achieve the best.

> — Roscoe Drummond, syndicated column,
> April 17, 1966

There is a tremendous new opening here for realizing the dream of the Great Society in the great area of Asia.

> — Vice President Hubert H. Humphrey,
> quoted in *New York Times*, April 20, 1966

I came away from South Vietnam two weeks ago with the feeling that the military operation is going quite well. . . . There are a number of new developments which we now have in the hands of the troops out there, and many, many more which we are working on with the best scientific and technological brains. . . . Infra-red radar sensors . . . used for locating trucks and camp fires. . . . The heat of that truck is picked up and reflected in the aircraft . . . then be relayed back to the attacking force which can bring in the airpower to strike them.

Another interesting device . . . is a device for detecting vehicle movement by sound. This is done by emplanting . . . under the ground a small object. . . . At a remote location . . . as the truck passes by this is indicated on the receiver. . . . We have . . . a seismographic type of device. . . . This is again buried under the ground. When a Viet Cong or a North Vietnamese approaches within a given distance of this, a seismic effect is reflected . . . is then broadcast back to the listening post. . . . There is . . . a starlight scope. It picks up the light of the stars and magnifies that light on a scope so that you can see in the darkness. . . . This is being used effectively.

> — Deputy Secretary of Defense Cyrus R. Vance,
> *Issues & Answers*, ABC, April 24, 1966

I have nothing but the highest praise for Secretary of State Rusk, for the job he is doing. . . . The larger war phase . . . can be brought under control.

> — Senator Henry M. Jackson, Democrat of
> Washington, *Meet the Press*, NBC,
> April 24, 1966

There is a struggle for power in South Vietnam today. . . . That struggle indicates how well the military operation has gone. A year ago there was no struggle for power. . . . Today . . . the power groups within South Vietnam are now positioning themselves to see who is going to run the country. . . . This is not a sign of weakness. It is indeed the best evidence that considerable progress has been made in defeating the enemy.

> — Vice President Hubert H. Humphrey,
> address, AP annual luncheon meeting,
> New York City, April 25, 1966

Well, we're not winning; we don't see daylight.

> — Senator Barry Goldwater, Republican of
> Arizona, interview, *U.S. News & World Report*,
> April 25, 1966

Many people feel today, they say, we should not be there in Vietnam. Well, whether we should or not, we are. . . . It is a fact.

> — Vice President Hubert H. Humphrey,
> April 25, 1966

You don't demean the Chief Magistrate of your country at a time like this when the war is on. You stand up to be counted.

> — Senator Everett M. Dirksen, Republican of
> Illinois, Minority Leader, Mexico City, quoted
> by *Time*, April 29, 1966

I believe that we shall overcome.

> — Vu Van Thai, South Vietnam Ambassador to
> U.S., Berkeley, Calif., quoted by *Time*,
> April 29, 1966

I don't think we are asserting an arrogance of power in respect to Vietnam. I think we are accepting the responsibility. . . . I have been for this struggle. . . . I back the President.

> — Senator Jacob J. Javits, Republican of New
> York, *Issues & Answers*, ABC, May 1, 1966

Saigon is an American brothel.

> — Senator J. William Fulbright, May 5, 1966

TOP SECRET

I . . . feel it is quite possible the military effects of a systematic and sustained bombing of POL [petroleum, oil, lubricants] in North Vietnam may be more prompt and direct than conventional intelligence analysis would suggest.

> — Presidential Assistant for National Security
> Walt W. Rostow, memorandum to Secretary
> of State Dean Rusk, May 6, 1966

Our position . . . has steadily improved. Though U.S. casualties continue to mount, the Vietcong's mount faster. . . . General Westmoreland is far better prepared than a year ago. . . . Politically the case is different. . . . Thich Tri Quang's Buddhist movement . . . helped overthrow the French, the Diem regime and several of the revolving-door governments in Saigon since then. He and his friends are dedicated nationalists who believe that Buddhism is the soul and conscience of Vietnamese freedom; they are anti-foreign, anti-Catholic and anti-Ky. . . . Tri Quang . . . Meanwhile we can . . . accept Ambassador Lodge's one-word strategy recommendation, which is "persistence"—including persistent military pressure on the Vietcong.

> — Editorial, *Life*, May 6, 1966

Mr. Schlesinger is not an expert on Asia. He took a very small role in Asian questions when he was in government. I worked on Asia for 25 years and I don't think I am going to get into a discussion with Mr. Schlesinger on Asia. . . . I don't want to engage here today with Senator Fulbright in a personal discussion. . . . I must say I was disturbed by the characterization of a city of two-and-a-half million people, a proud and sensitive people, as "an American brothel." . . . This reflects unfairly and inaccurately upon what our men are doing out there. The overwhelming majority of our men are fighting, standing guard, patrolling, carrying rice to people who are hungry, running aid stations for those who are sick, teaching classes, building schools, and doing the things that are necessary to help the South Vietnamese people get on with the job.

— Secretary of State Dean Rusk,
Issues & Answers, ABC, May 8, 1966

In Washington, officials were talking cautiously of a possible turning point in 1967.

— *U.S. News & World Report*,
May 9, 1966

U.S. bombs have had a noticeably adverse effect on Viet Cong morale and expectation of victory. . . . It appears the Viet Cong is losing what support it had from the rural population. . . . I am cautiously optimistic about the war. . . . We believe we are gaining.

— Secretary of Defense Robert S. McNamara
to Senate Foreign Relations Committee,
May 11, 1966

The expenditure on artillery and mortar shells, machine gun and rifle bullets alone in Vietnam is seven million dollars a day.

— *San Francisco Chronicle*, May 12, 1966

I don't think the elections will result in a Communist or neutralist government. But if they do, we will fight. I don't care if they are elected or not, we'll fight.

— President Nguyen Cao Ky,
quoted in *Time*, May 13, 1966

Sober military professionals claim that the war in Vietnam is being won. And these claims must be examined seriously. . . . Enemy deaths are now running at a rate of nearly 1,000 a month. At that rate, the virtual destruction of the hostile forces is not unthinkable. In that sense, victory is a possibility.

> — Joseph Kraft, syndicated column cabled from
> Ankhe, South Vietnam, May 13, 1966

You read, you're televised to, you're radioed to, you're preached to, that it is necessary that we have our armed forces fight, get killed and maimed, and kill and maim other human beings including women and children because now is the time we must stop some kind of unwanted ideology from creeping up on this nation. The place we chose to do this is 8,000 miles away with water in between. I believe there's record of but two men walking on water and one of them failed.

I want to tell you, I don't think the whole of South East Asia, as related to the present and future safety and freedom of the people of this country, is worth the life or limb of a single American. I believe that if we had and would keep our dirty, bloody, dollar-crooked fingers out of the business of these nations so full of depressed, exploited people, they will arrive at a solution of their own. That they design and want. That they fight and work for . . . and not the American style, which they don't want and above all don't want crammed down their throats by Americans.

> — General David M. Shoup, former
> commandant, Marine Corps, Los Angeles,
> May 14, 1966

The war goes well.

> — Ward Just, Washington Post Foreign Service,
> *Washington Post*, May 15, 1966

I ask you to join hands and trust ourselves to God's hands. . . . In the Southeast Asia Treaty Organization, we said that if any nation that is a part of that treaty . . . finds itself under attack and asks for our help, they will get it. And they are getting it tonight in Vietnam. . . . We shall seek an honorable peace. . . . The road ahead is going to be difficult. There will be some "Nervous Nellies" and some who will become frustrated and bothered and break ranks under the strain, and some who will turn on their leaders, and on their country, and on their own fighting men. . . . We can't get peace just for wishing for it. We must get on with the job.

> — President Lyndon B. Johnson,
> Chicago, May 17, 1966

There are indications that the military conflict may be starting to go our way.

> — S. J. Deichman, Institute for Defense
> Analyses, Washington "think-tank"; "Limited
> War and American Defense Policy,"
> *Washington Post*, May 22, 1966

Once again, the total of U.S. battle dead in one week of the Vietnamese war has exceeded the number of South Vietnamese troops killed.

> — *U.S. News & World Report*,
> May 30, 1966

Peace does not come just because we wish for it. . . . There is no going back . . . We can only go forward. . . . Loss of life only obscures the progress that is being made. . . . I believe that South Vietnam is moving toward a government that will increasingly reflect the true will of its people. . . . We must persevere.

> — President Lyndon B. Johnson,
> speech, Arlington National Cemetery,
> May 30, 1966

I don't think we should panic because we have some problems. . . . We will achieve our objectives here and there. . . . As a people we are doing well.

> — President Lyndon B. Johnson,
> impromptu press conference in cabinet room,
> May 31, 1966

The British Government . . . fully supports American policy in Vietnam. . . . I don't believe that a negotiated settlement is possible . . . until the Viet Cong and the North Vietnamese realize that they cannot win.

> — Edward Heath, leader,
> British Conservative party,
> *Meet the Press*, NBC, June 5, 1966

What the Hanoi government is now doing looks like a desperate last attempt to win.

> — Joseph Alsop, syndicated column,
> June 6, 1966

The conflict in Vietnam is confusing for many of our people.

> — President Lyndon B. Johnson,
> speech, Arlington National Cemetery,
> quoted by *Time*, June 10, 1966

The situation is full of promise.

> — Joseph Alsop, syndicated column,
> quoted by *Time*, June 10, 1966

I don't know any subject on which the American public has been more informed than Vietnam.

> — Secretary of State Dean Rusk,
> June 11, 1966

The Washington conclusion is that some sort of overture from North Vietnam will come within a month or two.

> — *Newsweek*, June 13, 1966

I urge you to remember that Americans often grow impatient when they cannot see light at the end of the tunnel.

> — President Lyndon B. Johnson,
> speech before State Department officials,
> quoted by *Time*, June 17, 1966

Prisoners and defectors are reporting hunger as a problem in Red ranks. The Allies are capturing their rice hoards and denying them the rice harvest. . . . U.S. commanders . . . are spoiling for a fight they are confident they can win. . . . U.S. Commander William C. Westmoreland has been promised everything he needs to win the war—and has been getting it. Allied troops already outnumber Giap's forces in the South by over 4 to 1, and there are more to come: an estimated 100,000 more U.S. fighting men to be added to the 275,000 who are now "in-country" by the end of this year.

> — *Time*, June 17, 1966

We have been able to overcome all difficulties. The fight against the Communists will soon be crowned with success and the next year will witness a . . . final victory.

> — President Nguyen Cao Ky, June 19, 1966

Some U.S. officials have grown so optimistic they privately speculate the Viet Cong . . . have lost confidence in their ability to achieve a military victory. As a result, these Americans say, the Reds may soon begin to seek a peaceful settlement of the conflict.

> — *Newsweek*, June 20, 1966

Top Secret

Strikes to commence with initial attacks against Haiphong and Hanoi POL on same day if operationally feasible. Make maximum effort to attain operational surprise.

> — Joint Chiefs of Staff, cablegram to Admiral
> U. S. Grant Sharp, commander in chief,
> Pacific forces, June 22, 1966

Ambassador Henry Cabot Lodge of the United States praised the South Vietnamese Government today for its aggressiveness on the battlefield and for the stand it took in putting down recent dissidence [of the] Buddhist and student opposition to the regime of Premier Nguyen Cao Ky.

> — *New York Times*, dispatch from Saigon,
> June 26, 1966

The military side of the war is going better than I expected several months ago. . . . We will maintain pressure on Hanoi. . . . I would hope that the leaders in Hanoi will understand the message. . . . Bombing . . . has achieved a number of results. It has greatly increased the cost of infiltrating men and material into the South. I think that has had a very real effect on the morale of the fighting forces of the Viet Cong. . . . I think that there is a growing apprehension in North Vietnam that this is going to be a very costly business for them. . . . There are reasons to be gratified. . . . American power . . . has been very effective in wearing down the belligerence and the aggression of the other side. . . .

> — Under Secretary of State George W. Ball,
> *Meet the Press*, NBC, June 26, 1966

Basically, I would support what we are doing. . . . I think we have a responsibility to the people in Vietnam. . . . I am in the Senate and I enjoy being in the Senate and I don't know where I am going to end up.

> — Senator Robert F. Kennedy,
> *Issues & Answers*, ABC, June 26, 1966

The military prospects in South Vietnam are somewhat better.

> — *New York Times*, June 27, 1966

The defense of South Vietnam is going well and encouraging progress has been made there.

> — Secretary of State Dean Rusk,
> Canberra, Australia, June 27, 1966

Another turning point in the war . . . we are now gaining. . . . It may even be possible to see light at the end of the tunnel.

> — Joseph Alsop, syndicated column,
> June 27, 1966

For the first time in memory, prayer sessions will be a regular weekly feature for the White House staff.

> — *Newsweek*, June 27, 1966

I'm much more optimistic . . . than I was when I left there a year ago.
. . . I'd say I'm a tiny bit more optimistic—or, rather, less pessimistic—
than I was. . . . The Vietnamese Army has been doing very, very well
there for months and months. . . . There is a chance—a very good
chance—that Communist North Vietnam will become convinced—
within, say, the next two years—that they cannot win. . . . Let's say I'm
cautiously optimistic. . . . I am not downhearted. . . . I will not be
surprised if . . . the Communists in Hanoi . . . just decide to call it
quits. . . .

> — Robert P. Martin, associate director,
> international staff, *U.S. News & World Report*,
> June 27, 1966

The weapons sounded terrifying and stupendous, like a chorus of
kettledrums played by giants. Its sight is equally stunning, with hundreds
of incandescent bursts of light. . . . This is a "C.B.U.," a military
abbreviation that stands for "Cluster Bomb Unit," one of the United
States weapons that are tending to invalidate some of the axioms of
guerrilla warfare. Military spokesmen in Vietnam are forbidden by
Washington to discuss this and other unusual weapons, but journalists in
the field know about them from witnessing their use and talking to
combat soldiers.

A cluster bomb is a canister containing more than 800 bomblets with
fat orange noses and folding silvery-tailed fins. As a fighter-bomber
sweeps in for attack, compressed air blows the bomblets out of the
canister and they fall to earth in a destructive and demoralizing pattern
of pyrotechnics. It is much like throwing 800 hand grenades at the enemy
at once, except that the bomblets seem to be more powerful and lethal
than hand grenades. The noise alone is overpowering.

Now, a new and more devastating C.B.U. has been developed. It
spews both napalm and lethal steel pellets from bomblets. The weapon
has been used to silence anti-aircraft positions in North Vietnam. This
new weapon is a part of the most impressive arsenal of conventional
firepower ever brought to bear in warfare. The United States forces can
shower hundreds of 750- and 500-pound bombs on guerrilla concentrations from flights of heavy B-52 bombers that the Viet Cong can never
see nor hear. . . .

A new "star-light" telescopic sight that gathers and amplifies the dim
light of a night scene, has been used by Air Force C-47 planes carrying
three guns that can put out a total of 18,000 machine-gun bullets a
minute. . . . Viet Cong units are harassed by highly-sensitive airborne
infra-red devices and other intelligence systems that spot their hidden
campsights and leave them open to air attack. . . .

The Viet Cong and North Vietnamese have a technological device of their own that has proved a surprisingly effective counter-measure to the United States firepower. It is a shovel about two and a half feet long with a bamboo handle and a steel blade. "These people are the damnest diggers I ever saw," said an American infantryman recently. "They dig a foxhole straight down and then they hollow out a little chamber back in the side of it to slip into when they hear the jets. Nothing but a direct hit will get them. You just can't hurt them too much with bombing and artillery when they are in their holes." . . .

In less than six months since the beginning of this year, American forces have suffered 15,000 casualties.

> — Charles Mohr, *New York Times*,
> June 28, 1966 dispatch from Saigon

277 magazine publishers . . . are attending the 47th annual management conference of the Magazine Publishers Association at the Greenbrier Hotel. . . . In a poll conducted here today, 44 percent said the best course to follow in Vietnam is "As is." 25 percent thought the United States should escalate the war, and 13 percent favored withdrawal. . . . The publishers also picked Gov. George Romney as the most likely Republican presidential nominee.

> — AP dispatch from White Sulfur Springs, W.
> Va., June 28, 1966

Your Daddy may go down in history as having started World War III. You may not wake up tomorrow.

> — President Lyndon B. Johnson to daughter
> Luci, quoted by President at White House
> party, June 28, 1966

41 Navy and Air Force strike aircraft today inflicted heavy damage on North Vietnam's major petrolem facilities at Haiphong and Hanoi. These facilities represent over 60 percent of North Vietnam's remaining oil-storage capacity. . . . I think you can recognize . . . with attacks on three targets, two of which contain over 60 percent of the total remaining [petroleum] capacity, there is bound to be a restriction of the total movement capability of the North. . . . They have only a limited rebuilding capability. . . . So it would be very difficult for them to rebuild.

> — Secretary of Defense Robert S. McNamara,
> June 29, 1966

I approve of it [bombing Hanoi and Haiphong].

> — Senator Richard B. Russell, June 29, 1966

This decision, of which the President informed me before taking action, was, in my opinion, a military necessity and I support it.
— Former President Dwight D. Eisenhower, Gettysburg, Pa., June 29, 1966

The bombing will, over a period, stop the use of trucks.
— Senator Stuart Symington, former Secretary of the Air Force, June 29, 1966

We all have a responsibility to American boys who are over there. Obviously the President is going to do everything he knows to do to further the cause of victory.
— Governor John Connally, Democrat of Texas, *Meet the Press*, NBC, July 3, 1966

General Westmoreland . . . I was tremendously impressed with him personally . . . a very able military leader and at the same time seems to understand political and military concepts. He has done this to a very heavy degree in South Vietnam, and in my candid opinion, he is one of the key reasons that we seem to be somewhat more successful there.
— Governor William Scranton, Republican of Pennsylvania, *Meet the Press*, NBC, July 3, 1966

Our diplomatic reports indicate that the opposing forces no longer really expect a military victory in South Vietnam. . . . We had very encouraging reports from a good many of our allies [about U.S. bombing near Hanoi and Haiphong]. . . . We think we pursued the right course. . . . I think we did the right thing at the right time.
— President Lyndon B. Johnson, LBJ Ranch, Tex., July 5, 1966

Condolence payment in the equivalent of $33 was made to each of the families of seven children killed accidentally by an Air Force weapon. The money in crisp new Vietnamese banknotes accompanied by a letter of "sympathy for the loss which you have suffered." *
— *New York Times*, July 5, 1966

Information coming back through several channels from South Vietnam . . . indicates that the North Vietnamese at long last are coming to the realization that they are not going to have military success in the South.
— Under Secretary of State George W. Ball, July 6, 1966

* In Congress it was reported that the cost of killing one guerrilla was $400,000.

Intelligence sources indicate the North Vietnamese . . . no longer expect a military victory. This is hopeful. . . . There has been a profound alteration of the outlook in South Vietnam. . . . That outlook has been further improved by the suppression of the Buddhist extremists. . . . If the North Vietnamese and the Vietcong have got the message, it is good news indeed. If they have not received the plain message . . . there is no alternative now but to speak louder and clearer.

— Editorial, *Washington Post*, July 7, 1966

American pilots who in one year have forged a brilliantly successful new tactical role for air power over Viet Nam, showed last week that the U.S. can succeed. On the ground, American fighting men are not only taking on wily veterans of guerrilla warfare, but are also inflicting losses that no foe can afford to take indefinitely.

— *Time*, July 8, 1966

There are some signs of improvement in the past year.

— *London Economist*, July 9, 1966

I am cautiously optimistic. . . . The Vietcong are suffering severe setbacks . . . and an erosion of morale. . . . We're gaining militarily.

— Secretary of Defense Robert S. McNamara,
July 9, 1966

Military activities should be left to the military. . . . This has been a turning point and we are winning a military victory in Vietnam. I don't think there is any question about it.

— Senator George Murphy, Republican of
California, *Meet the Press*, NBC, July 10, 1966

The President has certainly made it very plain that he is determined, and Mr. McNamara is very careful in talking about it. When he got back yesterday, he told the truth, that things are getting better, and we have every right to be proud of the way our men are fighting and the achievements of our men. . . . The President has a very important objective in Vietnam in showing to the world what America can do.

— W. Averell Harriman, ambassador-at-large,
Issues & Answers, ABC, July 10, 1966

Guerrilla warfare, inspired by one nation against another, cannot succeed. . . . Do not mistake our firm stand for false optimism.

— President Lyndon B. Johnson,
address, July 13, 1966

We feel an inner confidence about the war.

> — Walt W. Rostow, July 14, 1966

Fighting is going badly for the Viet Cong.

> — Roscoe Drummond, *Washington Post*,
> July 17, 1966

I think that the Central Intelligence Agency is but a small part of the national effort to perpetuate truly democratic ideals and freedoms around the world.

> — Admiral William F. Raborn, former director,
> CIA, *Meet the Press*, NBC, July 17, 1966

We have been achieving, I think, very good success from a military standpoint in the South. The enemy has been suffering very substantial losses. He has lost large quantities of food and other types of supplies, with the result that he has not been able to mount the monsoon offensive. . . . Things are going very well militarily. . . . We do know they are feeling the cost of this aggression. We hope they will ponder long and hard and realize that if they continue this aggression they will continue to pay the cost. And therefore we hope they will see the wisdom of trying to seek a peaceful solution.

> — Deputy Secretary of Defense Cyrus R. Vance,
> *Face the Nation*, CBS, July 17, 1966

If I were in North Vietnam [and] if I looked at the rate of attrition of the Viet Cong forces, I would be very depressed indeed.

> — Under Secretary of State George W. Ball,
> quoted by *U.S. News & World Report*,
> July 18, 1966

We are winning the war militarily and can keep on winning it militarily.

> — Major General Harry W. O. Kinnard, former
> commander, 1st Air Cavalry Division, U.S.
> Army, quoted by *U.S. News & World Report*,
> July 18, 1966

They have had smashing defeats. . . . Today there must be some hard thinking taking place in Hanoi. Our adversary must know that time is not on his side.

> — Vice President Hubert H. Humphrey, speech,
> Los Angeles, quoted by *U.S. News & World
> Report*, July 18, 1966

More manpower will be required. . . . On the military front our troops under General Westmoreland are giving an excellent account of themselves. . . . We shall persist. We shall send General Westmoreland such men as he shall require and request.

— President Lyndon B. Johnson,
July 20, 1966

Our brave fighting men have now turned the tide of battle. The initiative is no longer with the enemy. The initiative is with us. This must have surprised no one so much as it surprised the leaders in Hanoi.

— President Lyndon B. Johnson,
Fort Campbell, Ky., July 23, 1966

The fact is that American soldiers—who are now doing almost all the fighting—are violating the Geneva Convention relative to the Treatment of Prisoners of War every day. It is a violation for soldiers of one army to turn over prisoners of war to soldiers of another army. And that is precisely what we do.

Every correspondent in Vietnam knows this, and has seen it for himself. An American unit will move into a village, or an area, and round up every male. A South Vietnamese liaison officer will then interrogate each man, and if he believes the man is a Viet Cong guerrilla, or even a sympathizer, the man will be taken off to a detainment camp.

After detailed interrogation, he is usually executed.

That is why there are no huge POW camps springing up in the American West, as they did during the Second World War, and why, in South Viet Nam, officials only smile at your naïveté when you ask to visit an internment camp.

— Pete Hamill, *New York Post*,
July 25, 1966

New winds are blowing in Asia.

— Secretary of State Dean Rusk, July 1966

The tide has turned in Vietnam.

— *U.S. News & World Report*, July 25, 1966

I find that our effort is not appreciated. But what is more significant, it is not understood. If our aims were better understood, our effort would be more appreciated.

— Former Vice President Richard M. Nixon,
Paris, July 29, 1966

The Columbia Broadcasting System says about $15,000 a week in cash from a Saigon race track goes into a personal account of South

Vietnamese Premier Nguyen Cao Ky, who frequently draws large sums in cash from the account. The report last night from CBS correspondent Bill Stout said . . . $5000 to $15,000 were frequently paid directly to Ky in cash. . . . Stout approached Ky at a ceremony and asked him how the money was spent. "We use it for social welfare activities," Ky replied, "give it to hospitals or wounded. . . . That's no problem concerning me . . . because, concerning me, the flow of money is never a problem."

— *Washington Post*, July 29, 1966

Yes, I think we are winning the war. . . . I think we have pushed them back to the jungle areas. . . . The majority of the people and the rich areas are now under our control. . . . Once they lost control of the Delta . . . they will no longer be able to sustain their war efforts. . . . There is no doubt that we'll ever accept negotiations with the Communists in the South. About the end, I can see one thing: They will fade away, go back to the guerrilla tactics. . . . I am sure we are going to win.

— President Nguyen Cao Ky,
interview, *U.S. News & World Report*,
August 1, 1966

When you pick a man like General Westmoreland, the cream of the crop, and then take the next two in line and make them his deputies, you can't find anything better. We sent him the best of weapons and according to the last reports we have got 290,000 men over there. . . . If he can't win this war, certainly we can't win it here sitting up on Capitol Hill. . . . How many you have to have, I can't say, but Westmoreland would probably have the best estimate of what he needs. If we need more troops, all right. How many, I don't know. . . . I just know that we can't retreat and we can't surrender. We wouldn't dare to. . . . We made our promises. . . . We thought it was going to be only a little bit. . . . I guess the first contingent in there was about 6,000. Now it has ballooned and ballooned, and it may balloon some more before we get through. But the fact of the matter is that we have an obligation, and we have got to fulfill it. . . .

— Senator Everett M. Dirksen, Republican of
Illinois, Minority Leader, *Meet the Press*,
NBC, August 7, 1966

The four leading U.S. contractors in Vietnam are Brown & Root of Houston, Tex.; Morrison-Knudsen, Boise, Ida.; J. A. Jones, Charlotte, N.C.; Raymond International, New York, N.Y. At this writing the combine employs 38,745 South Vietnamese. An estimated 10 percent are considered members of the Viet Cong.

— *Parade*, August 7, 1966

A highly successful operation. The enemy has been set back again.

> — General William C. Westmoreland on
> "Operation Hastings" in Quang Tri Province,
> where U.S. Marines lost almost 200 killed, one
> of heaviest tolls of war, quoted by *Newsweek*,
> August 8, 1966.

Withdrawal would be disastrous. . . . Negotiations are likely when Hanoi realizes that its political apparatus in the countryside is being systematically reduced, and that this process will accelerate the longer the war lasts. . . . The war in Vietnam is a crucial test of American maturity.

> — Dr. Henry Kissinger, Professor of
> Government, Harvard; member, Center for
> International Affairs; consultant, National
> Security Council, *Look*, August 9, 1966

It is not too late to win. . . . U.S. troop strength in South Vietnam should be doubled to a figure of 500,000. . . . We must find and fix the main force of the enemy, and force him to expend his supplies in action. . . . The war must ultimately be won on the ground by destroying or breaking up the main-force units of the Vietcong. . . . The American and South Vietnamese military can launch search-and-destroy and search-and-clear operations. . . . The pacification program—in the past mishandled and underemphasized—has this year started slowly but well. . . . The enemy cannot win in a military sense; he is stymied on the field of battle.

> — Hanson W. Baldwin, military editor,
> *New York Times*, quoted in *Look*,
> August 9, 1966

Our cause in South Vietnam is not immoral. . . . It is not likely that a victorious NLF would treat with restraint . . . the Catholics.

> — Herman Kahn, director, Hudson Institute,
> former member, RAND Corporation, author,
> *On Escalation: Metaphors and Scenarios*,
> consultant, U.S. government, quoted in *Look*,
> August 9, 1966

I don't see any change for the worst at all. Our plane losses are under those we estimated. Our helicopter losses are under those we estimated. You sometimes, as you know, have heavier losses than you expect.

> — President Lyndon B. Johnson,
> August 9, 1966

In two or three years, or even before, the Communists will accept defeat.

> — President Nguyen Cao Ky, August 13, 1966

The war in Vietnam . . . our economy is able to stand it. . . . Businessmen who had questions now feel that actions that he [The President] has taken in Vietnam are the kind of actions that ought to be taken. By and large I believe the business community supports the President.

> — Sol M. Linowitz, chairman of the board, Xerox
> International, *Meet the Press*, NBC,
> August 14, 1966

As far as Vietnam is concerned, the Urban League takes no position on Vietnam.

> — Whitney M. Young, Jr., executive director,
> National Urban League, *Meet the Press*, NBC,
> August 14, 1966

In Japan American war orders are giving business a more welcome spurt. *How big a spurt?* Around *1.5 billion dollars* in direct and indirect business this year, says the Ministry of International Trade and Industry in Tokyo. Some bankers call this conservative. . . . Experts call war orders main factor in ending Japan's 18-month economic stagnation. Now business is sponging up excess capacity that plagued most Japanese industries.

> — *U.S. News & World Report*, August 15, 1966

The war in Vietnam is going well in many respects.
> — *Time*, August 19, 1966

TOP SECRET

I return [from Vietnam] *more optimistic than ever before.* The cumulative change since my last visit is dramatic. . . . Indeed, I'll reaffirm even more vigorously my prognostication of last November (which few shared then) that growing momentum would be achieved in 1967 on almost every front in Vietnam. Wastefully, expensively, but nonetheless indisputably, we are winning the war in the South. Few of our programs—civil or military—are efficient, but we are grinding the enemy down by sheer weight and mass and the cumulative impact of all we have set in motion is beginning to tell. Pacification still lags the most, yet even it is moving forward. . . . Our side now has in presently programmed levels all the men, money and other resources needed to achieve success.

> — Robert W. Komer, Special Assistant to
> President for Peaceful Reconstruction in
> Vietnam, "Vietnam Prognosis for 1967–68"
> *Pentagon Papers*, mid-August 1966

How long is the tunnel of war to extend in Vietnam? Is there now light at the end of that tunnel? If not, what is it going to take to bring light?

> — *U.S. News & World Report*, August 22, 1966

We are beginning to see some signs of success of this strategy. The Viet Cong monsoon offensive, which we know from captured documents it was their intention to carry out during the period May to October, has not materialized because of Westmoreland's tactics of carrying out spoiling operations based on intelligence he has received. . . . The number of defections this year has doubled compared with the past year. No doubt this is a sign of erosion of morale.

> — Secretary of State Dean Rusk,
> August 25, 1966

We are beginning to see some signs of success. . . . No doubt there is a sign or erosion of [enemy] morale.

> — Former Secretary of State Dean Acheson,
> August 25, 1966

The commander of the U.S. 1st Infantry Division took pains today to absolve the 7th Air Force for any blame in the accidental dropping of napalm on his troops. . . . Gen. Dupuy . . . said at a press briefing in Saigon: . . . "This is a rough business. When you're only off by 50 meters and the planes are going 150 or 200 miles an hour, these things are going to happen."

> — R. W. Apple, Jr., *New York Times*,
> August 27, 1966

Critics who picket the White House with signs calling the President of the United States a murderer . . . are really helping the enemy.

> — George Meany, president, AFL/CIO,
> *Meet the Press*, NBC, August 28, 1966

They have got to come to a recognition that the attempt to take over South Vietnam by force isn't going to succeed. . . . Very definitely we are sharply reducing the rates of infiltration of men and equipment. . . . We never thought we could choke it off. No student of bombing would have thought that.

> — Assistant Secretary of State for Far Eastern
> Affairs William P. Bundy, *Meet the Press*,
> NBC, September 4, 1966

The thing that impressed me most was the tremendous progress that's been made in the seven months since my last inspection—progress that augurs of a definite victory. . . . The magnitude of the effort . . . it is all just tremendous. That's No. 1. No. 2 is the progress made in the pacification of the countryside in the Northern Provinces where the Marines are located, and the success that we're having in the search-and-destroy operations. There is a very definite and noticeable progress. . . . We've been expanding the perimeters. . . .

This is the thing that really makes me feel optimistic. . . . I feel that within a reasonable time we're going to be able to amalgamate these beachheads into a single beachhead, which will be proof not only to our own people that our programs are succeeding out there, but also a clear signal to Ho Chi Minh that he's losing. . . .

We have two programs under way. . . . One is our search-and-destroy operation; the other is pacification. . . . The phrase really describes it very well. We search for organized units of the enemy until we locate them. Once they are located, we immediately get out there, usually by helicopter, and strike and try to destroy or fragment them. . . . Find the enemy, fix him and kill him. . . .

We aren't taking as many prisoners as we'd like. But I saw about 20 during this Operation Colorado. There had been about 20 prisoners captured. . . . I know I sound optimistic to you, and I'm enthusiastic about what I see, because I'm convinced, if we keep on with what we're doing, that we can bring a satisfactory close to this conflict in South Vietnam.

> — General Wallace M. Greene, Jr., commandant, Marine Corps, interview, *U.S. News & World Report*, September 5, 1966

I support the President. I think he is doing everything in God's green earth to achieve peace.

> — Governor Edmund G. (Pat) Brown, Democrat of California, *Meet the Press*, NBC. September 11, 1966

TOP SECRET

As of July 1966 the U.S. bombing of North Vietnam has had no measurable direct effect on Hanoi's ability to mount and support military operations in the South at the current level.

> — CIA/DIA [Defense Intelligence Agency] Report, September 12, 1966

The North Vietnamese cannot take the punishment any more in the South. The bombing has helped some, but the real influence is simply our military prowess. I think we can bring the war to a conclusion within the next year, possibly within the next six months.

> — Brigadier General S. L. A. Marshall, military
> expert, quoted in *Newsweek*,
> September 12, 1966

I do not think we are overcommitted. I think there are very great dangers in being undercommitted.

> — Secretary of State Dean Rusk, before Senate
> Preparedness Investigating Subcommittee,
> quoted by *Newsweek*, September 12, 1966

Undeniably, it is a mark of some progress that now, at last, South Vietnam will have elections.

> — *Newsweek*, September 12, 1966

Today the tide has turned . . . in Vietnam.

> — President Ferdinand E. Marcos of The
> Philippines, September 15, 1966

Bundy and Johnson were right, of course.

> — Editorial, *Life*, September 16, 1966

I think it [the war] can go on as long as it has to go on to achieve peace in Vietnam.

> — Nicholas Katzenbach, before Senate Foreign
> Relations Committee, September 27, 1966

Gen. Giap continues to make his incredible mistake of facing U.S. firepower.

> — *America*, magazine published by Jesuits of
> U.S. and Canada, October 1, 1966

The most recent polls I have seen indicate that the people still want this war prosecuted to an honorable end.

> — Senator Everett M. Dirksen, Republican of
> Illinois, *Face the Nation*, CBS, October 2, 1966

I am supporting the American position as announced by Ambassador Goldberg. . . . I am not for unilateral or immediate withdrawal.

> — Senator Paul H. Douglas, Democrat of Illinois,
> *Meet the Press*, NBC, October 2, 1966

In North Vietnam, the Reds are being bombed and hurt.

> — *U.S. News & World Report*, October 3, 1966

I view Vietnam as a problem of order.

> — Eugene V. Rostow, before Senate Foreign
> Relations Committee, October 4, 1966

I feel we are entitled to take a considerable degree of confidence from what has thus far been accomplished out there. . . . We must have been doing something right.

> — Deputy Under Secretary of State U. Alexis
> Johnson, address, New York City,
> October 4, 1966

Personally, I may not be able to say that bombing raids originate from Thailand, because I was not at the airport and I did not receive any official report on those questions.

> — Foreign Minister Thanat Khoman of
> Thailand, *Issues & Answers*, ABC,
> October 9, 1966

The Vietnamese people have become mere pawns in the struggle. . . . The United States can no longer make any pretense of fighting to safeguard South Vietnam's independence. The presence of 317,000 American troops in the country has made a mockery of its sovereignty and the military junta in Saigon would not last a week without American bayonets to protect it. . . . In the final analysis, American strategy in Vietnam consists in creating a killing machine in the form of a highly equipped expeditionary corps and then turning this machine on the enemy in the hope that over the years enough killing will be done to force the enemy's collapse through exhaustion and despair. . . .

> — Neil Sheehan, *New York Times Magazine*,
> October 9, 1966

Within six, eight, ten or twelve months—before the end of 1967, at any rate—the chances are good that the Vietnamese war will look successful. We are much closer to the end of the "military war" than most people . . . even dare to hope.

> — Joseph Alsop, syndicated column,
> October 1966

The Prime Minister [Prince Souvanna Phouma of Laos] and I met at

9:30 and . . . I pointed out to him that it must be obvious to the aggressors that they cannot succeed.

— President Lyndon B. Johnson,
news conference, New York City,
October 12, 1966

U.S. pilots flew 386 sorties—individual flights—and claimed they destroyed or damaged more than 475 enemy sampans, bunkers, fortified positions and huts.

— AP dispatch from Saigon, October 12, 1966

Soldiers in the airmobile division's continuing Operation Irving said they had killed three Vietcong and . . . seized an enemy field hospital and a cache of ammunition.

— *New York Times*, dispatch from Saigon,
October 13, 1966

[We have] progressed very satisfactorily . . . the rate of progress had exceeded our expectations . . . more than we would have forecast a year ago.

— Secretary of Defense Robert S. McNamara,
Saigon, October 13, 1966

In Asia over the last year, I have felt that there is an encouraging mood of new confidence. . . . The North Vietnamese and the Viet Cong monsoon offensive that gave us concern failed.

— President Lyndon B. Johnson,
news conference, October 13, 1966

The progress in the past 12 months has exceeded our expectations.

— Secretary of Defense Robert S. McNamara,
October 14, 1966

TOP SECRET

We have done somewhat better militarily than I anticipated. We have by and large blunted the communist military initiative . . . our program of bombing the North has exacted a price. My concern continues, however, in other respects. . . . Enemy morale has not broken. . . . The one thing going for us in Vietnam over the past year has been the large number of enemy killed-in-action resulting from the big military operations. . . . The enemy must be taking losses . . . at the rate of 60,000 a year. The infiltration routes would seem to be one-way trails to death. . . . Yet there is no sign of an impending break in enemy morale and it appears that he can more than replace his losses by infiltration from North Vietnam and recruitment in South Vietnam. Pacification is a bad disappointment. We have good grounds to be pleased by the recent elections . . . but . . . pacification has gone backward . . . guerrilla forces are larger; attacks, terrorism and sabotage have increased in scope and intensity; more railroads are closed and highways cut; the rice crop . . . is smaller; we control little, if any, more of the population; the VC political infrastructure thrives in most of the country, continuing to give the enemy his enormous intelligence advantage; full security exists nowhere (now even behind the U.S. Marines' lines and in Saigon); in the countryside, the enemy almost completely controls the night. Nor has the ROLLING THUNDER program of bombing the North either significantly affected infiltration or cracked the enemy morale of Hanoi. There is agreement in the intelligence community on these facts. In essence, we find ourselves—from the point of view of the important war (for the complicity of the people)—no better, and if anything worse off. . . . The discouraging truth is that, as was the case in 1961 and 1963 and 1965, we have not found the formula. . . .

> — Secretary of Defense Robert S. McNamara, memorandum to President Lyndon B. Johnson, October 14, 1966

I can say for the information of the American people that the military situation in South Vietnam is considerably improved from the Allied point of view, that our military successes have been very important, and they have been, as I indicated, successes. Our military activities have been successes. . . . Militarily we have gained many victories. Militarily we have administered a series of defeats on the enemy. Militarily we have proved our strength and our ability to conduct a struggle in this kind of an environment such as you find in Southeast Asia. . . . I can only say that we are going to redouble our efforts.

> — Vice President Hubert H. Humphrey, *Issues & Answers*, ABC, October 16, 1966

The most important weapon in Vietnam is patience. . . . Our military strategy is already quite clear.

> — President Lyndon B. Johnson, Honolulu, October 17, 1966

It would be idiotic to deal with the Viet Cong.

> — Colonel R. L. Houston (ret.), former deputy military adviser, Canadian section, International Control Commission, Vietnam, 1960 and 1961, interview, *U.S. News & World Report*, October 17, 1966

Uncle Ho will not accept the fact that he's losing. To give him another clear signal that he is losing, the Marines will step up its pacification program. It could turn into a snowballing affair and bring success throughout all of South Vietnam.

> — General Wallace M. Greene, Jr.,
> October 20, 1966

I believe there is a light at the end of what has been a long and lonely tunnel.

> — President Lyndon B. Johnson,
> Canberra, Australia, October 21, 1966

[We] have now seized the initiative. . . . The pressure on the Viet Cong, measured in terms of the casualties they have suffered, the destruction of their units, the measurable effect on their morale, has been greater than we anticipated.

> — Secretary of Defense Robert S. McNamara,
> quoted by *Time*, October 21, 1966

They have patience. So have we. And I think we just have to wait and see what develops.

> — Ambassador Arthur J. Goldberg, U.S.
> representative to UN, *Issues & Answers*, ABC,
> October 23, 1966

The Vietcong army is getting weaker and weaker. The units now arriving from the North are not as good as their predecessors. Some of them fight barefoot. Not enough food. Malaria takes its toll. The long march, the poor food, the sickness and the continual bombing of the Ho Chi Minh Trail drain their strength. Hanoi, too, will break. . . . Have they any chance of succeeding? Can they defeat the Americans? . . . No. Their military achievements are steadily declining. The situation is not any different from what it was 12 years ago, when they fought the French. . . . Their frontal attacks . . . are doomed to failure. . . . I cannot imagine a more inaccurate judgment than that of Giap on the fighting skill of the American Army. His basic concept, as expressed in his writings, is also overgeneralized.

The Americans in 1966 have infinitely more guns than the French possessed in 1954 and they are much better. And not only guns; also warplanes and helicopters and tanks and equipment and ammunition and money. Giap's second mistake lies in his estimate of the feeling of the American Army. The American Army is not tired and is not getting tired of the fighting in Vietnam. It does not involve very strenuous or prolonged physical effort: troops are flown everywhere and do relatively little moving on foot. The weather is much more agreeable than weather in Europe or Korea. . . . They go on leave to places like Hong Kong, Bangkok and Honolulu. They never had a war with such advantages: planes, artillery, armor, modern communications, aircraft carriers, helicopter-cavalry, against an army that has none. . . . The American Army, as a whole, as a military body, gets satisfaction out of every day it spends in Vietnam. . . . Most . . . would volunteer for service in Vietnam if they were not posted there. . . .

I do not think the Vietcong can defeat the American Army in the way they did the French.

> — Major General Moshe Dayan of Israel,
> *Washington Post*, October 23, 1966

The election of 40 or more Republicans to the House will serve notice to the enemy in Vietnam that the United States is not going to do what the French did 10 years ago: cut and run.

> — Richard M. Nixon, *Meet the Press*,
> NBC, October 23, 1966

The leaders of seven nations in the Asian and Pacific region held a summit conference in Manila on October 24 and 25, 1966, to consider the conflict in South Vietnam. . . . The participants were Prime Minister Harold Holt of Australia, President Park Chung Hee of the Republic of Korea, Prime Minister Keith Holyoake of New Zealand, President Ferdinand E. Marcos of the Philippines, Prime Minister Thanom Kittikachorn of Thailand, President Lyndon B. Johnson of the United States of America and Chairman Nguyen Van Thieu and Prime Minister Nguyen Cao Ky of the Republic of Vietnam. . . . This conference symbolizes . . . our high hopes. We are united in our determination. . . . We shall continue our military and all other efforts as firmly and as long as may be necessary . . . our united purpose is peace. . . . We are united. . . . The Government of Vietnam described the significant military progress . . . the accelerating efforts of the Government of Vietnam to forge a social revolution of hope and progress.

> — Joint communiqué, Manila Summit
> Conference, October 24, 1966

Additional troops are needed.

> — General Wallace M. Greene, Jr., Manila,
> October 24, 1966

The President may soon be gaining very greatly by substantial success in the Vietnamese War. . . . Within 6, 8, 10 or 12 months—before the end of 1967 at any rate—the chances are good that the Vietnamese war will look successful. We are much closer to the end of what Premier Nguyen Cao Ky calls the "military war" than most people here, including most people in the Government, even dare to hope.

> — Joseph Alsop, syndicated column,
> October 24, 1966

Nail the coonskin to the wall.

> — President Lyndon B. Johnson,
> advice to U.S. troops at Cam Ranh Bay,
> Vietnam, October 25, 1966

I am speaking to you this morning from Manila, only a few hours after my trip to Vietnam at our base on Cam Ranh Bay. . . . We saw much progress toward attaining [our] goals in Vietnam. . . . We received an eloquent and encouraging report from Gen. Westmoreland. . . . And I pray to God that our adversary may soon discover that he cannot succeed.

> — President Lyndon B. Johnson,
> Manila, October 27, 1966

The meeting in Manila . . . brought forth . . . the determination that the Army of South Vietnam be more intensively trained in matters of pacification. . . . I can say this, that President Johnson is giving us strong leadership.

> — Vice President Hubert H. Humphrey,
> *Meet the Press*, NBC, October 30, 1966

I have no magic wand.

> — President Lyndon B. Johnson,
> during Asian trip, quoted by *Newsweek*,
> October 31, 1966

The tide is turning politically and militarily in Vietnam. . . . A change in the climate is evident—resistance to Communist influence grows with the confidence that the Communists will not prevail. Election of the Constituent Assembly marks a new phase in a trend toward political stability that coincides with and may be largely due to military successes.

> — Richard C. Hottelet, CBS correspondent,
> *The Reporter*, November 3, 1966

"Nobody can accuse us of a soft attitude," said the President. "If anyone doubts the basis of our commitment, they will find we have more troops in Viet Nam than there are words in the *Webster's New*

Dictionary." Not yet. The U.S. has 336,000 troops there; *Webster's* has 450,000 words.

> — *Time,* November 4, 1966

You will recall that the military outlook was very dark indeed in the summer of 1965. . . . The scene has changed dramatically. . . . I think it is clear to all that today a military victory is beyond their grasp. . . . Their sanctuaries which once existed deep in the jungle are no longer free from attack. Food for the enemy is a problem, an increasing problem. It is no longer plentiful. His medical supplies are often short. Disease, particularly malaria, is affecting his troops. . . . The monsoon offensive . . . has been thwarted. . . . Nevertheless . . . the North Vietnamese soldiers and the Viet Cong soldiers, while clearly affected by the pressures being brought to bear upon them, are fighting on stubbornly. . . . I would hope that the adversary would see the utter futility of continuing. . . . They refuse to do that. Now, I don't know why. . . . There is no question, however, that . . . victory . . . is beyond their grasp. . . . Fortunately, the military situation has now improved. . . . The military operations continue to be successful. Our forces maintain the initiative. Our losses are light.

> — President Lyndon B. Johnson,
> news conference, LBJ Ranch,
> November 5, 1966

The support of the flag, the support of the troops, the support of the President's position . . . has been an overwhelming majority.

> — Senator Thurston B. Morton, Republican of
> Kentucky, *Meet the Press*, NBC,
> November 6, 1966

Electronic devices that can spot cigarettes and belt buckles from an airplane several thousand feet high are being used nightly in Viet Nam to ferret out the Communists, an American military source said today. . . . "The metal sensing gear is just as sensitive, but doesn't even need heat. . . . They fly over. . . . If there are half a dozen guys down there with belt buckles or knives or guns or anything made of metal, the plane will know it. In come the bombers and boom! No more belt buckles or people either. It's amazing."

> — *New York World-Journal-Tribune*,
> AP dispatch from Saigon, November 10, 1966

We're going to out-guerrilla the guerrilla and out-ambush the ambush. . . . And we're going to learn better than he ever did because we're smarter, we have greater mobility and firepower, we have more endurance and more to fight for. . . . And we've got more guts. . . . In war you have to pay a price.

> — General William C. Westmoreland,
> quoted by *Life*, November 11, 1966

In the past year, North Vietnamese and Viet Cong troops have achieved not a single victory worth writing home to Hanoi about, while the Communist homeland absorbs an ever-increasing rain of American bombs. U.S. manpower and firepower poured into the conflict since the summer of 1965 have made the Allies largely master of the battlefield. . . . Hungry, wet and hurting, the Viet Cong have turned from wooing to coercing the local peasantry to get food, money and fresh recruits. For lack of visible progress, and thanks to day and night harassment, Viet Cong soldiers are more and more presenting morale problems for the enemy. . . . Most Saigon observers think the long awaited signal for peace from Hanoi will not be far behind.

> — *Time*, November 11, 1966

If the U.S. fails to reach a settlement in Vietnam, it will not be the fault of Pope Paul VI or . . . W. Averell Harriman. In early November, the Pope received Mr. Harriman in Rome. . . . Mr. Harriman said he had found U.S. bombing in Vietnam "not popular in some quarters" and "not well understood."

> — *U.S. News & World Report*,
> November 14, 1966

TOP SECRET

A substantial air interdiction campaign is clearly necessary and worthwhile. . . . But at the scale we are now operating I believe our bombing is yielding very small marginal returns, not worth the cost in pilot lives and aircraft.

> — Secretary of Defense Robert S. McNamara,
> memorandum to President Lyndon B.
> Johnson, November 17, 1966

The entire Vietnamese Army will switch to a pacification role in 1967 and leave major fighting to American troops.

> — Tran Van Do, South Vietnamese foreign
> minister, quoted by *Los Angeles Times*,
> November 18, 1966

Our capacity to defeat the big Communist units and destroy redoubts is so well demonstrated that I would expect a very different military situation indeed here by next year. . . . Yes, we have reached a turning point . . . it is still clear to all that the Viet Cong cannot possibly win and that we cannot possibly be defeated. Because . . . the situation in this country is better than it has ever been before.

> — Ambassador Henry Cabot Lodge,
> interview, *U.S. News & World Report*,
> November 21, 1966

This is a major victory. From now on it is search and pursue. We hope they'll stay and fight. Frankly, I think our chances of a large engagement now are slim. We're in here too strong.

> — Major General William E. DePuy,
> commander, First ("Big Red One") Infantry
> Division, regarding "Operation Attleboro,"
> War Zone C, South Vietnam's Tay Ninh
> Province near Cambodian border, quoted by
> *Time*, November 21, 1966

We now have in Vietnam a well-balanced military force . . . giv[ing] renewed confidence . . . encouragement and hope. . . . The initiative has swung to our side. . . . The ratio of friendly troops killed in action compared with the number of enemy killed . . . is very much in [our] favor. . . . The ratio is increasing almost every month in our favor. . . . During the month of September, it was running better than 6 to 1. . . . Never before in the history of warfare have men created such a responsive logistical system.

> — General William C. Westmoreland,
> interview, *U.S. News & World Report*,
> November 28, 1966

Out at Bien Hoa air base, I encountered a Forward Air Controller (FAC) . . . he leads in the napalm-splashing Air Force Supersabres and Thunderjets. But I'm astonished that he only arrived on the job in Viet Nam two weeks ago, and has been bringing in dozens of air strikes per day. "How do you locate the correct targets out there anyway?" I ask him. "It's tricky," he confesses modestly. "But I'm learning—mostly by trial and error."

> — Barry Cunningham, *New York Post*,
> December 3, 1966

Every Prime Minister or even Minister said: "I'm here for two months, so money, money, and if necessary I'll go abroad."

> — President Nguyen Cao Ky, December 3, 1966

We are in a much stronger position than two years ago. . . . They will not be able to succeed here.

> — Secretary of State Dean Rusk, Saigon,
> December 9, 1966

We cannot accept a Communist seizure of Vietnam. . . . There is no
question that the bombings have hurt the North, and hurt it badly. . . .
The war cannot be lost militarily. . . . It can also be won.

> — Robert A. Scalapino, Professor of Political
> Science, University of California, Berkeley,
> quoted by *New York Times Magazine*,
> December 11, 1966

The GI is achieving victory on battlefields. . . . GI Joe is shattering
the illusion that the Communist jungle fighter is invincible. . . . From
one senior U.S. officer comes this comment: "Our troops have dealt the
Communists murderous punishment . . . our boys have shown they can
win at the enemy's own game in the jungle."

> — *U.S. News & World Report*,
> December 12, 1966

Only now does Hanoi seem to be groping for a new theology to sustain
the Viet Cong in the face of continued reverses.

> — *Time*, December 16, 1966

The time has been long overdue . . . to win the war in South Vietnam.
This can be accomplished by employing the U.S. Army . . . to isolate
the Vietnam battlefields and interdict the enemy on the ground. . . . The
U.S. can do anything in this world that she wants to do—so let's get on
with this task and get it cleared up. The steps outlined above will make it
a different war—and a winning one in Vietnam.

> — General John K. Waters (ret.), former
> commanding general, U.S. Army, Pacific, *U.S.
> News & World Report*, December 19, 1966

The successive raids, two weeks apart, on Yen Vien and Van Dien
may well have made the Communists feel that the noose was dangerously tightening around Hanoi.

> — *Time*, December 23, 1966

Less than victory is inconceivable.

> — Francis Cardinal Spellman, archbishop of
> New York, Saigon, December 24, 1966

The immense influx of American manpower and firepower, and the
ruthless use of the latter, have made the South Viet-Nam war, in the
short-run, militarily "unlosable."

> — Dr. Bernard B. Fall, *Viet-Nam Witness*

We must all hope . . . that there can be progress. . . . I would not be in favor of stopping the bombing or of prolonged pause in the bombing unless there is some reason to think that it would have an effect.

> — McGeorge Bundy, president, Ford
> Foundation, *Meet the Press*, NBC,
> December 25, 1966

This war in Vietnam is, I believe, a war for civilization. . . . We cannot yield. . . . American troops are the defense, protection and salvation not only of our country, but, I believe, of civilization itself.

> — Francis Cardinal Spellman,
> December 26, 1966

The side which has its feet on the ground at the right time and in the right place will win.

> — Sir Robert Thompson, British civil servant in
> Malaya, head, British Advisory Mission,
> Saigon, until March 1965, consultant to
> President Ngo Dinh Diem, The Pentagon,
> White House; *Defeating Communist
> Insurgency*, 1966

If General Westmoreland's theory is correct, the disheartening shock of the crushing of the main forces will cause the local and guerrilla forces to give up the fight. . . . Final victory will then be in sight. . . . In Washington, there is a wave of pessimism . . . these spasms of gloom are always to be distrusted, and have often been the harbingers of decisive success. . . . There are some encouraging indicators.

> — Joseph Alsop, syndicated column,
> December 28, 1966

[The Vietcong] just might fade.

> — Ambassador Henry Cabot Lodge,
> December 1966

A 250,000-MAN FRENCH EXPEDITIONARY FORCE CAME THIS WAY AND WAS DESTROYED. DON'T LET IT HAPPEN TO YOU.

> — V-C sign posted on a road in Vietnam, 1966

I think there is a possibility [of peace in 1967]. The task of diplomacy is to proceed on the basis of optimism. . . . One basis for optimism is that the other side must surely now understand that they are not going to succeed. . . . Maybe that will . . . change their political approach.

> — Secretary of State Dean Rusk,
> *Face the Nation*, CBS, January 1, 1967

There is only one liberator in the country, me.
> — President Nguyen Cao Ky, interview,
> Tonsannhuet Airbase, Vietnam, January 1,
> 1967

We are involved because the nation's word has been given that we would be involved.
> — Secretary of State Dean Rusk to 100 student
> leaders, January 4, 1967

Vietcong Morale: It sags, prompting hope that time no longer favors Hanoi . . . that is sparking a new gleam of hope for U.S. forces in Vietnam.
> — *Wall Street Journal*, January 5, 1967

I expect . . . the war to achieve very sensational results in 1967.
> — Ambassador Henry Cabot Lodge,
> January 8, 1967

The position of Hanoi's forces at the front is gravely deteriorating.
> — Joseph Alsop, syndicated column, January 9,
> 1967

We ought not even to consider civilians. We bombed Japanese and German cities in World War II.
> — Congressman L. Mendel Rivers, Democrat of
> South Carolina, chairman, House Armed
> Services Committee, quoted by *U.S. News &
> World Report*, January 9, 1967

I believe . . . you are not only serving your country but you are serving God, because you are defending the cause of righteousness, the cause of civilization and God's cause.
> — Francis Cardinal Spellman to men in the
> Philippines who had fought in Vietnam,
> quoted by *U.S. News & World Report*,
> January 9, 1967

The village of Bensuc . . . will be swept from the face of the earth. "This is probably the only military or political solution for this place," said an American colonel.
> — *New York Times*, January 11, 1967

Wherever they looked last week, the leaders of North Viet Nam saw trouble. . . . Below the 17th parallel, the U.S. and its allies were preparing a knockout blow.
> — *Time*, January 13, 1967

The solution in Vietnam is more bombs, more shells, more napalm . . . till the other side cracks and gives up. . . . We're winning the war. We're killing VC, guerrillas, Main Forces, destroying their bases, destroying caches of food and weapons, we're getting more Chieu Hoi [defectors]. . . . The 1st Division is doing one thing: killing guerrillas.

> — Brigadier General William C. DePuy,
> commanding general, 1st Division, Lai Khe,
> South Vietnam, January 13, 1967

Our kids are learning to fight back.

> — John Steinbeck, novelist, dispatch
> from Saigon, *Washington Post*,
> January 15, 1967

The Archbishop of Canterbury defends the U.S. right to be in Viet Nam because it is there "with the right motive."

> — *Time*, January 20, 1967

Ambassador Lodge . . . looks for a "sensational" improvement in our military situation this year. . . . What we have already accomplished and begun, justify the energetic support of our present policies in Vietnam.

> — Editorial, *Life*, January 20, 1967

It is perfectly clear that we must take whatever measures are necessary to ensure our ability to support our forces in the event the conflict does continue beyond June 30, 1967.

> — Secretary of Defense Robert S. McNamara,
> before joint session, Senate Armed Services
> Committee and Subcommittee of Department
> of Defense Appropriations, January 23, 1967

In my opinion, the time has not come for such drastic, unilateral action as pulling out of Vietnam.

> — Senator Vance Hartke, Democrat of Indiana,
> member, Senate Finance Committee, quoted
> by *U.S. News & World Report*,
> January 23, 1967

The situation in Vietnam is . . . not hopeless. . . . We just can't quit.

> — Senator Daniel B. Brewster, Democrat of
> Maryland, member, Senate Armed Services
> Committee, quoted by *U.S. News & World
> Report*, January 23, 1967

I am no puppet of the United States or anyone else. That is my answer to Mr. Fulbright. He is a colonialist.

> — President Nguyen Cao Ky, news conference,
> Christchurch, N.Z., January 23, 1967

If I were a Vietcong, I would be somewhat discouraged.

> — Lieutenant General Jonathan O. Seaman,
> commander, Operation Cedar Falls,
> Saigon, January 23, 1967

You've got to forget about this civilian stuff. Whenever you drop bombs you're going to hit civilians; it's foolish to pretend you're not.

> — Former Senator Barry Goldwater,
> New York City, January 23, 1967

The United States is doing very well. . . . I see a little progress being made since my last trip out there in December 1965. . . . I feel the mere fact that the Ky regime has lasted this long is an indication of some progress. . . . I'm convinced that the bombing . . . is definitely hurting. . . . We'll need more troops in Vietnam.

> — Senator Henry M. Jackson, Democrat of
> Washington, member, Senate Armed Services
> Committee, quoted by *U.S. News & World
> Report*, January 23, 1967

I've been in Southeast Asia twice since September, 1965, and I frankly am somewhat encouraged. . . . The next thing that needs to be done is to continue to keep the pressure on. . . . I am generally in favor of continuing the war along policy lines the Administration has followed. . . . In my personal opinion I think that by this time next year we'll be talking about pulling military people out of Vietnam.

> — Senator Howard W. Cannon, Democrat of
> Nevada, member, Senate Armed Services
> Committee, major general, U.S. Air Force
> Reserve, quoted by *U.S. News & World Report*,
> January 23, 1967

Some are worried about civilians killed in North Vietnam. I'd rather see them weep a little over some of our aviators who are being killed.

> — Senator Sam J. Ervin, Jr., Democrat of North
> Carolina, member, Senate Armed Services
> Committee, quoted by *U.S. News & World
> Report*, January 23, 1967

No, the U.S. should not pull out of Vietnam. Until . . . an honorable settlement, we cannot and will not withdraw from Vietnam.

> — Senator Mike Mansfield, Democrat of
> Montana, Senate Majority Leader, quoted by
> *U.S. News & World Report*, January 23, 1967

Militarily, in South Vietnam we are doing much better. . . . It is curious that such a tremendous propaganda effort has developed against the unintentional killing of relatively few civilians in North Vietnam.

> — Senator Stuart Symington, Democrat of
> Missouri, member, Senate Armed Services
> Committee, former Secretary of the Air Force,
> quoted by *U.S. News & World Report*,
> January 23, 1967

The war . . . is not hopeless. There is every reason for confidence that we will be able to defeat the main-force Viet Cong and North Vietnamese. . . . It would be unthinkable for us to leave Vietnam on any terms except those which are entirely honorable. . . . We cannot back out now.

> — Senator John C. Stennis, Democrat of
> Mississippi, chairman, Preparedness
> Subcommittee, quoted by *U.S. News & World
> Report*, January 23, 1967

Victory can be achieved in the Vietnam war. . . . We've got the highest caliber of professional military men in our history.

> — Senator John Tower, Republican of Texas,
> member, Senate Armed Services Committee,
> quoted by *U.S. News & World Report*,
> January 23, 1967

The information I have indicates that our military situation in Vietnam has considerably improved over the past year. Moreover, the South Vietnamese Government . . . has shown qualities of endurance which have been encouraging. The Viet Cong and North Vietnamese by now must realize, therefore, that they cannot hope for the military victory which was once virtually in their grasp, and, with our continuing build-up in the South and the movement of our forces into the Mekong Delta, we can hope for further improvement.

> — Senator Robert C. Byrd, Democrat of West
> Virginia, member, Senate Armed Services
> Committee, quoted by *U.S. News & World
> Report*, January 23, 1967

I think it will come to an end. . . . Their aggressive adventures will not succeed. . . . I believe we should continue what we're doing in the military field. Within two years, we should see some clear signs pointing toward another avenue—negotiations.

> — Senator Daniel K. Inouye, Democrat of Hawaii, member, Senate Armed Services Committee, quoted by *U.S. News & World Report*, January 23, 1967

Vietnam has not become a hopeless war. I believe that military successes, together with the efforts that are bound to be made on pacification, will eventually bring home to Ho Chi Minh and his boys the news that we've been trying to get to them for some time, and hopefully within a year or so bring this thing to a conclusion. . . . I refuse to accept the idea that conduct of the war is a bad job.

> — Senator Thomas J. McIntyre, Democrat of New Hampshire, member, Senate Armed Services Committee, quoted by *U.S. News & World Report*, January 23, 1967

67% of the Vietnamese now live in areas secure from the Vietcong.

> — Robert W. Komer, quoted in dispatch from Reuters, January 25, 1967

The captain in the green beret said, "The Catholics in the village have cooperated completely. But the Buddhists are still sitting on the fence."

> — *Life*, January 27, 1967

Nothing I had read, no photographs I had seen prepared me for the immensity of the American effort. . . . We have committed more troops to Vietnam than were necessary to fight the North Koreans and Chinese combined in 1950. . . . Each American soldier carries six times the firepower he had in World War II. . . . The total number of airfields in South Vietnam is now 282, one of the highest in the world. Will these become the Stonehenges—or, more appropriately, the Angkor Wats—of Vietnam, the relics of a civilization that passed that way. . . .

This lavish use of firepower, whether effective or not, contributes to the cost of killing the enemy, which is calculated at $400,000 per soldier—including 75 bombs and 150 artillery shells for each corpse. . . . Foremost Dairies has a contract (for $18 million) with the Navy to build and operate a plant at Chu Lai and one at Da Nang which will produce each day for the U.S. armed forces 9,000 gallons of reconstituted milk, 2,500 gallons of ice cream and 3,000 pounds of cottage cheese. . . . Things look more optimistic at the Saigon offices of the great consortium known as Raymond Morrison–Knudsen Brown & Root and J. A. Jones, whose $1 billion contract (the biggest in history) for airfields, piers and other heavy construction will be completed sometime in 1968. . . .

There is little doubt that this is a poor boy's war, with a heavy percentage of Negroes (up to 30% in some extra-pay airborne units). . . . What we have achieved in Vietnam is the equivalent of a half-million-man Foreign Legion. As professionals, our troops don't flinch from the unpleasant duty of killing a 90-pound underdog. . . . One finds many officers who are serving their second tour in Vietnam . . . a few who are in the country for the third time. A colonel in the Vietnamese IV Corps in the Mekong Delta said one day, "I was one of those who told McNamara in 1964 that the war would be over by the end of 1965; I swear I thought it would be." . . .

The Vietcong's resolution bewilders other American soldiers. A lieutenant in the 25th Division shook his head and said, "I just don't understand what motivates these people." I was to hear the same remark dozens of times throughout Vietnam. . . . A private in Saigon: "The only thing to do is to kill everybody in the country over five years old." A sailor in My Tho: "Pretty soon we'll have the country paved over. Then we won't have to worry about it any more." A facetious reporter: "General Westmoreland, there are 15 million people in South Vietnam. We put that many people in uniform in World War II. Why not mobilize enough troops to give every South Vietnamese a personal American bodyguard?" . . .

The South Vietnamese armed forces . . . poor in performance and in motivation . . . is being relegated to rural pacification (which is probably the worst place to put them: they systematically steal from the peasants).

— Robert Sherrod, *Life*, January 27, 1967

The enemy's chance for a military victory is gone. . . . The North Vietnamese have learned that there is an increasing toll to pay for aggression.

— General Earle G. Wheeler, chairman, Joint
Chiefs of Staff, news conference, mid-January
1967, quoted by *U.S. News & World Report*,
January 30, 1967

I have no doubt at all that the bombing has made it much more difficult for them. . . . The effort of the Viet Cong and the North Vietnamese . . . has been frustrated. The forces that are present there inflict very severe casualties upon them . . . so we think we are making headway.

— Secretary of State Dean Rusk,
interview for British television,
January 31, 1967

I have been dismayed by what seems to me the overly pessimistic view.
. . . Unless we commit the folly of abandoning the field in Vietnam to
communist subversion, Chinese prestige will probably go on fading. . . .
If we were more optimistic in our approach to Asia, I believe we would
perhaps do a better job there. . . . The United States is by far the
strongest country in the world.

> — Edwin O. Reischauer, former ambassador to
> Japan, professor, Harvard University, *Reader's
> Digest*, February 1967

We felt that it [bombing] would make the North Vietnamese
pay a much heavier price for what they were doing and . . . make
the infiltration more difficult. We think it has achieved all of those
expressed purposes.

> — President Lyndon B. Johnson,
> news conference, White House,
> February 2, 1967

I feel our weapons have an edge in each category. . . . The Viet Cong
still use some very crude weapons. . . . We do have night-viewing
devices. We got them after we arrived in Vietnam. They are excellent,
and I think they give us a big edge. . . . I can't tell you much more,
except to say again we do have such gadgets and we like them. We also
have sentry dogs and scout dogs to help spot the VC at night. The dogs
are very good on sentry work—there's no question about that. But when
it comes to scouting for the enemy, there are some real problems. . . .
Whether the average North Vietnamese soldier is frightened or motivated, he keeps going. . . . They tend to do some awfully stupid things,
and I've often wondered why.

> — Major General H. W. O. Kinnard, former
> commander, 1st Cavalry Division, Vietnam,
> interview, *U.S. News & World Report*,
> February 6, 1967

The strain of war on North Vietnam's economy is beginning to fray
the morale of many of its citizens. . . . That's the reading of experts in
Vietnamese affairs here in Hong Kong. . . . "The leaders have almost
talked themselves into a slightly suicidal state of mind," says a recent
visitor to Hanoi. . . . The hardships have been worsening steadily and
no end is in sight. . . . Hanoi's own ability to maintain enthusiasm . . .
appears . . . to be deteriorating. . . . The pangs of hunger have started
in the North. . . . In all North Vietnam last year, only some 1,000 pumps
were put to use on farms. . . . Waste is feeding the country's inflation.
. . . Enthusiasm for the war is waning.

> — *Wall Street Journal*, dispatch from Hong
> Kong, February 7, 1967

Something is starting to move.

> — General Maxwell D. Taylor,
> quoted by *Time*, February 10, 1967

I think the bombing is warranted. . . . Let me define what I mean by winning. My view of winning is that we must end up with a South Vietnam that is . . . standing on its own feet. . . . If you want to win this war, you must . . . start creating the kind of police force that a stable country requires. . . . The main effort would be concentrated on what is known as pacification. . . . I honestly don't see that America could pull out in the present circumstances. It would be a humiliating defeat. . . . I think that we should settle down and win the war in the South. . . . I think organization is really the key to the problem.

> — Sir Robert Thompson, expert on guerrilla
> warfare, former head, British Advisory
> Mission, Saigon, author, *Defeating Communist
> Insurgency: Malaya and Vietnam*; interview,
> *U.S. News & World Report*, February 13, 1967

The impact of the bombing can be judged in part by the great efforts of North Vietnam to force us to stop bombing.

> — Secretary of Defense Robert S. McNamara,
> news conference, February 15, 1967

His Excellency Ho Chi Minh,
President, Democratic Republic of Vietnam

Dear Mr. President:
   I am writing to you in the hope that the conflict in Vietnam can be brought to an end. . . . I believe that we both have a heavy obligation to seek earnestly the path to peace. . . . If you have any thoughts . . . it would be most important that I receive them as soon as possible.

Sincerely,
Lyndon B. Johnson

February 8, 1967

To His Excellency Mr. Lyndon B. Johnson,
President, United States of America

Your Excellency:
   On February 10, 1967, I received your message. This is my reply. Vietnam is thousands of miles away from the United States. The Vietnamese people have never done any harm to the United States. But contrary to the pledges made by its representative at the 1954 Geneva

conference, the U.S. Government has ceaselessly intervened in Vietnam, it has unleashed and intensified the war of aggression in South Vietnam with a view to prolonging the partition of Vietnam and turning South Vietnam into a neo-colony and a military base of the United States. For over two years now, the U.S. Government has, with its air and naval forces, carried the war to the Democratic Republic of (North) Vietnam, an independent and sovereign country. The U.S. Government has committed war crimes, crimes against peace and against mankind. In South Vietnam, half a million U.S. and satellite troops have resorted to the most inhuman weapons and the most barbarous methods of warfare, such as napalm, toxic chemicals and gasses, to massacre our compatriots, destroy crops, and raze villages to the ground. In North Vietnam, thousands of U.S. aircraft have dropped hundreds of thousands of tons of bombs, destroying towns, villages, factories, schools. In your message, you apparently deplore the sufferings and destruction in Vietnam. May I ask you: Who has perpetrated these monstrous crimes. . . . The Vietnamese people deeply love independence, freedom and peace. But in the face of the U.S. aggression, they have risen up, united as one man, fearless of sacrifices and hardships. They are determined to carry on their resistance until they have won genuine independence and freedom and true peace. Our just cause enjoys strong sympathy and support from the peoples of the whole world, including broad sections of the American people. The U.S. Government . . . must cease this aggression. That is the only way to the restoration of peace. The U.S. Government must stop definitively and unconditionally its bombing raids and all other acts of war against the Democratic Republic of Vietnam, withdraw from South Vietnam all U.S. and satellite troops, recognize the South Vietnam National Front for Liberation, and let the Vietnamese people settle themselves their own affairs. . . . You suggested direct talks between the Democratic Republic of Vietnam and the United States. If the U.S. Government really wants these talks, it must first of all stop unconditionally its bombing raids and all other acts of war. . . . The Vietnamese people will never submit to force, they will never accept talks under the threat of bombs. Our cause is absolutely just. It is to be hoped that the U.S. Government will act in accordance with reason.

Sincerely,
Ho Chi Minh

February 15, 1967

I chase every peace feeler, just as my little beagle chases a squirrel.

— President Lyndon B. Johnson, to group of
White House Fellows, quoted by *Time*,
February 17, 1967

We've reached a point where all the king's horses and all the king's men are not going to move us out of our position.

— President Lyndon B. Johnson,
February 20, 1967

Cost to the U.S. from six years of American involvement in Vietnam now is put at 1,172 fixed-wing aircraft. In addition, more than 600 helicopters are said to have been destroyed. The dollar cost, according to estimates, could run up to 3 billion dollars.

— *U.S. News & World Report,*
February 20, 1967

The best way to make Communists is to put the Americans into a place where there were no Communists before.

— Prince Norodom Sihanouk,
Prime Minister of Cambodia,
February 24, 1967

I can't recall a single instance when the Secretary of State and the Secretary of Defense have differed on bombing policy and not a single instance when their recommendations have differed on particular bombing targets.

— Secretary of Defense Robert S. McNamara,
February 24, 1967

I think we are doing better in Vietnam. I think we are doing better than even some of us think.

— Former Senator Barry Goldwater,
Face the Nation, CBS, February 26, 1967

"A new wind rising out of the war in Vietnam is sending straws around the world. Yugoslav diplomats from Hanoi report: "They know now they cannot win."

— *U.S. News & World Report*,
February 27, 1967

It will be difficult for the V-C to maintain its strength in the South in 1967. Like Mr. [David] Lilienthal, I sense a growing mood of confidence in South Vietnam that the outcome of the conflict is no longer in doubt.

— Robert W. Komer, press briefing by Komer
and Lilienthal after returning from Vietnam,
February 27, 1967

I have never observed two men who I thought could represent the State and Defense Departments more successfully and also the national interest more cooperatively [than Rusk and McNamara]. . . . No one has ever expected, except those who want to stop it, that bombing will stop infiltration. So that is my comment on your question. We never thought it would stop infiltration. . . . Probably we lost a billion dollars in planes.

> — President Lyndon B. Johnson,
> February 27, 1967

At this point of 1967 we are enjoying a greatly improved military situation in Vietnam as compared with a year ago. I am confident that a year from now our military progress will have been at least as great and probably greater than in the calendar year 1966. . . . I think it should be rather apparent by now, both to the North Vietnamese and to the Viet Cong, that they are not going to win a military victory. . . . The enemy "doth protest too much"—he clearly feels that the air campaign is hurting him. . . . Our bombing is highly effective. . . . One of General Westmoreland's most serious problems is trying to figure out ahead of time precisely what the enemy is going to do. . . .

Our casualties, by the way, have been less than we anticipated—a little under 5,000 dead last year. . . . Napalm is a very effective weapon for certain purposes. It is particularly effective against troops. . . . To get rid of a Viet Cong or a North Vietnamese trooper . . . you have to have a direct hit. . . . Napalm, by virtue of its splashing and spreading, can get into . . . defensive positions . . . incapacitates the crew and sometimes destroys the weapon. . . . I think we have succeeded in giving to General Westmoreland as good officers as are available. . . . There's just no question about it—he's got a good first team out there.

> — General Earle G. Wheeler, chairman, Joint
> Chiefs of Staff, interview, *U.S. News & World
> Report*, February 27, 1967

TOP SECRET

I return more optimistic than ever before. The cumulative change since my first visit last April is dramatic, if not yet visibly demonstrable. . . . Wastefully, expensively, but nonetheless indisputably, we are winning the war in the South. Few of our programs—civil or military— are very efficient, but we are grinding the enemy down by sheer weight and mass. And the cumulative impact of all we have set in motion is beginning to tell. Pacification still lags the most, yet even it is moving forward. . . . Our side now has in presently programmed levels all the men, money and other resources needed to achieve success.

> — Robert W. Komer, memorandum to President
> Lyndon B. Johnson, February 28, 1967

The Treasury announced today that it would deny all applications to send dollars to such organizations as the Canadian Friends Service Committee for the purchase of medical supplies to be shipped to North Vietnam.

> — *New York Times*, February 28, 1967

I would hate to be a VC and know that I have no safe haven in South Viet Nam any more.

> — Lieutenant General Jonathan O. Seaman,
> commander, "Operation Junction City,"
> quoted by *Time*, March 3, 1967

Ho's hardened veterans are getting weary of the war.

> — *Time*, March 3, 1967

I don't believe that the bombing up to the present has significantly reduced, nor any bombing that I could contemplate in the future would significantly reduce, the actual flow of men and matériel to the South.

> — Secretary of State Robert S. McNamara, secret
> testimony to Senate Armed Services and
> Appropriations Committees in January,
> released in late February, *Time*, March 3, 1967

Strengthening of allied forces in 1966, under the brilliant leadership of General Westmoreland, was instrumental in reversing the whole course of this war. . . . General Westmoreland's strategy is producing results . . . our military situation has substantially improved . . . our military success has permitted the groundwork to be laid for a pacification program which is the longrun key. . . . It is not the position of the American government that the bombing will be decisive.

> — President Lyndon B. Johnson, address to joint
> session of Tennessee legislature, Nashville,
> March 15, 1967

Contraction of Vietcong strength in the countryside shows nowadays. . . . For proof of this erosion and loss of heart . . . Tons of documents have been captured in the "Cedar Falls" and "Junction City" operations: and these documents all tell . . . how much has been accomplished . . . and how much more can be accomplished.

> — Joseph Alsop, syndicated column,
> March 17, 1967

I don't believe we should stop the bombings and hope that the other side comes to the table.

> — Right Reverend James A. Pike, former
> Episcopal bishop of California, quoted by
> *Time*, March 17, 1967

During a 45-minute meeting in his White House office on Feb. 6, Johnson castigated Kennedy for his stance on Viet Nam. "If you keep talking like this, you won't have a political future in this country within six months. . . . In six months all you doves will be destroyed." At one point, Johnson used the phrase, "The blood of American boys will be on your hands." Finally, the President told Kennedy, "I never want to hear your views on Viet Nam again." He also reportedly said to the Senator: "I never want to see you again." Bobby, for his part, is said to have called the President a s.o.b. and to have told him at one point: "I don't have to sit here and take that————."

> — *Time*, March 17, 1967

The Navy's A-6 Intruder jets are using a secret satellite to guide them to targets in North Vietnam. Insiders say the satellite, launched piggy-back in a scientific package from Cape Kennedy, gives precise navigational fixes that permit the fighters to make accurate air strikes either at night or in poor weather.

> — *Newsweek*, March 20, 1967

Now, suppose we go to the conference table in Vietnam. We have no right to expect that we would get any better deal than we got in Korea. . . . The alternative is to defeat the enemy. . . . We can't get out, in my opinion, because we'd lose all of Southeast Asia.

> — General Mark W. Clark, former commander,
> UN forces, Korea, U.S. commander, Italy,
> World War II, president, The Citadel,
> intervew, *U.S. News & World Report*, March
> 20, 1967

The enemy is suffering heavy casualties and there is evidence his morale is declining. . . . The enemy's losses from all causes have doubled in the last year. These losses seem to be increasing. . . . The number of prisoners taken by the Vietnamese and their allies during the past year have multiplied by four. . . . The number of Viet Cong defections has doubled and the rate continues to rise. The number of weapons lost by the enemy has multiplied by 2½ times during the past year.

On the other hand, the weapons lost by the Vietnamese forces has been reduced by approximately one-half. . . . Our military operations have opened up 18 percent of the road that was not open . . . a year ago.

. . . The enemy . . . now has in South Vietnam an estimated 154 . . . battalions. . . . Only one half of these are . . . fully combat-effective. . . . Desertions in the ranks of the Vietnamese armed forces have been cut in half. . . . Leadership . . . is improving. . . . Discipline and administration are also improving. Morale is obviously also on the incline. . . . In summary, we have much to be encouraged about.

> — General William C. Westmoreland,
> report to President Lyndon B. Johnson,
> Guam, March 20, 1967

There are many signs that we are at a favorable turning point. Your fighting men . . . now hold the initiative and are striking heavy blows against the strongholds and refuges of the Viet Cong. . . . There are many other things I could cite that give us encouragement.

> — President Lyndon B. Johnson to President
> Nguyen Cao Ky, remarks opening Guam
> Conference, March 20, 1967

We must convince Hanoi that its cause is hopeless . . . we must, Mr. President, work for an honorable peace.

> — President Nguyen Cao Ky to President
> Lyndon B. Johnson, Guam, March 20, 1967

We will win this war.

> — Lieutenant General Nguyen Van Thieu,
> Guam, March 20, 1967

This is a war of attrition . . . a very long stage down the road to eventual success has been covered during Cabot Lodge's term of service.

> — Joseph Alsop, syndicated column,
> March 20, 1967

President Johnson and Chairman Thieu and Prime Minister Ky reviewed the encouraging progress. . . . Discussion covered the military front, where the initiative lies increasingly with the allied forces and where the leaders of North Vietnam must recognize the futility of their effort. . . . They found that . . . the pacification and revolutionary development program was now beginning to show encouraging results. . . . They noted the successful maintenance of financial stability. . . . They heard from Dr. Vu Quoc Thuc and Mr. David Lilienthal of the long-range economic planning now getting underway. . . . The Vietnamese and American leaders also took note of the forth-coming meetings in Washington of SEATO. . . . The latter will . . . provide an opportunity for them to review progress. . . .

> — Joint communiqué on Guam Conference,
> March 21, 1967

Vietnam . . . the impressions of one of our senior staff members who went there for a firsthand look at all aspects of the war. . . . How *the war is going: The Reds are losing, we are gaining* . . . it is true . . . there's ample evidence of it. . . . *Red troops are being mauled.* . . . *They are giving up ground.* . . . We are going to increase the pressure on *the Reds* from now on. *This will require more U. S. troops.* . . . *The BAREST chance exists that peace may come before the fall.* As the communists begin to see that they are going to take a bad beating . . . they might decide to ask for peace talks.

> — *The Kiplinger Washington Letter,*
> March 24, 1967

Destroy . . . their entire productive capacity. We must be willing to continue our bombing until we have destroyed every work of man in North Vietnam.

> — General Curtis E. LeMay, USAF (ret.),
> speech to Channel City Club,
> Long Beach, Calif., March 26, 1967

If you crowd in too many termite killers, each using a screwdriver to kill the termites, you risk collapsing the floors or the foundation. In this war we're using screwdrivers to kill termites because it's a guerrilla war and we cannot use bigger weapons. We have got to get the right balance of termite killers to get rid of the termites without wrecking the house.

> — General William C. Westmoreland,
> quoted by *Newsweek*, March 27, 1967

The military situation in Viet Nam gave ample cause for confidence. South Viet Nam's Premier Nguyen Cao Ky said that the Communist forces in his country are "on the run" and pictured the supply system in the North as "in near paralysis."

> — *Time*, March 31, 1967

There is legitimate and growing hope that the long-awaited "light at the end of the tunnel" has begun to glimmer.

> — Editorial, *Life*, March 31, 1967

'Absentee landlords are still riding in with pacifying troops,' reports the *London Times*, 'not merely to grab back their lands but to extort back rents for the time they fled the Viet Cong.' Although an old law limits rents to 25 percent of the crop, the *Times* reports that 'landlords still extort rents as high as 60 percent.'

> — Clayton Fritchey,
> *Washington Evening Star*, March 31, 1967

Let there be no doubt in the mind of Ho Chi Minh or anyone else that the American people will persevere in their fundamental support of the South Vietnamese.

> — Senator Edward Brooke, Republican of
> Massachusetts, maiden speech in Senate,
> quoted by *Time*, March 31, 1967

I don't have to tell you men that the enemy struck out. . . . The victory you had yesterday was one of the most successful single actions of the war.

> — General William C. Westmoreland, Tay Ninh
> Province, after bloodiest week thus far (to both
> sides) of war, quoted by *Newsweek*,
> April 3, 1967

The best we can hope for from the war . . . would seem to be our present limited warfare to pacify South Vietnam.

> — Edwin O. Reischauer,
> former ambassador to Japan,
> *Look*, April 4, 1967

By late 1966 more than 1,000,000 artillery shells were fired monthly. U.S. war planes and Navy ships added their firepower. . . . U.S. infantry commanders as a matter of course called in air strikes and artillery whenever the enemy was encountered, even snipers. The firepower of Allied forces, more than anything else, has changed the war's nature, according to military authorities. . . . As more troops arrive, a need for even more is seen.

> — *Christian Science Monitor*,
> dispatch from Saigon, April 5, 1967

America needs to tell the world of the lives it is saving. . . . We need to be known as a nation of peacemakers, not just peace marchers. . . . What Mrs. Humphrey and I found in Europe that broke our hearts was that all the Continent hears of America is bombing, riots taking place. . . . That's what some people think is news! . . . I've been wanting to get this off my chest. . . . The Job Corps and the poverty program . . . That's news! That's what America needs to tell the world!

> — Vice President Hubert H. Humphrey, speech
> to National Council of Jewish Women,
> Atlanta, April 13, 1967

The other side is having considerable difficulty in maintaining their forces. . . . We have seen some very favorable signs that we are making headway. . . . I would think we made very, very substantial headway during 1966.

> — Secretary of State Dean Rusk,
> *Meet the Press*, NBC, April 16, 1967

It can be said now that the defeat of the Communist forces in South Vietnam is inevitable. The only question is, how soon?

> — Richard M. Nixon, April 17, 1967

The military picture is favorable. . . . The enemy . . . is taking great casualties and he does have logistics problems.

> — General William C. Westmoreland,
> April 24, 1967

Many communities in Vietnam are living a better life because of the encouragement and help our American troops have given to them. A true missionary zeal among our troops is commonplace. . . . I am constantly impressed. . . .

> — General William C. Westmoreland,
> New York City, April 24, 1967

TOP SECRET

Westmoreland was quoted as saying that without the 2⅓ additional divisions which we had requested "we will not be in danger of being defeated but it will be nip and tuck to oppose the reinforcements the enemy is capable of providing." In the final analysis we are fighting a war of attrition in Southeast Asia. Westmoreland predicted that the next step if we are to pursue our present strategy to fruition would probably be the second addition of 2⅓ divisions or approximately another 100,000 men. Throughout the conversations he repeated his assessment that the war would not be lost but that progress would certainly be slowed down. To him this was "not an encouraging outlook but a realistic one." When asked about the influence of increased infiltration upon his operations, the general replied that as he saw it "this war is action and counteraction. Anytime we take an action we expect a reaction." The President replied: "When we add divisions can't the enemy add divisions? If so, where does it all end?" Westmoreland answered: "The VC and DRV strength in SVN now totals 285,000 men. . . . If we add 2½ [sic] divisions, it is likely the enemy will react by adding troops." The President then asked "At what point does the enemy ask for volunteers?" Westmoreland's only reply was, "That's a good question." . . . The President closed the meeting by asking: "What if we do not add the 2⅓ divisions?" General Wheeler replied first, observing that the momentum would die, in some areas the enemy would recapture the initiative.

> — Assistant Secretary of Defense for
> International Security Affairs John T.
> McNaughton, memorandum of conversation
> between President Johnson and Generals
> Wheeler and Westmoreland, April 27, 1967

Now this is what the war in Vietnam is all about—control of the people. . . . [General Giap] has been proven wrong. . . . We will prevail in Vietnam. . . . [Our policy] is producing results. . . . [The] enemy's tactic has failed.

> — General William C. Westmoreland,
> speech to joint session of Congress,
> April 28, 1967

The American attitude toward the war is wholesome.

> — General William C. Westmoreland,
> Honolulu, April 30, 1967

The Commandant of the Marine Corps has called the Vietnam War "the most pressing problem" America faces, more important than conditions in city slums.

> — General Wallace M. Greene, Jr.,
> address to American Legion,
> Boston, April 30, 1967

General Maxwell D. Taylor . . . as military adviser to the late President Kennedy laid down in 1961 the original strategy. . . . *The strategy has worked*—brilliantly. In a manner altogether astounding to behold, the whole course of the battle has been turned around. From being on the verge of losing its position in South Vietnam lock, stock, and barrel, the U.S. has driven the main enemy army to the brink of defeat. Never in modern times has there been a smoother, surer, swifter reversal in the tide of a . . . struggle.

> — "The War We've Won," *Fortune*, April 1967

Overlooked in the Vietnam turmoil is this fact: For the first time, principles of free enterprise—not French socialism—have the upper hand in South Vietnam. New chiefs of the country's economy, Nguyen Huu Hanh and Pham Kim Ngoc, are rated as *tough and realistic*. Joint Vietnamese–U.S. committees now oversee the economy. They put pressure on lower echelons for action.

> — *U.S. News & World Report*, May 1, 1967

Gen. Westmoreland needs more troops. . . . If Gen. Westmoreland is thus enabled to resume maximum pressure on the enemy, the best forecast is that the worst of the war should be over before end of this year. . . . If the new threat in the North . . . is beaten back, in sum, the road for the Hanoi war-planners should be downwards.

— Joseph Alsop, syndicated column, May 3, 1967

TOP SECRET

On the ineffectiveness of the bombing as a means to end the war, I think the evidence is plain. . . . Ho Chi Minh and his colleagues simply are not going to change their policy on the basis of losses from the air in North Vietnam. No intelligence estimate that I have seen in the last two years has ever claimed that the bombing would have this effect. . . . The real justification for the bombing, from the start, has been double—its value for Southern morale . . . and its relation to Northern infiltration. . . . The tactical bombing of communications and troop concentrations . . . seems to me sensible and practical. It is strategic bombing that seems both productive and unwise. It is true, of course, that all careful bombing does some damage to the enemy. But the net effect of this damage upon the military capability of a primitive country is almost sure to be slight.

— McGeorge Bundy, memorandum to President
Lyndon B. Johnson, May 4, 1967

Several indices clearly point to steady and encouraging success.

— General William C. Westmoreland,
quoted by *Time*, May 5, 1967

TOP SECRET

We have never held the view that bombing could stop infiltration. We have never held the view that bombing of the Hanoi-Haiphong area alone would lead them to abandon the effort in the South. We have never held the view that bombing Hanoi-Haiphong would directly cut back infiltration. We have held the view that the degree of military and civilian cost felt in the North and the diversion of resources to deal with our bombing could contribute marginally—and perhaps significantly—to the timing of a decision to end the war.

— Walt W. Rostow, memorandum to Secretary
Rusk, Deputy Secretary of Defense Vance,
Under Secretary of State Nicholas deB.
Katzenbach, Assistant Secretary of Defense
McNaughton, Assistant Secretary of State
Bundy, and CIA Director Richard Helms,
May 6, 1967

For policy makers wrestling with the dilemma of Vietnam . . . as a model for South Vietnam they are looking to Chung Hee Park, the newly re-elected President of Korea, and the regime he heads as a way out in Saigon. Behind this prospect is a conviction that Vietnam is not ready for party politics and civilian government. . . . The theory is that the military in a developing country has a greater concern for the national interest. . . . It should surprise no one that the chief propounder of this theory is that brilliant theoretician, Walt Rostow, the No. 2 adviser to the President on foreign policy. . . . As a theoretician Rostow has few rivals and certainly not in government. . . . He makes the parallel between Seoul and Saigon seem not only inevitable but right, and the course of military authority equally inevitable for new nations struggling toward stability.

> — Marquis Childs, syndicated column (United Features), *Washington Post*, May 8, 1967

We are trying to help the Vietnamese ignite a social revolution. . . . I'd like to get everybody to come to Vietnam. I don't know a person who has spent a few weeks who has not been impressed.

> — Barry Zorthian, chief, U.S. public relations and psychological warfare in Vietnam, quoted in *Life*, May 12, 1967

The French are weak, cowardly and intelligent. The Americans are strong, courageous and stupid.

> — General Charles de Gaulle, quoted by T. R. Tournoux in *The Tragedy of the General*

Since we got here in October, 1965, we have killed 8,583 Viet Cong and we ourselves have lost fewer than 800. So the kill ratio is 10 to 1, more than double that of other Allied forces. . . . I think we have done a good job. . . . the most important thing, I think, is to . . . instill confidence. . . . We are Oriental. . . . I do hope to conclude this war as soon as possible. The best way to end it is in victory. . . . We, therefore, have to apply more pressure on them . . . bombings and naval-gunfire support, to squeeze them. . . . More bombings, I think, will force our enemy to accept peace talks.

> — General Chae Myung-shin, chief, Korean forces in Vietnam, interview, *U.S. News & World Report*, May 15, 1967

We are making good headway every day, and the enemy is losing ground every day. Time is no longer on his side. . . . When they are destroyed, North Vietnam will have lost its fight. The war will be over.

. . . The most significant progress you can make in a war of this type is in the antiguerrilla war . . . we have done a lot of antiguerrilla and pacification work. We've destroyed many thousands of guerrillas . . . but we don't have forces enough. . . . It is a matter of time. We can destroy the infrastructure and the guerrillas, but the problem is having security there after you've done that. . . . That is why we need more troops. . . . We are making progress.

> — General Lewis W. Walt, commandant, U.S. Marine Corps, interview, *U.S. News & World Report*, May 22, 1967

We are confident of the successful outcome of this struggle.

> — President Nguyen Van Thieu, May 30, 1967

Whatever happens in Vietnam, I can see nothing but military victory.

> — Former President Dwight D. Eisenhower, West Point, June 2, 1967

Without American money, guns, food, medicine and supplies, we of the National Liberation Front would have a hard time surviving.

> — Major Pham Van-linh, logistics officer, National Liberation Front (Vietcong), interview, Saigon, June 1967

What I am is a revolutionary. . . . You must admit that things are a lot better than they were 16 months ago.

> — President Nguyen Cao Ky, interview with Kermit Lansner, managing editor, *Newsweek*, June 5, 1967

So the war goes on. Like a buzzard, the olive-green helicopter banked and wheeled over the burned-out village.

The village was a dust heap. The sienna-colored huts had been flattened by repeated air strikes. Trails of fresh blood splashed a crazy path among the broken coconut palms.

A top sergeant is busy emptying his back pack to make room for a mother-of-pearl Buddhist altar looted from the ruins. . . . A bulldozer heaves aside the one remaining wall of someone's home. On it is scrawled in English, "G.I., PLEASE DON'T BURN MY HOME!" . . . Another First Cav trooper is giving out black playing cards. On one side is a death's-head skull with paratrooper wings. Beneath this is the legend "Death From Above." The idea, I am told, is psywar at the company level. When Charlie returns to find his family dead, he is expected to get the message. The cards are stuck in dead mouths.

"What's the bulldozer doing here?" I asked.

"The captain is looking for rice and weapons—they've got to be buried somewhere!"

"What about the villagers?"

"Screw the villagers. Everyone here was VC."

> — Desmond Smith, "There Must Have Been
> Easier Wars," *The Nation*, June 12, 1967

The policy of the United States is to support fair, free, and honest elections in South Vietnam.

> — Ambassador Ellsworth Bunker,
> to newsmen, June 29, 1967

The United States is confident that the efforts by South Vietnam and its allies will continue to bring improvements. The important thing to bear in mind is that . . . the most significant indicators of military success may be found not in battle reports and casualty statistics but in the evidence that the country is moving forward . . . holding village and hamlet elections. . . . The remarkable progress being made . . . augurs well for the future.

> — Secretary of State Dean Rusk,
> interview with Swedish newsman,
> July 1, 1967

The 470,000 U.S. troops in South Vietnam should be sufficient to deal with enemy forces.

> — *Newsweek*, July 3, 1967

The war will end with the fadeout of V-C activity.

> — Henry Cabot Lodge, quoted in *New York
> Times*, July 7, 1967

TOP SECRET

In a series of suddenly executed offensive operations undertaken by General Westmoreland last April in which a total of 12,000 of the enemy have been killed in action, the enemy has been kept off balance and his time schedule has been disrupted. It seems apparent that the main effort of the enemy to achieve his summer campaign objectives has been postponed from May until at least July. General Westmoreland's strategy of anticipating enemy threats has paid off handsomely. . . . An encouraging element of these recent operations has been evidence of increased effectiveness of the Vietnamese Armed Forces.

> — Ambassador Ellsworth Bunker, July 7, 1967

The war is not a stalemate. We are winning it slowly but steadily. North Vietnam is paying a tremendous price with nothing to show for it in return.

> — General William C. Westmoreland,
> Saigon, July 7, 1967

First we beat the hell out of them, then we talk with them.

> — President Nguyen Van Thieu,
> quoted by *Time*, July 7, 1967

Our casualties are high but we also have inflicted very high casualties on North Vietnamese army units. I anticipate the enemy will receive a very heavy pounding.

> — Secretary of Defense Robert S. McNamara,
> following visit to DMZ, Vietnam,
> July 9, 1967

I went into several hamlets on the banks of the canal. There I saw sampan shops, carpenter shops . . . that are back in business. This time there is demonstrable progress, demonstrable in the sense that the Vietnamese military are performing better. . . . The 1st Division . . . has a string of unbroken successes. . . . They have cleaned out an enormous number of VC, captured rice and this sort of thing in the coastal area north of Danang, north of Hué, actually.

> — General Harold K. Johnson, chief of staff,
> U.S. Army, news conference, White House,
> July 12, 1967

Substantial progress has been made on nearly all fronts. . . . The political scene has changed. . . . The nation now has a constitution. . . . The election . . . will be held. . . . This is tremendous progress. . . . There has been a very substantial improvement in the economy. . . . I met with the . . . senior Vietnamese commanders. . . . Korean and New Zealanders . . . and . . . U.S. officers—all of the military commanders stated that the reports that they read in the press of military stalemate were—to use their words—the "most ridiculous statements that they ever heard." In their view, military progress had occurred and was continuing. . . . Pacification . . . will increase. . . . What we are really trying to do here is engage in nation building. . . . The most dramatic change I saw . . . was the opening of the roads. . . . Highway No. 1 . . . has gradually reopened. . . . As a matter of fact, day before yesterday, the route from the southern border of the II Corps to Dong Ha . . . was opened for traffic. . . . As I flew over this road after this long stretch was opened, literally hundreds of bicycles and . . . cars and trucks . . . were using it. . . . Some more troops will be needed.

> — Secretary of Defense Robert S. McNamara,
> news conference, White House,
> July 12, 1967

We have tried to evaluate our successes—they are many. . . . We are generally pleased with the progress that we have made militarily. We are very sure that we are on the right track. We realize that some additional troops are going to be needed and are going to be supplied.

> — President Lyndon B. Johnson, joint news
> conference with McNamara, Wheeler, and
> Westmoreland, July 13, 1967

We have there 450,000 or 460,000 and we have on the order of 20,000 or 30,000 to go. They will be supplied within the next few weeks.

> — Secretary of Defense Robert S. McNamara,
> joint news conference, July 13, 1967

The statement that we are in a stalemate is complete fiction. It is completely unrealistic. During the past year tremendous progress has been made. . . .

> — General William C. Westmoreland, joint news
> conference, White House, July 13, 1967

It is also a war of attrition against the Marines. "It isn't great sport any more," says a Marine veteran. "You know—a 7-to-1 ratio of Communist casualties to the U.S.'s. It is now about 3-to-1, and in some places 2 to 1, and even occasionally 1 to 1."

> — *Time*, July 14, 1967

The other side is hurting, and they are hurting very badly. I think there is military progress.

> — Secretary of State Dean Rusk, July 18, 1967

The wailing of women and the stench of burned bodies greeted the troops as they marched in Bagia. A United States Air Force officer said, "When we are in a bind we unload on the whole area. We kill more women and children than we do Vietcong, but the Government troops just aren't available, so this is the only answer."

> — AP dispatch, July 18, 1967

In my view the clash of regular armies could end in Vietnam during this calendar year. I expect some sort of settlement in 1967 or early 1968.

> — Frank N. Trager, Professor of International
> Affairs, N.Y.U., expert on Southeast Asia,
> interview, *American Legion Magazine*,
> July 1967

My duty is to crush all disturbances of whatever origin.

> — President Nguyen Cao Ky, commenting on
> Thich Tri Quang, leader of the Buddhist
> opposition, *Time*, August 11, 1967

The troops will be brought home in 18 months.

> — General Harold K. Johnson, chief of staff,
> U.S. Army, August 12, 1967

It is simply not correct that there is a military stalemate in Viet-Nam. There is a vast amount of information to prove that we are slowly but steadily making progress. If you look at the situation two years ago and compare it with the situation today, there cannot be any doubt in any fair mind that much progress has been made. . . . Both the morale and the performance of the South Vietnamese Armed Forces has improved dramatically. Two years ago, the Communist forces were on the offensive and were winning significant victories against the ARVN. Now, the Communists are on the defensive and ARVN units have recently scored some signal victories. It has been a year since Communist forces won a significant victory. . . . The Viet Cong, all over the country, are experiencing severe manpower problems. Food has become a critical problem. . . . Considerable progress has been made on the economic, social and political fronts.

> — From secret Department of Defense paper,
> August 13, 1967

An American officer said to me, "The only immorality is to kid ourselves. If there's no light at the end of the tunnel, it's up to *us* to say so. But if there is light at the other end of the tunnel, we have to stay."

> — Theodore H. White, "Saigon," *Life*,
> September 1, 1967

I have just had the greatest brainwashing that anyone can get when you go over to Vietnam, not only by the generals, but also by the diplomatic corps over there, and they do a very thorough job.

> — Governor George Romney, Republican of
> Michigan, Detroit, September 4, 1967

In my opinion our new air effort against North Vietnam is making a major contribution to the achievement of our objectives.

> — Admiral Thomas H. Moorer, chief of naval
> operations, quoted by *Newsweek*,
> September 4, 1967

Here's one reason the war in Vietnam drags on and on: the Viet Cong have been hurt surprisingly little by those much-heralded search-and-destroy operations. A Pentagon analysis of combat operations in South Vietnam for the six months ending last Feb. 1 showed that each U.S. battalion (800 men) engaged in search-and-destroy missions killed an average of less than two Viet Cong guerrillas a day and captured but one enemy rifle every two days.

> — *Newsweek*, September 4, 1967

Last spring I felt we had a year to win it, but now I think I ought to move that date ahead.

> — Brigadier General S. L. A. Marshall, military
> historian, quoted by *Time*, September 8, 1967

We're really doing the job now.

> — Brigadier General J. M. Philpott, director,
> Intelligence, U.S. 7th Air Force, quoted by
> *Time*, September 8, 1967

I think we are making steady progress—not spectacular progress. . . . I think we are making steady progress. This is a situation which cannot be solved overnight. It takes time. It takes patience. It takes steady application of pressure. . . . It is a question of keeping on the pressure, gradually moving ahead.

> — Ambassador Ellsworth Bunker,
> *Face the Nation*, CBS, September 10, 1967

We are very definitely winning in Vietnam. . . . There has been a marked turnabout. . . . By the end of 1965, with the advent of U.S. forces, we had arrested—I think that is the best term—the downhill slide. . . . There began to be evidence of an upward turn in August of 1966. This has continued, and now there is a forward movement everywhere. . . . As concerns television . . . you tend to get a repetitive picture of misfortune in Vietnam. And when you get this over a period of time, about the only thing it can induce is an attitude of pessimism back home. . . .

Success feeds on success, and I think that we have a momentum going now that we have not had before, and in order to increase this momentum and to bring the active hostilities to a conclusion faster, we want to reinforce success. . . . I think we have come a very long way in the past two years—and I see no reason why we can't keep this momentum going.

— General Harold K. Johnson,
interview, *U.S. News & World Report*,
September 11, 1967

In early August a Marine battalion burned perhaps 500 houses in the embarrassing presence of a television camera crew. . . . Around them is some evidence that the war is hard for the Vietnamese, too. Although Defense Department spokesmen had criticized the Columbia Broadcasting System for saying that 150 were burned in Camne, marines and Vietnamese officials insist that the correct figure was 500.

— Charles Mohr, *New York Times*,
September 15, 1967

Hanoi may be ready to talk peace. . . . We know they are having shortages of supplies. . . . We know that the bombings are being tremendously effective. The psychological effect of the bombings alone has been one of the most effective things.

— Senator George Murphy, Republican of
California, September 17, 1967

I'm explaining what the President is trying to do in Vietnam. . . . Every American citizen should be proud and should support him. It takes three things to be a great President and Lyndon Johnson has them all.

— Presidential Assistant Jack Valenti,
September 17, 1967

"I don't want to sound too optimistic," said one Pentagon general, "but I think we're turning the corner with these elections and the heartening military progress we're making in the ground war. I fully agree with Johnny Johnson [Army Chief of Staff Harold K. Johnson]." . . . U.S. intelligence now professes to detect a drop in over-all enemy strength, the first in two years.

— *Newsweek*, September 18, 1967

Latest intelligence reports on the movement of arms and men from the north show a sharp decline. . . . There is also reason to believe that Ho Chi Minh may be having far more serious manpower problems than generally realized.

— Joseph Alsop, syndicated column,
September 25, 1967

We'll be able to withstand just about any type of minor attack.

> — Frank J. Martin, architect who designed new
> U.S. Embassy Chancery in Saigon, at
> dedication ceremony, September 29, 1967

There is progress in the war itself, steady progress . . . dramatic progress. . . . The campaigns of the last year drove the enemy from many of their interior bases. The military victory almost within Hanoi's grasp in 1965 has now been denied them. The grip of the Viet Cong on the people is being broken. . . . Reason will at last prevail. . . . Hanoi will realize that it cannot win. . . . The keepers of peace . . . will prevail.

> — President Lyndon B. Johnson,
> speech at San Antonio,
> September 29, 1967

America is too young to die! Meet your challenge! The tocsin sounds, your country calls. We will walk this road together. Tell us your story, and I give you my word you will not bear this cross alone.

> — Congressman L. Mendel Rivers, Democrat of
> South Carolina, chairman, House Armed
> Services Committee, address, 89th annual
> conference, National Guard Association,
> quoted by *Time,* September 29, 1967

This is not 1948; LBJ is not Harry Truman; and Vietnam is not Korea.

> — Editorial, *New Republic,*
> September 30, 1967

The enemy has suffered a crushing defeat. . . . He has had a severe setback. He has had heavy casualties. He has a weather problem. The enemy losses as seen at Conthien are great.

> — General William C. Westmoreland,
> Saigon, October 4, 1967

Anyone not a rigorous pacifist must at least consider the argument that this war, evil as it is, is the lesser of available evils, intended to forestall worse wars.

> — John Updike, novelist, letter to *New York
> Times,* week of October 1, 1967, quoted by
> *Time,* October 6, 1967

"Liberals" . . . are wrong, I would think, in their proposed solution, which is for the Government to get out of Vietnam.

> — Daniel Patrick Moynihan, director,
> Harvard-M.I.T. Joint Center for Urban
> Studies, remarks to ADA, quoted by *U.S.
> News & World Report*, October 9, 1967

It appears near-certain that the abandonment of the siege of Conthien marks the real end of the long, bloody phase of the war. . . . If this is true, we are half-way to victory, and maybe a good deal more than half-way. . . . The skill of Gen. William C. Westmoreland . . . always cheated the Hanoi war planners of their longed-for "victory." No U.S. battalion had been annihilated. Still worse, V.C. recruitment in the South had continuously declined, and enemy losses . . . had continuously, cruelly risen. . . . The Conthien plan, therefore, has to be understood as a last desperate attempt. . . . Fortunately there are also documents which make the foregoing speculation into a near-certainty.

> — Joseph Alsop, syndicated column,
> Saigon, October 11, 1967

I am encouraged by progress toward peace in South Vietnam. . . . We shall continue our effort. . . . I know that some reporter in Saigon invented the word "stalemate." Ambassador Bunker doesn't believe there is a stalemate. Our military authorities do not believe there is a stalemate. . . . Despite all the tongues-in-cheek, despite all the skepticism, the South Vietnamese have come through with what really ought to be considered almost a miracle. . . . The South Vietnamese have been moving steadily. . . . The economic situation has been improving. In other words, the Viet Cong have not achieved their objective. The country is moving ahead. And I see no reason for us to be gloomy simply because it is not over yet. . . . The situation is moving. . . . When you look at the total situation, it's moving; and I have no reason myself whatever to subscribe to this notion of a stalemate. It's not a stalemate at all.

> — Secretary of State Dean Rusk,
> news conference, October 12, 1967

The war is going along quite steadily in our favor.

> — Admiral U. S. Grant Sharp, October 13, 1967

Con Thien is a Dienbienphu in reverse.

> — General William C. Westmoreland,
> quoted by *Time*, October 13, 1967

You do not demean the ruler. It don't sound good and it don't look good. . . . Do we quit? Do we retreat? . . . I learned long ago that it is

the hit dog that yelps. They are being hit. They are being hurt, and they
are beginning to yelp.

> — Senator Everett Dirksen,
> quoted in *Time*, October 13, 1967

The Vietcong appears to be falling apart at the seams.... We are now
running into 13-to-16-year-olds who break and run as soon as we hit them.

> — General George P. Seneff, former commander,
> U.S. Army aviation forces, Pentagon news
> conference, October 13, 1967

We have no choice but to persevere.

> — Vice President Hubert H. Humphrey,
> Doylestown, Pa. October 15, 1967

The cause in Vietnam is one which *can* be won and is *being* won. . . .
The Vietcong and North Vietnamese forces lost over 100,000 men last
year. . . . They are losing men at about double that rate at the present
time. . . . The loss . . . should raise serious doubts among the leaders
in the North . . . as to the feasibility of continuing the struggle. . . . As
an indicator of progress in pacification, there has been an encouraging
increase in Government control. . . . We should note . . . the most
dramatic note of political progress. . . . This evidence of growing
political maturity is most encouraging. . . . Hanoi . . . cannot win a
military victory in the South and will inevitably pay an increasing price
in the North. . . . This war can be won and is being won. . . .
Fortunately, the assets and resources of the North are strictly limited and
clearly inadequate. It is they who started a war which cannot be won,
and it is their leaders—not ours—who should be meditating upon the
inevitability of failure. Although they may cling to the hope for the
collapse of our determination, events will, I think, prove it vain.

> — General Maxwell D. Taylor, president,
> Institute for Defense Analyses, Washington
> "think-tank," *New York Times Magazine*,
> October 15, 1967

I know of no significant opinion in this country supporting a
withdrawal and an abandonment of Vietnam and Southeast Asia.

> — Secretary of State Dean Rusk, interview with
> foreign press, USIA transcription,
> October 16, 1967

The U.S. military command rates the battle of the Demilitarized Zone
as the "worst defeat" of the war for North Vietnam.

> — *U.S. News & World Report*, dispatch from
> Saigon, October 16, 1967

In the South where the enemy deliberately mixes in with the population, a massive toll is taken among civilians by artillery and aircraft. There are estimates that up to 5,000 casualties die each month, with 10,000 wounded. . . . The American command estimates that up to 40,000 Viet Cong and North Vietnamese regulars have been slain this year alone. But the figure is known to contain a large number of civilians. After a battle, all the dead other than allied troops are counted as enemy, even women and children.

— AP dispatch, October 24, 1967

The enemy has now been broken up by the growing pressure of U.S. search-and-destroy operations, its supply bases destroyed, and its links to friendly villages disrupted . . . proving how successful U.S. tactics have been, one more small nail in the Vietcong coffin.

— Rowland Evans and Robert Novak,
syndicated column, October 27, 1967

What sustains Hanoi? At first and until recently, the hope of military victory in the South. That possibility is now beyond their reach. . . . The South Vietnamese have adopted a new constitution and elected a President and Vice President and . . . village and hamlet leaders. Perhaps Hanoi has hoped to build up international pressures to cause us to alter our course. That is not occurring. I have just completed meeting with about 90 foreign ministers. . . . I can tell you that we are not under pressure from other governments to pull out of Vietnam.

— Secretary of State Dean Rusk,
address at Columbus, Ind., October 30, 1967

The military situation is very encouraging now, and I can say that we are winning the military war. The situation has improved very much in comparison with 1965 and early 1966. Politically, I believe that we are now on the way. . . .

— President-elect Nguyen Van Thieu,
interviewed before October 31 inauguration,
U.S. News & World Report, October 30, 1967

Vietnam is our greatest adventure, and a wonderful adventure it is! . . . I think we are winning this struggle. I don't say it has been won. I say we are winning it.

— Vice President Hubert H. Humphrey,
Saigon, November 1, 1967

I believe that we are making progress. I believe that we are doing what we ought to do. I think we are going to continue doing what we ought to do.

> — President Lyndon B. Johnson,
> news conference, White House,
> November 1, 1967

Vice President Hubert H. Humphrey chose to soft-pedal Washington's desire for swift improvements in South Vietnam during his meetings with President Nguyen Van Thieu and Vice President Nguyen Cao Ky. . . . Humphrey's major message to the leaders of Vietnam's new government was that the Johnson Administration is determined to stick by its present policy. Humphrey also stressed that although "there obviously is a vocal element in the United States that represents dissent from our policy, the majority of Americans support the U.S. role in Vietnam."

> — *Washington Post*, dispatch from Saigon,
> November 1, 1967

Vietcong terrorists shelled the Presidential Palace here last night just after Vice President Hubert H. Humphrey arrived for a reception given by Lieut. Gen. Nguyen Van Thieu, South Vietnam's new President. . . . The shelling was done with a 61-mm mortar. Three rounds landed inside the Palace walls. . . . A few rushed to the veranda, apparently thinking that what they heard was a fireworks display or a military salute to Thieu and Air Vice Marshal Nguyen Cao Ky, the country's new Vice President. Westmoreland, resplendent in a bemedaled white uniform, was under no such illusions. "Probably 75-mm recoilless," he declared. He was wrong about the weapon, but right about its not being friendly.

> — *Washington Post*, dispatch from Saigon
> November 1, 1967

The U.S. is not going to pull out. . . . We're there, and we're not going to leave. I don't care how many demonstrations you have. The nation is committed.

> — Vice President Hubert H. Humphrey,
> Kuala Lumpur, Malaysia, November 2, 1967

We believe the tide has turned and the enemy strength is on the decline.

> — Confidential report to Secretary of State Dean
> Rusk from Saigon, based largely on captured
> documents, quoted by Drew Pearson,
> syndicated column, November 2, 1967

Increasingly the President and his top lieutenants on the White House Staff and in the Cabinet appear more insulated from the rest of the nation. More and more they talk to each other, reassuring themselves of the wisdom and justice of their course.

> — *Wall Street Journal*, November 3, 1967

Our humiliation in Viet Nam would persuade guerrilla nuclei here of the efficacy of "national liberation" wars. Our adversaries know, even if we do not, that revolutionary warfare in Viet Nam is directly linked to the fate of South America.

> — C. L. Sulzberger, *New York Times* columnist,
> writing from Latin America,
> quoted in *Time*, November 3, 1967

Our premature withdrawal . . . would put all the free nations now along the Pacific coast of Asia into great and immediate jeopardy. . . . Because we know that Communism hates Christianity, we would soon expect religion to disappear in Asia. . . . Am I an incurable pessimist? Far from it. I think we are winning. . . .

> — Senator Wallace F. Bennett, Republican of
> Utah, speech in Senate, quoted by *U.S. News
> & World Report*, November 6, 1967

The war—the military war—in Vietnam is nearly won.

> — Orr Kelly, *Washington Evening Star*,
> November 7, 1967

I am more encouraged than at any time since I arrived here. The enemy is literally on the verge of starvation.

> — General William C. Westmoreland,
> Saigon, November 7, 1967

We military people are all very optimistic. We see the situation getting steadily better. . . . I know he [the enemy] isn't going to do very well. He just isn't going to make it. He's been in a losing situation for 18 months. We've gone into his base areas. We've burned his rice, captured his weapons and medicine. He's hungry, he's sick and he's hurting. . . . By next year at this time, he's going to be in bad shape. Personally, I have doubts he can hang on.

> — Brigadier General A. R. Brownfield, deputy
> assistant chief of staff, U.S. Military Assistance
> Command (MACV), Saigon, quoted by
> *Washington Evening Star*, November 7, 1967

South Vietnam has made more progress toward constitutional government in 13 months while fighting a war than the United States made in
the first 13 years after the American Revolution.

> — President Lyndon B. Johnson,
> November 9, 1967

We are on the offensive; territory is being gained. We are making
steady progress.

> — Vice President Hubert H. Humphrey,
> television interview, NBC,
> November 10, 1967

Our statesmen will press the search for peace to the corners of the
earth.

> — President Lyndon B. Johnson,
> November 11, 1967

Napalm . . . adheres to whatever it touches and continues burning.
. . . Napalm is one of the cheapest and most effective weapons invented
in the 20th century. . . . The napalm now used in Vietnam is known as
napalm-B. . . . It consists of 50% polystyrene, 25% benzine, and 25%
gasoline. It is packaged by the American Electric Co. of Paramount,
Cal., which makes the casings for the ingredients manufactured by Dow
Chemical of Torrance, Cal. Napalm burns at a heat approaching 2100
degrees centigrade. It develops high concentrations of deadly carbon
monoxide. Dropped on or near air raid shelters it causes the inmates to
die of asphyxiation. . . . White phosphorus is generally used to ignite
napalm. . . . Victims of a napalm attack frequently continue to smolder
when the phosphorous particles are imbedded in their skin. . . .
According to Drs. Peter Reich and Victor Sidel, writing in the *New
England Journal of Medicine*, and citing the *Chemical Engineering News*,
March 14, 1966, current production of napalm-B in the U.S.A. is
approaching 50 million pounds per month.

> — *Parade*, November 12, 1967

They don't bomb us, so they can't talk about "we won't bomb you if
you don't bomb us." We will continue to supply our troops at the front
[during the bombing pause] so they will continue to supply theirs. Yet we
expect them not to, I presume, as a reciprocal act.

> — General James M. Gavin (ret.),
> November 12, 1967

I have never been more encouraged in my four years in Vietnam.

> — General William C. Westmoreland,
> November 15, 1967

The war gains are very encouraging.

> — General William C. Westmoreland, calling for
> more troops, November 16, 1967

General Westmoreland expressed cautious optimism.

> — Senator Richard B. Russell, after General
> Westmoreland briefed Senate Armed Services
> Committee, November 16, 1967

We are making progress. We are pleased with the results that we are getting. We are inflicting greater losses than we are taking. . . . Overall, we are making progress. . . .

> — President Lyndon B. Johnson,
> news conference, White House,
> November 17, 1967

I hope they try something because we are looking for a fight. They want to put on a show of strength to make it appear to the American public that they are strong. Well, they are being defeated at every turn.

> — General William C. Westmoreland,
> quoted by *Time*, November 20, 1967

A CBU victim, if hit in the stomach, is simply slit from the top of the stomach to the bottom and the contents of the stomach emptied out on the table and fingered through for "frags." . . . When the sorting is done the entrails are replaced and the stomach sewed back up like a football. This "football scar" has become the true badge of misery in South Vietnam.

> — Frank Harvey, *Air War: Vietnam*

We're winning. . . . It is pretty obvious that about all the enemy can do is resort to guerrilla tactics.

> — Admiral U. S. Grant Sharp, commander,
> U.S. forces, Pacific (CINCPAC),
> Honolulu, November 21, 1967

We have reached an important point when the end begins to come into view. . . . The enemy has not won a major battle in more than a year. . . . His Viet-Cong military units can no longer fill their ranks from the South. . . . His guerrilla force is declining at a steady rate. Morale problems are developing within his ranks. . . . We are making progress. . . .

> — General William C. Westmoreland,
> address to National Press Club,
> November 21, 1967

The war of attrition is effective. . . . The ranks of the Vietcong are thinning steadily. . . . 45% of the North Vietnamese-VC-main-force units are combat-ineffective. . . . It's the beginning of a great defeat for the enemy.

> — General William C. Westmoreland,
> The Pentagon, November 22, 1967

The informed leaders and analysts . . . have the . . . basic assumption: that the North Vietnamese can no longer carry the huge manpower burden. . . . Men of great experience and sound instinct, notably including Gen. William C. Westmoreland. . . . Any hunch of General Westmoreland's must be profoundly respected, for no one else has anything approaching comparable experience.

> — Joseph Alsop, syndicated column,
> November 24, 1967

It can no longer be argued that we do not have a plan and a timetable and a grand strategy. . . . The program laid out by General Westmoreland last week is nearly overpowering in the precision of its promises and the almost total absence of qualifications or doubt. The strategy, quite simply, is to "weaken the enemy." . . . The plan comes in a procession of astonishingly detailed steps. . . . Right now, we are moving along nicely into Phase Three "when the end begins to come into view." . . . So we also have a clear purpose. . . . Perhaps . . . he is right in his latest judgment that the "enemy's hopes are bankrupt." . . . The Westmoreland Plan, in short, is encouraging. . . . It relieves some doubts. . . . It points persuasively to a time when the war will wither away.

> — Editorial, *Washington Post*,
> November 26, 1967

"Doves" . . . may yet be left on a limb—victims of their own lack of information and understanding. *War in Vietnam*, changing sharply for the better, provides the reason. . . . *1967* is a year in which the tide definitely has turned for the better.

> — *U.S. News & World Report*,
> November 27, 1967

If you're chasing some people and they just step over into Cambodia or Laos, it wouldn't bother me. I'd go at 'em. . . . I'd go in wherever his base was.

> — Dwight D. Eisenhower, CBS-TV,
> November 28, 1967

They think we're in a bad way. . . . I just don't believe the American people are that weak. . . . They're not going to give up and get out. And as soon as the Communists realize that, maybe we will have a stop—cessation in the fighting.

> — General of the Army Omar N. Bradley,
> CBS-TV, November 28, 1967

There are a few IOs [Information Officers] out here who are not playing on the team. On occasion these guys have downgraded one or another of the programs the U.S. is trying so hard to make work in Vietnam—and have done their sounding off to the press yet! . . . To argue your case in the press is not to show the courage of your convictions; it's a betrayal of a trust. It's disloyal.

> — USARV directive, Vietnam, December 1967

Robert W. Komer, Chief of U.S. pacification programs, announced that two-thirds of the people of South Vietnam now live in secure areas under South Vietnamese control. The computerized Hamlet Evaluation System provides a detailed monthly check on the allegiance of the South Vietnamese living in the country's 12,600 cities and hamlets. It shows the "secure population has increased more than a million since last January. . . . I think it's getting a pretty accurate picture," said Komer.

> — New York Times, December 1, 1967

When the Communists feel that this effort has not succeeded, they will stop the effort. . . . They just stop. This is what they did in Korea. They just stopped. After a while they got tired of it. . . . They don't want to negotiate. I say that's fine. I hope they stay that way.

> — Former Secretary of State Dean Acheson,
> interview on public television, NET,
> December 3, 1967

We are making steady progress all the time.

> — General Creighton W. Abrams, Jr.,
> U.S. News & World Report,
> December 4, 1967

We have reached an important point, when the end begins to come into view.

> — General William C. Westmoreland to special
> council of war at White House, reported by
> Newsweek, December 4, 1967

The U.S. has now dropped more bombs on North and South Vietnam than it dropped on Europe during World War II. Top Air Force leaders said they found this total "stupifying" but attributed it to the unique nature of the bombing in the Vietnam War. They said the B-52s, which carry 30 tons of bombs each, pushed the total up as they bombed large areas of the countryside instead of precision [bombing]. . . .

As of Nov. 15, the U.S. Air Force and Navy had dropped 1,630,500 tons of bombs on North and South Vietnam since July 1965 . . . 100 pounds of explosives for every person living in North and South Vietnam. Over 12 tons of bombs for every square mile of territory in both countries. Double the tonnage of bombs U.S. dropped during the Korean War. Triple the tonnage dropped by American planes in the Pacific Theater during World War II.

The U.S. dropped 635,000 tons of bombs during the Korean War and 502,781 tons in the Pacific Theater during World War II, according to Pentagon figures. Slightly more than half—about 53%—of the Vietnam War total landed in North Vietnam and the rest in South Vietnam.

> — *New York Post*, December 5, 1967

In large areas of the country, you couldn't believe there was a war going on.

> — David Lilienthal, emissary of President
> Johnson, after fact-finding mission to Vietnam,
> whose private company, Development and
> Resources Corp., had contract as consultant to
> South Vietnamese government; above quote
> reported by *Washington Post*,
> December 7, 1967

If the Administration were to negotiate a settlement that paved the way for an early Communist take-over, then it will mark the total eclipse of America as a great nation and the beginning of the end for the entire free world.

> — Senator Thomas J. Dodd, Democrat of
> Connecticut, December 8, 1967

The war will rock along as in the past.

> — General Earle G. Wheeler, chairman,
> Joint Chiefs of Staff, quoted by *Newsweek*,
> December 11, 1967

I see no changes in Vietnam policy.

> — Secretary of Defense Robert S. McNamara,
> quoted by *Newsweek*, December 11, 1967

Our military position is greatly improved.

> — Walt W. Rostow, memorandum,
> December 12, 1967

The bombing in the North is having an important attritional effect. They're under tremendous manpower strain. Their casualties are going up at a rate they cannot sustain. . . . I honestly believe we are on a rising curve. I see light at the end of the tunnel.

> — Walt W. Rostow, *Look*, December 12, 1967

TOP SECRET

The U.S. bombing of North Vietnam has had no measurable effect on Hanoi's ability to mount and support military operations in the South. . . . Since the beginning of the ROLLING THUNDER air strikes on NVN, the flow of men and materiel from NVN to SVN has greatly increased, and present evidence provides no basis for concluding that the damage inflicted on North Vietnam by the bombing program has had any significant effect on this flow. In short, the flow of men and materiel from North Vietnam to the South appears to reflect Hanoi's intentions rather than capabilities even in the face of the bombing.

> — Institute of Defense Analyses, JASON
> Division, top secret report, "The Bombing of
> North Vietnam," December 16, 1967

TOP SECRET

NVN has transmitted many of the material costs imposed by the bombing back to its allies. Since the bombing began, NVN's allies have provided almost $600 million in economic aid and another $1 billion in military aid—more than four times what NVN has lost in bombing damage. If economic criteria were the only consideration, NVN would show a substantial net gain from the bombing, primarily in military equipment. Because of this aid . . . NVN's economy continues to function. NVN's adjustments to the physical damage, disruption and other difficulties brought on by the bombing have been sufficiently effective to maintain living standards, meet transportation requirements, and improve its military capabilities. NVN is now a stronger military power than before the bombing, and its remaining economy is more able to withstand bombing.

> — Institute of Defense Analyses, JASON
> Division, top secret report, "The Bombing of
> North Vietnam," December 16, 1967

Your company is performing a service for our armed forces—a service that plays a vital role. . . . Students who interfere with Dow's job recruiters . . . are misdirecting their efforts.

> — Secretary of Defense Robert S. McNamara,
> letter to Dow Chemical Company, quoted by
> *U.S. News & World Report*, December 18, 1967

Incessant U.S. bombing in Vietnam—now greater than the level of World War II—is creating a growing food shortage among enemy civilians and troops. That is the latest report from intelligence sources in Washington.

> — *U.S. News & World Report,*
> December 18, 1967

We will never recognize the National Liberation Front as a government or even as a legitimate political party.

> — President Nguyen Van Thieu,
> December 20, 1967

We are defeating this aggression. The use we are making of air power in all its forms is a major reason the plans of the enemy are doomed to fail. . . . Your cause is a just one. . . . The spirit of America is the steadfastness and resolve of a nation holding firmly. . . . From our course we shall not turn.

> — President Lyndon B. Johnson,
> Korat Air Base, Thailand, December 23, 1967

I don't know how I might have decided it had I been in the White House at the time. I do remember reflecting at the time it happened that I thought President Kennedy did the right thing in approving the sending of 16,000 troops plus military advisors into the area. We can win this war.

> — Former President Dwight D. Eisenhower,
> Indio, Calif., December 23, 1967

There seems little reason to doubt that Hanoi has abandoned hope of conquering South Vietnam. . . . The enemy has been defeated in every important campaign. . . . The enemy can no longer find security. . . . The allies are winning, and the enemy is being hurt. . . .

> — Hanson W. Baldwin, *New York Times,*
> December 26, 27, 28, 1967

Crops may be grown only to be destroyed by one side or the other. . . . Planes of the United States and South Vietnamese air forces drop napalm bombs on these crops. . . . The war has consistently seen more civilians killed than Viet Cong. Between 1961 and 1964, even modest estimates of the casualties indicated that more than half a million . . . civilians had been killed. Under these circumstances, is it a matter for surprise that more and more Vietnamese are drawn to the ranks of the National Liberation Front?

> — Thich Nhat Hanh, *Vietnam: Lotus in a*
> *Sea of Fire*

In 1967 the "Free World Forces" in Vietnam—Americans, Vietnamese, and Koreans, with additional small contingents of Australians, Thais and Filipinos—had reached a combined total of 1,300,000 men . . . 2,000 tactical jet aircraft and the B-52s of the Strategic Air Command.

— Frances FitzGerald, *Fire in the Lake*

I support America's present policy. . . . The Communists . . . have simply to be convinced that they can never win. They will collapse then.

— Kingsley Amis, in *Authors Take Sides on Vietnam*, 1967

It is dishonest of those who demand the immediate withdrawal of all American troops. . . . American troops, alas, must stay in Vietnam.

— W. H. Auden, in *Authors Take Sides on Vietnam*, 1967

The Americans are in Vietnam to discourage, to contain, and to outwit the advance of Communism. This is something which we should certainly support. . . . One thing is certain: the Americans are there to stay until they win . . . the Communists . . . will call a halt and go away.

— Nicholas Monsarrat, in *Authors Take Sides on Vietnam*, 1967

I . . . support my Government's stand in Vietnam. . . . I am not unhappy about our defense of South Vietnam. . . . I support my Government's position.

— James A. Michener, in *Authors Take Sides on Vietnam*, 1967

It is easy to say that the Americans should get out of Vietnam, and equally easy to say that the Communists should be driven out of Vietnam. I say neither.

— Malcolm Muggeridge, in *Authors Take Sides on Vietnam*, 1967

I do not see how we can abdicate our burdensome position in South Vietnam.

— John Updike, in *Authors Take Sides on Vietnam*, 1967

The battlefield has a rhythm of its own.

— Vietcong leader, December 1967

We *must* keep the pressure on North Vietnam, and I think the bombing is doing that quite effectively. . . . There is certainly no stalemate. We're making solid progress in South Vietnam. . . .

> — Admiral U. S. Grant Sharp,
> interview, *Reader's Digest*, January 1968

Tet was a sobering experience from which American officials in Washington still have not recovered. Could the estimates ever be trusted again? "It is very strange," said an embassy official in Saigon. "After Tet, Washington became very pessimistic, and we became very optimistic. Before, it was the other way around."

> — Ward Just, "Notes on Losing a War," *The Atlantic Monthly*, 1968

TOP SECRET

The cost and difficulties of the war to Hanoi have sharply increased. . . .

> — Admiral U. S. Grant Sharp, cablegram to Joint Chiefs of Staff headed "Year-End Wrap-Up Cable," January 1, 1968

I see not a single unfavorable trend.

> — Robert W. Komer, General Westmoreland's civilian deputy, quoted by *Newsweek*, January 1, 1968

While you are not winning now, you certainly are not losing. . . . I would not negotiate at present myself. I don't think you are in the right position to negotiate.

> — Sir Robert Thompson, adviser to U.S. and South Vietnamese governments, expert on pacification, quoted by *Newsweek*, January 1, 1968

At midweek, 14 eminent scholars, including Asian specialists A. Doak Barnett of Columbia University and former Ambassador to Tokyo Edwin O. Reischauer, issued a document that warned of "disastrous" consequences of a U.S. defeat. "To accept a Communist victory in Vietnam," declared the authors of the report, "would . . . deeply affect the morale—and the policies—of our Asian Allies."

> — *Newsweek*, January 1, 1968

[The enemy] can't point to a single victory in Vietnam.

> — President Lyndon B. Johnson,
> quoted in *Newsweek*, January 1, 1968

I do not believe the Americans can win militarily unless they make
Vietnam their 51st state.

> — General André Beaufré, senior French
> commander during Indochinese war, quoted
> by *Newsweek*, January 1, 1968

We expect our gains of 1967 to be increased manyfold in 1968. . . .
[Pacification] is expected to gain considerable headway during the next
six months. Impact on the enemy should be increased casualties,
desertions, sickness and lowered morale. . . . His in-country recruiting
potential will be reduced by acceleration of our military offensive and
pacification efforts. . . . Our forces have been able to detect impending
major offensives and to mount spoiling attacks. . . . The enemy did not
win a major battle in 1967.

> — General William C. Westmoreland, Saigon,
> January 1, 1968, classified report to
> Washington, obtained by *New York Times* and
> published March 21, 1968

We are very hopeful that we can make advances toward peace. . . .
We feel that the enemy knows that he can no longer win a military
victory.

> — President Lyndon B. Johnson,
> news conference, Johnson City, Tex.,
> January 1, 1968

TOP SECRET

Over the entire period of the bombing, the value of economic
resources gained through foreign aid has been greater than that lost
because of the bombing.

> — "The Bombing," top secret paper, Systems
> Analysis Office, Department of Defense,
> January 2, 1968

Some 20,000 "phantom soldiers" are still in the ranks—soldiers who
have defected to civilian life but who still remain on the active rolls in
exchange for letting their officers pocket their pay. Graft runs right up
the command line in many units. The going price for a province chief's
chair can be $25,000, an investment quickly earned back via shakedowns
of the local population and kickbacks on licenses and shipments of goods.

> — *Time*, January 5, 1968

There is good reason to believe, as 1968 starts, that this year is really
going to see the beginning of the end of the war here in Vietnam.

> — *U.S. News & World Report*,
> dispatch from Saigon, January 8, 1968

The Vietnam war is really an "administrative" war, and the side with superior administration is likely to win. . . . Hanoi . . . has no detailed blueprint for victory at all. . . . I now want to put myself on record as arguing that the current state of gloom represents an excessive swing. . . . The Tet offensive . . . indicates little or nothing about the accuracy of the pre-Tet intelligence estimates. . . .

The Christian just-war doctrine [is a] classic Christian concept. . . . Burning an evacuated village may be a legitimate act of war. . . . One of the things that Vietnamese complain a great deal about is the harassing and interdiction fire. But I don't believe this has killed anybody who is not guilty.

> — Dr. Herman Kahn, director, Hudson Institute, consultant, Rand Corporation, White House, *On the Possibility for Victory or Defeat*, reprinted in *Can We Win in Vietnam?* (1968)

Viet Cong . . . are poorly motivated and poorly trained. . . . ARVN now has the upper hand completely. . . . The military situation in the Delta will be very favorable in one to two years. . . . I think we have the force to win. . . . We have gained the upper hand.

> — Brigadier General William R. Desobry, senior U.S. military adviser, Mekong Delta, *Los Angeles Times*, dispatch from Saigon, January 9, 1968

The war is definitely not stalemated. . . . The Viet Cong had a bad year in 1967. . . . They are in trouble. . . . 1968 holds little prospect for being a good year for them.

> — General Harold K. Johnson, chief of staff, U.S. Army, speech to Headline Club, Chicago, January 11, 1968

BULLETIN

SAIGON (AP)—THE VIET CONG SHELLED SAIGON ITSELF EARLY WEDNESDAY IN A STUNNING FOLLOWUP TO ITS ATTACKS ON EIGHT CITIES.

FIRST REPORTS SAID ROCKET OR MORTAR ATTACKS LANDED NEAR INDEPENDENCE PALACE, SEAT OF THE GOVERNMENT IN THE HEART OF SAIGON, OTHER GOVERNMENT BUILDINGS AND THE U.S. EMBASSY.

THE ATTACK STARTED AROUND 3 A.M. LESS THAN 24 HOURS AFTER THE SERIES OF LUNAR NEW YEAR'S DAY ATTACKS AGAINST SEVEN LARGE PROVINCIAL CAPITALS AND THE KEY CITY OF DA NANG, SECOND LARGEST CITY IN SOUTH VIETNAM.

SAIGON (UPI)—AMERICAN TROOPS WEDNESDAY LAUNCHED A HELI-

COPTER ASSAULT ON THE U.S. EMBASSY HERE TO ROOT OUT COMMUNIST SUICIDE SQUADS OCCUPYING PART OF THE BUILDING.

AS U.S. MILITARY POLICE ATTACKED COMMUNIST POSITIONS IN THE EMBASSY FROM THE STREET LEVEL HELICOPTERS TOOK TROOPS TO THE ROOF OF THE EIGHT STORY [*sic*] BUILDING TO ROOT THEM OUT FLOOR BY FLOOR.

COMMUNIST TROOPS INSIDE THE BUILDING OPENED FIRE ON THE HELICOPTERS AS THEY CAME IN FOR LANDINGS.

> — AP and UPI teletype dispatches,
> 1st day of Tet offensive, January 31, 1968

The situation is getting more serious. . . . I declare a state of martial law throughout the nation from today until further notice.

> — President Nguyen Van Thieu, Saigon,
> January 31, 1968

In my opinion this [the Tet offensive] is a diversionary effort.

> — General William C. Westmoreland,
> Saigon, February 1, 1968

We have known for some time that this offensive was planned by the enemy. . . . The stated purposes of the general uprising have failed . . . that has come as a complete failure. . . . The ability to do what they have done has been anticipated, prepared for, and met. . . . As a military movement it has been a failure. . . . I do not believe they will achieve a psychological victory. . . . We feel reasonably sure of our strength.

> — President Lyndon B. Johnson, news
> conference, White House, February 2, 1968

[The Vietcong is] about to run out of steam.

> — General William C. Westmoreland,
> news conference, Saigon, February 2, 1968

THE PRESIDENT ASKS ME IF THERE IS ANY REINFORCEMENT OR HELP THAT WE CAN GIVE YOU.

> — General Earle G. Wheeler, secret cablegram to
> General William C. Westmoreland, 4th day of
> Tet offensive, February 3, 1968

. . . The North Vietnamese and the Viet Cong have not accomplished . . . their major objectives. . . . The North Vietnamese have suffered very heavy penalties in terms of losses of weapons. . . . The balance has definitely moved toward the South Vietnamese. . . . I don't think any of us predicted seven years ago or 15 years ago the deployment of 500,000 men to Vietnam. I know I didn't.

> — Secretary of Defense Robert S. McNamara,
> *Meet the Press*, NBC, February 4, 1968

It became necessary to destroy the town to save it.

> — U. S. Army Major, referring to Ben Tre,
> South Vietnam, February 7, 1968

More force will have to be applied to stabilize the situation. . . . The right thing for this country to do is the hardest thing. It is to hold firm.

> — Joseph Kraft, syndicated column,
> February 6, 1968

We have dropped 12 tons of bombs for every square mile of North and South Vietnam. Whole provinces have been destroyed. More than two million South Vietnamese are now homeless refugees.

> — Senator Robert F. Kennedy,
> February 8, 1968

QUERY: DO YOU NEED REINFORCEMENTS? OUR CAPABILITIES ARE LIMITED. WE CAN PROVIDE 82ND AIRBORNE DIVISION AND ABOUT ONE HALF A MARINE CORPS DIVISION, BOTH LOADED WITH VIETNAM VETERANS. HOWEVER, IF YOU CONSIDER REINFORCEMENTS IMPERATIVE, YOU SHOULD NOT BE BOUND BY EARLIER AGREEMENTS. . . . UNITED STATES GOVERNMENT IS NOT PREPARED TO ACCEPT DEFEAT IN VIETNAM. IN SUMMARY, IF YOU NEED MORE TROOPS, ASK FOR THEM.

> — General Earle G. Wheeler, secret cablegram to
> General William C. Westmoreland,
> February 8, 1968

Whose side are you on? Now, I'm Secretary of State of the United States, and I'm on our side! . . . None of your papers or your broadcasting apparatuses are worth a damn unless the United States succeeds. They are trivial compared to that question. So I don't know why, to win a Pulitzer Prize, people have to go probing for the things that one can bitch about when there are 2,000 stories on the same day about things that are more constructive.

> — Secretary of State Dean Rusk to newsmen,
> February 9, 1968

I don't want any damned Dienbienphu.

> — President Lyndon B. Johnson to Joint Chiefs
> of Staff during White House discussion of Khe
> Sanh, *Time*, February 9, 1968

We cannot know what the morrow will bring. . . . I can, and I do, tell you that in these long nights your President prays. . . . It's just a bunch of blarney. . . . When I hear this argument that we can't protect freedom in Europe, Asia or our own hemisphere and still meet our domestic problems, I think this is a phoney argument. It's just like saying I can't take care of Luci because I have Lynda Bird. . . . The nights are very long. The winds are very chill. Our spirits grow weary and restive as the springtime of man seems farther and farther away.

> — President Lyndon B. Johnson to White House presidential prayer breakfast, quoted by *Time*, February 9, 1968

We Americans will never yield. . . . We feel reasonably sure of our strength.

> — President Lyndon B. Johnson, at Medal of Honor ceremony in White House, quoted by *Time*, February 9, 1968

I think it is fair to say that additional funds are likely to be required.

> — Senator Mike Mansfield, quoted by *Time*, February 9, 1968

NEEDLESS TO SAY, I WOULD WELCOME REINFORCEMENTS AT ANY TIME THEY CAN BE MADE AVAILABLE. (A) TO PUT ME IN A STRONGER POSITION TO CONTAIN THE ENEMY'S MAJOR CAMPAIGN IN THE DMZ–QUANG TRI–THUA THIEN AREA AND TO GO ON THE OFFENSIVE AS SOON AS HIS ATTACK IS SPENT. (B) TO PERMIT ME TO CARRY OUT MY CAMPAIGN PLANS DESPITE THE ENEMY'S REINFORCEMENTS FROM NORTH VIETNAM, WHICH HAVE INFLUENCED MY DEPLOYMENTS AND PLANS. (C) TO OFFSET THE WEAKENED [SOUTH] VIETNAMESE FORCES RESULTING FROM CASUALTIES AND TET DESERTERS. REALISTICALLY, WE MUST ASSUME THAT IT WILL TAKE THEM AT LEAST 6 WEEKS TO REGAIN THE MILITARY POSTURE OF SEVERAL WEEKS AGO. . . . (D) TO TAKE ADVANTAGE OF THE ENEMY'S WEAKENED POSTURE BY TAKING THE OFFENSIVE AGAINST HIM.

> — General William C. Westmoreland, secret cablegram to General Earle G. Wheeler, February 9, 1968

It is becoming clearer and clearer that the Vietcong attack on the cities and towns of South Vietnam resulted in a serious and potentially shattering defeat.

> — Joseph Alsop, syndicated column, February 12, 1968

Reducing the intensity of the war tempo . . . *could materially improve* [sic] *the course of our staying the course for an added number of grinding years without rending our own society.*

> — Under Secretary of Air Force Townsend
> Hoopes, letter to Secretary of Defense Clark
> Clifford, February 13, 1968, re reducing level
> of bombing in North (italics in original).

I believe we're stronger today. . . . The Viet Cong created considerable damage . . . but that does not necessarily mean that we're not stronger. . . .

> — Ambassador Ellsworth Bunker, interviewed in
> Saigon, taped September 16, 1968, *Face the
> Nation*, CBS, February 18, 1968

The North Vietnamese . . . after this year they will be weaker and weaker and they cannot win the war either politically nor militarily. So the guerrilla by itself will not be decisive [sic] and they have no hope to win the war, for I believe that it is the last year for the V.C. . . . They are hurt very severely in North Vietnam after three years of bombing, and they have lost many countryside areas, so they have difficulty to recruit men, to have supplies, and, most important, they are believing now, they are like fish thrown out of water because they have no people in the countryside. . . . We continue to move forward on our pacification program. . . . I believe the V.C. have met with complete failure with the Tet offensive. . . . In three weeks they have suffered 40,000 casualties.

> — President Nguyen Van Thieu, interview,
> Saigon, taped February 23, 1968, *Face the
> Nation*, CBS, February 25, 1968

We also have great opportunities. . . . All our forces there [Vietnam] . . . inflicted a very significant defeat on the enemy.

> — General Earle G. Wheeler,
> Bangkok, February 25, 1968

The allegation that casualties inflicted on the enemy are padded . . . is not the case. I have given my personal attention to the matter and . . . I am confident that the officially reported enemy killed in action figures are conservative. . . . His ability to pursue a protracted war has been reduced by the losses. . . . In sum, I do not believe Hanoi can hold up under a long war. The present enemy offensive attitude may indicate that Hanoi realizes this, also. They have run into a buzz saw. . . . Additional U.S. forces will probably be required. With additional troops we could more effectively deny the enemy his objectives and capitalize on his recent defeats.

— General William C. Westmoreland,
news conference, Saigon, February 25, 1968

TOP SECRET

The enemy failed to achieve his initial objective but is continuing his effort . . . many of his units were badly hurt. . . . Enemy losses have been heavy. . . . Morale in enemy units . . . probably has suffered severely. . . . If the enemy synchronizes an attack against Khe Sanh/ Hué-Quang Tri with an offensive in the highlands . . . we must be prepared to accept some reverses. For these reasons, General Westmoreland has asked for a 3 division-15 tactical fighter squadron force. . . . The enemy has been hurt badly in the populated lowlands.

— General Earle G. Wheeler,
memorandum to President Johnson,
February 27, 1968

Persevere in Vietnam we must and we will. . . . We stand at a turning point. The enemy . . . has failed. . . . Our answer, here at home, in every home, must be: no retreat. . . .

— President Lyndon B. Johnson,
remarks at Dallas, February 27, 1968

For seven years . . . you have brought a new dimension to defense planning and decision-making.

— President Lyndon B. Johnson,
presenting Medal of Freedom to Secretary of
Defense Robert S. McNamara,
February 28, 1968

The Chairman of the Joint Chiefs of Staff . . . has returned from Saigon to recommend a substantial addition to . . . troop strength. . . . He should do so. . . . Every six days, the enemy is losing the equivalent of one month of VC recruitment. . . . As the captured documents continue to pour in, moreover, it becomes clearer and clearer that the Tet-period attacks on the cities were a major disaster for Gen. Giap. . . . The Hanoi war-planners . . . have experienced a grave setback.

— Joseph Alsop, syndicated column,
February 28, 1968

TOP SECRET

Additional forces would serve to forestall the danger of local defeats. . . . With the total additive combat forces requested it will be possible to deal with the invader from the north and to face with a greater degree of confidence the potential tank, rocket and tactical threat.

> — General William C. Westmoreland,
> February 29, 1968

The South Vietnamese have much to be desired. I don't think you could compare the American people to any other people and certainly not the people of Southeast Asia. . . . You cannot expect and you cannot get as much from them. . . . They have their weaknesses. . . . They have their inefficiencies.

> — President Lyndon B. Johnson,
> remarks, Beaumont, Texas, March 1, 1968

Men may debate and men may dissent, men may disagree—but there does come a time when men must stand. And for Americans, that time has now come.

> — President Lyndon B. Johnson, address to U.S.
> sailors on deck of carrier *Constellation*, quoted
> by *Time*, March 1, 1968

The gods of war were in their favor.

> — Lieutenant General Robert E. Cushman, Jr.,
> commander, I Corps forces, U.S. Marine
> Corps, regarding enemy successes at Citadel in
> Hué, quoted by *Time*, March 1, 1968

As far as a military victory is concerned, I believe in a great respect we have already attained a type of victory in South Vietnam. I believe our presence there, our successful presence there, has many times justified the cost to us in our men and in our treasure. . . . We have extended this shield. I believe we must continue to do it.

> — Clark Clifford, testifying before Senate Armed
> Services Committee prior to confirmation of
> nomination as Secretary of Defense, quoted in
> *Reader's Digest*, March 1968

I pledge to you new leadership will win the war and win the peace in the Pacific.

> — Richard M. Nixon, Nashua, N.H.,
> March 5, 1968

We are there not just to save the South Vietnamese . . . if we lose there, before you know it, they would be up to the beaches of Hawaii.

> — Senator Strom Thurmond, Democrat of South
> Carolina, March 14, 1968

What is happening in Vietnam today is not blitzkrieg; it is kamikaze—
a desperation move on their part. They have taken tremendous losses.
. . . I believe that the next several months could bring us much closer to
victory. . . . I am encouraged. . . . Hué is not really as badly shattered
as we are led to believe. . . . It is humiliating that we could be caught off
guard, that this thing could happen. But there are pluses. . . . They
cannot take the losses they have taken in this war of attrition over the
years. . . . I think it is the most un-Giap thing that Giap has ever done.
. . . He would not have done it if he had not been desperate. . . .

And here is an interesting development. . . . The local guerrillas . . .
were destroyed. . . . There is just no Vietcong anymore. . . . This is
not the sort of picture I have been getting listening to the television. I do
not watch much television any more. I get too mad. I lose my temper.
. . . The impression grows that the South Vietnamese Army is no
damned good. I am asked, "How can the North Vietnamese be so much
better motivated than our people?" In the first place, they aren't. They
are not 7 feet tall. They put their trousers on one leg at a time like
anybody else. South Vietnam's defection rate is going down and theirs is
going up. . . . So they are in pretty bad shape. . . .
> — Jim Lucas, Scripps-Howard correspondent, to
> Senate Judiciary sub-committee,
> March 14, 1968

We are beginning to enter a higher level of American democracy. We
are beginning to fulfill the promise of American democracy. . . . We
do not deny for a single moment that we have suffered reverses, that
we have had difficulties in Vietnam, but we have a confidence that if we
prevail . . . with perseverance . . . if we persevere with courage that we
can ultimately succeed. . . . If you try to take the temperature report
each day, Mr. Scali, and then report it as a sort of final observation, you
are going to get into trouble. . . . I think you should be a little more
patient. . . . This is a painful war. This is a very discouraging operation
at times. . . . But the President . . . has said that we will persevere. He
said we have the ability, the capacity. . . . We are making a very careful
evaluation of everything in Vietnam. . . . We do not see that our course
. . . is wrong. We think that it is basically sound.
> — Vice President Hubert H. Humphrey,
> *Issues & Answers*, ABC, March 17, 1968

Napalm is being burned in South Vietnam in a steadily increasing
volume. Figures compiled by the Defense Department show the Air
Force alone has dumped more than 100,000 tons of napalm on Vietnam
since 1963. The Navy also drops napalm bombs, and the Army uses large
quantities in flame-throwers, but they have not compiled tonnage figures.
The Air Force used nearly 55,000 tons of napalm in 1966 alone, far

outpacing the 32,215 tons dropped in the 3-year Korean war. . . . The big 1966 jump in napalm in Vietnam paralleled development of a hotter compound called napalm B, capable of turning truck engines into liquid steel. . . .

> — AP dispatch from Washington,
> March 18, 1968

Make no mistake about it—we are going to win.

> — President Lyndon B. Johnson,
> Minneapolis, Minnesota, March 18, 1968

Make no mistake about it—America will prevail. . . . Today we are the Number One Nation. And we are going to stay the Number One Nation.

> — President Lyndon B. Johnson,
> March 19, 1968

Total cost of Operation Rolling Thunder—the bombing of North Viet Nam—and "Steel Tiger" (Laos) over the past three years runs about $8 billion. This includes about $2 billion for the 800 planes lost and perhaps another $1 billion for a thousand planes damaged. About a million tons of bombs have been dropped ($2 billion), and operating costs were about $3 billion.

> — *Newsweek*, March 25, 1968

I know of no general of U.S. forces who has led his men more brilliantly.

> — Former Secretary of Defense Robert S.
> McNamara, referring to General
> Westmoreland, quoted by *Time*, April 1, 1968

If there is any way General Westmoreland could go, it would be up.

> — President Lyndon B. Johnson,
> quoted by *Time*, April 1, 1968

Only the G.O.P. can get us out of Vietnam.

> — Senator Thurston B. Morton,
> *Saturday Evening Post*, April 6, 1968

The enemy failed to achieve his military objective . . . the advantage [is] being taken of the enemy's weakened military position. . . . Militarily, we have never been in a better relative position in South Vietnam. . . . In view of the sensitive nature of the present situation, I have nothing further to say.

> — General William C. Westmoreland,
> remarks to press, White House, April 7, 1968

In a long life of service to my country, I have never encountered a situation more depressing than the present spectacle of an America deeply divided over a war. . . . What has become of our courage? . . . patriotism? . . . One large defeatist group proclaims loudly and positively that "we can never win the Vietnam war." Others insist, contrary to the best military judgment and to clear evidence, that our air strikes "do no good." . . .

Some Americans publicly burn their draft cards. . . . The "peaceful" antiwar demonstrations frequently get out of hand. These militant peace-at-any-price groups are a small minority, but all too often they get away with such illegal actions. . . . There is no reason to tolerate this arrogant flouting of the law. . . . It should be stopped—at once. Their action . . . is rebellion, and it verges on treason. . . . It is unthinkable that the voices of defeat should triumph in our land.

> — Dwight D. Eisenhower, *Reader's Digest*,
> April 1968

Nothing if not realistic, prominent Roman Catholics have begun talking about a migration out of Viet should the time come that peace talks seemed headed toward a coalition. They have considered Australia, according to one Catholic source. "But the Australian Government doesn't like Asians. They may try Canada."

> — *New York Times Magazine*, April 7, 1968

The enemy . . . failed.

> — President Lyndon B. Johnson, message to U.S.
> armed forces, Southeast Asia, on lifting of
> siege at Khe Sanh, April 8, 1968

We have never been in a better relative position.

> — General William C. Westmoreland,
> April 10, 1968

The days are long gone when Americans can say that Asians are not our kind of people.

> — President Lyndon B. Johnson,
> Honolulu, April 17, 1968

Relentless U.S. bombing also has hurt the Communists in North Vietnam far more than is generally recognized, officials say.

> — *U.S. News & World Report*, April 22, 1968

[The Vietnam war] costs us some $1.5 billion a year in foreign exchange. . . . We simply must be prepared to shoulder this kind of financial burden.

> — David Rockefeller,
> President, Chase Manhattan Bank,
> quoted by *New York Times*, April 25, 1968

President Johnson's decision to stick it out in Vietnam was crucial in achieving progress. . . . In short, the logic of our involvement is the same today as it was in 1956 or 1962.

> — John P. Roche, former professor of history and
> politics, Brandeis University, Special
> Consultant to President since 1966; *The
> Democrat*, April-May 1968

I think they are making progress.

> — President Lyndon B. Johnson,
> May 3, 1968

The morale of U.S. troops remains high. . . . In the nearby town of Sangpai, they can buy a drink and find friendly feminine companionship. Another morale-booster is the growing action itself. "When you get soldiers involved in an operation," says Lieut. Colonel Frank Ramano, "their morale soars. They don't like boredom."

> — *Time*, May 3, 1968

The Vietnamese are coming along.

> — General Creighton W. Abrams, U.S.
> commander, Vietnam, quoted by *New York
> Times Magazine*, May 3, 1968

I have said about Vietnam that history is going to determine whether it was a good idea or a bad idea.

> — George W. Ball, U.S. Permanent
> Representative-Delegate to UN, *Meet the
> Press*, NBC, May 5, 1968

Don't lets leave 500,000 boys and girls out there without an honorable settlement. Don't be weak and give in. Let us have no appeasement. We must be strong but not cruel. This is a sad war. The only war that was a happy one was World War One. People used to dance in the streets to see the boys go away. . . . But we haven't been in a happy war since then.

> — Governor Roger Branigin, Democrat of
> Indiana, May 9, 1968

Civilization simply cannot afford . . . politicians who demand that . . . the national duty in Vietnam be discarded to provide huge make-work programs in the city slums with money diverted from Vietnam.

> — Governor Ronald Reagan, Republican of
> California, speech, New Orleans, May 1968

We will never cede an inch of land . . . we will never set up a coalition government with the NFLSV [NLF], and we will never recognize the NFLSV as a political entity equal to us, with which we must negotiate on equal footing.

> — President Nguyen Van Thieu, May 9, 1968

It is claimed this is a civil war. We do not see it that way. We see it as your President sees it—And because we see it that way, we contribute. We don't contribute a great deal. But . . . we do what we can.

> — Australian Prime Minister John G. Gorton,
> address to National Press Club, Washington,
> May 28, 1968

[Our forces have] vividly demonstrated to the enemy the futility of his attempts to win a military victory in the South. . . . We shall not be defeated.

> — President Lyndon B. Johnson,
> LBJ Ranch, May 30, 1968

The enemy's . . . only victories in the last few years have been in the propaganda field. . . . I am confident the enemy is receiving false reports from his field commanders. This partially explains his alleged exaggerated battlefield successes. . . . In summary, the enemy seems to be approaching a point of desperation; his forces are deteriorating in strength and quality. I forecast that these trends will continue. . . . Time is on our side.

> — General William C. Westmoreland,
> LBJ Ranch, May 30, 1968

This is the greatest victory in the history of warfare.

> — General James F. Hollingsworth, U.S. adviser,
> Military Region III, commenting on battle of
> Anloc, June 15, 1968

As of midnight on Sunday, June 23, the Viet Nam conflict became the longest war ever fought by Americans. It was 2,376 days since Dec. 22, 1961, when Viet Cong bullets killed the first American soldier. The U.S.

death toll to date: 25,068. The previous longest U.S. conflict: the War of Independence, which lasted 2,375 days and, according to the Revolutionary Army's records, cost 4,435 dead.

> — *Time*, June 22, 1968

Our side is getting stronger whereas the enemy is getting weaker. . . . Resolve is still the key to success.

> — General William C. Westmoreland, Saigon,
> before leaving Vietnam, quoted by *Newsweek*,
> June 24, 1968

I think we have some bits and straws to indicate that there is some movement [toward peace] now.

> — Secretary of Defense Clark M. Clifford,
> quoted by *Newsweek*, July 1, 1968

We're closer to an era of real global peace than any time since 1914 [*sic*]. They have been tactically defeated.

> — Walt W. Rostow, July 5, 1968

There is in Washington today a strong sense that a major turn has been made in the long and bloody Vietnam War and that its end, if not yet clearly in sight, is somewhere over the horizon. . . . Somehow the war is going to end and sooner rather than later. . . . The mood persists in Washington that the end somehow will, indeed, come into sight.

> — Chalmers Roberts, *Washington Post*,
> July 7, 1968

I want . . . to settle it in an honorable way, to produce a genuine peace. I think we can get it. . . . That process has already started in Paris. . . . I really believe that for a candidate . . . to spell out what would be the ingredients of an acceptable political settlement would be a great disservice to the men who are conducting our negotiations in Paris. . . .

> — Vice President Hubert H. Humphrey,
> *Issues & Answers*, ABC, July 7, 1968

We're gaining militarily. . . . I am cautiously optimistic.

> — Secretary of Defense Robert S. McNamara,
> Honolulu, July 18, 1968

Today, we pay tribute to what you and your countrymen have done. . . . That is truly remarkable progress—almost unprecedented progress.

> — President Lyndon B. Johnson, remarks of
> welcome to President Nguyen Van Thieu,
> Honolulu, July 18, 1968

I feel that we have every reason to look to the future with confidence. . . . I look forward to constructive steps. . . .

> — President Nguyen Van Thieu,
> Honolulu, July 18, 1968

We are in Vietnam whether we like it or not. . . . I am against the Viet Cong being involved in the government. . . . I don't think they deserve to be in the government. . . . And also we should stop these folks in this country from advocating Communist victory. . . . I am tired of our children and grandchildren—stop them how? By indicting a professor who makes a speech calling for a Communist victory. . . . By a man who raises money, blood and clothes . . . on the college campuses and flies a Viet Cong flag. That is not dissent, that is treason. . . . You don't have a right to call for a Communist victory and the average man on the street is sick and tired of it.

> — Governor George C. Wallace of Alabama,
> presidential candidate, *Face the Nation*, CBS,
> July 21, 1968

QUESTION: Does this mean the tide has finally turned in the war?
ANSWER: Yes. . . . We have the initiative. . . . The morale of enemy troops is now at a very low point. . . . In fact, the general trend has been continuously unfavorable to the Communists. They are weakening every day. Although we have the advantage over the enemy, we need time to achieve complete success . . . the Communists . . . will gradually fade away. . . . We have . . . to bring an early end to this war. . . . Right now, with the behavior we have seen of the Hanoi delegation in Paris, I have not yet seen any light at the other end of the tunnel. . . . They have failed in all their major objectives. So I think that Giap is in deep trouble now.

> — President Nguyen Van Thieu,
> interview, *U.S. News & World Report*,
> August 5, 1968

I pledge to you tonight that the first priority foreign policy objective of our next Administration will be to bring an honorable end to the war in Vietnam. . . . My fellow Americans, the dark long night for America is about to end.

> — Richard M. Nixon,
> Presidential Nomination acceptance speech,
> Republican National Convention,
> Miami, Florida, August 8, 1968

French Political Scientist Raymond Aron has astutely pointed out . . . "Either the Viet Cong will rule in Saigon tomorrow or they won't."

> — *Time*, August 9, 1968

I can tell you that I believe that peace is going to come—that is, if we are steady. . . . So, my friends, let's not be hoodwinked. Let's not be misled . . . the people must understand one thing: We are not going to stop the bombing.

> — President Lyndon B. Johnson,
> VFW Convention, Detroit, August 9, 1968

Well, let me just say a word about Vietnam. . . . If I can lend one little word of optimism today, which I do very carefully and with prudence and caution, I would say that the negotiations . . . are at a serious stage.

> — Vice President Hubert H. Humphrey,
> *Issues & Answers*, ABC, August 11, 1968

The exercise of power involves pain. . . . To endure the pain of power, a nation needs a conviction of its own righteousness. Our agonized effort . . . is surely at least as righteous as imperial Britain's wars against the "lesser breeds without the Law." And yet we have no Kipling to celebrate the war in Vietnam, and a sense of our righteousness is precisely what we wholly lack.

> — Stewart Alsop, column, *Newsweek*,
> August 12, 1968

I would never accept any Communist to run in an election in Vietnam. . . . When we say one man, one vote, we mean the vote would be given to Vietnamese citizens who deserve it.

> — President Nguyen Van Thieu,
> Bienhoa, South Vietnam, August 27, 1968

Our forces have achieved an unbroken string of victories which, in the aggregate, is something new in military history.

> — General Earle G. Wheeler,
> chairman, Joint Chiefs of Staff,
> August 31, 1968

Just to stop the bombing, without any indication that it will lead to anything but just stopping the bombing, I don't think is a very prudent act. . . . I am not the President, gentlemen, and I don't think it helps to play President. . . . I believe the war should be brought to a halt, but I don't believe it should be brought to a halt at the expense of the safety and the security of the people of South Vietnam. . . . I don't see any prospect at all that we are going to be bogged down in Asia for 5 or 10 years. I don't see that as a possibility.

> — Vice President Hubert H. Humphrey,
> *Issues & Answers*, ABC, September 8, 1968

The American attitude toward the war is wholesome.

> — General William C. Westmoreland,
> New Orleans, La., September 10, 1968

Within the past month or so I have been beginning to feel that we are on the verge of a breakthrough.

> — George W. Ball, after resigning as ambassador
> to UN to become foreign policy adviser to
> Vice President Hubert H. Humphrey, *Face the
> Nation*, CBS, September 18, 1968

I urge a course of firmness and fortitude. . . . The road ahead has a turning. . . . The Vietnam conflict is a test . . . of our character.

> — Congressman Walter H. Judd, member, House
> Foreign Affairs Committee, former missionary
> in Asia, *Reader's Digest*, September 1968

The conflict in Vietnam demands something more than impatience. It demands steadfastness.

> — President Lyndon B. Johnson,
> September 19, 1968

I never meant to indicate there was a plan to end the war.

> — Spiro T. Agnew, Republican vice-presidential
> candidate, Honolulu, September 21, 1968

[From] what I have seen and read and heard and briefings I have had from military friends . . . you do not have to have an additional million troops in South Vietnam. You can win the war with conventional weapons with the manpower that you have.

> — Governor George C. Wallace of Alabama,
> presidential candidate, *Face the Nation*, CBS,
> September 22, 1968

Within a year, the U.S. is convinced, the tide of battle will turn decisively in Vietnam—and serious business can get started.

> — *U.S. News & World Report*,
> September 23, 1968

There is growing hope for an end to this war, perhaps sooner than many yet dare to think.

> — Robert W. Komer, civilian administrator,
> Pacification Program, Saigon,
> September 23, 1968

[The war is] well on its way to an honorable political solution.
> — George W. Ball, former UN ambassador,
> September 26, 1968

I would use anything we could dream up, including nuclear weapons.
. . . We seem to have a phobia about nuclear weapons. . . . I think there
are many times when it would be more efficient to use nuclear weapons.
However, the public opinion in this country and throughout the world
would throw up their hands in horror when you mention nuclear
weapons, just because of the propaganda that's been fed to them. I don't
believe the world would end if we exploded a nuclear weapon. . . . At
Bikini . . . the fish are back in the lagoons; the coconut trees are growing
coconuts; the guava bushes have fruit on them; the birds are back. As a
matter of fact, everything is about the same except the land crabs . . .
the land crabs are a little bit "hot" and there's a little question whether
you should eat a land crab or not.
> — General Curtis E. LeMay, former commander,
> Strategic Air Force and chief of staff, Air
> Force, news conference announcing candidacy
> for vice president, Pittsburgh, October 3, 1968

Those who have had a chance for four years and could not produce
should not be given another chance.
> — Richard M. Nixon, presidential candidate,
> October 9, 1968

It has never been clearer that the enemy will fail. . . . [It] has suffered
a clear and significant defeat. . . . One day the war in Vietnam will end
. . . the day will surely come. . . .
> — President Lyndon B. Johnson, remarks of
> welcome to Prime Minister Holyoake of New
> Zealand, White House, October 9, 1968

We are very pleased that the casualties are no higher than they are. We
lost 100 American lives last week.
> — President Lyndon B. Johnson,
> October 24, 1968

I've made my statement in Vietnam. I listen and watch very carefully
as to what is happening. I believe there are indications that bear some
significance. . . . There have been very low casualties. There are
sensitive negotiations underway. And I believe that I make my greatest
contribution to the success of these negotiations by maintaining discreet
silence. . . . Am I hopeful? The answer is Yes.
> — Vice President Hubert H. Humphrey,
> *Meet the Press*, NBC, October 27, 1968

. . . I would continue the bombing. . . . I just can't see how the United States, with its great strength, cannot win a victory against a small, backward country like North Vietnam. . . . I think that if we tell them we are going to win, then set about doing it, we will have a victory in very short order.

> — General Curtis E. LeMay, vice-presidential
> candidate, American Independent Party, *Face
> the Nation*, CBS, October 27, 1968

Light at the end of the tunnel? Some American troops may be pulled out of Vietnam early next year . . . to demonstrate how well the war is going.

> — *U.S. News & World Report*,
> November 18, 1968

The South Vietnamese and the Americans have the upper hand on the military side.

> — Sir Robert Thompson, Special Advisor to the
> President; British citizen; beneficiary of a
> $100,000 contract for support and advice
> regarding the Saigon Police Department from
> the Department of Defense; London,
> December 14, 1968.

Some critics today worry that our democratic, free societies are becoming overmanaged. I would argue that the opposite is true. . . . To undermanage reality is not to keep free [*sic*]. . . . Vital decision-making, particularly in policy matters, must remain at the top. This is . . . what the top is for.

> — Robert S. McNamara, *The Essence of Security*

I am now certain that if the North Vietnamese withdrew and the Americans pulled back to their bases, our forces could defeat the Viet Cong without help.

> — Premier Tran Van Huong
> of South Vietnam, December 18, 1968

If you stop bombing Hanoi, we will stop bombing Washington. Johnson and Rusk keep saying that they'll increase the pressure until they force us to the peace table. Well, you can note this. . . . We will not make peace under the heel of the aggressor. . . . We will not sell our fundamental right of independence for peace.

> — Prime Minister Pham Van Dong of North
> Vietnam, quoted by David Schoenbrun, 1968

TOP SECRET

What intelligence agencies like to call the "modern industrial sector" of the economy was tiny even by Asian standards, producing only about 12 percent of a GNP of $1.6 billion in 1965. There were only a handful of "major industrial facilities." . . . NVN's limited industry made little contribution to its military capabilities. NVN forces, in intelligence terminology, placed "little direct reliance on the domestic economy for material." . . . The idea that destroying, or threatening to destroy, NVN's industry would pressure Hanoi into calling it quits seems, in retrospect, a colossal misjudgment.

> — Pentagon historian's staff analysis, Office of Secretary of Defense Task Force, 1968

There are wars that are inevitable under the circumstances. The war in South Vietnam is one. The U.S. could not ignore the challenge. . . . We can and should think in terms of the defeat of the North Vietnamese. . . . To say that the United States cannot do this is a counsel of despair.

> — Drew Middleton, *America's Stake in Asia*, 1968

TOP SECRET

What became clearer and clearer as the summer wore on was that while we had destroyed a major portion of North Vietnam's storage capacity, she retained enough dispersed capacity, supplemented by continuing imports . . . to meet her ongoing requirements. [This] meant an ever mounting U.S. cost in munitions, fuel, aircraft losses, and men. By August we were reaching the point at which these costs were prohibitive. . . . The POL [petroleum, oil, lubricants] strikes had been a failure . . . there was no real evidence that NVM had at any time been pinched for POL. . . . The . . . failure . . . was reflected . . . in the undiminished flow of men and supplies down the Ho Chi Minh trail to the war in the South.

> — Pentagon historian's staff analysis, Office of Secretary of Defense Task Force, 1968

1969–1973

The three men picked . . . to handle Vietnam policy [Bunker, Lodge, and General Johnson] all believe that time and the course of the fighting are running in American favor now and that there need be no hurry in pushing along the peace road.

> — *Christian Science Monitor*, January 9, 1969

The prospects, I think, for peace are better today than at any time. . . . The North Vietnamese know that they cannot achieve their aggressive purposes by force . . . it will yield no victory to the Communist cause. . . . I have been sustained by faith.

> — President Lyndon B. Johnson,
> State of the Union Address,
> January 14, 1969

I don't think that I understand the students, or I don't think that my generation understands the students. . . . Obviously, we don't understand.

> — President Lyndon B. Johnson,
> National Press Club, January 17, 1969

The peace we seek is . . . the peace that comes with healing on its wings, with compassion for those who have suffered, with understanding for those who have opposed us . . .

> — President Richard M. Nixon,
> January 20, 1969

Some light was finally showing at the end of the Vietnamese tunnel.

> — *Newsweek*, January 27, 1969

I am the most hopeful man you have ever known in your life.

> — Henry Cabot Lodge, U.S. chief negotiator at
> Paris peace talks, when asked about prospects
> for settlement of war, quoted by *Time*,
> January 31, 1969

I consider the Department of Defense to be a Department of Peace.

> — President Richard M. Nixon,
> press conference, February 6, 1969

We have the enemy licked now. He is beaten. We have the initiative in all areas. The enemy cannot achieve a military victory; he cannot even mount another major offensive. We are in the process of eliminating his remaining capability. . . . My optimism is based on hard military realities. The enemy has suffered staggering losses. . . .

Leadership and general caliber of troops are deteriorating rapidly. The Vietcong has been . . . decimated. . . . For the past year we have been looking at an increasingly anemic military capability. . . . General Abrams has taken the initiative from the enemy in brilliant fashion. . . . In retrospect, the Tet offensive may have been the turning point in the war, where the enemy once and for all lost the South Vietnamese people. . . . Our intelligence is too good and our forces are too strong for him. . . . [The South Vietnamese] have come a long way.

In recent months, they have been displaying an increased morale, proficiency and dedication. The main reason is that they are receiving much better training. . . . And there have been intangible factors, including . . . an awareness that the war is being won. . . . Our current authorized strength is 549,500. . . . This should be ample to do the job, particularly in view of the enemy's fast-deteriorating military posture. . . . The enemy is beaten.

> — Admiral John S. McCain, Jr., commander in
> chief, Pacific, interview, *Reader's Digest*,
> February 1969

The enemy has lost the war militarily. The signs of deterioration are plain. . . . Clearly we have crossed the ridge line of the war.

> — Hanson W. Baldwin, retired military editor,
> *New York Times*, in *Reader's Digest*, February
> 1969

Recent reports have indicated a noticeable improvement in the effectiveness of the South Vietnamese forces . . . the South Vietnamese forces will be able to play a greater military role.

> — Senator Daniel K. Inouye, Democrat of
> Hawaii, quoted in *U.S. News & World Report*,
> February 10, 1969

[Peace may come in the] next few months.

> — Senator Claiborne Pell, Democrat of Rhode
> Island, quoted in *U.S. News & World Report*,
> February 10, 1969

A truce and a cease fire . . . is possible . . . and likely within two or three months.

> — Senator John J. Sparkman, Democrat of Alabama, quoted by *U.S. News & World Report*, February 10, 1969

The chances are that the next 12 to 24 months will witness a dramatic tapering-off of hostilities, and conceivably a complete cease-fire.

> — Senator Thomas J. Dodd, Democrat of Connecticut, quoted by *U.S. News & World Report*, February 10, 1969

It will be my policy as President to issue a warning only once, and I will not repeat it now. Anything in the future that is done will be done. There will be no additional warning. The Communist offensive . . . is less than that of last year. . . . Now, this offensive has failed. . . . It has failed to achieve any significant military breakthrough. It has failed to break the back of the Government of South Vietnam. . . . We will not tolerate a continuation of this kind of attack. . . . We have made, we think, some progress. We are going to make some more.

> — President Richard M. Nixon, news conference, March 4, 1969

The basic military situation in Vietnam is far better than it was. . . .

> — Stewart Alsop, column, *Newsweek*, March 10, 1969

On March 4 . . . I issued what was widely interpreted as a warning. It will be my policy as President to issue a warning only once, and I will not repeat it now. Anything in the future that is done will be done. There will be no additional warning. I think [there] is significant progress. . . . Our casualties for the immediate past week went from 400 down to 300.

> — President Richard M. Nixon, news conference, March 14, 1969

We will be going forward. . . . The South Vietnamese will be going forward. . . . I think we have had too many prophecies and too many forecasts. . . . I have tried to avoid that.

> — Secretary of Defense Melvin Laird, *Meet the Press*, NBC, March 23, 1969

The idea of finishing a defense wall across South Vietnam to stymie invaders from the North is just about dead. The wall was conceived in 1966 by "whiz kids" working for Robert S. McNamara, then Secretary of

Defense. . . . It was to have cost 1.6 billion dollars over three years. Something less than 1 billion—it is estimated—has so far been spent on it. Shortly before he left the Pentagon, Mr. McNamara said: "The McNamara Line is no longer referred to as that, because it is successful." His successors didn't agree. . . . Melvin R. Laird, the present Secretary, told Congress: "The original plan did not work out as expected."

> — *U.S. News & World Report*, March 31, 1969

We think we're on the right track.

> — President Richard M. Nixon,
> quoted by *Newsweek*, April 7, 1969

The Administration's assessment is that North Vietnam now wants peace. An agricultural country like North Vietnam must be close to exhaustion after fighting an industrial power like the United States for so long. North Vietnamese manpower losses have been staggering. Best U.S. judgment: half a million North Vietnamese troops killed, another quarter of a million put out of action permanently by wounds or illness.

> — *U.S. News & World Report*, April 21, 1969

The Nixon Administration is now embarking on a plan that could lead the way out.

> — Chalmers M. Roberts, *Washington Post*,
> April 27, 1969

The U.S. bombing effort in both North and South Vietnam has been one of the most wasteful and expensive hoaxes ever to be put over on the American people.

> — General David M. Shoup, former
> commandant, U.S. Marine Corps, *Atlantic*,
> April 1969

The war will end within two years.

> — President Nguyen Van Thieu, May 3, 1969

I want to end this war. The American people want to end this war. The people of South Vietnam want to end this war. But . . . a great nation cannot renege on its promises.

> — President Richard M. Nixon, May 14, 1969

The day the United States decides to withdraw its forces, all other problems will be solved and the Paris deadlock will be broken. It is this decision we demand and it is the key to all other issues.

> — Premier Pham Van Dong of North Vietnam,
> interview, May 17, 1969

The Americans are too anxious to get peace. . . . In the meantime our government is trying to win over the people of South Vietnam. . . . They [the enemy] are on the downward slope here.

> — Premier Tran Van Huong of South Vietnam, interview, May 18, 1969

"Hamburger Hill" was a tremendous, gallant victory and some people are acting like it was a catastrophe.

> — Major General Melvin Zais, who ordered paratroopers onto "Hamburger Hill" for 11 assaults, at cost of 46 U.S. dead, 308 wounded, quoted by *U.S. News & World Report*, June 2, 1969

The Pentagon is buying $4 million worth of "noiseless button bomblets" . . . for the Vietnam war. The bomblets transmit a radio signal when stepped on and are useful when buried around U.S. installations or along jungle trails used by the enemy.

> — *Newsweek*, June 2, 1969

Quiet confidence . . . emanates from the Nixon Administration. . . . This confidence is based partly on the situation in South Vietnam. . . . The military and political situation in South Vietnam really is much better. . . . The Saigon government now controls more people. . . . The Communist "infrastructure" shows real signs of unraveling. . . . The Viet Cong is having severe recruiting and disciplinary problems. . . .

> — Stewart Alsop, column, *Newsweek*, June 9, 1969

Our mountains will always be,
our rivers will always be,
our people will always be;
The American invaders defeated,
we will rebuild our land
ten times more beautiful.

> — Ho Chi Minh, written few months before death, 1969

I do not want to leave any doubt on this score: President Thieu is the elected President of Vietnam. . . . There is no question about our standing with President Thieu. . . . I think we are on the right road in Vietnam.

> — President Richard M. Nixon, news conference, White House, June 19, 1969

The prospects for peace are brighter now than they have been for a long time.

> — Hubert H. Humphrey, New York City,
> quoted by *Time*, June 20, 1969

Hanoi has nothing to gain by waiting.

> — President Richard M. Nixon, July 11, 1969

I think we've certainly turned the corner.

> — Secretary of Defense Melvin Laird to Senate
> Foreign Relations Committee, July 15, 1969

Out here in this dreary, difficult war, I think history will record that this may have been one of America's finest hours, because we took a difficult task and we succeeded.

> — President Richard M. Nixon to U.S. troops,
> Headquarters, 2d Brigade, 1st Infantry
> Division, Di An, South Vietnam, 13 miles
> north of Saigon, July 20, 1969

South Vietnam is now strong and steadily growing stronger. . . . In two years we will be so strong that the Communist Army of North Vietnam will have to withdraw completely. . . . Don't think that being President is a sinecure. I have been President for the last two years and all I know is that my hair has turned gray.

> — President Nguyen Van Thieu, July 23, 1969

We are re-evaluating our tactics in Vietnam.

> — President Richard M. Nixon
> to newsmen, Guam, July 25, 1969

We trust that the war in Vietnam can be brought to a successful conclusion. . . . I happen to be an optimist. . . . We can see the exciting possibilities for progress.

> — President Richard M. Nixon, toast to
> President Ferdinand Marcos, Phillippines,
> state dinner, Manila, July 26, 1969

[The U.S.] has turned the corner so far as Vietnamization of the war and a reduction of troops.

> — Secretary of Defense Melvin Laird,
> *Face the Nation*, CBS, July 27, 1969

I think we have to do everything we can to build up the deterrent effect of American presence in Asia. . . . I wouldn't do very much more than he [President Nixon] is doing. I think he is trying to end it on an honorable basis. . . . There is progress being made and it is moving steadily. I am encouraged on that part of it. . . . There is some possibility that this war in Vietnam . . . would end simply through withering away.

> — Former Secretary of State Dean Rusk,
> *Issues & Answers*, ABC, July 27, 1969

The Viet Cong military machine is running out of steam. . . . Evidence of Allied successes is piling up. . . . Saigon seems to be ruling more effectively in the cities and villages. Actions against the guerrilla "infrastructure" . . . are hurting the Reds.

> — *U.S. News & World Report*, July 28, 1969

There is hope in this part of the world for fresh U.S. support—and money. At the heart of it all is a 25-to-50-billion-dollar project to tame the mighty Mekong River. . . . Experts . . . say it could take a generation to finish. Costs could soar to double the present 25-billion-dollar estimate.

> — *U.S. News & World Report*,
> dispatch from Bangkok, July 28, 1969

President Thieu is one of the four or five best politicians in the world.

> — President Richard M. Nixon,
> Saigon, August 1, 1969

Very exciting horizons . . . 5 or 10 years from now: . . . We can detect anything that perspires, moves, carries metal, makes a noise, or is hotter or colder than its surroundings. . . . This is the beginning of instrumentation of the entire battlefield. . . . You begin to get a "Year 2000" vision of an electronic map with little lights that flash for different kinds of activity. This is what we require for this "porous" war, where the friendly and the enemy are all mixed together.

> — Leonard Sullivan, deputy director, Research
> and Development for Southeast Asian
> Matters, quoted in *Congressional Record*,
> August 8, 1969

I can understand the anguish of the younger generation. . . . They see no great purposes in the world. But conscientious objection is destructive of a society. . . . Conscientious objection must be reserved for only the greatest moral issues, and Vietnam is not of this magnitude.

> — Dr. Henry Kissinger to college students,
> quoted in *Look*, August 12, 1969

Top Secret

It has been estimated that approximately 52,000 civilians were killed in NVN by U.S. air strikes.

> — National Security Study Memorandum
> NSSM-1, 1969

Do I approve of what the President has done in Viet Nam? Of course I do. . . . We are on the right course.

> — Hubert H. Humphrey, interviewed by *Time*.
> August 15, 1969

I don't see anything improper in the relationship between the military and industry. . . . There are tens of thousands of companies doing defense work. . . . And it is all done through the free-enterprise system.

> — Roger Lewis, president and chairman of the
> board, General Dynamics, quoted by *Look*,
> August 26, 1969

It is shocking to realize that Congress was not asked for specific authority for the sending of America's soldiers to South Vietnam and, indeed, that the government of South Vietnam did not make a written, formal request for these troops.

> — Senator J. William Fulbright,
> September 3, 1969

Vietnamization . . . is going very well indeed.

> — Joseph Alsop, syndicated column,
> September 17, 1969

Time, the weapon employed so well by the enemy, is beginning to work against him now.

> — General Leonard Chapman, commandant,
> U.S. Marine Corps, quoted by *Time*,
> September 19, 1969

They say this village is 80 percent VC supporters. By the time we finish this it will be 95 percent.

> — American officer, quoted by *New York Times*,
> September 24, 1969

As many as 2,000,000 Vietnamese may be directly dependent upon wages paid by the Americans. . . . In effect, the war has created a terribly artificial situation in which many depend upon employment that can't last, a black market that must someday wane, and thievery that will someday have fewer available victims.

> — George W. Ashworth, *Christian Science Monitor*, September 26, 1969

I would point to some progress. . . . Once the enemy recognizes that it is not going to win its objectives by waiting us out, then the enemy will negotiate and we will end this war by the end of 1970. . . .

Now, I understand that there has been and continues to be opposition to the war in Vietnam on the campuses, and also in the Nation. As far as this kind of activity is concerned, we expect it. However, under no circumstances will I be affected whatever by it. . . .

> — President Richard M. Nixon, Address to the Nation, September 26, 1969

We will not stop short of victory, no matter what happens in Washington.

> — President Nguyen Van Thieu, news conference, Vung Tau, South Vietnam, September 26, 1969

There are no American combat forces in Laos.

> — President Richard M. Nixon news conference, September 26, 1969

I am the youngest politician in the world. Now, the President of the United States is so sophisticated for me. It's a very big President for a small President like me. But I don't believe that the United States has to withdraw. The United States has to make the Vietnamese people an army. . . . The problem is not to stick [*sic*] and run but to help this small country to grow up and to be strong themselves, and strong, big with themselves. . . . The United States can . . . help us economically and in more sophisticated weapons, like atomic warfare that we have not. . . . You have a direct responsibility . . . to defend the freedom in Southeast Asia, in South Vietnam. . . . You have not to abandon . . . you should stand somewhere in the world. . . .

> — President Nguyen Van Thieu *Issues & Answers*, ABC, September 28, 1969

There may be one more offensive. The enemy has about one offensive left in him. After that, that enemy is a defeated enemy.

> — Senator Hugh Scott, Republican of Pennsylvania, Senate Minority Leader, *Face the Nation*, CBS, October 5, 1969

I think we have made tremendous progress with the steps we have taken in the Vietnamization of the war. I think the South Vietnam government is stronger politically than it has ever been. . . . Certainly the military preparedness and military capability of the South Vietnamese is much greater.

> — Vice President Spiro T. Agnew,
> *Issues & Answers*, ABC, October 5, 1969

I judge that we are on the right track.

> — General Earle J. Wheeler,
> Chairman, Joint Chiefs of Staff, Saigon,
> October 7, 1969

[To pull our troops out of Vietnam] would be to abandon an objective, to betray our allies and, I believe, to imperil Australia's future security.

> — Prime Minister John Gorton of Australia,
> October 8, 1969

Vietnamization is on schedule and in some places ahead of schedule.

> — General Earle Wheeler, chairman, Joint Chiefs
> of Staff, planeside conference following return
> from Vietnam, October 9, 1969

It may be that Vietnam will destroy all those who touch it.

> — Dr. Henry Kissinger, quoted by Hugh Sidey,
> *Life*, October 10, 1969

I'm not going to be the first American President who loses a war.

> — President Richard M. Nixon to Republican
> congressional and party leaders, Camp David,
> Md., quoted by *Time*, October 10, 1969

I will say confidently that looking ahead just three years, the war will be over. It will be over on a basis which will promise lasting peace in the Pacific.

> — President Richard M. Nixon, at White House
> dinner for Board of Directors, AP, October 12,
> 1969

We are on the road to peace. . . . There is nothing to be learned from demonstrations.

> — President Richard M. Nixon, in letter to
> university student Randy J. Dicks, on the
> Vietnam moratorium demonstrations,
> October 13, 1969

I am determined against a coalition government in South Vietnam.

> — President Nguyen Van Thieu,
> Hué, October 15, 1969

It's not very healthy to be in the opposition in Vietnam. If you want to learn about the status of the non-Communist opposition, go to Con Son [offshore prison island]. That's where you'll find the largest gathering.

> — Pham Ba Cam, Hoa Hao leader, quoted by
> Terence Smith, *New York Times*, October 24,
> 1969

Tonight I want to talk to you on a subject of deep concern to all Americans . . . the war in Vietnam. . . . Let me begin by describing the situation I found when I was inaugurated. . . . No progress had been made. . . . The war was causing deep division at home and criticism from many of our friends as well as our enemies abroad . . . there were some who urged I end the war at once . . . this would have been a popular and easy course. . . . This was the only way to avoid allowing Johnson's war to become Nixon's war. . . . I could only conclude that the precipitate withdrawal of American forces from Vietnam would be a disaster. . . . For the United States, this first defeat in our nation's history would result in a collapse of confidence in American leadership . . . precipitate withdrawal would thus be a disaster of immense magnitude [resulting in] our defeat and humiliation. . . .

Let me turn . . . to a more encouraging report. . . . I, therefore, put into effect another plan to bring peace . . . the Nixon Doctrine. . . . We are an impatient people. . . . The South Vietnamese have continued to gain in strength. . . . Enemy infiltration . . . is less than 20 percent of what it was. . . . United States casualties have declined. . . . I am glad to be able to report tonight progress . . . has been greater than we anticipated . . . our timetable for withdrawal is more optimistic now than when we made our first estimates. . . .

In speaking of the consequences of a precipitate withdrawal, I mentioned that our allies would lose confidence in America. Far more dangerous, we would lose confidence in ourselves . . . inevitable remorse and divisive recrimination would sear our spirit as a people. . . . I have chosen a plan for peace. I believe it will succeed. . . . Let historians not record that when America was the most powerful nation in the world we passed on the other side of the road. . . . Let us . . . be united against defeat. Because let us understand: North Vietnam cannot defeat or humiliate the United States. Only Americans can do that. . . .

> — President Richard M. Nixon,
> Address to the Nation, White House,
> November 3, 1969

In 1969 the U.S. set a goal for the Phoenix program to "neutralize" 20,000 NLF agents during the year, and at the end of the year GVN authorities reported 19,534 agents "neutralized." The figure was unsettling in that there had been no corresponding decline in American estimates of NLF agents at large. Who, then, were the 19,534 people . . . ?
. . . A large percentage of the "neutralized agents" were simply people whom the Phoenix herded in and out of the police stations in order to fill their quotas. . . . A conscientious village chief discovered the local Phoenix agent was extorting gold and jewelry from the people of the village on the threat of arresting them as "Viet Cong agents." When the village chief attempted to tell the district chief about the racket, the Phoenix agent had him figured as a "Viet Cong suspect."

> — Frances Fitzgerald, *Fire in the Lake*

Dear Mr. President:
I wanted to take this opportunity to reaffirm . . . my desire to work for a just peace. . . . There is nothing to be gained by waiting. Delay can only increase the dangers and multiply the suffering. The time has come to move forward at the conference table for an early resolution of this tragic war.

> — President Richard M. Nixon, letter to Ho Chi
> Minh, July 15, 1969, released by White House,
> November 3, 1969

To His Excellency Richard Milhous Nixon,
President of the United States, Washington.
Mr. President:
I have the honor to acknowledge receipt of your letter. The war of aggression of the United States against our people, violating our fundamental national rights, still continues in South Vietnam. The United States continues to intensify military operations, the B-52 bombings and the use of toxic chemical products multiply the crimes against the Vietnamese people. The longer the war goes on, the more it accumulates the mourning and burdens of the American people.
I am extremely indignant at the losses and the destruction caused by the American troops to our people and our country. I am also deeply touched at the rising toll of death of young Americans who have fallen in Vietnam by reason of the policy of governing circles. Our Vietnamese people are deeply devoted to peace, a real peace with independence and real freedom. They are determined to fight to the end, without fearing the sacrifices and difficulties in order to defend their country and their sacred national rights.
The overall solution in 10 points of the National Liberation Front and the Provisional Revolutionary Government of the Republic of South

Vietnam is a logical and reasonable basis for the settlement of the South Vietnamese problem. It has earned the sympathy and support of the peoples of the world. . . . In your letter you have expressed the desire to ask for a just peace. For this the United States must cease the war of aggression and withdraw their troops from South Vietnam, respect the right of the population of the South and of the Vietnamese nation to dispose of themselves, without foreign interference. . . . This is the path that will allow the United States to get out of the war with honor.

> — Ho Chi Minh, letter to President Richard M.
> Nixon, August 25, 1969, released by White
> House, November 3, 1969

At the end of 1970 we will replace all American combat troops.

> — Vice President Nguyen Cao Ky,
> Dalat, South Vietnam, November 5, 1969

There is one very, very large development that may take place. Nobody knows at this point whether it will prove out or not. That is oil exploration that is going on in the Gulf of Thailand . . . and there are now six companies, five of them American, that are now carrying out explorations. . . . Now if that develops, it of course will be a very major additional American investment in the country.

> — Ambassador to Thailand Leonard Unger,
> testimony before Senate Foreign Relations
> Committee, November 11, 1969

We have been successful. This may not be a victory in the usual sense of the word, but it is nevertheless success. . . . I know that in some quarters it has become fashionable to downgrade the qualities of the Vietnamese fighting forces. . . . There is no question in my mind that their performance is improving. . . . The pacification program this year has made steady progress.

> — Ambassador Ellsworth Bunker, interview,
> Saigon, *U.S. News & World Report*, November
> 17, 1969

There is remarkable progress.

> — David Packard, Deputy Secretary of Defense,
> after 6-day visit to Vietnam, November 21,
> 1969

[In] a new Pacific age . . . a new order will be created by Japan and the United States.

> — Premier Eisaku Sato of Japan,
> quoted by *New York Times*,
> November 22, 1969

. . . bomb craters beyond counting, the dead gray and black fields, that have been defoliated and scorched by napalm, land that has been plowed flat. . . . And everywhere can be seen the piles of ashes forming the outlines of huts and houses, to show where hamlets once stood.
— *New York Times Magazine*, November 23, 1969

There was about 40 or 45 people that we gathered in the center of the village . . . men, women, children . . . babies. And we all huddled them up. . . . Lt. Calley . . . started shooting them. And he told me to start shooting. So I started shooting, I poured about four clips into the group. . . . I fired them on automatic . . . you just spray the area . . . so you can't know how many you killed . . . so we started to gather them up, more people . . . we put them in the hootch, and we dropped a hand grenade in there with them . . . they had about 70 or 75 people all gathered up. So we threw ours in with them and Lt. Calley . . . started pushing them off and shooting . . . off into the ravine. It was a ditch. And so we just pushed them off, and just started using automatics on them . . . men, women, children . . . and babies . . . after I done it, I felt good, but later on that day it was gettin' to me. . . . It just seemed like it was the natural thing to do at the time.
— Private Paul Meadlo, Americal Division, interview on CBS-TV, November 24, 1969

I think our policy is . . . sound. . . . We are the strongest nation in the world. . . . When we say something it carries a great weight . . . it just carries weight because of the prominence and prestige and importance of the United States. . . .
— Secretary of State William P. Rogers, interview, NET, November 26, 1969

TOP SECRET

The regime [in North Vietnam] was quite successful . . . in using the bombing threat as an instrument to mobilize people. . . . The general populace found the hardships of the war more tolerable when it faced daily dangers from the bombing than when this threat was removed. . . . There is no evidence to suggest that these hardships reduced to a critical level NVN's willingness to resolve or continue the conflict. On the contrary, the bombing actually may have hardened the attitude of the people and rallied them behind the government's programs.
— National Security Study Memorandum NSSM-1, 1969

The [Symington subcommittee] hearings showed, for example, that the United States has been paying for the Philippine troop commitment in

Vietnam. It has also shown that, without this payment, the Philippines would not have sent a single man to help the United States in Vietnam. . . . Administration officials admitted paying the Philippines some $40 million to send the troops to Vietnam. . . . The U.S. paid South Korea and Thailand as well.

> — William Selover, *Christian Science Monitor*,
> November 28, 1969

We should be proud of our country because the Americal Division rules of engagement are based on Judeo-Christian traditions and are moral, unlike those of the enemy.

> — Lieutenant Colonel James E. Shaw,
> chief chaplain, Americal Division,
> Chulai, South Vietnam, November 29, 1969

The only good Dink is a dead Dink.

> — Specialist-4 James Farmer, Americal Division,
> quoted by *New York Times*, Chulai, South
> Vietnam, November 29, 1969

What is behind the flurry of optimistic reports? . . . The South Vietnamese are starting to roll up their sleeves. . . . The enemy, at the same time, is finding the war increasingly difficult going by all the statistics available. In short, there has been a significant turn for the better. . . . There is evidence of a Vietnamese determination that has long been lacking.

> — *U.S. News & World Report*, December 1, 1969

This must be just about the first time in the history of warfare that a nation has thought it could prevail by withdrawing combat troops and reducing its military presence.

> — Walter Lippmann, *Newsweek*,
> December 1, 1969

In the Mekong Delta, U.S. military advisers at My Tho told a UPI correspondent, Robert Kaylor, that the government's pacification program was still being hampered by the effects of indiscriminate killing of civilians by U.S. 9th Infantry Division troops. . . . "You can't exactly expect people who have had parts of their family blown away by the 9th to be wholeheartedly on our side," said a U.S. source, a member of a pacification team.

> — *Boston Globe*, December 1, 1969

We are at war with 10-year-old children. It may not be humanitarian, but that's what it's like.

> — Staff major, Americal Division, quoted by
> Henry Kamm, *New York Times*, December 1,
> 1969

The only concrete progress here is agreement on the shape of the table.

> — Ambassador Henry Cabot Lodge, concluding
> service as chief American delegate to Paris
> peace talks, at 45th plenary session,
> December 4, 1969

As far as . . . [the My Lai massacre] is concerned, I believe that it is an isolated incident. We have 1,200,000 Americans who have been in Vietnam. . . . They built roads and schools. They built churches and pagodas. The Marines alone this year have built over 250,000 churches, pagodas and temples for the people of Vietnam.

> — President Richard M. Nixon,
> news conference, December 8, 1969

TOP SECRET

In spite of these extra demands, it appears that NVM has enough manpower to continue the war at the high casualty rates sustained in 1968. . . . It is generally agreed that the bombing did not significantly raise the cost of the war to NVM. . . . MACV finds it has effectively blocked these [infiltration] roads 80% of the time and therefore caused less traffic to get through. OSD/CIA/State [OSD—Office of Secretary of Defense] agree that enemy traffic on the roads attacked has been disrupted. However, they point out that the enemy uses less than 15% of the available road capacity, is constantly expanding that capacity through new roads and bypasses, and our air strikes do not block but only delay traffic. . . . JCS/MACV and OSD/CIA agree that we destroy 12% to 14% of the trucks observed moving through Laos and 20% to 35% of the total flow of supplies in Laos. To MACV/JCS, the material destroyed cannot be replaced so that our air effort denies it to the VC/NVA forces in South Vietnam. In complete disagreement, OSD and CIA find that the enemy needs in SVN (10 to 15 trucks of supplies per day) are so small and his supply of war material so large that the enemy can replace his losses easily, increase his traffic flows slightly, and get through as much supplies to SCN as he wants to in spite of the bombing.

> — National Security Study Memorandum
> NSSM-1, 1969

Sir Robert Thompson, who led the victory over Communist guerrillas in Malaya and is now a Rand Corp. consultant, recently returned to Viet Nam to sound out the situation for President Nixon. He told the

President last week . . . "things felt much better and smelled much better over there."

> — *Time*, December 12, 1969

It is encouraging, I believe, to look at the situation in Vietnam. . . . We have had success this year in Vietnamizing the war. . . . Infiltration is below 1968. . . . Vietnamization . . . has been moving along on schedule and we are very pleased. . . . It is moving forward on a very progressive basis. . . . I am not going to get into any predictions or forecasts. I think we have had too much of that. . . . We are moving forward. . . .

> — Secretary of Defense Melvin Laird,
> *Issues & Answers*, ABC, December 14, 1969

When the decision was made, I went along. I didn't say much but I went along. . . . We can't be there forever, but think what has been accomplished. There is a new self-confidence in Southeast Asia . . . we've walked the extra mile.

> — Senator Hubert H. Humphrey, Democrat of
> Minnesota, interview, *Newsweek*,
> December 15, 1969

I have asked for this television time tonight to give you a progress report. . . . Ambassador Lodge has had to leave his assignment in Paris because of personal reasons. I have designated Philip Habib, one of our most experienced Foreign Service officers . . . as the acting head of our delegation with the personal rank of Ambassador. . . . Let me turn now to the progress of . . . Vietnamization. . . . I have a much more favorable report to give to you tonight. . . . Let me share with you how I reached this conclusion. . . . It is most important to get independent judgments. . . . Several months ago I read a book by Sir Robert Thompson, a British expert. . . . On October 7 I met with Mr. Thompson and asked him to go to Vietnam. . . . His full report . . . must remain confidential since it bears on . . . security. . . . But let me read to you from his summary of his findings:

> I was very impressed by the improvement in the military and political situation in Vietnam as compared with all previous visits. . . . A winning position . . . has been achieved. . . . The greatest need is confidence. . . . Continuing U.S. support . . . will increase the confidence already shown by many South Vietnam leaders.

Mr. Thompson's report, which I would describe as cautiously optimistic, is in line with my own attitude and with reports I have received from other observers and from our own civilian and military leaders in

Vietnam. There is one disturbing new development, however. . . .
Enemy infiltration has increased substantially. . . . I am announcing
tonight a reduction in our troop ceiling. . . . I have consistently said we
must take risks for peace. . . . Reduction of our forces . . . marks
further progress. . . . Hanoi should abandon its dream of military
victory. . . . I am glad that I was able to report tonight some progress.
. . . Thank you and goodnight.

> — President Richard M. Nixon,
> Address to the Nation, December 15, 1969

They [the Americans and South Vietnamese] can win. . . . We—
meaning the West—have not understood how badly they [the North
Vietnamese] have been hurt.

> — Sir Robert Thompson, British guerrilla expert,
> former Secretary of Defense, Federation of
> Malaysia, head of British Advisory Mission,
> Vietnam, consultant to Rand Corporation and
> to President Nixon, quoted in *Washington
> Post*, December 17, 1969

There is abundant evidence that the North Vietnamese tire not only of
the rigors of the war but of the manifest futility of it . . . 100,000
Vietcong have defected. . . . The enemy . . . is reeling from successive
disasters. . . . The bright side of it . . . is that something like an entire
generation of North Vietnamese males has been killed during the past
seven or eight years. . . . Did I forget to mention that there are only
75,000 Vietcong? . . . We are, in fact . . . winning the war.

> — William F. Buckley, Jr.,
> column from Hong Kong, December 20, 1969

The North is suffering heavy casualties in the South. Since the *Tet*
offensive, nearly two years ago, more than 300,000 Northern troops—at
a conservative estimate—have died in the South. There isn't a single
family in the North that hasn't lost a husband or a son. And the war, still
going on, is a drain on the North. . . . Buildings in Hanoi are crumbling
from a lack of maintenance. . . . Only one hospital in Hanoi is still
above ground. . . . There is no industry to speak of, no production of
chemical fertilizer. The steel plant is idle. There's a great shortage of
coal. Gasoline is reserved for military transport. Electricity is rationed in
Hanoi and, in the summer, is available in homes for only an hour a day.
. . . In the winter, electricity is on for an additional hour. . . . All the
thermal power centers were knocked out. . . .

It's impossible to find the simplest items—buttons, safety pins, pens,
wire and wool anywhere. . . . You can't even find chalk for the

blackboards in the schoolrooms. Friends of mine who visited Haiphong said the city reminded them of Berlin in 1945. It's a ruined, ravaged city. . . . North Vietnam is in ruins. I'd say the air war put the country back 20 years. . . . It is now impossible for the North to conquer the South.

> — Pierre Darcourt, French journalist, Paris,
> quoted by *U.S. News & World Report*,
> December 22, 1969

Enemy infiltration has dropped. . . . The climate of world opinion toward the United States has greatly improved. . . . I am cautiously optimistic. . . . The South Vietnamese . . . are taking hold.

> — Secretary of State William P. Rogers,
> news conference, December 23, 1969

The Viet Cong are no longer 10 feet tall. They are more like frightened 16-year-olds. . . . The thing that surprised me more than anything else was the extent to which the government has regained control in the countryside. . . . The war isn't won, but we're in a position from which we could win.

> — Sir Robert Thompson,
> quoted in *Time*, December 26, 1969

President Thieu has made amazing progress.

> — Vice President Spiro T. Agnew to reporters on
> plane en route from Saigon to Guam, AP
> dispatch from Guam, December 28, 1969

They just might make it. The South Vietnamese just might be able to hold their own. . . . This is the admittedly rather timid conclusion that this reporter has reached. . . . There has been a very big change for the better. . . . We Americans have learned a lot about fighting this kind of war.

> — Stewart Alsop, column, *Newsweek*,
> December 29, 1969

The local defeat of the armed enemy can all be clearly seen.

> — General William C. Westmoreland, quoted in
> *The Battle for Khe Sanh*, published by U.S.
> Marine Corps, 1969

Almost any statement about Vietnam is likely to be true.

> — Dr. Henry Kissinger, *Foreign Affairs*, 1969

Why does the whole world respect Ho Chi Minh and Defense Minister

Giap? Why? Who are they? . . . Why can't we find a man in the South and make him respected by the whole world?

> — Vice President Nguyen Cao Ky, 1969, quoted by Luce and Sommer, *Vietnam: The Unheard Voices*

Morale is higher than it ever was.

> — Vice President Spiro T. Agnew, winding up 24-hour visit to South Vietnam, January 2, 1970

The Republic of Vietnam exhibit[s] an ever-increasing capacity to build their nation on firm foundations.

> — Annual U.S. AID Report, presented to Ambassador Ellsworth Bunker by Donald G. MacDonald, director, USAID mission, Saigon, January 5, 1970

I believe peace will come in two to three years when the Communists are completely defeated.

> — President Nguyen Van Thieu, news conference, January 9, 1970

[The people massacred at My Lai] got just what they deserved.

> — Senator Allan Ellender, television interview for Louisiana station, January 15, 1970

We are cautiously optimistic. . . . There is a growing confidence in South Vietnam. . . . The result will be valuable for the future security of the area. . . . We believe we are on the right track. . . . We hope that we may become more successful.

> — Secretary of State William P. Rogers, speech to Conference for Editors and Broadcasters, January 15, 1970

The U.S. Army will forbid newsmen to speak with American war prisoners when they are released by the Vietcong because some of them have spoken well of their captors, informed military sources said today. Commanders made the decision . . . after three Americans released in November and two in December spoke highly of the enemy. One said he could never fight the Vietcong again. . . . Sources said the Army may make an exception if a former prisoner is found during debriefings to be hostile to his captors. News conferences also may be permitted . . . after a "readjustment" period.

> — *Washington Post*, UPI dispatch from Saigon, January 16, 1970

We're cautiously optimistic. So far, the program has worked out quite well, and we have reason to think that it will continue to work out successfully. But we are a little bit cautious about making predictions. . . . The President . . . has a program and is going to carry it out. . . . We have every reason to think that it will work. . . . I mean that there is no prospect of a negotiated settlement. There is always the possibility of success. . . . South Vietnam is certainly not going to accept a coalition government. . . . We are reasonably satisfied with the progress that has been made these last 12 months. . . . The rate of infiltration is down. So the whole war has changed. . . . It's working. . . . It's quite satisfactory. I think everyone who goes to Vietnam comes back with that conclusion. I haven't talked to anyone recently . . . who hasn't come back with the conclusion that the program is working rather well.

> — Secretary of State William P. Rogers,
> interview, *U.S. News & World Report*,
> January 26, 1970

I have accomplished the objectives I went to Paris to achieve—the beginnings at least of peace in Vietnam.

> — Ambassador R. Sargent Shriver, letter of
> resignation to President Richard M. Nixon,
> January 27, 1970

The enemy has not had much success with his military efforts.

> — Ambassador Ellsworth Bunker, Saigon,
> January 29, 1970

We are moving on schedule on Vietnamization. . . .

> — President Richard M. Nixon,
> news conference, January 30, 1970

The Tet offensive . . . was a disaster, a debacle, and a serious military loss [for the enemy]. I don't think that ever got communicated to the American people.

> — Former President Lyndon B. Johnson,
> televised reminiscences,
> CBS, February 6, 1970

Nothing has happened so far to indicate that Vietnamization will not work, while there is some very limited evidence that it might.

> — Marsh Clark, *Time* Saigon Bureau chief,
> quoted by *Time*, February 9, 1970

There is positive progress in Vietnamization.

> — Secretary of Defense Melvin Laird, to
> newsmen on departure from Vietnam,
> February 13, 1970

The program to neutralize the Vietcong infrastructure in South Vietnam is called Phoenix. . . . Some war critics in the U.S. have attacked Phoenix as an instrument of mass political murder. . . . Phoenix is an offspring of the CIA and because its operations have always been obscured by the cloak of official secrecy, the Foreign Relations Committee may discuss the program in a closed session. But Phoenix's secrets are not well-kept in Vietnam. The . . . program does involve killing.

American statistics on Phoenix results (which are radically more conservative than the Vietnamese figures) show 19,534 . . . "neutralized" during 1969—6,187 of them killed. . . . Phoenix was the idea of the CIA, and until last July it was run by the agency. Phoenix operations conducted by Provincial Reconnaissance Units have involved assassinations. . . . The central government assigns Phoenix quotas to the provinces. Thus a province chief has to report neutralization of a certain number . . . every month to stay in good. "They will meet every quota that's established for them," one American adviser noted. But meeting the quotas often means disregarding any standards.

> — Robert G. Kaiser, Jr.,
> dispatch from Saigon, *Washington Post*,
> February 17, 1970

Over the past two years, there has been a substantial strengthening of all the tools with which the Government and the people of Vietnam are fighting this war, and at the same time there has been a weakening on the Communist side.

> — Ambassador W. E. Colby, deputy to General
> Creighton W. Abrams, Jr., before Senate
> Foreign Relations Committee, February 17,
> 1970

We have been making progress in security. . . . We have had the opportunity to achieve progress. . . . I have become so confident that we are going in the right direction. . . . I had the utmost confidence that [Vietnamization] was the right direction to go in Vietnam. . . . I see a very low probability of the enemy being able to substantially roll back the pacification program that has been achieved. . . . He does not have anywhere near the men to even make a dent in pacification. . . . Right now all expectations are that the current stability will continue.

The American presence today is necessary. . . . The present government is the most efficient government that I have seen in Vietnam since 1962. . . . Most civilian deaths would probably occur in an area where the conflict was going on. . . . SENATOR CASE: [Deleted.] MR. VANN:

[Deleted.] SENATOR CASE: Will you break that down? MR. VANN: [Deleted.] . . . SENATOR FULBRIGHT: Yes. MR. VANN: [Deleted.] SENATOR FULBRIGHT: Three years? MR. VANN: [Deleted.] SENATOR FULBRIGHT: Is it too far to see beyond that? MR. VANN: [Deleted.]

> — John Paul Vann, deputy for CORDS (Civil
> Operations & Rural Development Support
> program), before Senate Foreign Relations
> Committee, February 18, 1970

The solatium payment [compensation to Vietnamese civilians killed by military action] for those over 15 years of age that are killed is 4,000 piasters [about $7.00]. Those under 15 years old is 2,000 piasters [about $3.50]. They do not keep figures on the number of payments that have been made. However, the total payments made last year amounted to 114,713,440 piasters or $972,000.

> — Information supplied Senate Foreign
> Relations Committee by John Paul Vann,
> chief, U.S. pacification program, February 18,
> 1970

. . . Claims of progress in Vietnam have been frequent during the course of our involvement there—and have often proved too optimistic. . . . The American people must have the full truth. . . .

> — President Richard M. Nixon, 1st Annual
> Report to Congress on U.S. Foreign Policy for
> the 1970s, February 18, 1970

The enemy grows weaker as our side grows stronger. . . . President Nixon's Vietnamization plan shows real signs of working.

> — Edmund A. Gullion, dean, Fletcher School of
> Law and Diplomacy, Tufts University, former
> State Department official, former deputy chief,
> American mission in Saigon, member,
> Citizen's Committee for Peace With Freedom
> in Vietnam, *Reader's Digest*, February 1970

SENATOR FULBRIGHT: Did you get the figures on the cost of the training of pilots?

GENERAL CLEMENT [Brig. Gen. Wallace Clement, director, MACV Training Directorate]: Yes, sir . . . the estimated cost . . . for fiscal year 1970 is [Deleted].

FULBRIGHT: [Deleted].

CLEMENT: Yes, sir.

FULBRIGHT: What do you estimate it costs to train one pilot? . . .

CLEMENT: For a UH-1 helicopter pilot [Deleted]. For a jet pilot [Deleted].

FULBRIGHT: . . . Is there any reason why these figures should be . . . secret?

CLEMENT: Sir, these are confidential figures.

FULBRIGHT: Why? . . . Is it simply to keep the American people ignorant of how much the war costs them? . . .

CLEMENT: No, sir.

FULBRIGHT: Then what is the reason? Just give us a good reason.

CLEMENT: I am sure the training costs . . . is a security matter. . . . I really do not know the exact reason . . . but I do understand . . . the security aspects.

FULBRIGHT: Maybe you want to speak for yourself and tell us the reason. Why is the cost of jet pilot training confidential? . . .

MR. KNAUR [Peter R. Knaur, Office of Assistant Secretary of Defense]: Actually, I do not think it is in the general's or my purview to know why. I mean, it is a decision made by the responsible officials.

FULBRIGHT: Who?

KNAUR: This, sir, would fall within the Security Review Branch of the Pentagon.

FULBRIGHT: Why is it that the cost of training a Vietnamese to fly a jet is confidential? I cannot imagine why it should be, other than the fact that you are afraid it might disillusion the Congress and the American people. . . .

SENATOR MANSFIELD: I think I can show stories out of the *U.S. News & World Report*.

KNAUR: The fact that a figure exists in the paper does not declassify it. . . .

FULBRIGHT: [Deleted].

CLEMENT: Yes, sir.

FULBRIGHT: What is 1970?

CLEMENT: [Deleted].

FULBRIGHT: [Deleted].

CLEMENT: Yes, sir.

FULBRIGHT: How is that broken down?

CLEMENT: [Deleted].

FULBRIGHT: [Deleted].

CLEMENT: [Deleted].

FULBRIGHT: [Deleted]. That [Deleted] is a year or is it total? Say 18 months at the outside it costs [Deleted]. Does that not strike you as very expensive?

CLEMENT: Yes, sir; I do think that training is expensive. . . .

FULBRIGHT: And in rough figures how much is that worth?

CLEMENT: About $250,000 per helicopter. . . .

FULBRIGHT: How many helicopters have we lost in Vietnam?
CLEMENT: . . . 1,500, sir.

> — Testimony before Senate Foreign Relations
> Committee, March 3, 1970

Estimated Department of Defense outlays in support of Southeast Asia operations: $104,603,000,000.00.

> — Department of Defense information supplied
> to Senate Foreign Relations Committee,
> March 4, 1970

Vietnam has been good for the Marines, and the Marines have been good for Vietnam.

> — Lieutenant General Herman Nickerson, Jr.,
> U.S. Marine Corps, Danang, South Vietnam,
> March 9, 1970

The nature and diversity of our efforts . . . have been, I think, unprecedented. . . . I think more South Vietnamese . . . have access to a range of producer and consumer goods which have expanded their social and economic horizons. . . . South Vietnam is generously endowed with natural resources. . . . The whole gamut of potential Vietnamese exports in the 1970's is really very favorable. A study completed for AID just last December by David Lilienthal's Development & Resources Corp. suggests potential export earnings in 1980 could be as high as $425,000,000. . . . The Bank of America and Chase Manhattan are doing rather nicely. . . . Our [civilian AID] employment peaked last June at 10,272. . . . Vietnamese, American [at] a 25-percent differential . . . over basic salary. . . . [The] percentage of A.I.D. personnel abroad in Vietnam [is] 40.3 percent. . . . The average wage would be $28,000 to $34,000 total average cost. . . . $67,000 at the highest and $16,000 at the lowest. . . .

SENATOR FULBRIGHT: Do you supply any cover or money to the C.I.A.?

MR. MCDONALD: Mr. Chairman, I have been instructed to say that all comment on such questions must be made in executive session and by other appropriate officials than myself.

> — Donald G. McDonald, director, Agency for
> International Development, Vietnam, before
> Senate Foreign Relations Committee, March
> 17, 1970

The office in Saigon which I head . . . is called the Joint U.S. Public Affairs Office or JUSPAO. This office, which was established in 1965,

includes American military and civilian personnel . . . to provide policy
guidance for all U.S. psychological operations in Vietnam [and] media
materials in support of U.S. policy in Vietnam. . . . American civilian
positions [are] 132; American military positions [are] 118. . . . The . . .
total budget available to me for JUSPAO's operations [are] $10,900,000.
. . . It does not include military salaries. . . . They would be in addition.
. . . [In addition] there are 761 U.S. military psyops field personnel and
50 serving on staff or as advisers to the Vietnamese, for a total of 811.
. . . [Among] the civilian component of JUSPAO there are six people
who speak Vietnamese. . . .

The average pay of a USIA employee with JUSPAO . . . including
allowances, minus housing, would be about $28,900 . . . housing is
furnished. . . . The combination of my salary and allowances, again
making no provision for my housing, is $45,473. . . . I am furnished with
housing [and automobile]. . . . Beginning in 1965, propaganda leaflets
were dropped from aircraft over North Vietnam . . . designed generally
to convince North Vietnam that [they] would fail. . . . At its peak, the
program involved some 25 million leaflets per month. . . . We publish
. . . posters . . . 1.73 million copies . . . 24 million plus . . . maga-
zines, newspapers, and pamphlets . . . somewhere in the vicinity of 1.5
billion [leaflets] primarily distributed by the military.

SENATOR FULBRIGHT: Could you say whether any CIA personnel are
using the USIA as cover?

MR. NICKEL: Comment on such a question must be made in executive
session by other appropriate officials, Mr. Chairman.

> — Edward J. Nickel, Director, Joint U.S. Public
> Affairs Office, Saigon, before Senate Foreign
> Relations Committee, March 19, 1970

I was asked to bring in a body count, not to bring in prisoners. I did
what I felt my superior officers wanted me to do.

> — 1st Lieutenant James B. Duffy, court-martial
> for murder of civilian Vietnamese, quoted by
> *Newsweek*, April 13, 1970

The war is winding down.

> — President Richard M. Nixon, April 29, 1970

An atheist could not be as great a military leader as one who is not an
atheist. I don't think you will find an atheist who has reached the peak in
the Armed Forces.

> — Admiral Thomas H. Moorer, chairman, Joint
> Chiefs of Staff, statement at U.S. District
> Court, Washington, in support of compulsory
> chapel attendance at service academies,
> *Washington Post*, April 29, 1970

To protect our men who are in Vietnam . . . I have concluded that the time has come for action. . . . This is the decision I have made. In cooperation with the armed forces of South Vietnam, attacks are being launched this week to clean out major enemy sanctuaries of the Cambodian-Vietnam border. . . . Tonight American and South Vietnamese units will attack the headquarters for the entire Communist military operation in South Vietnam. . . .

This is not an invasion of Cambodia. The areas in which these attacks will be launched are completely occupied and controlled by North Vietnamese forces. . . . The action I have taken tonight is indispensable for the continuing success of [our] withdrawal program. . . . Tonight I again warn the North Vietnamese that if they continue to escalate the fighting . . . I shall meet my responsibility as Commander in Chief of our Armed Forces to take the action I consider necessary. . . .

We will not be humiliated. We will not be defeated. . . . We live in an age of anarchy, both abroad and at home. We see mindless attacks on all the great institutions which have been created by free civilizations in the last 500 years. . . . If, when the chips are down, the world's most powerful nation, the United States of America, acts like a pitiful, helpless giant, the forces of totalitarianism and anarchy will threaten free nations and free institutions throughout the world. . . . No one is more aware than I am of the political consequences of the action I have taken. . . . I know that a peace of humiliation for the United States would lead to a bigger war or surrender later. . . .

I would rather be a one-term President and do what I believe is right than to be a two-term President at the cost of seeing America become a second-rate power and to see this nation accept the first defeat in its proud 190-year history.

> — President Richard M. Nixon,
> April 30, 1970

It [renewing bombing in North Vietnam] is not a new policy at all. We have before on previous occasions made these attacks when it was necessary to protect reconnaissance flights, part of the arrangement made with North Vietnam when we stopped the bombing.

> — Secretary of State William P. Rogers,
> Washington, May 1, 1970

You know, you see these bums, you know, blowing up the campuses. Listen, the boys on the college campuses today are the luckiest people in the world—going to the greatest universities—and here they are burning up the books. I mean storming around about this issue, I mean you name it, get rid of the war, there'll be another one.

> — President Richard M. Nixon, addressing
> Department of Defense employees, The
> Pentagon, May 1, 1970

They [the enemy] have been in a war for years and years and they're quite debilitated and decimated and I don't think they're capable, with any kind of resistance, to continue this fight.

QUESTION: You mean "light at the end of the tunnel"?

ANSWER: Yes. Exactly.

> — Vice President Spiro T. Agnew,
> *Face the Nation*, CBS, May 3, 1970

We don't intend to become involved militarily in support of any Cambodian government. . . . I'm talking about United States troops, or air support. . . . We have no present plans to embark on that kind of program.

> — Secretary of State William P. Rogers,
> May 13, 1970

The single greatest reason to hope . . . is the vital Mekong River delta, where the Vietcong have been losing the guerrilla war for over a year and may well have lost it entirely by the end of 1970. This remarkable turnabout . . . stems from the fact that the Vietcong are being systematically pushed out of populated regions into the wilderness. . . . The Mekong delta is one of growing stability.

> — Rowland Evans and Robert Novak,
> syndicated column, May 13, 1970

I wish to make it clear that we will not let our hands be bound by anyone any more. . . . Our armed forces have the capability of mounting military operations independently in Cambodia as well as Vietnam. We will continue to maintain our military presence in Cambodia . . . to provide protection for the lives and property of 600,000 resident Vietnamese in Cambodia.

> — Vice President Nguyen Cao Ky,
> May 21, 1970

A dink in the open is fair game.

> — American briefing officer,
> quoted by *New York Times*, May 21, 1970

When the Cambodians can fight the North Vietnamese and Viet Cong by themselves, we will go home.

> — Vice President Nguyen Cao Ky,
> quoted by *Time*, May 25, 1970

The allied drive into Cambodia—after two weeks of operations—is being judged an enormous military success.

> — *U.S. News & World Report*, May 25, 1970

Current actions in Cambodia should be viewed as part of the President's effort to withdraw United States forces from combat in Southeast Asia.

> — John Stevenson, legal adviser, State
> Department, to Hammarskjold Forum, New
> York City Bar Association, May 28, 1970

Everyone can see the fighting spirit of the Vietnamese and their capacities. They are not so weak as rabbits as some people think. I've been around all the corps areas. . . . Everywhere I see big, big spirit. For years our troops have not clearly seen the reason why they could not destroy the enemy. But now they realize that the enemy are Vietnamese just as we are. We can prove to ourselves that we are capable of destroying the enemy. . . . If in a year, there's still a big internal problem, then I don't know whether I will run [for President], but I'll consider it. I must serve my country.

> — Vice President Nguyen Cao Ky,
> interview, *Newsweek*, June 1, 1970

Cambodia has been a bonanza for ARVN. Nothing helps like kicking the hell out of the other guy.

> — Major General Hal D. McCowan, top U.S.
> adviser, delta region, quoted by *Time*, June 8,
> 1970

I love the fight.

> — Lieutenant General Do Cao Tri, commander,
> ARVN "Operation Total Victory," quoted by
> *Time*, June 8, 1970

I like the presence of pretty ladies—aristocratic, high-class ladies. It is one of the reasons why most people are jealous of me. I frequent not low people, but maintain some class in my relations. . . . People are jealous. But my private life has nothing to do with my official life. And if I have the money, I have the right to . . . buy myself a car and have a nice villa.

> — Lieutenant General Do Cao Tri, commander,
> III Corps region around Saigon, later
> commander, South Vietnamese troops,
> Parrot's Beak, Fishhook, quoted by *Newsweek*,
> June 8, 1970

No one can say now we lack fighting spirit.

> — Minister of State Phan Quang Dan,
> quoted by *Newsweek*, June 8, 1970

In the past, foreign investors have been somewhat wary of the over-all political prospect for the [South Asia] region. I must say, though, that the U.S. actions in Vietnam this year . . . have considerably reassured both Asian and Western investors.

> — A vice president, Chase Manhattan Bank, 1965, quoted by *New York Times*, June 20, 1970

This operation in Cambodia has been a tremendous military success. . . . I think this is a big plus. . . . I believe that the military operation in Cambodia will be . . . successful, far beyond the expectations of any of those who planned it. . . . We know the enemy has been hurt and we also know that the South Vietnamese forces have been able to show their strong military capability. . . .

I believe that the progress that the Administration will make in Vietnam will be successful. . . . The economy will be turned around so that there will be optimism. . . . Inflation will be declining. . . . Employment will be going up and unemployment will be going down. . . . You are going to see a growing decline in the rate of inflation.

> — Congressman Gerald R. Ford, Republican of Michigan, House Minority Leader, *Issues & Answers*, ABC, June 22, 1970

The Cambodian operation to date has been analyzed. . . . The statistics are impressive. . . . They leave no doubt that the enemy has been hurt. . . . The sheer magnitude of the impact . . . on the enemy's capability to fight is hard for many to comprehend. . . . Plans are disrupted, units decimated, communications destroyed. . . . Their capabilities as soldiers are seriously impaired. . . . Not even the jungle can hide the facts. Not even the cleverest propaganda from the leaders in Hanoi can minimize the military debacle they have suffered.

> — Colonel William C. Moore, USAF, former member, Strategic Plans Group, Joint Chiefs of Staff, quoted by *U.S. News & World Report*, June 22, 1970

They told me that this place was 90 per cent destroyed. Why, it's not more than 70 per cent destroyed.

> — Robert W. Komer, chief, U.S. pacification, Central Vietnam, after Tet offensive, quoted by Stanley Karnow, *Washington Post*, June 28, 1970

Charlie is on the run everywhere. He's whipped.

> — Colonel William Pietsch, chief military aide, U.S. Diplomatic Mission, Phnom-Penh, Cambodia, quoted by *Newsweek*, June 29, 1970

The morale and self-confidence of the Army of South Vietnam is higher than ever before.

> — President Richard M. Nixon, June 30, 1970

Indiana Republican Rep. Bray, who recently served as one of Nixon's fact-finders in Indochina, claims the big toes of Cambodian soldiers are prehensile, invaluable for climbing trees, so the Cambodians will be good jungle-fighters.

> — *Wall Street Journal*, July 10, 1970

We will have victory in the near future.

> — Premier Lon Nol of Cambodia, Phnom-Penh,
> *Washington Post*, July 15, 1970

We cannot have peace overnight. . . . Peace will come with the strength of our army. . . . I am ready to smash all movements calling for peace at any price because I am still much of a soldier. We will beat to death the people who are demanding immediate peace.

> — President Nguyen Van Thieu, Saigon,
> July 15, 1970

It takes 100,000 bullets, statistically speaking, to kill or maim a Vietcong. This is the conclusion of a classified Defense Department study, which puts the total number of small arms rounds fired in combat each year at 2.5 billion. Bullets cost a nickel to a dime apiece. To gun down a Vietcong with small arms fire, therefore, costs the taxpayers between $5,000 and $10,000.

There are no figures for the estimated 80 percent of all casualties caused by artillery, bombs, mines and other methods of mayhem. The classified study, prepared under contract with Secretary of Defense Melvin Laird's office, relies upon the controversial body counts. . . . Critics say the body counts are too high. If this is true, it takes more than 100,000 bullets to do in a Vietcong.

> — Jack Anderson, syndicated column,
> July 21, 1970

The Senate Thursday passed an amendment to prohibit the United States from paying South Korean and Thai troops serving in Vietnam larger overseas and combat allowances than are paid to American troops. . . . Thai lieutenant generals in Vietnam were paid an overseas allowance of $5,400 a year by the United States while American officers of the same rank get a $780 allowance. A Thai private gets $468 in overseas allowances above his base pay, compared with $96 for an American private.

— *Arkansas Gazette*, dispatch from Washington, August 21, 1970

A Thai lieutenant general in Vietnam . . . receives $5,400 a year in extra pay, while U.S. officers—including generals—receive a uniform $780.

— *Newsweek*, August 31, 1970

By the South Vietnamese estimates and our estimates and also by Cambodian estimates—and they should certainly be in a position to know—somewhere in excess of 50 per cent of all the Viet Cong and North Vietnamese forces in Cambodia have been eliminated.

— Vice President Spiro T. Agnew, aboard Air Force Two en route to Honolulu from Bangkok, August 31, 1970

Vietnamization is working well.

— Vice President Spiro T. Agnew, San Diego, California, September 11, 1970

The U.S. has never sought to widen the war. What we do seek is to widen the peace.

— President Richard M. Nixon, October 7, 1970

We have walked nine-tenths of the road to peace and we are seeing the light at the end of the tunnel.

— President Nguyen Van Thieu, October 31, 1970

Despite the promising progress of the South Vietnamese air force, some U.S. airmen are reluctant to give up an American combat role. "My men grumble that they are frustrated—that there are no good targets left any more," says one U.S. air force wing commander. "But I always remind them of the plight of pilots back in the States. 'Let's face it,' I tell them, 'Viet Nam is the only place in the world today where you can drop real bombs.' "

— *Newsweek*, November 2, 1970

We've got to get the profits up.

— Assistant Secretary of Defense David Packard, November 3, 1970, when average profit on war contracts was running 66.1%

The war will be over by 1972.

> — President Richard M. Nixon,
> quoted by *Time*, November 8, 1970

This was not a failure. . . . These men knew full well the chance that there might not be POWs present. . . . I would like to tell you, Mr. Chairman, that we have made tremendous progress so far as intelligence is concerned.

> — Secretary of Defense Melvin Laird, testimony
> before Senate Foreign Relations Committee
> explaining futile raid into North Vietnam to
> rescue U.S. prisoners not there, November 24,
> 1970

I am not sure I know what you mean by "intelligence failure."

> — Colonel Arthur Simons, U.S. Army, in charge
> of rescue raid on empty POW camp in North
> Vietnam, November 24, 1970

[We now have in the U.S.] a centralized state, far more powerful than anything else, for whom the enemy is not simply the Communists but everything else, its own press, its own judiciary, its own Congress, foreign and friendly governments—all these are potentially antagonistic.

It has survived and perpetuated itself, often using the issue of anti-Communism as a weapon against other branches of government and the press, and finally, it does not necessarily for the benefit of the Republic but rather for its own ends, its own perpetuation; it has its own codes which are quite different from public codes. . . .

> — Neil Sheehan, writing of *Pentagon Papers*

Increasingly, North Vietnam is being beset by low morale, food and manpower shortages, a stagnant economy, corrupt officials and feuding leaders. . . . Clearly, the North Vietnamese people are tired of war. Morale—at home and in the Army—is sagging. . . . Juvenile delinquency is rampant in North Vietnam. Pornography, prostitution and petty theft are problems. A black market thrives, diplomats in Hanoi report. . . . Consumer goods are scarce. Food is rationed. . . . Industry —not yet recovered from three years of U.S. bombing—is hard hit by absenteeism, poor management and . . . "incorrect ideologies." . . .

In some factories, workers put in only four or five hours a day—if they show up for work at all. Quality of goods is poor. . . . American officials cite these examples . . . : The country's only steel mill—wrecked by U.S. bombers—still has not been put back into production. The production of coal, North Vietnam's major export, is far behind 1970 goals mainly because antiquated open-pit mining methods are being used. North Vietnam's collective leadership . . . has been unable to halt the nationwide deterioration.

> — *U.S. News & World Report*, November 30, 1970

The object of our long agony in Vietnam . . . has been achieved . . . victory has at last been won.

> — Stewart Alsop,
> column, *Newsweek*, December 7, 1970

He [Captain Edward Medina, the company commander] ordered the village burned, the animals shot, the wells contaminated and every living thing in that area killed.

> — George W. Latimer, Lieutenant Wm. L.
> Calley's chief defense counsel, in opening
> statement, December 10, 1970, same day
> President Nixon called North Vietnam "an
> international outlaw."

I think President Nixon wants to get out. I would have been proceeding that way, but a little more carefully. We have to be careful not to let Thieu and Ky collapse.

> — Senator Hubert H. Humphrey,
> December 10, 1970

Before the year is over, the outcome in Vietnam will pretty certainly be clearly knowable. There, the outlook is so hopeful that the people who have prated about an "unwinnable war" will be wise to start pondering their explanations after-the-fact.

> — Joseph Alsop,
> syndicated column, January 1, 1971

Somewhere in the continental shelf off the South Vietnamese shore lies hidden one of the most spectacular deposits in the world.

> — *Economic Report*, Saigon, January 1971

Sure, some of the villages get bombed, but there's no other way to fight a war out here, for God's sake. It's a war, and the civilians have to suffer. We did it at Cherbourg, didn't we?

> — L. Hafner, U.S. deputy director, Agency for
> International Development, Laos, January 4,
> 1971

We now see the end. . . . We are on the way out. . . . 1971, in essence, will be a good year. . . . We can now see the end. . . . Our Vietnamization policy has been very carefully drawn up . . . and it is

working. . . . Before we can really get the lift of a driving dream, we
have to get rid of some of the nightmares. . . . One of the nightmares is a
war without end. We are ending that war.

> — President Richard M. Nixon, White House
> "conversation" with representatives of three
> networks and PBS, January 4, 1971

In Cambodia . . . despite setbacks, U.S. military observers in Southeast Asia are not pessimistic about the situation.

> — *Time*, January 4, 1971

Another . . . turning point may be just ahead in Vietnam. . . . To
begin with, the South Vietnamese Army has at last got the number of the
North Vietnamese Army. . . . The Northern troops have either suffered
heavy defeat, or have simply run like rabbits. . . . The Southerners have
been continuously and aggressively tangling with the Northerners. . . .
The results . . . make a great many pompous spouters look exceedingly
silly. . . . It is abundantly clear, moreover, that the South Vietnamese
are only just beginning. . . . The question, then, is whether we
Americans are going to imitate the French.

> — Joseph Alsop,
> syndicated column, January 20, 1971

I don't think Cambodia is deteriorating as much as has been reported.

> — Admiral Thomas Moorer, chairman, Joint
> Chiefs of Staff, Phnom-Penh, quoted by
> *Newsweek*, January 25, 1971

You know, a lot of people ask me how I feel about the Vietnam
conflict. . . . It knocks me out when I see a politician get on television
and say, "We want peace." Who the hell doesn't want peace? But we
want a peace we can be proud of. . . . Ladies and gentlemen, when you
hear politicians running on a peace platform, suspect them! . . . But I
guarantee you we'll be out of this thing. . . . This Administration will
have our kids back by the end of 1971, but I want to tell you one thing:
we're not leaving there in defeat. We haven't made this sacrifice for
naught.

> — Bob Hope, comedian, South Bend, Ind.,
> quoted by *Life*, January 29, 1971

Over the years eight journalists, including myself, have slipped into
Long Cheng and have seen American crews loading T-28 bombers while
armed CIA agents chatted with uniformed Thai soldiers and piles of raw
opium stood for sale in the market (a kilo for $52). It's old hat by now,

but Long Cheng is still so secret that in the past year both the U.S. embassy press attaché and the director of USAID's training center were denied clearance to visit the mountain redoubt. The CIA not only protects the opium in Long Cheng and various other pick-up points, but also gives clearance and protection to opium-laden aircraft flying out.

> — Carl Strock, *Far Eastern Economic Review*,
> January 30, 1971

All refugees talk about the bombing. They don't like [it]. But even if you found an example in which it was proven conclusively that houses were bombed, so what?

> — J. Williamson, chief, USAID Refugee Relief,
> Vientiane, Laos, February 2, 1971

This limited operation is not an enlargement of the war.

> — State Department policy statement, explaining
> South Vietnamese invasion of Laos, February
> 8, 1971

The U.S. should stay in Asia. . . . There is greater support than most newspaper and intellectual comment would indicate. . . . But there are problems: . . . people generally do not understand what we are doing in Vietnam. Almost no one has ever given a reasonable explanation of it. Why? Because it is hard to explain. . . . You see, the U.S. military believe they've basically won the war in Vietnam. I would tend to agree with them.

> — Dr. Herman Kahn, "Foreign-Affairs Expert
> . . . noted strategist," *U.S. News & World
> Report*, February 8, 1971

Richard M. Nixon is beginning to appear as one of our better war presidents.

> — Joseph Alsop,
> syndicated column, February 12, 1971

The President is aware of what is going on in Southeast Asia. That is not to say there is something going on.

> — Ronald L. Ziegler, White House Press
> Secretary, quoted in *Newsweek*, February 15,
> 1971

VIETNAM GI: We're gonna invade Laos.
REPORTER: Where did you hear that?
VIETNAM GI: The mama-san who cleans my hooch told me.

> — *Newsweek*, February 15, 1971

The plan is underway to give the South Vietnamese Air Force an interdiction capability.

> — Secretary of Defense Melvin Laird,
> CBS News Special Report, February 16, 1971

I am not going to place any limitation upon the use of air power. . . . The Laotian operation . . . has gone according to plan. . . . The North Vietnamese have to fight here or give up the struggle. . . . The operation in the Chup Plantation, led by General Tri, is going along in a fashion much better than was expected, with a great number of enemy casualties and, as General Abrams put it, excellent performance. . . . Next year will be a year when the Vietnamization program's very success creates the point of greatest danger.

> — President Richard M. Nixon,
> news conference, Oval Room, White House,
> February 17, 1971

The Vietnam war has been won.

> — Major General George S. Eckhardt,
> commandant, Army War College,
> La Jolla, Calif., February 17, 1971

First you had Asians fighting the French. Then you had Asians fighting the Americans. Now you have Asians fighting Asians.

> — Jean Larteguy, French journalist and guerrilla
> historian (*The Centurions*), after Laotian
> invasion, quoted by *Time*, February 22, 1971

The overall objectives are being accomplished.

> — Congressman Gerald R. Ford,
> Republican of Michigan,
> February 23, 1971

I have been disturbed by reports, usually attributed to a junior officer in the field, that this operation has bogged down.

> — Lieutenant General John W. Vogt, Assistant
> Deputy Chief of Staff, Plans & Operations,
> Pentagon briefing, February 24, 1971

The operation is going according to plan.

> — Secretary of Defense Melvin R. Laird,
> February 24, 1971

Some of the heaviest antiaircraft fire of the war is downing an average of 10 American helicopters a day, pilots here report. . . . To date the U.S. command in Saigon has announced the loss of 29 helicopters in combat since the invasion began Feb. 8–18 in Laos, 11 in South Vietnam. . . . But the command figures do not include helicopters that are shot down and later recovered. Pilots and other military sources believe this category includes a third or more of the estimated fleet of 500-plus helicopters to support the Laos invasion. . . . Pilots earlier this week were ordered not to discuss downed but salvaged helicopters with newsmen.

> — Michael Parks, dispatch from Khe Sanh,
> *Baltimore Sun*, February 25, 1971

The South China Sea is going to be one of the biggest oil production areas in the world in the next few years.

> — Michael B. Morris, vice president, Eastern
> Hemisphere Operations, Continental Oil Co.,
> reported by *Business World*, March 6, 1971

This war is ending. In fact, I seriously doubt if we will ever have another war. This is probably the very last one. . . . I rate myself a deeply committed pacifist.

> — President Richard M. Nixon, interview with
> Cyrus Sulzberger, *New York Times*, March 9,
> 1971

Contrary to reports that you noticed in the last day or so in the papers, this was not a rout—this was an orderly retreat.

> — Vice President Spiro T. Agnew,
> Newton, Massachusetts, March 19, 1971

I found the nation in war. . . . And I have taken the nation quite a way since then. . . .

HOWARD K. SMITH: Sir, the other day, I think, in your press conference, you said that Communist traffic on the Ho Chi Minh trail had been cut by 55 percent. Now the same day the UPI quoted the military command in Saigon as saying it had been only 20 percent, which was quite a drastic difference. Can you match these—

THE PRESIDENT: Oh, yes. The military commander was actually completely correct and so was I. . . . The South Vietnamese have now passed a milestone . . . 18 out of 22 battalions, as General Abrams has pointed out, are doing extremely well and, he says, will come out with greater confidence and greater morale than before. . . . And here I come back to an expert, General Abrams, who tells it like it is and says it like it is. . . . The operation in Laos in this interim period has made considerable progress. . . . The South Vietnamese are achieving the capability of hacking it. . . . Now we are reaching the key point. . . . Let me say I know when we are getting out. We have a plan, it is being implemented. . . . But as far as a deadline is concerned, the next announcement, I am sure, will give some indication as to the end of the tunnel.

> — President Richard M. Nixon,
> interview with Howard K. Smith, ABC-TV,
> March 22, 1971

We cannot judge it [the Laos campaign] before it is concluded, and we cannot judge it after it is concluded.

> — President Richard M. Nixon,
> quoted in *Newsweek*, March 29, 1971

"Look at it this way," a doubtful American officer said. "The Vietnamese said they have killed nearly 14,000 Communists in Laos. If you figure that at least two are wounded for every soldier killed, that means at least 42,000 Communists were put out of action. Since there were supposed to be only 30,000 Communists in the area in Laos, they are now minus 12,000. Now the command says we killed something like 15,000 trucks along the trail since the dry season began in October," he continued. "They had only about 12,000, so again Hanoi is short, this time about 3,000 trucks. So, if they are minus 9,000 men and 3,000 trucks, it's a wonder they can still keep going."

> — Alvin Schuster, dispatch from Saigon,
> *New York Times*, April 1, 1971

The disruption of enemy supply lines, the consumption of ammunition and arms in the battle has been even more damaging to the capability of the North Vietnamese to sustain major offensives in South Vietnam than were the operations in Cambodia ten months ago. Consequently tonight I can report that Vietnamization has succeeded. . . . The American involvement in Vietnam is coming to an end.

> — President Richard M. Nixon,
> Address to the Nation, April 7, 1971

As long as the South Vietnamese have not yet developed the capacity to defend themselves, to take over from us the defense of their own country, a capacity that they rapidly are developing, we will have forces there. . . . We have some cards to play, too. . . .

> — President Richard M. Nixon, interviewed at
> annual dinner, American Society of
> Newspaper Editors, April 16, 1971

The Vietnamization plan is not completed yet. . . . It would take 15 or 20 more years before South Vietnam is capable of defending itself.

> — Vice President Nguyen Cao Ky,
> Saigon, April 18, 1971

I inherited this war. . . . Progress is being made.

> — President Richard M. Nixon,
> news conference, April 29, 1971

The war situation is serious but not desperate.

> — Vice President Nguyen Cao Ky,
> quoted in *Washington Post*, May 1, 1971

McGovern is a secret agent of international Communism. The day he comes here, I will kick him out personally. He has no proof that I am involved in smuggling, but we all have the proof that he is a Communist.

> — Vice President Nguyen Cao Ky,
> impromptu press conference, Saigon,
> quoted by *Newsweek*, May 3, 1971

In 1954 North Vietnam's top general, Vo Nguyen Giap, defeated the French at Dienbienphu, thereby establishing his reputation as a "military superman." . . . In fact, the record shows his over-all performance has been so poor that one wonders why he has not been fired. . . . In early 1968, Giap ordered the big Tet offensive. . . . In the final analysis, Tet was a serious tactical mistake and a strategic disaster. . . . The incursions into Cambodia by U.S. and South Vietnamese forces during May and June of 1970 smashed Giap's favorable position. . . . Leaders in Hanoi no doubt realize the full strategic significance of Giap's failures. . . . Positions they once enjoyed have been eroded badly, while Allied positions have improved markedly. . . . Clearly, Giap's military image is tarnished, and his chances to brighten his reputation do not appear promising.

> — Colonel William C. Moore, former planner,
> U.S. headquarters, Pacific, Strategic Plans
> Group, Joint Chiefs of Staff (USAF); *U.S.
> News & World Report*, May 3, 1971

South Vietnam is like a sinking boat . . . the people have lost faith in the Government. . . . Corruption is rampaging . . . officials have a price list for every transaction. . . . Jungle law rules in all government echelons. Corruption has become open, public . . . not only are the people writhing under social injustices, but they are also becoming more and more miserable because of the harsh economic measures decreed in the name of national necessity . . . with the people . . . near starvation

. . . while powerful and rich people continue to evade taxes and corruption continues to spread. . . .

A new class of profiteers has emerged, made up of those in positions of power and authority. . . . These people have been able to achieve for themselves a life of luxury, while other people are living in misery . . . our soldiers . . . are being given the lowest standard of living . . . war widows . . . have to take up indecent professions to live . . . honest civil servants are a forgotten class. The peasantry, which makes up the greater part of our society . . . are still being exploited by intermediaries. With the support of some people in power, rice dealers are free to exploit both peasants and consumers . . . the poor are still paying more taxes than the rich, as shown in the national budget documents.

> — Vice President Nguyen Cao Ky, speech,
> School of Social Welfare, Saigon, translated
> from Vietnamese by Saigon Bureau, *New York
> Times*; *Ibid.*, May 17, 1971

If it turns out that we can achieve our objectives in Vietnam, and I think that there is still a good chance that they [the South Vietnamese] can stand on their own feet . . . then on balance it [the Vietnam War] may turn out to be a good thing. . . . The Army is fighting effectively today in Vietnam.

> — Secretary of the Army Stanley Resor,
> news conference as outgoing secretary,
> The Pentagon, May 22, 1971

The Government of South Vietnam has progressed.

> — H. R. Rainwater, commander in chief,
> Veterans of Foreign Wars, to Senate Foreign
> Relations Committee, May 27, 1971

If a great war does break out, I implore all the supernatural spirits of the New Year to protect the Cambodian people.

> — Premier Lon Nol of Cambodia, April 1971,
> quoted in *Washington Post*, May 28, 1971

The Government's control of the Delta population has gone from less than three million in 1968 to 5.8 million today. In all, the Delta has 6.2 million people . . . the enemy [is] recognizing that military victory is not going to be achieved. . . . Actually, the whole nature of the war has changed. . . . I frankly anticipate that the Government is going to be successful. . . .

> — John Paul Vann, U.S. civilian director,
> Vietnam's 2nd Military Region, former Army
> officer, AID official, and until May 16 head of
> pacification program in Mekong River Delta;
> *U.S. News & World Report*, May 31, 1971

I think of the people—and the war has been going on a long
time—they are tired of the war. We are an impatient people. We like to
get results.

> — President Richard M. Nixon,
> news conference, June 1, 1971

We know the President has a program. He is going to follow it. . . .
We're getting out of Vietnam.

> — Secretary of State William P. Rogers,
> June 15, 1971

Now it is North Vietnam whose human and material resources are
strained to the breaking point.

> — *National Review*, June 29, 1971

Mr. Nixon is optimistic and I think that optimism is well founded.

> — Speaker of the House Carl Albert,
> Democrat of Oklahoma, July 2, 1971

I personally, I think, underestimated the persistence and the tenacity
of the North Vietnamese. . . . My generation has become old and tired.
. . . What I almost feel now is that this is another day. Perhaps in this
sort of thing the world has passed me by.

> — Former Secretary of State Dean Rusk, Today
> Show, NBC, interview, *Athens* (Ga.) *Daily
> News*, July 2, 1971

I have nothing new to say on Vietnam. . . . But that does indicate the
winding down of the war.

> — President Richard M. Nixon,
> remarks, July 6, 1971

I think when we get perspective the performance of the South
Vietnamese will appear remarkable. . . . There was the Tet attack. It was
clearly a major military failure on the part of the North Vietnamese. It
was clearly a major political failure. . . .
I suppose I was . . . a planner [of the war]. . . . If we walk away from
Asia now—the consequences will not be peace, the consequences will
be—larger war. . . . The pain was worth taking. . . . They have not won.
We don't know the answer in Vietnam. And in Asia . . . that is a very
different Asia we have now. . . . [Bombing] was effective to a degree.
. . . I think it reduced the flow of men and supplies. . . . I don't believe
it induced unity in North Vietnam. . . . I have greatly enjoyed the

academic environment. . . . I think I have come to be taken for what I am, a rather old teacher.

> — Dr. Walt W. Rostow, *Issues & Answers*, ABC,
> July 11, 1971

Agents fingered villages and villagers for extinction, the former by B-52 strikes and artillery fire, the latter by death, often after torture. A major at the Central Intelligence Agency operation headquarters in Da Nang . . . was the coordinator for the Phoenix program, a grisly operation which the House Subcommittee on Foreign Government Operations is desperately trying to uncover and stop. According to Ambassador William J. Colby, until recently in charge of the parent program, the Civil Operations and Rural Development and Support, run jointly by the U.S. and South Vietnam, the purpose of the exercise is "to provide permanent protection" for the villagers.

Permanent protection of a sort has been conferred on 20,578 Vietnamese. At least it is permanent. 20,578 have been killed under the program. . . . One is reminded of the official report of My Lai—in which it was recounted that the "civilians had been assisted to safety." . . . Phoenix is nothing but "a sterile, depersonalized murder program."

> — Mary McGrory, *Washington Evening Star*,
> August 3, 1971

The enemy doesn't have the punch that it had.

> — President Richard M. Nixon,
> news conference, August 4, 1971

As far as South Vietnam is concerned, its democratic processes . . . we believe that considerable headway has been made. We believe that the situation from that standpoint is infinitely better.

> — President Richard M. Nixon,
> news conference, September 16, 1971

President Nguyen Van Thieu has won his uncontested election to a second term. . . . In the unofficial results, Thieu won 94.3 per cent of the votes cast with 5.7 per cent against him, AP reported. . . .

> — *Washington Post*, dispatch from Saigon,
> October 4, 1971

I will have another announcement on Vietnam in November. . . . I will not speculate further on that. . . . I would strongly urge the members of the press not to speculate as to what I am going to say in

November. . . . The situation in South Vietnam has been that they have made great progress toward representative government there.

> — President Richard M. Nixon,
> news conference, October 12, 1971

Should we vainly play the game of democracy and freedom which will lead us to complete defeat, or should we curtail anarchical freedom in order to achieve victory. The government has made its decision. We have selected the way that will bring us to victory. . . . Democracy is a sterile game.

> — Prime Minister Lon Nol of Cambodia, radio
> address announcing establishment of military
> dictatorship, Phnom-Penh, October 20, 1971

No President ever escalated enough to satisfy the military, who always complained about civilian restrictions on military actions and kept insisting that they be allowed to bomb, shoot, and drown more and more Vietnamese.

> — Arthur M. Schlesinger, Jr., "Eyeless in
> Indochina," *New York Review of Books*,
> October 21, 1971

The Vietcong weakness in the countryside is grave already. It is increasing rapidly as well.

> — Joseph Alsop, syndicated column,
> October 22, 1971

There are more three and four star generals and admirals in uniform today than there were at the height of World War II . . . we have 190 more Generals and Admirals today than we had at the height of the Korean War.

> — House Appropriations Committee on 1972
> Defense Budget, quoted by *I. F. Stone's
> Bi-Weekly*, November 29, 1971

The town is destroyed. But you have to expect that.

> — Lon Non, younger brother of Lon Nol,
> commenting on use of air power to retake
> Cambodian town, December 12, 1971

Both Ford and American Motors plan joint ventures with local entrepreneurs to build assembly plants near Saigon. Some 18 oil companies are interested in exploration concessions off the Vietnamese coast, and several electronic concerns, including Chicago's Admiral

Corp., have had representatives in Saigon checking the market. . . .
American businessmen . . . see considerable advantage—both short-
and long-term—to be gained from Thieu's recently announced economic
reforms. . . . Last month's devaluation of the piaster . . . is to give U.S.
companies an edge over international competitors in selling to the
Vietnamese market.

> — *Business Week*, December 25, 1971

The issue of Viet Nam will not be an issue in the campaign, as far as
this Administration is concerned, because we will have brought the
American involvement to an end. . . . Ending the war in Viet Nam is
inevitable.

> — President Richard M. Nixon,
> interview, *Time*, January 3, 1972

Had I been elected, we would now be out of that war.

> — Senator Hubert H. Humphrey, announcing
> presidential candidacy, Philadelphia,
> January 10, 1972

The great advantage of secret negotiations is that you can leapfrog
public positions. . . . The reason why North Vietnam . . . won't
negotiate . . . is that their military prospects are unfavorable. . . . We
can contain them.

> — Dr. Henry Kissinger, White House briefing,
> January 26, 1972

Personally, I would expect the probable gains of victory to exceed its
anticipated costs by a substantial margin. . . . But even in victory we
cannot completely redeem the unheroic image created by many aspects
of our behavior in the course of the conflict. . . . A proper concept of
limited war is one in which the objectives are limited to something less
than total destruction of the enemy. . . .

The effort to split and defeat us is now in progress . . . with the abuse
of . . . freedom of press, speech and dissent. To cope with it, we need a
new concept of national security broad enough to assure that defensive
measures are taken against subversion in this form. Surely the defense of
our national unity merits a dedication of effort at least equal to that
which we have lavished in the past on the protection of our overseas
possessions.

> — General Maxwell D. Taylor, memoirs, *Swords
> and Plowshares*

. . . South Vietnam has made remarkable progress. . . . The Constitution is proving effective. . . . A consistent political evolution has taken
place. . . . The South Vietnamese presidential election in October 1971

we hoped . . . would be vigorously contested. . . . We were disappointed that the election was uncontested; but . . . others believed that opponents deliberately chose to embarrass President Thieu rather than contest an election they expected to lose. . . .

The achievements in 1971 were especially striking. . . . It is a courageous undertaking to move forward rapidly. . . . The Vietnamese look to their friends to assist them. . . . The unwise Congressional reduction of foreign assistance funds has hampered this effort. . . . South Vietnam will continue to need substantial U.S. support. . . . We must not expect instantaneous results, however.

> — President Richard M. Nixon, 3rd Annual
> Report on the State of U.S. Foreign Policy,
> February 9, 1972

Hanoi [is in an] unfavorable situation in a war they have all but lost. . . . The Thieu government is stronger in the rural areas . . . than ever before. . . . The ARVN, Air Force and Navy are gaining strength and capability every day. . . . Communist diplomats are trying desperately to win back in conference a war they have irretrievably lost on the ground.

> — Colonel Robert D. Heinl, Jr., North American
> Newspaper Alliance columnist, *Armed Forces
> Journal*, March 1972

The United States Navy has removed a secret team of warrior porpoises from Vietnam. . . . The six porpoises and their trainers had the job of guarding the harbor of the Cam Ranh Bay Air Base from Communist frogmen. Weapons were attached to their snouts. . . . Although their presence was known throughout the country, the Navy refused to answer questions about the porpoises. A Navy spokesman issued a brief communiqué Saturday saying only: "The collection of research data scheduled for the Republic of Vietnam concerning surveillance capabilities of porpoises was completed in late 1971 and the porpoises have been withdrawn. Further details are not available." . . . The sources said an assortment of different weapons, one representing a switchblade knife, were attached to the snouts of the porpoises.

> — UPI dispatch from Saigon, March 18, 1972

This is no time to push the panic button.

> — Editorial, *Washington Star*,
> April 4, 1972

I think the President is doing the right thing.

> — Senator Hubert H. Humphrey, commenting on
> resumption of bombing, Today Show, NBC,
> April 4, 1972

We have stopped them now.

> — Lieutenant General Hoang Xuan Lam, South
> Vietnamese commander, northern front; AP
> dispatch from Saigon, April 4, 1972

It is very difficult to evaluate at this point.

> — Admiral Thomas H. Moorer, chairman, Joint
> Chiefs of Staff, to Armed Forces Policy
> Council, April 4, 1972

There is considerable confidence in the inner circle here, reflecting confidence in Saigon.

> — Joseph Alsop, syndicated column,
> April 5, 1972

By and large, the South Vietnamese have fought well under the circumstances.

> — Admiral Thomas H. Moorer, April 6, 1972

I believe history will record our involvement in Vietnam as a very worthwhile and moral accomplishment, perhaps the most moral act that the United States ever performed.

> — Vice President Spiro T. Agnew, speech to 101st
> Airborne Division, Fort Campbell, Ky.,
> April 6, 1972

I served as a member of the administration that was involved in the escalation of this war in Southeast Asia. I heard every argument that has been said here today, every one. I want to tell you something. . . . Let me tell you . . . I heard it often, and I believed it. And quite frankly, in retrospect, what I heard did not make much sense, and in retrospect what I believed did not make much sense.

> — Senator Hubert H. Humphrey,
> speech in Senate, April 7, 1972

The Viet Cong are a declining force, pushed back into a few sanctuaries or mountain or marsh.

> — *London Economist*, April 8, 1972

The South Vietnamese are doing very well. . . . I think they are going to succeed.

> — Secretary of Defense Melvin Laird,
> April 10, 1972

I feel very comfortable about the situation. I think the situation is stable.

> — Congressman F. Edward Hébert, Democrat of
> Louisiana, chairman, House Armed Services
> Committee, April 11, 1972

The South Vietnamese are fighting very well.

> — Admiral Thomas H. Moorer to House Armed
> Services Committee, April 11, 1972

The South Vietnamese forces are doing very well . . . inflicting heavy casualties.

> — Jerry W. Friedheim, Defense Department
> spokesman, April 11, 1972

The ARVN forces have been giving a good account of themselves.

> — Robert J. McCloskey, State Department
> spokesman, April 11, 1972

Hell yes, I'm optimistic, we're killing him [the enemy] and that's what makes me happy.

> — Major General James Hollingsworth, senior
> American adviser for provinces around
> Saigon; Binhlong, quoted by Peter Osnos,
> *Washington Post*, April 12, 1972

We still feel that the South Vietnamese are doing well.

> — Jerry W. Friedheim, Defense Department
> spokesman, The Pentagon, April 12, 1972

The events of the last few days have proven the triumphant success of President Nixon's Vietnamization program. Vietnamization's success, of course, may not be enough to prevent the South Vietnamese army's defeat. . . . The Vietnamization program must now be counted a remarkable success, however the fighting comes out between the South and North Vietnamese armies.

> — Joseph Alsop, syndicated column, April 12,
> 1972

The offensive has failed.

> — General Hoang Xuan Lam of South Vietnam,
> April 10, 1972, quoted by *Washington Post*,
> April 12, 1972

They have got a lot of casualties. But no one cares about casualties now. Neither do I.

> — Lieutenant General Nguyen Van Minh,
> commander, South Vietnamese forces in
> provinces around Saigon, *Washington Post*,
> April 13, 1972

American B-52 bombers are now flying 1,800 sorties a month against targets in Indochina.

> — *Washington Evening Star*, April 13, 1972

Thousands of North Vietnamese troops stormed An Loc with tanks at dawn today and by late afternoon had taken half of the provincial capital 60 miles north of Saigon.

> — *Washington Evening Star*, dispatch from
> Saigon, April 13, 1972

The Army has "bottomed out" of its problems. . . . We're on our way up . . . the pendulum is beginning to swing.

> — General William C. Westmoreland, quoted by
> the Washington *Sunday Star*, April 16, 1972

This is the final battle.

> — President Nugyen Van Thieu, quoted in
> *Newsweek*, April 17, 1972

For a long time the North Vietnamese have been able to peddle, to sell a cruel hoax to a segment of the American people that somehow the war in Vietnam was a civil uprising. . . . The South Vietnamese forces have been acting courageously. . . . Now it's quite a different war we're fighting. . . . These attacks will . . . result in a failure of these offensives. . . .

The South Vietnamese . . . have been fighting well. They fought very courageously. . . . We can't now just turn tail and leave our friend and ally alone. . . . I think Vietnamization is working. . . . We are encouraged. They have about nothing left. . . . Do we think the South Vietnamese have the will to fight? . . . Of course, you never know for sure until they try it. . . .

> — Secretary of State William P. Rogers,
> testimony before Senate Foreign Relations
> Committee, April 17, 1972

I'm satisfied they [the North Vietnamese] are going to lose.

> — Senator George Aiken, Republican of
> Vermont, April 17, 1972

Reflecting the cynical view of more than a few American G.I.s . . .
one U.S. military adviser last week complained: "The colors in the South
Vietnamese flag are certainly appropriate—most of the people are
yellow, and the rest are Red."

— *Time*, April 17, 1972

I believe success is assured. . . . We have a plan. We have a program.
. . . We do not plan on failure. We plan on success.

— Secretary of Defense Melvin Laird
to Senate Foreign Relations Committee,
April 18, 1972

The antiwar activists in America do not realize what the Vietnam war
really means.

— David Lawrence, column, *U.S. News & World
Report*, April 24, 1972

Their attack is a proof that the war—the counterinsurgency war—has
succeeded, because they have abandoned this type of warfare and gone
to a purely conventional thrust, a thrust which is being defeated overall,
a thrust which will be defeated, and one which . . . will have proved to
be a strategic blunder, as was the Tet offensive of 1968.

— John Paul Vann, chief U.S. civilian adviser,
3rd highest-ranking official in Vietnam, ABC
Evening News, April 25, 1972

Gen. Abrams predicts in this report that there will be several more
weeks of very hard fighting in which some battles will be lost and others
will be won by the South Vietnamese.

— President Richard M. Nixon, April 26, 1972

There is no mistaking Hanoi's heavy defeat if you spend three days
. . . talking to commanders. . . . The South Vietnamese have been
moving forward. . . . The biggest single battle of the present fighting has
been, on balance, a solid, deeply reassuring success for the South
Vietnamese army. . . . ARVN has won the big one.

— Joseph Alsop, syndicated column,
April 26, 1972

Last week, by U.S. estimate, the total count of the military dead in
Viet Nam since 1961 passed 1,000,000. . . . U.S. bombers pounded the
North again. . . . "The North Vietnamese," said Secretary of State
William Rogers, "are the culprits in this."

— *Time*, May 1, 1972

Time is on our side. . . . The military situation is going to get better.

> — Congressman Gerald R. Ford, Republican of
> Michigan, House Minority Leader, after
> briefing by Admiral Thomas H. Moorer, May
> 3, 1972

The Communists will very likely lose a great deal.

> — Senator John Tower, Republican of Texas,
> quoted in *New York Times*, May 3, 1972

It is easy—and pretty shameful—to overstress . . . ARVN failures.
. . . Only fools expect that nothing will go badly. . . . To all appearances, at the moment, the position in the Northern provinces has
suddenly taken a very bad turn for the worse.

> — Joseph Alsop, syndicated column,
> May 3, 1972

Evidence grows every day that U.S. intelligence grossly underestimated both Hanoi's resources and its goals in the invasion of South
Vietnam.

> — Rowland Evans and Robert Novak,
> syndicated column, May 3, 1972

We are not defeated yet. We need people to fight. I like to fight. I've
been fighting for 23 years.

> — General Hoang Xuan Lam, South Vietnamese
> commander, Northern Military Region,
> Saigon, May 4, 1972

Maybe we don't have enough imagination.

> — Dr. Henry Kissinger, press conference,
> May 9, 1972

President Nixon announced tonight that he had ordered the mining of
all North Vietnamese ports.

> — *New York Times*,
> dispatch from Washington, May 9, 1972

Hanoi's losses have already been horrendous.

> — Joseph Alsop, syndicated column,
> May 10, 1972

I promise our armed forces will destroy the enemy. . . . The
Communists are strong temporarily, not forever. The few commanders

who have shown defeatist spirit will be punished severely. . . . This is
not a time for normal politics. We must all work to save the country.

> — President Nugyen Van Thieu,
> quoted by *Washington Post*, May 10, 1972

The Saigon Government today ordered an immediate change in the
military command in the Central Highlands, where enemy pressure has
been steadily mounting. Lieut. Gen. Ngo Dzu was relieved of his
command of the area, Military Region II. . . . He was replaced by Maj.
Gen. Nguyen Van Toan. . . . John Paul Vann, the senior U.S. adviser,
said he believed the change had come about because of pressure on the
President. . . . Mr. Vann . . . said of General Toan, "He'll either be
better or worse than General Dzu, or maybe similar."

> — Dispatch from Pleiku, South Vietnam,
> May 10, 1972

It [mining Haiphong] probably is going to be a turning point in the
war.

> — Secretary of State William P. Rogers,
> before Proxmire subcommittee, May 15, 1972

We are coming out of the woods. . . . There has been a turnabout in
South Vietnamese morale. They feel they have turned the corner and are
on the way back. . . . Basically the trend will be towards success. . . .
There has been a great deterioration in morale in Hanoi in recent weeks.

> — Vice President Spiro T. Agnew to reporters,
> May 19, 1972

Results on the battlefield have been encouraging.

> — Secretary of State William P. Rogers,
> press conference, May 19, 1972

Now there are almost no Vietcong.

> — Joseph Alsop, syndicated column,
> May 22, 1972

The Vietnam War itself is going to be determined on the battlefields.

> — *U.S. News & World Report*, May 22, 1972

We've got 'em beaten now. . . . They're beaten. They've failed.

> — General Creighton W. Abrams, Jr., U.S.
> commander, Vietnam, May 28, 1972

The outlook in the South no longer is so grim.

> — *U.S. News & World Report*, May 29, 1972

Vietnamization is astonishingly successful.

> — Secretary of Defense Melvin Laird,
> June 5, 1972

The winds of peace are stirring.

> — Secretary of Defense Melvin Laird,
> address at Naval Academy, Annapolis,
> June 7, 1972

I expect to succeed. . . . I expect to defeat—I expect the Vietnamese to defeat—the North Vietnamese force. I have predicted success since December.

> — John Paul Vann, chief American civilian
> adviser, Pleiku, June 7, 1972, quoted by
> Laurence Stern, *Washington Post*, June 8, 1972

The enemy is hurting.

> — Lieutenant General George J. Eade, head, Air
> Force planning office, Pentagon briefing,
> June 8, 1972

The South Vietnamese are more than holding their own.

> — Richard Valeriani, NBC Evening News,
> June 9, 1972

The situation . . . is improving. . . . American advisers are more confident than ever before.

> — Robert Wiener, ABC-TV News, June 9, 1972

The war in South Vietnam is going better than seemed probable or even possible a month ago. . . . The overall judgment is that the military capability of the North Vietnamese is likely to diminish rapidly from here on.

> — Crosby S. Noyes, column, *Washington Star*,
> June 11, 1972

Hanoi's great offensive in South Vietnam is an unqualified disaster. . . . North Vietnam's alleged human sea of manpower reserves is in fact a nearly empty barrel. . . . When experience shows that experts are total duds, they should be traded in.

> — Joseph Alsop, syndicated column,
> June 14, 1972

U.S. fighter-bombers pounded North Vietnam with a record number of raids . . . 340 raids Tuesday. . . .

> — *Washington Post*, AP dispatch from Saigon, June 15, 1972

Our forces not only have the ability to stand fast, but to fight back.

> — Bui Diem, South Vietnamese Ambassador, June 16, 1972

The enemy is beating himself to death. . . . I now have absolute certainty that [the Hanoi leaders] have committed a blunder equal to or greater than that of Tet '68. . . . The enemy has had it. . . . I would think the enemy is aware of their total disaster.

> — John Paul Vann, last letter written to Joseph Alsop before his death, quoted by Alsop, syndicated column, June 16, 1972

There is an atmosphere of confidence throughout the country now.

> — *London Economist*, June 24, 1972

A very special challenge was that of Vietnam. We have met that challenge successfully. . . . We are coming out of Vietnam. . . . Militarily and politically, Hanoi is losing. . . . Looking back over this nation's record in the field of foreign policy, Americans have a right to feel proud.

> — President Richard M. Nixon, quoted in *U.S. News & World Report*, June 26, 1972

If I were in Hanoi, I wouldn't negotiate. Why should I?

> — Dean Rusk, former secretary of state, to House Foreign Affairs Subcommittee, June 28, 1972

In order to save Hué we have to take Quangtri, and in order to save Quangtri they have to take Hué.

> — Top aide to President Nguyen Van Thieu, quoted by *Washington Post*, June 28, 1972

The war should end soon.

> — Ambassador Ellsworth Bunker, quoted by *New York Times*, June 29, 1972

The United States has been secretly seeding clouds over North Vietnam, Laos and South Vietnam to increase and control the rainfall for military purposes. . . . The disclosure confirmed growing speculation in Congressional and scientific circles about the use of weather modification in Southeast Asia . . . scientists are not sure they understand its long-term effect on the ecology of a region.

> — *New York Times*, dispatch from Washington,
> July 3, 1972

The resumed Paris talks will lead to the ending of the war before the presidential election in November.

> — Victor Zorza, *Washington Post*,
> July 12, 1972

I have no comment on where Henry Kissinger is, period.

> — White House Press Secretary Ronald L.
> Ziegler, July 18, 1972

Senate Republican leader Hugh Scott will nominate President Nixon for the Nobel peace prize to be awarded next winter, Scott's office said yesterday. . . . The nomination must be submitted to Stockholm by Feb. 1.

> — *Washington Post*, UPI dispatch, July 19, 1972

Muted optimism at the highest levels here about a Vietnam settlement is based on the hard conviction that a massive Communist offensive against Hué, expected soon, will be crushed before October. . . . Hanoi is believed to have scraped the bottom of its manpower barrel.

> — Rowland Evans and Robert Novak,
> syndicated column, *Washington Post*,
> July 28, 1972

I think that either we will have a negotiated settlement before the election . . . or we will have one very soon after.

> — Secretary of State William P. Rogers,
> interview, Knight newspapers,
> August 16, 1972

The enemy initiatives have dropped off. They've taken very severe local defeats. ARVN morale is on the rise, and at this juncture they're as strong if not stronger than before they were attacked. I would see an improving situation for the South Vietnamese.

> — General Alexander Haig, national security
> affairs adviser to Dr. Henry Kissinger,
> interviewed by Lloyd Shearer, *Parade*,
> August 20, 1972

The current North Vietnamese offensive in South Vietnam is proving as costly and terrible a failure as the Tet offensive of 1968

> — Joseph Alsop, syndicated column,
> September 1, 1972

North Vietnam is hurting.

> — *U.S. News & World Report*, September 4, 1972

I would be willing to die to defend the South Vietnamese.

> — Mrs. Pat Nixon, news conference,
> Chicago, September 18, 1972

The northern high command faces a bleak prospect. To be specific, the North Vietnamese forces have now disastrously failed.

> — Joseph Alsop, syndicated column,
> September 18, 1972

The influential . . . Vatican newspaper . . . *L'Osservatore Romano* is . . . broadening the area . . . for pointed editorial comment. *L'Osservatore* . . . recently carried an editorial declaring that Sen. George S. McGovern's presidential campaign was helping North Vietnam and the Vietcong. . . . Since the editorial was signed by Frederico Alessandrini, the Vatican press spokesman, it was taken to represent a certain coolness toward McGovern on the part of the highest levels of the Vatican.

> — William Tuohy, dispatch from Vatican City,
> *Washington Post*, September 20, 1972

We have made so much progress.

> — President Richard M. Nixon,
> Atlanta, October 12, 1972

Peace is at hand. . . . We are confident.

> — Dr. Henry Kissinger, announcing a proposed
> 9-point cease-fire, Washington, October 26,
> 1972

Peace is within reach. . . . I am confident we will succeed in achieving our objective.

> — President Richard M. Nixon,
> Washington, October 26, 1972

There is every chance of a cease-fire by November 7.

> — Victor Zorza, *Washington Post*,
> October 27, 1972

We are on the eve of a cease-fire.

> — Prince Souvanna Phouma, Premier of Laos,
> Vientiane, October 27, 1972

A cease-fire can come only when I myself take a pen and sign the agreement.

— President Nguyen Van Thieu, Saigon,
October 27, 1972

The movement toward peace in a land weary of war is irreversible.

— Marquis Childs, syndicated column,
October 31, 1972

SAIGON—South Vietnam intensified its propaganda campaign against a cease-fire. . . . A team of 56 psychological warfare officers spread through Saigon to "explain" . . . the arguments raised by President Thieu.

— *Washington Post*, October 31, 1972

Hanoi has accepted near-total defeat. . . . Anyone with practical common sense should be able to see . . . Hanoi's acceptance of near-total defeat. . . . The numerous American politicians and thinkers who endlessly said . . . we could never get an honorable settlement . . . look pretty silly.

— Joseph Alsop, syndicated column,
November 1, 1972

President Nixon reiterated yesterday that the United States would not be rushed into an agreement . . . presidential press secretary Ronald L. Ziegler told reporters.

— *Washington Post*, November 1, 1972

We have reached a substantial agreement.

— President Richard M. Nixon,
nationwide TV address, November 3, 1972

The North Vietnamese . . . were being hurt very badly. . . . I don't think they could achieve any real military victory of great significance.

— Patrick J. Honey, Asian expert, in charge of
North Vietnamese studies at London
University, interviewed in London by *U.S.
News & World Report*, November 6, 1972

An honorable, even a successful settlement of the Vietnamese war at last seems to be within reach. . . . A whole new structure of primary world relationships . . . gives wholly new hope for the world's future. And it could never have happened without Vietnam.

— Joseph Alsop, syndicated column,
November 15, 1972

Vo Tanh Vinh, the deputy chief of Binhlong Province, said today the government has agreed to compensate families of civilians killed or wounded in fighting at Anloc, a provincial capital 60 miles north of Saigon. Government sources quoted Vinh as saying the government would pay families 6,000 piasters (about $13) for each adult killed; 3,000 piasters ($6.50) for each child killed.

> — *Washington Post*, dispatch from Saigon,
> Nov. 17, 1972

We are proceeding with a constructive attitude. . . . President Nixon is confident.

> — Ronald L. Ziegler, White House press
> secretary, November 26, 1972

Nixon has become one of the great peacemakers in history.

> — Dr. Norman Vincent Peale, pastor,
> Marble Collegiate Church, New York City,
> November 26, 1972

The Pentagon [announced that] more North Vietnamese and Vietcong soldiers have been killed in 1972 than in any year since 1969.

> — *Washington Post*, November 28, 1972

I don't think we should pull the rug out from under him [President Nixon].

> — Speaker of the House Carl Albert, Democrat
> of Oklahoma, December 27, 1972

The U.S. Command reported Wednesday that American warplanes made almost 1,500 strikes. . . .

> — *Washington Post*, dispatch from Saigon,
> December 28, 1972

Mademoiselle, I am not so mysterious as many believe. On the contrary, I'm a very open man. I hide nothing . . . and I don't listen to those who advise me. . . .

I have to recall that I represent South Vietnam. As President Thieu I cannot afford the luxury of being an open enemy of the United States. . . . The Americans say there are 145,000 North Vietnamese troops in South Vietnam; I say there are 300,000, and perhaps many more. . . . The gradualism of President Johnson in the Vietnam war was untenable. He never realized this simple truth: either you make a war or you don't. . . . For years they bomb, they stop bombing, they bomb again, they reduce, they escalate, they reduce, over the 20th parallel, under the 20th parallel . . . what's that?! A war? Mademoiselle, that's not war. *Cela n'est pas la guerre, c'est une demie guerre.* That's half a war. Until today we have had a *demie guerre,* half a war. . . .

Had the Americans persisted, in 1966 the war would have been over. But the Americans do not persist. They kill for five minutes; then they give four minutes breathing space; then they kill again. . . . They are Vietnamese like me. Deep in my heart, I don't like it. But I also know that to stop the war we have to bomb them. . . . The North Vietnamese . . . suffer . . . they are short of food. . . . They are short of enthusiasm because of the expeditionary corps in the South. . . . They have lost 1,057,000 men since 1964. Look, I have it in my secret documents. . . . Vietnamization has worked marvelously . . . everything has worked out as I said. . . .

The Americans have shown too much concern for their 500 prisoners in Hanoi, and now the North Vietnamese use them as some merchandise to impose political conditions on us. It's disgusting. . . . Democracy as they have it in America or as you have it in Europe cannot exist here as yet. We aren't ready for it. . . .

Mademoiselle, *j'aime la vie.* I love life. . . . At Quang Tri, at Binh Long, at Kontum, I said my prayers to the Holy Virgin. . . . Every Sunday morning I attend Holy Mass in my chapel and every day I pray. I prayed for my troops to take back Quang Tri. . . . I went to the church of Saint Mary of the Advent and I prayed in the middle of the Communist artillery's assault. I also prayed when Dr. Kissinger was here and kept asking for things I couldn't accept. I'm a real Catholic. I was converted after eight years of thinking about it. My wife was already a Catholic. . . . Mademoiselle, I like to do well whatever I do, whether being converted, playing tennis, riding a horse, waterskiing, staying in office as President. I like to assume my responsibilities, and this is why I don't share the power and I'm the chief. *Oui, je suis le chef.* Mademoiselle, *demandez moi: qui est le chef ici? Moi! C'est moi! C'est moi le chef.* I am the chief.

C'est tout? Is that all? I hope you are satisfied, Mademoiselle. I hope you are because I did not hide anything from you. . . . I'm made like that. Would you have ever expected to find a guy like that? *Un type comme ça? Merci,* Mademoiselle. And, if you can, please pray for peace in Vietnam. . . . Sometimes I feel like there isn't anything else to do, anymore, but pray to God.

> — President Nguyen Van Thieu, interview with
> Oriana Fallaci, Saigon, December 30, 1972
> (for Rizzoli Press Service—L'Europeo),
> English translation, *New Republic,* January 20,
> 1973

I'm still optimistic. . . . Dr. Kissinger is optimistic.

> — Howard K. Smith, ABC-TV,
> January 3, 1973

Again the drama of peace weighs upon all our thoughts, especially in Vietnam.

> — Pope Paul VI, St. Peter's Square,
> Vatican City, January 7, 1973

David Packard, former Deputy Defense Secretary, got a $269 million bonus last year. That's how much the value of his stockholdings in Hewlett-Packard Co. rose in 1972. As of last week-end, Packard was worth $582 million in Hewlett-Packard stock, which soared last year to record levels.

> — Chicago Daily News Service,
> January 7, 1973

The South Vietnamese are now capable of defending themselves.

> — Secretary of Defense Melvin Laird,
> January 8, 1973

It sounds encouraging to me. . . . Progress seems to be made in Paris. . . . Once again my hopes have been raised that perhaps an agreement is at hand. . . . There is a ray of light. Maybe this time we will be able to see that ray of light at the end of the tunnel.

> — Senator Mike Mansfield, January 15, 1973

Trust me.

> — President Richard M. Nixon, personal
> message to President Nguyen Van Thieu,
> reported by AP, Saigon, January 16, 1973

U.S. planes bombarded Indochina with 95,490 tons of bombs in December . . . the Pentagon reported Tuesday.

> — Wire service dispatches from Washington,
> January 17, 1973

We are quite close to a conclusion.

> — Foreign Minister Tran Van Lam of South
> Vietnam, January 19, 1973

Agreement on Ending the War and Restoring Peace in Vietnam
CHAPTER VIII—THE RELATIONSHIP BETWEEN THE UNITED
STATES AND THE DEMOCRATIC REPUBLIC
OF VIETNAM

Article 21: . . . The United States will contribute to healing the wounds of war and to postwar reconstruction of the Democratic Republic of Vietnam and throughout Indochina.

Done in Paris this twenty-seventh day of January, One Thousand Nine Hundred and Seventy-Three, in Vietnamese and English. The Vietnamese and English texts are official and equally authentic.

For the Government of the United States of America

William P. Rogers
Secretary of State

The last soldier to die in the Indochina War has not yet been born.
— Editorial, Paris newspaper, January 28, 1973

We think we have taken a big step. . . . We have finally achieved a peace with honor. . . . It would have been a peace with dishonor had we . . . "bugged out" and allowed what the North Vietnamese wanted: the . . . goal they have failed to achieve. Consequently, we can speak of peace with honor. . . . Now, as far as amnesty is concerned . . . amnesty means forgiveness. We cannot provide forgiveness for them. . . . Those who deserted must pay their price.
— President Richard M. Nixon,
news conference, February 1, 1973

The decision to resume the bombing in the middle of December was perhaps the most painful, the most difficult and the most lonely the President has had to make.
— Dr. Henry Kissinger, February 1, 1973

SAIGON—The leaders of all eight delegations to the two-Vietnam peace-keeping commissions held their first joint meeting today in an atmosphere of optimism about the prospects for implementing the Paris agreement.
— *Washington Post*, February 5, 1973

I think the best thing we can do for the time being is remain quiet and give peace time to be consummated. I don't think now is a good time to rock the boat.
— Senator Mike Mansfield, Democratic majority
leader, February 7, 1973

It has been worthwhile.

> — President Richard M. Nixon,
> Jacksonville, Fla., February 16, 1973

Intense fighting continued on Vietnam's traditional battlefields despite pleas from the International Joint Military Commission to make the three-week-old cease-fire a genuine peace. . . . Since the cease-fire became effective at 8 a.m. Saigon time January 28, the South Vietnamese have reported 8,296 dead, including 7,018 Communists, 1,218 government troops and 60 civilians. Nearly 6,000 troops have been wounded, according to Saigon.

> — Wire service dispatches, February 19, 1973

The most selfless purpose that any nation has ever fought a war . . . was our goal and we achieved that goal.

> — President Richard M. Nixon,
> Columbia, S.C., February 20, 1973

I think it is safe to say the North Vietnamese will not keep up this pressure.

> — Champassak Sisouk, Laotian Finance Minister
> and Minister of Defense, February 22, 1973

Mr. Nixon and Kissinger have come through with an agreement. Those who said it couldn't be done their way have been proved wrong.

> — Kenneth Crawford, *Washington Post*,
> February 24, 1973

North Vietnamese planes have begun using the old American airstrip at Khesanh in the northwest corner of South Vietnam. . . . Those who used to shell the Khesanh runway are now improving it for their own use.

> — *Washington Post*, dispatch from Saigon,
> March 6, 1973

We think there is good reason to believe that a renewal of North Vietnamese aggression could be contained.

> — Secretary of Defense Elliot Richardson, to
> House Appropriations Subcommittee on
> Defense, April 3, 1973

SAIGON—American B-52s and F-111 swing-wing fighter bombers pounded insurgent forces Tuesday in some of the heaviest air attacks of the Cambodian war. . . . Approximately 60 B-52s in Southeast Asia participated in the massive bombings.

— Associated Press story, April 3, 1973

You can be sure that we stand with you as we continue to work together to build a lasting peace.

— President Richard M. Nixon, to President Nguyen Van Thieu, in Washington, April 3, 1973

I am very confident that our army and our people are able to defend themselves. . . . We can take off in a comparatively short time provided we are helped in the beginning.

— President Nguyen Van Thieu, remarks to National Press Club, Washington, April 5, 1973

President Thieu is a tremendous leader.

— Vice President Spiro T. Agnew, Washington, April 5, 1973

I am convinced that we can do it. North Vietnamese divisions . . . could not defeat us and we are certainly not going to lose now. It is our turn to chase them.

— Major General Sesthene Fernandez, commander-in-chief, Cambodian armed forces, Phnom Penh, May 2, 1973

The attainment of an honorable settlement in Vietnam was the most satisfying development of this past year.

— President Richard M. Nixon, Foreign Policy Report to the Congress, May 3, 1973

We are not pessimistic. We are not too pessimistic.

— Dr. Henry Kissinger, news briefing, Washington, May 3, 1973

We have already passed the most critical stage. . . . They could not defeat us. We are certainly not going to lose now.

— Major General Sosthene Fernandez, commander-in-chief of the Cambodian armed forces, Phnom Penh, May 21, 1973

American B-52 bombers dropped about 104,000 tons of explosives on Communist sanctuaries in neutralist Cambodia during a series of raids in 1969 and 1970 that were later disguised as attacks in South Vietnam, the Pentagon said yesterday. . . . The secret bombing was acknowledged by the Pentagon Monday after a former Air Force major, Hal M. Knight, described how he falsified reports on Cambodian air operations and destroyed records on the bombing missions actually flown.

— *Washington Post*, July 19, 1973

For the first time in a decade people holding French passports outnumber Americans here. . . . "French economic interests in South Vietnam remained very strong throughout the war," one French source said. French companies hold monopolies or near monopolies in the rubber, beer, soft drink, cigarette, match, textile, tea and coffee industries.

— *Los Angeles Times* dispatch from Saigon,
July 26, 1973

The White House said yesterday the United States "would continue to provide all possible economic, diplomatic and military support" to the Cambodian government.

— Associated Press story, August 3, 1973

An American B-52 bombed a Cambodian naval base Monday. . . . 100 men, women and children were killed and 30 others were wounded. . . . Pentagon spokesman Jerry W. Friedheim said that the base was hit when part of the bomb load from a B-52 fell short of its target. . . . A State department spokesman described the bombing as "very distressing."

— Dispatch from Phnom Penh, August 7, 1973

Oh, the Government definitely has control over most of the people.

— Dr. Gerald C. Hickey, Cornell University,
formerly of Michigan State University, the
Rand Corporation and the National Academy
of Sciences, "America's top expert on the
social structure and politics of rural Vietnam,"
U.S. News & World Report, August 13, 1973

Your country belongs to the Western seas, ours to the eastern. As the horse and the buffalo differ, so do we—in language, literature, customs. If you persist in putting the torch to us, disorder will be long. But we shall act according to the laws of heaven, and our cause will triumph in the end.

> — Vietnamese proclamation to first group of French sailors venturing up Saigon River in 19th century; from Buttinger's *Vietnam: A Dragon Embattled*, citing Pierre Dabezies, *Forces politiques au Viet-Nam*

Why should we take Chinese troops, horses, money and supplies and waste them in such a hot, desolate and useless place? It is definitely in the class of not being worth it. . . . Even if we chase away the [Vietnamese rebels] how can we guarantee that there will not be more . . . again coming out to cause trouble? The environment of that place is inhospitable. It is not worth any great involvement.

— Chinese Emperor Ch'ien-lung, 1789

The enemy must fight his battles far from home for a long time. . . . We must weaken him by drawing him into protracted campaigns. Once his initial dash is broken, it will be easier to destroy him. . . . When the enemy is away from home for a long time and produces no victories and families learn of their dead, then the enemy population at home becomes dissatisfied and considers it a Mandate from Heaven that the armies be recalled.

Time is always in our favor. Our climate, mountains and jungles discourage the enemy; but for us they offer both sanctuary and a place from which to attack.

— Marshal Tran Hung Dao, Vietnamese general
who defeated Mongols, 1280 A.D.

Index

441